THE PARSIS OF INDIA

Preservation of Identity in Bombay City

JESSE S. PALSETIA

MANOHAR
2008

First published 2001

This reprint edition 2008 is for sale in South Asia only

ISBN 81-7304-781-2

Published by
Ajay Kumar Jain *for*
Manohar Publishers & Distributors
4753/23 Ansari Road, Daryaganj
New Delhi 110 002

Typeset by
Ajay Arts
Delhi 110 006

Printed by
Lordson Publishers Pvt. Ltd.
Delhi 110 007

THE PARSIS OF INDIA

CONTENTS

LIST OF ILLUSTRATIONS

PREFACE

In appreciation of their efforts on behalf of the freedom struggle in South Africa, and in appeal for their continued support, M. K. Gandhi noted the legacy of the Parsis of India: "It is one of the supreme wonders of God that, though the Parsee community does not number more than a hundred thousand in the whole world, it has made a name for itself everywhere by virtue of its many illustrious qualities. It can be said that it is this community, which holds power in India. Bombay is the real capital of India, [and] it owes its prosperity mainly to the Parsees."[1] Gandhi's assessment is but one of many that have sought to understand the ability of the Parsis of India to survive and prosper as a community and people over the centuries since their arrival in India.

The focus of this work is to examine and account for the ways in which the Parsis have historically sought to safeguard and preserve their identity in India. The work focuses on the major events, issues, and themes that relate to the Parsis' attempts to safeguard and shape their identity, principally in Bombay from the seventeenth century to the first decades of the twentieth century. The arrival of the Iranian Zoroastrians to India, where they came to be known as Parsis, had posed the dilemma of how to maintain a sense of common identity in the midst of coexisting and integrating into the broader fabric of Indian civilization. Each chapter seeks to explore the way by which the Parsis safeguarded identity at a given historical moment. The Parsis pass through key phases that witness them develop from an insular group to a community of pluralistic outlook. At the same time, underlying Parsi attempts to safeguard identity is the theme and process of continuity of historical response.

The work includes six major chapters, an introduction, and a conclusion in the form of an epilogue. The Introduction provides an overview of the Parsis' arrival and settlement in India, prior to the rise of Bombay, and examines the themes and processes involved in the Parsis' attempts to preserve identity in the Indian setting. The Introduction takes account of the Parsis' transition from Iran to India and their emergence as a distinct community in India. The history of the Parsis in the provincial setting is prelude to the tremendous changes that would affect the Parsis

[1] From *Indian Opinion*, 20.2.1909, in *The Collected Works of Mahatma Gandhi*, vol. 10, September 1908-November 1909 (Ahmedabad, 1966), 193-4.

in the urban setting of colonial Bombay, and which forms the major focus of the work.

Chapter One focuses on the rise of the Parsi community in Bombay, and the moral and economic supports to community and identity that take shape in the urban setting. An examination of the role and place of charity within the Parsi community, and the Parsis' pre-eminence in trade and commerce provide insight into the Parsis' adaptation in the new setting, and the building of the foundation and base for the subsequent growth of the community under colonialism.

Chapter Two examines the factors that made for leadership of the community among the wealthy and influential Parsi merchant-princes of early Bombay, and the rise of the institution of the Parsi Punchayet of Bombay as the internal government of the Parsis. The chapter examines the ability of the Parsis to exploit the new opportunity made available in Bombay to safeguard, preserve, and redefine identity with the establishment of the Punchayet, and prior to the great influence of Western ideas on the community. The chapter takes account of the community norms and the social ideology that emerges among the Parsis in the urban setting and which, for a time, unite the Parsis in support of the Punchayet. The chapter then focuses on the decline of the Punchayet and the processes that make for the rise of alternative models for safe-guarding identity.

Chapter Three examines the challenge posed to Parsi religious identity by the conversions of Parsi boys in Bombay, by the Reverend Doctor John Wilson. The chapter provides a unique picture of the challenge faced by the Parsis from the Christian missionaries, and how the most accommodating of communities under colonialism reacts in antagonism to a perceived threat from the colonial environment. It reflects that amidst the Parsis' continuing progress and socialization under colonialism, their religious identity remained inviolable. Of central focus is the ability of the Parsis as a community to withstand the challenge posed by the Christian missionaries, while in general affected by the impact of the colonial environment.

Chapter Four examines the Parsis' response to the changing social milieu of mid-nineteenth century Bombay. The influence of Western education and British values on the Parsis, and the attempts by the Parsis to direct social progress to their advantage amidst social and cultural change, are examined. The chapter in particular focuses on the rise of the Parsi reformers, as a new centre of authority among the Parsis, and the consequences of the reformers' reform movement.

Chapter Five concentrates on the attempts by the Parsis to shape their identity through legislative and legal channels. The chapter first examines the Parsis' attempts, at mid-nineteenth century, to fashion and have enacted a Parsi law code that deals with the issues of (intestate) inheritance and succession, and marriage and divorce. The section notes the pressures of the colonial environment and, in particular, the effect of British legal norms on the Parsis, which shape the Parsis' responses. The chapter then deals with an important legal case in the history of the Parsi community, known as the Parsi Punchayet Case of 1906-08. The Parsi Punchayet Case involved the Parsis turning to the law courts to settle issues relative to their identity, specifically the issue of conversion and membership in the community, and the consequences of their actions. Finally, the chapter examines the evolution of Parsi thought by the early twentieth century and a second important legal case, known as the Rangoon Navjote Case of 1915-18. This section seeks to provide historical context to the changes the Parsis had undergone since the middle of the nineteenth century, and that shaped their arguments over identity and modernity.

Chapter Six examines the diversification of Parsi opinion over politics, specifically the rise of political nationalism among some Parsis, and the tension this creates within the Parsi community as to political allegiances and identity. The chapter traces the public career of Dadabhai Naoroji (1825-1917), his ties to the Parsis, and the influences that shaped his identification with the Indian nationalist movement. The chapter also examines the efforts and difficulties of the Parsis Sir Pherozeshah M. Mehta (1845-1915) and Sir Dinsha E. Wacha (1844-1936) to associate the Parsis with Indian nationalism. The rise of the Parsis in the Indian nationalist movement provides insight into the evolution and maturation of a segment of Parsi opinion towards a broader sense of identity, as well as the problematic nature of the transition for the Parsis.

Finally, the Epilogue presents an overview of the present-day Parsis and is included to both update the historical narrative, and demonstrate the relevance of the historical narrative to the issues that continue to preoccupy the Parsis of India.

The book is a reprint of my *Parsis of India* of 2001. While events continue to shape the narrative on the Parsis, many of the themes raised in the book remain constant. I tender a grateful thanks to all those who made both the original work and the reprint possible. No major work of research can be produced without the assistance and goodwill of many individuals, and in the case of a work on the Parsis, the aid of members of the community. In particular, no major work of research whose primary centre of research is India can proceed without the assistance of parties without whose help the researcher is lost. It is in Bombay that the overwhelming part of the research for the work was conducted, and I should like to thank those individuals who familiarized me with the sources of research in the city, and those individuals associated with many institutions that facilitated my work. I wish to acknowledge with gratitude the advice offered to me on conducting research during my initial sojourn in Bombay by the late Professor D. N. Marshall, former librarian and professor emeritus of library science at the University of Bombay. I wish to thank and acknowledge: the chief secretary, secretaries, and staff of the Bombay Parsi Punchayet for their assistance, valued time, and good wishes; Jamshed Kanga, former president of the Bombay Parsi Punchayet for meeting with me; the late Jer A. Dhondy, the director of the *Jam-e-Jamshed* newspaper; Jehan Daruwala, the editor of the *Bombay Samachar* newspaper; the librarians and staff of the J. N. Petit Library; and the editors and secretaries at *Parsiana*. The above individuals and the staff of the institutions evinced all the finest traditions and generosity that is associated with the Parsis. In addition, I am grateful for the assistance and professionalism of the staff at the University of Bombay Library, and the Maharashtra State Archives.

I should like to thank my professors for their patient expectations and thoughtful commentaries offered me on my research, and whose knowledge and experience I have benefited from over many years. In particular, I should like to extend appreciation to N. K. Wagle, professor emeritus of Indian history at the University of Toronto, whom I account my teacher and friend. In addition to his time, patience, and overwhelming goodwill towards me, Professor Wagle's insights into Indian life and history, and his appreciation for the historical process continued to inspire and motivate my understanding of the historical material.

I should further like to take the opportunity to thank the many individuals who made possible my accommodation in Bombay, who assisted my introduction to various parties on behalf of my research, and who encouraged and assisted my work in innumerable ways. I wish to acknowledge: the late Mr. and Mrs. H. A. Havaldar, Mr. and Mrs. J. Irani, Dastur and Mrs. S. N. Panthaky, Mr. and Mrs. F. G. Achhadwala, and Mr. and Mrs. R. A. Sui. I owe an especial thanks to Jim S. Palsetia for his assistance in the production of my thesis and book, without whose very generous help, time, and goodwill the work could not have emerged.

I must thank Brill and Manoḥar Publishers for the publication and reprint of my work respectively. The publishers' dedication to Parsi and Zoroastrian studies and Indology has immeasurably benefited the academic genre over many decades.

Finally, I dedicate this work to the memory of my parents: to my father who died long before this work was contemplated but whose example has sustained me in all my endeavours; and to my mother who passed away some months after the completion of my original thesis. To my mother I owe an ultimately ineffable debt of thanks for her support of my goals. Her assistance and patience were instrumental in the completion of the work, and her ever-present good humour and companionship filled my years.

JESSE S. PALSETIA

INTRODUCTION

THE PATTERN OF SETTLEMENT

The Parsis are a community in India that trace their ancestry and religious identity to pre-Islamic, Zoroastrian Iran (pre-651 C.E.). The Parsis presently number approximately 110,000 individuals worldwide, and over 70,000 individuals in India.[1] The Parsis are the descendants of Iranian Zoroastrians who migrated to and settled in India in order to preserve their Zoroastrian religion. Zoroastrianism is the religion associated with the teachings and revelation of the Iranian prophet and priest Zarathustra, or Zoroaster as referred to by the ancient Greeks. Zarathustra and his religious message date from the second millennium B.C.E. (*c.* 1200-1000 B.C.E.). Zoroastrianism was the first major religion of Iran and a living faith in the ancient world. It developed following the division between the Indo-Iranian 'Aryan' peoples who migrated from the steppes of Asia to the Middle East, Iranian Plateau, and north-western India, during the second

---

[1] *Census of India 1981, X: Greater Bombay*, Government of India, records 71,630 Parsis in India, of which 68,676 individuals are in Greater Bombay. See also Malini Karkal, *Survey of the Parsi Population of Greater Bombay, 1882* (Bombay, 1984); Sapur F. Desai, *Statistics of World Zoroastrians with Special Reference to Indian Zoroastrians* (Bombay, 1964). John R. Hinnells, "South Asian Diaspora Communities and Their Religion: A Comparative Study of Parsi Experiences," *South Asia Research* 14, 1 (Spring 1994): 62-104, and "The Zoroastrian Diaspora in Britain, Canada, and the United States," in *The South Asian Religious Diaspora in Britain, Canada, and the United States*, eds. H. Coward, J. R. Hinnells, and R. B. Williams (Albany, 2000), 35-54, offers estimates from research surveys of the number of Zoroastrians outside India to include: Britain, 5,000; USA, 6,500; Canada, 4,500; Australia, 300; Pakistan, 3,000; Hong Kong, 150; Kenya, 80. The estimates of the number of Zoroastrians in Iran vary considerably. Information based on official statistics places the population at 50,000 individuals out of a world Zoroastrian population of 150,000. See P. Greenway and D. St. Vincent, *Iran*, lonely planet series (May 1998), 214. Estimates that are more conservative place the number of Iranian Zoroastrians at 20,000 individuals. See also J. K. Amighi, *The Zoroastrians of Iran: Conversion, Assimilation, or Persistence* (New York, 1990). *Hamazor: The Bulletin of the World Zoroastrian Organisation*, January-February 1993 (Bombay, 1992), notes the Zoroastrian population of Hong Kong to be less than 200 individuals. See also K. N. Vaid, *The Overseas Indian Community in Hong Kong* (Hong Kong, 1972).

half of the second millennium B.C.E. The Indo-Aryans settled in India, while the Iranians settled in greater Iran. Early Zoroastrianism forms a unique tradition that shares with Indo-Aryan religion traits, while also providing the basis upon which a more elaborated tradition emerges among the Iranian peoples.

The long history of Zoroastrianism makes it difficult to characterize the religion without reference to either speculation or debate. The representations of Zoroastrianism and its history are largely reconstructions of traditions from the combined evidence of religious texts. The oldest writings associated with Zarathustra are the *Gāthās:* a collection of esoteric songs, poems, and thoughts in an Old Iranian language, later referred to as Gāthic Avestan or Old Avestan. Zarathustra's religion is considered dualistic, i.e., a religion in which good and evil in the world is attributed to antagonistic good and evil spirits. Zoroastrianism, however, represents an original attempt to unify the existing ancient Iranian dualistic tradition within an ethical framework. The religion of Zarathustra was both revolutionary in its conceptualization and innovative in its observance.

Zarathustra conceived and revealed a vision of creation as inhabited by the all-good and benevolent spirit of Ahura Mazdā (Wise Lord) in continuous conflict with evil forces known as the *daēvas.* Ahura Mazdā is head of a group of divine beings called *ahuras*, and in the *Gāthās* has no direct counterpart among the *daēvas*. The *ahuras* and the *daēvas* are personifications of broader ahurian and daēvic concepts and ideals in opposition to one another in the cosmos, principal among which include truth (Avestan *asha*) and falsehood (*druj*) respectively. In the Zoroastrian story of creation, Ahura Mazdā created humanity as part of the struggle between good and evil. The power of humanity lies in the free and conscious choice to follow either good or evil in life, and thereby influence both one's individual fate and the fate of all humanity. Early Zoroastrianism held human nature to be essentially good, breaking with older Middle Eastern traditions about the inherent baseness of humanity, and modern Zoroastrianism continues to summarize the duty of humans as to follow the path of good thoughts, good words, and good deeds. In the final transfiguration of the world, Ahura Mazdā, Zarathustra, and the truthful among humans triumph over evil.

Zoroastrianism was practised under all the Iranian dynasties of antiquity, and became the official imperial religion under the Sasanian dynasty, until its fall in 651 C.E. Under the Sasanians, the extant religious texts were canonized, and elaborate religious rituals and a fully developed theology marked Zoroastrianism. The evolution and transformations of Zoroastrianism are the consequences of its history. The Parsis of India would be greatly affected by its variegated history. The Parsis incorporated the entire tradition of Zoroastrianism from Zarathustra through Sasanian Zoroastrianism as part of their religious heritage. They would seek to preserve its essential elements while reinterpreting Zoroastrianism in the context of their own evolution as a community.[2]

The Zoroastrians of India came to be known as Parsis, i.e. 'Persians' (inhabitants of the Iranian province of Persis, modern Fars) and as their name implies, for the Parsis, the sense of their ancestral past remains both relevant and important. The Parsis also refer to themselves as 'Zarāthustrians,' 'Zarthosti,' 'Māzdayasnāns,' to signify their religious identity as followers of the message of Zarathustra and as worshippers of Ahura Mazdā. In India, the Parsis became a prosperous and influential community, retaining the characteristics of an ethnic and religious minority. The story of the Parsis begins with their arrival in India, which, according to Parsi tradition, was in the eighth century C.E. The account of the Persian refugees' exodus from Iran and their arrival in India is almost entirely based on two narrative works in Persian: *the Qisseh-i Sanjan* or Story of Sanjan written in 1599, by the Parsi priest Behman Kaikobad Sanjana; and the *Qisseh-i Zartushtian-i Hendustan*, written by the Parsi Shapurji Maneckji Sanjana in Navsari between 1765 and 1805.[3] The trad-

[2] The literature on Zoroastrianism is extensive and varied. For an understanding of Zoroastrian history and themes, see Mary Boyce, *Zoroastrians: Their Religious Beliefs and Practices* (London, 1979); idem, *Zoroastrianism: Its Antiquity and Constant Vigour* (Costa Mesa, 1992); M. A. Dandamaev and V. G. Lukonin *The Culture and Social Institutions of Ancient Iran*, trans. P. Kohl and D. J. Dadson (Cambridge, 1989), 320-47; Albert de Jong, *Traditions of the Magi: Zoroastrianism in Greek and Latin Literature* (Leiden, 1997); Jacques Duchesne-Guillemin, *Religion of Ancient Iran*, trans. K. M. JamaspAsa (Bombay, 1973); Gherardo Gnoli, *Zoroaster's Time and Homeland: A Study on the Origins of Mazdeism and Related Problems* (Naples, 1980); Helmut Humbach, *The Heritage of Zarathustra: A New Translation of the Gāthās* (Heidelberg, 1994); *The New Encyclopaedia Britannica*, 15th ed., s.v. "Zoroastrianism and Parsiism." See also Chapter Four.

[3] The chronology and dates for the Parsis' arrival in India vary exceedingly, to the point that it is not possible to give an authentic date based on either the *Qisseh-i Sanjan* or the *Qisseh-i Zartushtian-i Hendustan* for the Parsis' arrival in India. Based on a pamphlet written in 1826 by Dastur A. Kamdin, tradition holds the Parsis to have arrived in India in 716 C.E. See K. N. Seervai and B. B. Patell "Gujarat Parsis from Their Earliest Settlement to the Present Time," in *Gazetteer of the*

itional accounts together relate the peripatetic wanderings of the Zoroastrians following the defeat of the last Sasanian king, Yazdagird III, at the battle of Nihavand in 642 C.E., by the Muslim Arabs. The Zoroastrians first migrated to Khurasan, where they stayed for a hundred years, and then migrated to the island of Hormuz in the Persian Gulf, where they resided for some fifteen years, before finally undertaking the sea voyage to India. The Persian refugees first landed on the island of Diu, off the Gujarat coast, where they remained for some nineteen years, before finally arriving on the western coast of India, at or near what would become the Gujarat town of Sanjan.[4]

The traditional accounts of the Parsis' arrival in India leave as many questions as they provide answers to the migration and settlement of the Parsis in India.[5] No exact dates are provided for the year in which the Persian refugees began their wanderings from place to place in Iran or their arrival in India. The chronologies of the accounts militate against the Parsis arriving in the eighth century. The narratives, however, provide an appreciation of the Parsis' traditional

---

Bombay Presidency, vol. 9, part 2, ed. J. M. Campbell (Bombay, 1899), 185. The Parsi writer Jivanji Jamshedji Modi (1854-1933) accepted the eighth century as the period for the arrival of the Parsis to India, and cited the year to be 785 C.E. See J. J. Modi, *A Few Events in the Early History of the Parsis and Their Dates* (Bombay, 1905), 9-10. A recent survey of the dates and literature on the Parsis' arrival and settlement in India accepts that the Parsis landed in India sometime around 780 C.E. See H. E. Eduljee, *Kisseh-i-Sanjan* (Bombay, 1991). The main challenge to the traditional date(s) and period for the Parsis' arrival in India lies in calculating the arrival to have been sometime in the tenth century. In 1870, the Parsi scholar Kharshedji Rustomji Cama (1831-1909) noted discrepancies in Kamdin's calculation of the year for the Parsis' arrival in India, and cited the year 936 C.E. as the more likely date. See M. M. Murzban, *The Parsis*, vol. 1 (1917; reprint, Bombay, 1994), 49-50. The latter date was also accepted by the Parsi historian S. H. Hodivala, "Jadi Rana and the Kisseh-i-Sanjan," in *Studies in Parsi History* (Bombay, 1920), 67-91. Western scholarship also cites the tenth century as the period for the probable arrival of the Parsis to India, see Carlo G. Cereti, *An 18th Century Account of Parsi History: The Qesse-ye Zartoštiān* (Naples, 1991); idem, "The Qesse-ye Zartoštiān-e Hendustān and the Qesse-ye Sanjān: Notes on Parsi History," in *Proceedings of the Second European Conference of Iranian Studies* (Rome, 1995), 141-52; Boyce, *Zoroastrians*, 157.

[4] S. H. Hodivala, "The Kisseh-i-Sanjan Translated," in *Studies in Parsi History*, 92-117; J. J. Modi, "Qisseh-i Zartushtian-i Hendustan," *Journal of the K. R. Cama Oriental Institute* 17 (1930): 1-63; 19 (1931): 45-57; 25 (1933): 1-147.

[5] The reliability and authenticity of the traditional narratives have been questioned. See G. K. Nariman, "Was it Religious Persecution Which Compelled the Parsis to Migrate from Persia to India?" *Islamic Culture* 7 (Hyderabad, 1933); B. N. Bhatena, *Kisseh-i-Sanjan, A Palpabie Falsehood* (Benares, 1944).

understanding of their history that is of considerable importance and value. By tradition, the members of the Parsi community of India are held to be the descendants of the original Persian pilgrims and refugees who landed on the western coast of India. Furthermore, the narratives provide an appreciation of the broad themes of early Parsi history, which along with the historical data available are useful in drawing certain conclusions. A plausible account would suggest that a band of Zoroastrians from the area of Khurasan migrated to India following along trade routes that were known between the two countries, or along a course that took them to a land that had some ancient religious connection for them. The reason for the Zoroastrians' exodus lay in the loss of political and social power in Islamic society, and growing religious intolerance and persecution that were the result of changing political and religious factors in Iran, as early as the eighth century. Conversion of Zoroastrians to Islam proceeded for various reasons both individual and communal, including for personal gain and incentive to maintain social status and freedom, and as a result of persecution. The level and frequency of religious persecution, if not systematic following the conquest of Iran, was pervasive over time. The traditional accounts of the emigration of the Zoroastrians to India should not discount the possibility of more than one migration. The earliest physical evidence of a Zoroastrian community in India, that of the Kanheri cave inscriptions, dates from the tenth century. The changing nature of politics in Iran and its effect on the Zoroastrians, and the evidence available on the dispersal pattern of the Parsis in Western India further suggest of migrations subsequent to that described in the traditional narratives.[6]

---

[6] On trade routes existing between Iran and India and their significance to the Parsis' exodus, see K. Inostransev, "The Emigration of the Parsis to India and the Musalman World in the Midst of the VIIIth Century," trans. L. Bogdanov, *Journal of the K. R Cama Oriental Institute* 1 (1922): 33-70; V. Fiorani Piacentini, *L'Emporio ed il Regno di Hormuz* (Milano, 1975); Andre Wink, *Al-Hind: The Making of the Indo-Islamic World* (Oxford, 1990). On early Zoroastrian influences in India, see A. S. Altekar, "The Extent of the Sassanian Political Domination in India," in *M. P. Kharegat Memorial Volume*, vol. 1 (Bombay, 1953), 215-25; D. R. Bhandarkar, "Parasikas," in *M. P. Kharegat Memorial Volume*, vol. 1 (Bombay, 1953), 196-8. On conversions and the situation of the Zoroastrians in Islamic Iran, see Richard W. Bulliet, *Conversion to Islam in the Medieval Period: An Essay in Quantitative History* (Cambridge, Mass., 1979); David Morgan, *Medieval Persia, 1040-1797* (New York, 1988), 15; Jamsheed K. Choksy, "Zoroastrians in Muslim Iran: Selected Problems of Coexistence and Interaction During the Early Medieval Period," *Iranian Studies* 20, 1 (1987): 17-30; idem, *Conflict and Cooperation:*

The arrival of the Parsis in India posed the question of how the small minority would integrate itself into the new dominant social milieu while retaining the essence of its identity. The history of the Parsis in India is that of their attempts to maintain their Zoroastrian identity in the midst of accommodation to the Indian milieu. The traditional narratives of the Parsis relate the process of assimilation and acculturation that had begun with their integration into the Indian setting. Parsi tradition holds that on arriving in India, the Parsis were hesitantly welcomed by the local Hindu ruler of Gujarat, identified as Jādi Rana. Conditions were attached to the Parsis' settlement in the territory of the local rajah. These conditions included the Parsis forsaking their weapons and becoming peaceable subjects of the rajah, adopting the local language and dress, and observing the performance of their marriage ceremonies after sunset; or in general observing their ceremonies in the manner of the locals. In addition, the Parsis were asked to explain their religion to the rajah and his subjects.[7] The conditions the Zoroastrians were asked to comply with describe the cultural assimilation of the Parsis in India. The justification of the Parsis' cultural assimilation to the Indian setting, as conditional to their compact made in Sanjan, forms part of the historical aetiology of the community. With the exception of their religion, the Parsis believed their assimilation to the Indian cultural milieu as conditional to their acceptance and safe existence in India.

The unique cultural configuration of the Parsi community taking shape is evidenced in the tales of the Parsis' settlement in India. The process of the Parsis casting their cultural characteristics, and distinguishing their customs and norms from other Indians gains significance in the new setting. The Parsis' acculturation and assimilation

---

Zoroastrian Subalterns and Muslim Elites in Medieval Iranian Society (New York, 1997), 13-47, 69-93.

[7] A Parsi oral tradition relates that a Parsi priest recited the sixteen Sanskrit *Shlokas* (distich verses) before the Hindu rajah to explain the religion and customs of the Zoroastrians. The Sanjan *Shlokas* appear to be the oldest Parsi literature in India. Debate surrounds the identity of the author, and whether he was a Parsi or a Hindu. The composition of the Sanskrit *Shlokas* suggests that the Parsis had sufficiently integrated into Indian society to explain their religion in a uniquely Indian medium and context. For translations and discussion of the *Shlokas*, see James Burgess, "Translation of the Sanjan S'lokas," *The Indian Antiquary*, July 5, 1872, 214-16; S. K. Hodivala, "The 16 Sanskrit Shlokas," in *Dastur Hoshang Memorial Volume* (Bombay, 1918), 70-94; Hans-Peter Schmidt, "The Sixteen Sanskrit Sanjan Slokas of Ākā Adhyāru," *Bulletin of the Deccan College Research Institute* 21 (1960-1): 157-96.

in India, in all likelihood, was a long process. The Parsis came to India with their own religious, cultural, and social norms. In particular, the Parsis guarded their religious norms. Over time the Parsis' religious, cultural, and social norms would evolve to meet their specific requirements in the Indian setting while co-existing alongside those of Indian society. Tradition holds that as a measure of their secure settlement in Sanjan, and in honour of their safe deliverance by God, the Parsis consecrated their first *Ātash Bahrām* or sacred fire, *c.* 720 C.E. The *Ātash Bahrām* of the Parsis, which they venerated as the symbol of God, was consecrated with ritual objects specifically brought from Iran, signifying the spiritual and physical tie to the sacred fires of Iran. The Parsis have safeguarded this original *Ātash Bahrām* to this day.[8]

The fire-ritual belonged to the Indo-Iranian heritage of Zoroastrianism, in which fire is a central element of ritual and devotional worship. Notwithstanding their common origin, the Iranian and Indian fire-cults had their own characteristics; and this fact distinguished how the Parsis worshipped on arriving in India. The Sanjan fire remained the only sacred fire until the eighteenth century when a second sacred fire and temple were consecrated in Navsari. The Parsis maintained the tradition known in Iran of worshipping before lesser fires or hearth fires. The temple cult among the Iranians dates from Achaemenian times, and formed a non-idolatrous means of devotional worship. The development of the temple cult witnessed the veneration of sacred fires and lesser fires, and their sanctification in temples. Following the Arab conquest of Iran and through medieval times many fires and temples survived, but over time were reduced in number and became inconspicuous, surviving in a few places in a humble state, reflecting the state of the Zoroastrians of Iran.[9]

---

[8] The *Ātash Bahrām* of Sanjan by the eighteenth century would come to be known as the Iran Shah (Fire of the King of Iran), and was believed to have come with the Parsis from Iran. The *Ātash Bahrām* consecrated in Sanjan, from the fifteenth century was removed to Bansda, Navsari, Surat, and Bulsar before finally coming to reside in Udwada in 1742. The present fire-temple in Udwada was erected in 1829, through the liberality of Dadabhoy Pestonjee Wadia (1802-85). See W. Ramsay, "The Sacred Fire of the Parsis at Udwada," *The Indian Antiquary*, July 5, 1872, 213-14. On the fire-temples of the Parsis, see also Chapter One.

[9] The existence and history of the fire-temple in Iran is the subject of much discussion. See J. C. Heesterman, *The Broken World of Sacrifice: An Essay in Ancient Indian Ritual* (Chicago, 1993); Mary Boyce, "On the Zoroastrian Temple Cult of Fire," *Journal of American Oriental Society* 95 (1975): 454-65; De Jong, *Traditions of the Magi*, 343-50; B. M. Tirmidhi, "Zoroastrians and Their Fire

As the Parsi community grew, the Parsis' ritual observance of their religion witnessed the rise of temple-worship in India. The fire-temples of the Parsis take their designation from one of three grades of sacred fire they house, signifying the primacy of the fire. The first grade, *Ātash Bahrām*, is collected and consecrated from sixteen kinds of fire, and is kept perpetually alight and attended by the high priests. The *Ātash Ādarān*, literally fires, is consecrated from four kinds of fire, and maintained by priests with less elaborate ritual than the *Ātash Bahrām*, though with equal reverence. Finally, the *Ātash Dādgāh* is the fire of the household and requires no special ritual of consecration. The sacred nature of the Dadgah comes from the consecration of the fire-temple it abides in. Both the *Ādarān* and the *Dādgāh* fires are also kept in an agiary, which is the Parsi-Gujarati word for fire-temple.[10]

The Indian social and religious milieu influenced the development and nature of Parsi temple-worship, as the Parsis safeguarded their religious observance from the influence of the predominantly Hindu environment around them. The fire-temples were reserved exclusively for the use of Parsis, and the building of fire-temples paralleled the dispersion of the Parsis across Gujarat and India. The nature of temple-worship also became unique to the Parsis of India. The Parsis continued the Iranian practice of fire-oblation or 'feeding the fire' known as the *Būi* ceremony, accompanied by the *Ātash Niyāyesh* or supplication 'prayer to fire,' performed five times a day by the priest. The ceremony became more elaborate within the temple as priests fed the fire with sandalwood and other fragrant materials and developed unique sacerdotal customs and etiquette in service of the fire. Parsis also expanded on the practice in Iran of consecrating a fire on a stone slab or plinth, and enacted elaborate ceremonies for the 'enthronement' of a sacred fire in a temple, upon a large covered urn or censer, called an *āfargāniun*, situated on top of a slab.[11] Signifi-

---

Temples in Iran and Adjoining Countries from the 9th to the 14th Centuries as Gleaned from the Arabic Geographical Works," *Islamic Culture* 24, no. 4 (1950): 271-84.

[10] On the consecration of the fires and fire-temples, see J. J. Modi, *The Religious Ceremonies and Customs of the Parsees* (Bombay, 1937), 210-43; Mary Boyce, "On the Sacred Fires of the Zoroastrians," *Bulletin of the School of Oriental and African Studies* 31, no. 1 (1968): 52-68.

[11] See Boyce, *Zoroastrianism*, 85-7; idem, *Zoroastrians*, 62-5, 166-7, 172; M. N. Dhalla, History of *Zoroastrianism* (1938; reprint, Bombay, 1963), 221-2; Modi, *Religious Ceremonies and Customs*, 210-43, 273.

cantly, while the construction of fire-temples distinguished the nature of Parsis religious observance in India, temple-worship complimented older forms of Iranian and Parsi religious worship. Devotional practices as well as ceremonies such as those of marriage and the *Navjote* or religious çonfirmation are not of necessity performed in a fire-temple.

Following their settlement in Sanjan, the Parsis migrated and settled along the coast of Gujarat and its provincial centres. By the twelfth century, the Parsis had settled in Vankanir in Kathiawar, Broach, Variav, Anklesvar, Cambay, and Navsari.[12] At Broach the Parsis also built their first *dakhma* or Tower of Silence. A brick *dakhma* was built sometime before 1300, and a second Tower was built in 1309, to service the inhabitants of Broach and vicinity.[13] The *dakhma* is a circular, roofless walled structure, enclosing a central well (*bhandār*), built to consign the bodies of the deceased to be devoured by vultures and carrion crows or desiccated by the sun, as part of the Zoroastrian practice of excarnation of the dead. The ori gin of the *dakhma* is part of a long history of funerary traditions in the Iranian world. The Parsis retained and elaborated on the practice of exposure known to them from Iran, as part of the funerary ritual of Dakhmenashini.[14] Consignment of a corpse to the *dakhma* reflected the Parsi practice not to defile the natural elements, as enjoined in Zoroastrianism, and symbolized the Parsis' sense of equality in resting together. *Dakhmas* built in the provincial setting served the needs of local and neighbouring communities. By the late thirteenth century, the Parsis had established themselves sufficiently in the local environment that the *āthornans* or Parsi priesthood had divided ecclesiastical jurisdiction for Gujarat into five *panthaks* or districts, centred near Sanjan, Navsari, Anklesvar, Broach, and Cambay. The growth of Parsi priesthood in the provincial towns of Gujarat established these towns as the centres of traditional authority among the Parsis. In 1142, one Kamdin Zarthosht was the first priest to arrive in Navsari from Sanjan, to service the religious needs of the

[12] R. E. Enthoven ed., *The Tribes and Castes of Bombay*, vol. 3 (Bombay, 1922), 189; Modi, *A Few Events*, 11.

[13] Enthoven, *Tribes and Castes*, 189.

[14] See Mary Boyce, "Corpse, Disposal of, in Zoroastrianism," *Encyclopedia Iranica* 6 (1993): 279-86; Modi, *Religious Ceremonies and Customs*, 51-74; De Jong, *Traditions of the Magi*, 51-69.

growing Parsi population.[15] The Parsi priesthood is a hereditary occupational class following along the male line. The priests of Navsari are the descendants of two families of priests that settled in Navsari from the early thirteenth century. Navsari became the head-quarters of the Parsi priesthood and a centre of religious authority and learning. The other centres of Parsi settlement sent for priests from Navsari as their populations grew. In 1531, Manek Changa, the son of the great Parsi leader Changa Asa, erected a stone *dakhma* in Navsari, possibly replacing an earlier brick *dakhma*.[16]

Along with Navsari, Surat became a major centre of Parsi settlement. Surat grew to be a centre of Parsi concentration with its rise as a commercial centre from the sixteenth century. The first *dakhma* was erected possibly before 1600 by subscription of the Parsis, and in 1647, Nanabhoy Poojia Modi (died 1667) erected a second Tower. The growing wealth and population of Surat up to the nineteenth century would witness many additions to the *dakhma*. In 1823, two *Ātash Bahrām* temples were built in Surat in addition to a dozen lesser fire-temples.[17] Surat grew to become the principal centre of Parsi settlement and the virtual headquarters of the community prior to the rise of Bombay. Many of the Parsis who settled in Bombay traced their ancestry from Surat. Surat's relatively safe location encouraged its settlement, particularly following the Maratha incursions into Navsari in the eighteenth century. It was, however, the arrival of the European factories or merchant trading stations, from the sixteenth century, that accounts for Surat's rise to prominence. Surat became the major entrepôt for the European companies on the west coast of India and the centre of Parsi commercial concentration.

The Parsis of Gujarat functioned as agriculturalists, artisans, merchants, and revenue collectors and, from the seventeenth century, commercial traders, and shipbuilders. The establishment of Parsi communities in the provincial centres of Gujarat inured the Parsis to the patterns and ways of Gujarat life for much of their history. The Gujarat Parsis adapted to the usages and customs of the local envi-

[15] B. B. Patell, comp., *Parsee Prakash*: *Being a Record of Important Events in the Growth of the Parsee Community in Western India, Chronologically Arranged*, 2 vols. (in Gujarati) (Bombay, 1888, 1910), 1:2, and R. B. Paymaster, 5 vols. (to 1942) (hereafter cited as *Parsee Prakash*); F. M. Kotwal and J. Boyd, *A Guide to the Zoroastrian Religion* (Harvard, 1982), 212.

[16] M. S. Commissariat, *History of Gujarat, 1297-1573* (Bombay, 1938), 184.

[17] Seevai and Patell, "Gujarat Parsis," 254.

ronment as, for example, in their inheritance patterns. At the same time, the Parsis' sense of their uniqueness fostered the belief that many of their customs were derived from their religious and historical heritage. A conservative and traditionalist ethos emerged in the provincial setting that contrasted to the culture the Parsis developed from the time of their settlement in Bombay, particularly in the nineteenth century. By the nineteenth century, the Parsis of Bombay became the principal community and its prosperous and influential nature made it the leader of the Parsi community of India as a whole.

The Parsis also integrated themselves into the local political culture. The Parsis professed loyalty to the various political administrations and regimes they ultimately found themselves under, whether Hindu rulers, Mogul emperors, or the British Raj. At times, the Parsis also suffered the consequences of their support of local allies against conquering regimes. Sometime in the tenth or eleventh century, the Parsis of Variav suffered military reprisal from the Rajput Prince of Ratanpur for their failure to pay tribute.[18] In 1297, the Parsis of Cambay suffered during the conquest of Gujarat by the Muslim Delhi Sultanate; and once again, in 1465, the Parsis were defenders of the realm against the Muslim Sultan Mahmud Begada.[19] Parsis also suffered the penalty for the breach of the laws and customs of the dominant ruling community. In the seventeenth century, a Parsi weaver from Broach named Camaji Homaji was put to death by Ahmad Beg, Nawab of Broach, for having called a Muslim an infidel and having refused an offer of converting to Islam in lieu of death.[20] The Parsis' socialization to the dominant political regime also offered them advantages. Individual Parsis assumed positions of power and prestige under various regimes. The Parsi priest Dastur Meherji Rana (*c.* 1510-91) of Navsari and his family were of service to the Mogul Emperor Akbar; and the Dordi family served the Mogul court in the reign of Jehangir. With the arrival of the Europeans in India, the Parsis functioned as traders and middlemen for many interests. Rustam Manock (*c.* 1635-1719) of Surat, was the greatest Parsi trader of his age, and was broker, ambassador, and plenipotentiary between the Europeans and the Mogul court. The ability to preserve identity, gain status and reputation, and avail new opportunities

---

[18] J. J. Modi, "A Note on the Parsee Massacre at Variav," *Journal of the K. R. Cama Oriental Institute* 2 (1923).

[19] S. H. Hodivala, "The Sack of Sanjan," in *Studies in Parsi History*, 37-66.

[20] Seervai and Patell, "Gujarat Parsis," 219.

for material gain through political collaboration was a pattern familiar to the communities and groups, and families and individuals in the history of India. The commercial and political ties the Parsis developed with Europeans particularly the British, from the seventeenth century, saw them become one of India's most influential communities.

In 1322, the first European account of the Parsis was made by the French missionary Jordanus, who noted the race of pagans that worshipped fire and exposed their dead to vultures in roofless towers. Jordanus described the Parsis of Broach. In 1323, the Italian monk Odoric noted practices by the Parsis of Thana similar to those observed by Jordanus in Broach.[21] From the sixteenth century, more accounts of the Parsis appear, starting with those of the Portuguese.[22] In 1615, Edward Terry, chaplain to Sir Thomas Roe, the ambassador to the Mogul Emperor Jehangir from 1615 to 1618, offered the first British account of the Parsis. Terry noted the race of heathens called Parsis, living among the Hindus, but in many ways differing from them. Terry would be one of the first Europeans to note the similarity of the Parsis to the other Indians around them, for example, in their occupations and livelihood. At the same time, he noted the unique religion of the Parsis: "For those Parsees, further, they believe that there is but one god, who made all things and hath a sovereign power over all."[23] From his observations of the religious beliefs and customs of the Parsis, it also appears that Terry was one of the first Europeans to directly converse with the Parsis and have their traditions explained to him. The need the Parsis felt to explain their religion and culture in a favourable way to outsiders to the community was measure of their conciliatory and adaptive nature.

The early history of the Parsis in India illustrates the imperatives that prevailed upon the minority in safeguarding its existence in the new and dominant social environment. The Parsis' ability to adapt to the social and cultural norms of the Indian setting reflected the extent

[21] See D. F. Karaka, *History of the Parsis*, 2 vols. (London, 1884), 1:40; R. B. Paymaster, *Early History of the Parsees in India* (Bombay, 1954), 36. N. K. Firby, *European Travelers and Their Perceptions of Zoroastrians in the 17th and 18th Centuries* (Berlin, 1988).

[22] See Garcia Da Orta, *Colloquies on the Simples and Drugs of India*, trans. Sir Clements Markam (London, 1913); Father Anthony Monserrate, *The Commentary of Father Monserrate S.J. On His Journey to the Court of Akbar*, trans. J. S. Hoyland (London, 1922).

[23] Paymaster, *Early History of the Parsees*, 38.

to which they had successfully integrated into Indian society. In large measure, this involved the Parsis' assimilating to the Indian setting. The Parsis' adoption and use of the languages of India was the most conspicuous example of their assimilation. Persian was effectively abandoned and forgotten in favour of a dialect version of the Gujarati in Western India.[24] Significantly, prayers and religious ritual continued to be recited in Avestan. The Parsis also adapted many of the practices and tendencies favoured by the various Indian communities that surrounded them, as for example, the adoption of Indian dress norms, and the observance of many of the festivals and ceremonies of India. The Parsis also adapted to the rules of purity and commensality practised in the Indian setting. They adhered to dietary regulations and restrictions alongside those followed by the Indian communities. For example, the Parsis followed the taboo against the eating of beef or pork, adhered to by Hindus and Muslims respectively, according to the practice of the particular local Hindu or Muslim community the Parsis neighboured.[25] Some of the social practices of the Indian setting would test and threaten the Parsis' exclusiveness. Child marriage, bigamy, and the worship and frequenting of non-Zoroastrian religious sites were practices adhered to by some Parsis. The Parsis, as a community, recognized these practices as borrowed from Hindus and Muslims, and as both foreign to their traditional norms and unsanctioned under Zoroastrianism. Repeated attempts would be made to remove these practices in the history of the Parsis. The antagonism of the Parsis to aspects of their social environment, in the midst of their general assimilation to it, evinced the agency of the Parsis to transform the terms of the encounter.

The same norms that encouraged the Parsis' assimilation to the Indian setting also isolated the Parsis as a community and fostered

---

[24] The Parsis fashioned their own Gujarati dialect or patois that utilized Persianized forms and vocabulary. During the nineteenth century, as the Parsis increasingly became Anglicized, the strength of Parsi-Gujarati was in decline. Today, Parsi-Gujarati has lost much of its uniqueness predominantly as a result of English usage among the Parsis. The decline in Gujarati literacy among new generations of Parsis, furthermore, is turning Parsi-Gujarati increasingly into a conversational language. See S. N. Gajendragadkar, *Parsi-Gujarati: A Descriptive Analysis* (Bombay, 1974); Bharati Modi, in *Parsiana*, January 1992.

[25] John Henry Grose, *A Voyage to the East Indies*, vol. 1 (London, 1766), 124, noted the custom of the Parsis to observe the dietary sensibilities of both their Hindu and Muslim neighbours, which Grose took to be a part of the 'covenant' made by their ancestors on first coming to India.

their exclusiveness. The caste customs and rules of purity and commensality practised in the Indian setting permitted the Parsis to remain apart from other Indian communities, without incurring their displeasure. The customs of the Parsis were left both undisturbed and free to change to meet their unique requirements. Whereas the Parsis adhered to local rules of purity and commensality, they also retained the purity laws mandated by their religion. Purity codes are a characteristic of Zoroastrianism and its dualistic belief in the struggle between good and evil in the spiritual and material worlds. The separation, protection, and purification of what is regarded as ritually pure from that which is polluted corresponds to the safeguarding and furtherance of good in the universe. Zoroastrian purity laws and codes are both complex and comprehensive, and bind the Zoroastrian in responsibility and obligation to observe ritual purity on behalf of oneself and others. The Parsis of India sought to maintain certain customs and prohibitions that were based on Zoroastrian religious theory. In particular, the Parsis sought to maintain those purity laws that directly affected their religious life.

The injunctions of Zoroastrianism centred on a defence of the seven elements of creation, and the obligation on every Zoroastrian to avoid coming into physical contact with ritual pollutants. Ritual pollution and impurity were defined as the onset and encroachment of decay, defilement, and death. Purity laws encompassed rules for the protection of the ritually pure from defilement, and purification following contamination and pollution. Parsis meticulously observed the protection and purification of metal, earth, water, fire, plants, and animals, as well as the rules regarding personal conduct and purity in daily life. Purity rules governed personal hygiene and daily ablutions, bodily excretions, childbirth, and sexual conduct and relations. For example, the proper ritual disposal of shorn hair and cut nails had to be observed, as both substances once removed from the body were considered the tools of evil, and were to be wrapped up and buried. The Parsis also continued the practice observed in Iran of secluding women during their menstrual period, as they were considered ritually impure during this time. This practice had ancient roots among the Indo-Iranians, and similar, if less severe, rituals of purification were observed among both Hindus in India and Muslims in Iran and elsewhere. Menstruating Parsi women were secluded and removed themselves to a special enclosure known as the *dashtānestān* or 'place of menstruating women,' which in medieval times consisted of a separate building, and in later periods a special room within the house. Contact between the women and others was limited and purifications were required of those who came into contact with the women. In respect of their own dietary laws, the Parsis also observed ritual dictates that divided living creatures into good and evil categories. The consumption of *khrafstra* or 'noxious' creatures believed the potential tools of evil was taboo, and their destruction was considered religiously meritorious among Zoroastrians. Parsis also abstained from consuming meat for a number of days following the death of a relation, or on special occasions and ceremonies, as it was considered inauspicious at this time.[26]

Rituals of protection and purification among the Parsis included the performance of devotional acts, and various forms of physical purification. Prayer was a central component of daily life among both laity and priests. Bracketing activities by prayer served to ritualize the function. Parsis recited various prayers known as the *bāj*, at the beginning of each of the five *gāhs* or watches of the day, on special occasions, and before and after engaging in many daily activities such as ablutions and eating. The *Kustī* ceremony composes the central prayer ritual of the Parsis, and consists in untying and tying the *kustī* or thread cord around the waist of the *sudra* or white undershirt worn by the initiated Zoroastrian. Parsis perform the *Kustī* ceremony daily, and the medieval Parsis preceded it with the performance of the *Pādyāb* ritual of washing parts of the body with *gōmēz* or unconsecrated bull's urine, as a ablutionary liquid, before engaging in religious activity. Parsi religious practice also included personal and vicarious ritual observance, performed on behalf of oneself or others, such as the confession of sins, or prayers in memory of the dead. As many of the purity rituals of the Parsis were simplified or came into disuse over time, prayer remained of or gained particular importance among the Parsis.[27]

---

[26] Modi, *Religious Ceremonies and Customs*, 167-77; Jamsheed K. Choksy, *Purity and Pollution in Zoroastrianism: Triumph Over Evil* (Austin, 1989), 78-104; Boyce, *Zoroastrians*, 44-5; Philippe Gignoux, "Dietary Laws in Pre-Islamic and Post-Sasanian Iran: A Comparative Survey," *Jerusalem Studies in Arabic and Islam* 17 (1994): 16-42; De Jong, *Traditions of the Magi*, 14-24.

[27] Modi, Religious Ceremonies and Customs, 86-101, 354-76; Choksy, *Purity and Pollution*, 53-62; Boyce, *Zoroastrians*, 138-9; Mary Boyce, "The Pious Foundations of Zoroastrians," *Bulletin of the School of Oriental and African Studies* 31, no. 1 (1968): 270-89.

The ceremonies surrounding death were particularly important as the greatest pollution resulted from contact with carrion (nasā). A special class of individuals existed to prevent physical pollution and minimize the contact between Parsis and the dead. The function of handling a corpse after death and carrying a corpse into the *dakhma*, as well as maintaining the *dakhma*, was exclusively assigned to a special hereditary class of corpse-bearers among the Parsis, known as *nasāsālārs*. In areas of greater Parsi population, a second set of individuals could also exist known as *khāndhiās*, to further minimize the degree of contact between Parsis and the dead, who performed the task of pall-bearers carrying a corpse upon an iron bier to the *dakhma* for obsequies. The *Barashnom* ceremony was the most elaborate Zoroastrian ritual purification, intended for the physical removal of extreme forms of pollution from an individual, and a process of reintegration undergone in order to renew contact with other Zoroastrians. The *Barashnom-e noh-shab* or 'ablution of the nine nights,' consisted of a Parsi undergoing successive ritual cleansings in retreat for nine nights in a secluded pit or area.[28]

The religious rituals of the early Parsis in India reflected the evolution of Zoroastrian religious observance in post-Sasanian times. Parsi observances and rituals, at the same time, underwent change in the Indian setting. The Parsis remained doctrinally orthodox while adaptive in their ritual observance. Over time, many of the purity laws were looked on more as ideals than as practical observances. Elaborate purification ceremonies and rites for relatively minor pollutions were increasingly dispensed with by Parsis, simplified, or became vicarious and were delegated to priests to act on behalf of the laity. The *Barashnom* was simplified, and over time was seen as a ceremony reserved predominantly if not exclusively for the priesthood. The *Rīman* ritual effectively superseded the *Barashnom* ceremony as a ritual ablution against carrion, eliminating the nine days and nights retreat in favour of an individual ritually traversing nine enclosures or 'pure' spaces within a short period of time. The *Rīman* ritual evolved following the development of the Parsi priesthood in Gujarat, and was practiced solely among the Parsis of India. The Parsis also gradually eliminated the killing of *khrafstra* or 'noxious'

[28] Modi, *Religious Ceremonies and Customs*, 102-48; Albert de Jong, "Purification in *absentia*: On the Development of Zoroastrian Ritual Practice," in Jan Assmann and Guy G. Stroumsa, ed. *Transformations of the Inner Self in Ancient Religions* (Leiden, 1999), 301-29.

creatures, yet maintained the theoretical link between certain creatures and evil. The diminution of this unique practice, as well as changes in the number and significance of festivals, were in all likelihood the result of acculturation and the changing relevance of certain cultural practices within the new social environment. Other practices continued until modern times and the influence of particularly Western influences on the Parsis. The practice of secluding women during their menstrual period was observed until the nineteenth century among orthodox Parsis.[29] Significantly, while the Parsis abandoned many of the purity dictates of their ancestors, they would compose new standards and conventions of community conduct and behaviour in benefit of Parsi identity in the Indian setting.

The Indian setting undoubtedly influenced other practices among the Parsis. The sacrifice of certain animals performed in Iran was abandoned in India. The Parsis increasingly venerated the cow and bull, and employed the latter in certain rites. The use of ritual cleansing and ablutionary agents such as bull's urine and hairs, and ash from sacred fires has an ancient history among the Indo-Iranian peoples. The evolution of purification rituals among the Parsis reflected the fidelity to religious laws under changing circumstances, and the exploitation of the opportunities available to preserve identity within the new social milieu. The Parsis utilized *nīrang* or consecrated bull's urine as a ritual-cleansing agent, and sanctified its use through the unique consecration ceremony of *Nīrangdin*. The use of the *varasyo* or white bull was also unique to the Parsis, and had an important role in the development of priestly power in India. Each *panthak* guarded the possession of the bull and distributed the 'ritual elements' associated with the bull to priestly locales under its jurisdiction for their use in religious rites. The influence of the Indian setting on the Parsis was also evident in the terminology the Parsis adopted to denote ceremonies and rites, as the Parsis increasingly employed Gujarati words or unique Parsi renderings to Zoroastrian ceremonies, and reassigned the names of ceremonies common to the Parsi and Iranian communities, thereby distinguishing their understanding of the ceremonies from that of the Iranian community.[30]

---

[29] Choksy, *Purity and Pollution*, 71-7; De Jong, "Purification in *absentia*" 301-29.

[30] Boyce, *Zoroastrianism*, 174-5; idem, *Zoroastrians*, 173-4; idem, "On the Calendar of Zoroastrian Feasts," *Bulletin of the School of Oriental and African*

The nature of caste-based India also aided the formation and concretization of other Parsi social patterns. The Parsis in India reaffirmed endogamy as a means of safeguarding identity. Endogamy, as the practice of marrying within the tribe or group, defined the social character of the Parsis. The Zoroastrians of Iran had their own custom of endogamy. Iranian society was based on a rigid hierarchy of four basic classes: priests, nobles, farmers/herdsmen, and artisans. Society was patriarchal and distinct marriage practices and customs existed to favour 'racial purity'. In the early Islamic period, both Zoroastrian purity laws and Islamic law forbade or limited the social contact between Zoroastrians and Muslims. The Zoroastrians of Iran grew more isolated over time, and the threat of the loss of group identity as a result of pressures to convert became ever-present.[31] In India, the Parsis were free to define their sense of group identity without fear of external threat. The caste customs and social structure of Indian society, theoretically, constrained the ability of Parsis to intermarry with members of other communities. In reaffirming endogamy as a means of consolidating group identity, the Parsis came to define themselves as a non-proselytizing community. Moreover, the Parsis of India evolved a strict endogamy along religious and ethnic lines. The protection of the religious identity became identified with marriage within the ethnic group of the Indian Zoroastrian community. For the Parsi, religious identity as a Zoroastrian and ethnic identity as a Parsi became synonymous. The reaffirmation of endogamy by the Parsis served to foster the sense of a self-conscious and self-defined community.

The ability of non-Hindu groups and communities to share characteristics of the Hindu social environment without conforming completely to the system is not unusual in the social milieu of India. Muslim, Christian, and Jewish communities in India have adopted caste-like divisions and categorizations. Unlike the Parsis, moreover, these communities having accepted converts have been known to reproduce social stratification and hierarchical divisions within their ranks. Muslims in India maintain caste distinctions based on ethnic

---

Studies 23 (1970): 513-39; Modi, *Religious Ceremonies and Customs*, 25-39; De Jong, *Traditions of the Magi* 338-42; Enthoven, *Tribes and Castes*, 464-5.

[31]Alessandro Bausani, *The Persians: From the Earliest Days to the Twentieth Century*, trans. J. B. Donne (London, 1971), 62-3; De Jong, Traditions of the Magi, 409-10, 424-32, 455; Choksy, *Conflict and Cooperation*, 76-93; idem, "Zoroastrians in Muslim Iran," 28.

and convert descent. Marriage patterns that support hereditary groupings as well as the practice of hereditary professions are also common among Indian Muslims communities. Christians maintain their cultural and religious distinctiveness from other Indians while converts tend to retain their caste status. Among the Jews of India, the Bene Israel community numbers some 5,000 individuals today, and resides predominantly in Maharashtra and along the Cochin coast. The Bene Israel community claims an 'ancient' heritage in India and has sought to maintain certain unique Jewish customs. At the same time, among the Bene Israel, distinctions and rankings based on both 'colour' and original ancestry have been noted.[32]

As measure of their distinct social organization, and in imitation of the terminology used among Indians, the Parsis would refer to themselves as a 'caste'. Essentially, Indian society came to see the Parsis as a distinct and different *jāti* or caste, writ large. The application of the term 'caste,' in the broader sense, to self-defined communities within Indian society, was maintained even in the nineteenth century when, for example, in Bombay City many groups coexisted and cooperated with one another in the development of a common civic culture. In such a setting, in a juridical sense, "caste comprised any well-defined native community governed for certain internal purposes by its own rules and regulations."[33] Many of the contemporary monographic sources on the Parsis, both Parsi and British, acknowledge and refer to the Parsi caste and the efforts undertaken by the Parsis to preserve the sense of their community consciousness. By the nineteenth century, the Parsis were an influential and important community determined to promote cooperation with the other Indian communities of Bombay, including the British, in the interests of the improvement of life in Bombay. At the same time, they remained ever conscious of the need to safeguard and distinguish their minority community identity.

---

[32] Imtiaz Ahmad, ed., *Caste and Social Stratification Among the Muslims* (Delhi, 1973); Romila Thapar, *A History of India* (New York, 1966), 294, 300-1; S. Benjamin, *The Bene-Israels of the Bombay Presidency* (Bombay, 1873); S. Strizower, "Jews as an Indian Caste," *Jewish Journal of Sociology* 1 (1959): 43-57; idem, *The Children of Israel*: *The Bene Israel of Bombay* (Oxford, 1971); Shirley Berry Isenberg, *India's Bene Israel: A Comprehensive Inquiry and Sourcebook* (Bombay, 1988); Oprah Slapak, ed., *The Jews of India: A Story of Three Communities* (Jerusalem, 1995).

[33] D. F. Mulla, *Jurisdiction of Courts in Matters Relating to the Rights and Powers of Castes* (Bombay, 1901), 2-3.

The Parsis' adoption of characteristics of the indigenous social environment had in all likelihood prevented their complete assimilation into Indian society. The ability of the Parsis to adopt characteristics of the indigenous social environment, and their ability to adapt these characteristics to their requirements is the striking feature of the Parsis' early history in India. The Parsis' sense of identity served to safeguard against those characteristics typically associated with the Hindu caste environment. The Parsis did not develop occupational specializations on any religious or ideological basis; and the Parsis did not develop a hierarchical system of social stratification that formed a caste system within their ranks. By adapting general aspects of the social environment to their social organization, to some extent, the Parsis were able to set the terms for their standing within the dominant social culture.

The Parsis recognized a moral and religious equality within the community, mindful of the socio-economic differences that existed between individuals. The practice of endogamy did not translate into strict marriage patterns among Parsis along lineal, kinship and clan lines, as among the Hindus, and which distinguish various socio-economic, occupational, and religious distinctions on a caste and subcaste level, as part of identity. Parsis took to the majority of livelihoods and professions. Many of the Gujarati names they adopted, particularly in the nineteenth century denoted the place where they settled and the professions they took up. Parsis, however, did not form any link between caste and occupational specialization. Parsis were not tied hereditarily to either the land they settled on or the profession they chose, and no hierarchy according to profession arose as existed among Hindu castes. Both the *āthornans* or Parsi priesthood and the *nasāsālārs* or corpse-bearers, functioned as hereditary occupational classes, followed along the male line. Both professions, to varying degrees, recognized the rules of purity and commensality in their dealings with the other members of the community. However, the males born into both classes were not bound to compulsorily follow the profession, and the professional duties of the members of the classes did not exclude them from participation in the life of the Parsi community.

The resistance to the development of caste divisions within the Parsi community was the result of an outlook that saw such divisions as antithetical to the Parsis' moral and religious values, and as counter-productive to the *raison d'être* of the community. The distinctiveness and exclusiveness the Parsis sought to maintain from the other Indian communities depended upon the regulation of the customs and practices of all those who called themselves part of the Parsi community. The emergence of subgroups or subcastes that could take on and develop separate and unique characteristics of their own, apart from the general body of Parsis, would have militated against the formation of a strong, singular identity among the Parsis. The practice of endogamy and the general disinclination on the part of the Parsis to accept 'converts' into the religion and community further militated against caste divisions arising as a result of any acculturative influence of contact between Parsis and new converts.[34] Unlike other non-Hindu communities in India that also find no ideological justification for a caste system within their respective religious traditions, but that reproduce caste-like social stratification, the Parsis maintained group identity without incidence of social schism. The historical imperative that shaped itself within the Parsi community in support of common identity combined religious ideology with social necessity to militate against caste divisions.

The evolution of leadership among the Parsis corresponded to the ability of the Parsis to utilize the mechanisms of their social environment in benefit of identity. The earliest form of authority among the Parsis was the guidance provided by the priest class. The spiritual authority of the Zoroastrian priest derived from the chain of spiritual authority that descended from Ahura Mazdā and Zarathustra. It gave to the priest his knowledge of religious tradition and literature and ability to judge in matters of faith, as well as his essential role in the performance of ritual and sacerdotal rites on behalf of the laity. The authority the priesthood retained upon the Parsis' arrival in India is inferred in the leadership role ascribed to priests in the traditional narratives, in both representing the Parsis before non-Parsis, and in the consecration and protection of the sacred fire in India. The growth of the Parsi community in India witnessed a corresponding change in priestly practice and development. A more specialized and hierarchically differentiated priesthood emerged than existed in Iran, to service the varied social and religious requirements of the Parsis.[35]

---

[34] Ahmad, *Caste and Social Stratification*, 13.

[35] On the history, authority, and structure of the Parsi priesthood, see Philip G. Kreyenbroek, "On the Concept of Spiritual Authority in Zoroastrianism," *Jerusalem Studies in Arabic and Islam* 17 (1994): 1-15; idem, "Zoroastrian Priesthood After the Fall of the Sasanian Empire," in *Transition Periods in Iranian History: Actes du*

The Parsi priesthood is ranked according to ritual duties into three grades: the *dastūr* (high priest), the *mōbad*, and the *hērbad* or *ērvad*. The Parsi priesthood has no head, or pope, though the members of great priestly families are the heads of *panthaks* or ecclesiastical districts.[36] The five *panthaks* of Sanjan, Navsari, Anklesvar, Broach, and Cambay that were established in the thirteenth century came to exercise both administrative and economic power. In addition to controlling the priesthood within their jurisdictions, the *panthaks* benefited from the wealth generated from fees paid to them from lesser districts. The priests could also collect substantial *ashōdād* or gratuities for religious rites performed, which constituted the chief means of support for a Parsi priest. In c. 1492, the *Ātash Bahrām* and priests of Sanjan came to reside in Navsari, upon an agreement arranged between the Sanjana and Bhagaria priests of Navsari. Disputes between priestly centres were settled by the exchange of missives, or adjudicated by convening *anjumans* or special conclaves of priests. In a serious dispute, where no agreement could be reached internally, the priests appealed to the local non-Parsi authority.[37]

The establishment of jurisdictions and the settlement of disputes suggest the comprehensive organization of the Parsi priesthood in Gujarat. Within the major provincial centres members of leading priestly family functioned both as mediators within and representatives of the Parsis outside the community.[38] The members of great priestly families held a special cachet inside and outside the Parsi community as individuals of responsibility and moral authority who

---

Symposium de Fribourg-en-Brisgau, 22-24 Mai 1985 (Paris, 1987), 151-66; Modi, *Religious Ceremonies and Customs*, 197-204.

[36] There are two degrees for the Parsi priesthood, known as the *Nāvar* and the *Martab*. Both degrees require having to master and recite religious texts, and undergo a succession of rites and ritual purifications before the priest may be deemed initiated. The latter degree qualifies a priest to perform the ceremonies of the inner fire-temple. See Modi, *Religious Ceremonies and Customs*, 197-209.

[37] In the eighteenth century, a dispute arose involving priestly jurisdiction between the Sanjana priests and the Bhagaria priests of Navsari. The Sanjana priests who had been limited to tending the *Ātash Bahrām* in Navsari sought to increase their priestly duties over the Bhagaria's right to perform all ecclesiastical duties in Navsari. The local Hindu prince a Damaji Rao adjudicated the dispute in favour of the Navsari priests. This led the Sanjana priests to remove the *Ātash Bahrām*, to whom it belonged, from Navsari. It eventually settled in the Gujarat town of Udwada. See Modi, *A Few Events*, 80.

[38] Documents bear the names of many *andhyarus* (Gujarati for those of priestly background) as arbiters in disputes between Parsis. See S. H. Hodivala, "Some Ancient Parsi Documents," in *Studies in Parsi History*, 189-253.

could be called on to represent Parsis involved in legal disputes or other difficulties with non-Parsi officials. It was a measure of the reputation of the priests of Navsari that between 1578 and 1579, Dastur Meherji Rana and the priests of Navsari visited the Mogul Emperor Akbar at Fatehpur Sikri to expound on the tenets of Zoroastrianism. They took part in religious discussions and debates between the representatives of different religious communities, which the Emperor had initiated between 1576 and 1579, during a period of personal religious inquiry. The influence of the Parsis on the enlightened Emperor was such that Akbar had incorporated Zoroastrian motifs, including the veneration of fire and the sun, and the use of Zoroastrian calendar names, into the syncretic religious royal cult he had initiated in 1582, known as the *Din-i-Ilahi*.[39] In appreciation for his services, Akbar had bestowed a large fief of land on Meherji Rana and, some years later, an equally large amount on his son Dastur Kaikobad. The visit of Dastur Meherji Rana to the Emperor had raised the profile of the Parsis and enhanced the reputation of the Meherji Rana family.[40] The situation of the Parsis with Indian political society albeit remained precarious, and even the Meherji Rana family was not immune from political prosecution, as Dastur Kaikobad and his relatives would spend time in Mogul prisons possibly involving revenue disputes with the Mogul government.[41]

The authority of the Parsi priesthood within the Parsi community would reach its height by the eighteenth century. The competition and rivalry for influence among the priestly centres were measure of their coveted leadership role. The destruction of Sanjan by the Muslims in 1478 and the transfer of the *Ātash Bahrām* to Navsari in *c.*1492 effectively had established the religious and territorial primacy of Navsari among priestly centres and over the Parsi community. In 1765, the second *Ātash Bahrām* of the Parsis was consecrated in Navsari, to replace the sacred fire that the Sanjana priests removed to Udwada.[42] The authority of Navsari was further enhanced with the commencement of the *Rivāyat* correspondence between the Parsis and the Zoroastrian priests of Iran. The *Rivāyat* correspondence, as it

---

[39] J. J. Modi, "The Parsis at the Court of Akbar and Dastur Meherji Rana," in *Contributions on Akbar and the Parsees*, ed. B. P. Ambashthya (Delhi, 1976); M. L. R. Choudhury, *The Din-i-Ilahi, or the Religion of Akbar* (Calcutta, 1952).

[40] Modi, "Parsis at the Court of Akbar," 9-12, 83.

[41] See Hodivala, "Some Ancient Parsi Documents," 189-253.

[42] See Ramsay, *The Indian Antiquary*, July 5, 1872, 213n.

is known, composes a corpus of religious and social questions by the Parsis to the Iranian priests and their answers that began in 1478 and continued until the eighteenth century. The *Rivāyats* evinced the dependence of the Parsis upon the Zoroastrian priests of Iran for answers to the proper observance of rituals, and the continued spiritual authority they held among the Parsis. The *Rivāyats* at the same time reflected the change Parsi ritual observance in India had undergone, as well as the state of knowledge among the Parsi priesthood. By the fifteenth century, an evolution occurred in many basic Parsi rituals—relating to consecration ceremonies, purity observance, and funerary customs and rites. The change that Parsi ritual observance underwent in India was as much a result of the necessity to meet the particular exigencies and requirements of the Parsis in the new setting as of declining religious knowledge among the priests. Ultimately, the transformation of Parsi ritual tradition as well as the growth of religious learning that the *Rivāyat* correspondence contributed to would alter the relationship between the Parsi and Iranian communities, and shift spiritual authority among the Parsis away from Iran to India.[43]

The *Rivāyat* correspondence is also significant in highlighting the growing influence of the *behdins* or laity in the Parsi community. The initiation of the *Rivāyat* correspondence had owed to the efforts of the Parsi leader Changa Asa of Navsari. The family of Changa Asa held high administrative office in Navsari under the Muslim Sultans of Gujarat. Both Changa Asa and his father Asa Rana were important in securing a reduction in the *jaziya* tax on non-Muslims for the Parsis. Changa Asa had negotiated the transfer of the *Ātash Bahrām* and priests of Sanjan to Navsari, and the sharing of priestly responsibilities. Changa Asa extolled on the need to resume communications with the priests of Iran to benefit Parsi knowledge, which led to the layman Nariman Hoshang of Broach undertaking the voyage.[44] Significantly, the termination of the *Rivāyat* correspondence by the Parsis in the eighteenth century may have been a result of the refusal of the lay leadership among the Parsis to accept any longer

---

[43] See B. N. Dhabhar, *The Persian Rivayats of Hormazyar Framarz and Others: Their Version With Introduction and Notes* (Bombay, 1932); J. J. Modi, "Darab Hormazdyar's Rivayat: A Few Notes in the Study of an Early Part of its Contents," *Journal of the K. R. Cama Oriental Institute* 22 (Bombay, 1932): 109-238; S. H. Hodivala, "The Dates of the Persian Rivayats," in *Studies in Parsi History*, 276-349; Paymaster, *Early History of the Parsees*, 66-84.

[44] Karaka, *History of the Parsis*, 1:4-7.

the claim of spiritual authority from the Iranian priesthood and their followers in India. Controversy had arisen among the Parsis over discrepancies in the customs of the Parsi and Iranian communities that the *Rivāyat* correspondence made evident, in particular as regarded the calendar. The Parsis' intercalation had come to differ from that performed in Iran, resulting in a difference of a month between the calendars of the two communities. In 1745, a group of Parsis adopted the Iranian calendar. A schism formed between those Parsis who recognized the Iranian calendar known as *Qadimis* (ancients), and the majority *Rasmis* or *Shāhānshāhis* (traditionalists) who maintained the claim of religious orthodoxy and continuity with their ancestors. The last four *Rivāyats* from 1743 onwards were exclusively between the *Qadimis* and Iranians. The calendar controversy aptly illustrated the evolution and consolidation of a unique Parsi tradition in India by the eighteenth century that was adhered to by the majority of Parsis. Furthermore, the disposition of that tradition would increasingly rest with a new class of Parsis. The growing economic power of the laity and its imperative to legitimize its authority through the defence of Parsi tradition would see it assume the leadership of the Parsi community.[45]

With the spread and growth of the Parsi community in Gujarat, lay and clerical leaders shared authority within the community. The institutions of social organization among the Parsis had to advance beyond those suited to only the priests. The Parsis utilized and adapted the social mechanisms and institutions within their environment to safeguard and preserve their religious and community identity. The institution of the caste punchayet or council of elders became an effective model for community government and a tool to strengthen Parsi identity. The punchayet form of organization was an indigenous model unknown to the Zoroastrians of Iran, and utilized by the Parsis to meet their community requirements in the Indian setting. 'Caste' punchayets were formed by the Parsis in the towns

---

[45] See B. B. Patel, "A Brief Outline of Some Controversial Questions That Led to the Advancement of the Study of Religious Literature Among the Parsis," in *K.R. Cama Memorial Volume* (Bombay, 1900), 170-82; D. N. Coorlawalla, "The Last Kabiseh," in *Dastur Hoshang Memorial Volume* (Bombay, 1918), 143-69; Mario Vitalone, *The Persian Revayat 'Ithother': Zoroastrian Rituals in the Eighteenth Century* (Naples, 1996); E. Bickerman, "The Zoroastrian Calendar," *Archiv Oriental* 35(1967): 197-207; Karaka, *History of the Parsis*, 1:114-15.

and locales where they settled to deal with the specific disputes and issues relative to the Parsi community. The nature of the Parsis' social organization was reflected in the nature of the Parsis' punchayets. Birth, wealth, and property did not automatically confer status among the Parsis, whether socially or in terms of requisite for leadership. The clerical and lay individuals who formed punchayets on behalf of the Parsis derived their authority from their background, character, and service to the community. The Parsis were under the jurisdiction of the local authority, Hindu or Muslim, in matters criminal and civil. The caste punchayet, however, provided the settlement of disputes between parties who were Parsi, as well the discussion of issues of concern to the entire community. Many issues were of a social and religious nature such as concerning marriage, adoption, excommunication, and priestly duties. In adjudicating private disputes between parties, the punchayet's authority was equally effective in providing the means to regulate the broader social, religious, and cultural concerns of the Parsi community. The punchayets did not pass laws, in a modern sense, but their regulations were binding upon the members of the community.

The Parsis of Navsari had formed a Punchayet in 1642, composed of priests and influential laymen. In Surat, the commercial nature of the town made for leadership among the class of merchants and brokers in its punchayet. By the mid-seventeenth century, Surat became the major centre of Parsi concentration largely as a result of the commercial trade in Western India. With the rise of Parsi wealth, a new class came to leadership among the Parsis, known as the *shetias*. The Parsi *shetias* effectively succeeded the Parsi priesthood as the centre of authority and leadership among the Parsis. The Parsi *shetias* reached the height of their authority in Bombay, where they utilized the punchayet and their ties to the British to assume authority over the Parsi community. In 1787, the British officially recognized the punchayet in Bombay as the internal government of the Parsis in Bombay. In the following decades, the Parsi Punchayet extended its influence over the whole of the Parsi community of Western India.

Parsi Identity in Colonial Times

In the centuries following their arrival in India and through medieval times, the processes by which the Parsis shaped their identity and sought to function in India took shape. The Parsis followed a pattern of assimilation and accommodation to new social norms, adaptation of social norms, mechanisms, and influences to their own requirements, and agency in leading change to the benefit of identity. This pattern of assimilation, accommodation, adaptation, and agency was repeated on their arrival in Bombay. A continuity of process in support of identity emerges, and which places the formation of identity under colonialism as a prominent chapter within that process. The challenges faced by the Parsis in the urban setting of nineteenth century Bombay presented the community with new threats to the collective identity, as well as new opportunities to safeguard it. The development of the Parsi community in Bombay takes place in the context of the recurring concern to preserve identity in a changing social environment.

The impact of colonialism on the Parsis was not unique among the communities of India; however, it was unusual for the pronounced effect it had in both shaping the Parsi identity and the understanding of that evolution.[46] Colonialism shaped the representation of the Parsis to the world and reshaped Parsi self-perceptions. The pervading influence of colonialism on the Parsis was such that the appreciation of their historical development was altered. The history of the Parsis from their arrival in India prior to their settlement in Bombay, a period of perhaps as much as a thousand years, was reinterpreted and downplayed in comparison to the history of the Parsis during their heyday in Bombay, particularly during the nineteenth century. The lack of monographic sources before the nineteenth century, in part, accounts for this outlook. In larger measure, the tremendous economic and social transformation the Parsis underwent during the colonial era inspired the majority of interest, and imposed on the historical imagination a view of a more static community in earlier centuries. The danger in any analysis of iden-

[46] The analysis of colonialism of late has concentrated on the dialogue and interdependence between the rise and ascendancy of colonialism and the 'construction' of the colonial world, or the representation of communities under colonialism. Colonialism and the history of conquest has come to be viewed as essential in shaping the European concept of its own identity, fostering views of nationality and culture that are distinguished and dichotomized from colonial cultures and peoples. Identity for colonial peoples, in turn, has been interpreted as largely being shaped and derived from the social and political shifts under the new conditions of colonialism. See Edward W. Said, *Orientalism* (New York, 1985); Ronald Inden, *Imagining India* (Oxford, 1990); Nicholas B. Dirks, ed., *Colonialism and Culture* (Ann Arbor, 1992).

tity under colonialism is to ascribe to the colonial setting the conditions under which identity is shaped altogether. The danger too often lies in viewing colonialism as the only subject, and seeing change as in large measure driven by, or limited to colonialism.[47]

The incorporation of the Parsis into the economic and political world of British power, from the late eighteenth century, evinced the successful transformation the Parsis effected from minority community in the provincial setting to influential colonial elite in the new urban setting of Bombay. The Parsis' cooperation with the British was primarily based on a keen appreciation of the new environment of opportunity the British were effecting in Western India, on the part of both individual Parsis directly in contact with the British and on the part of the community as a whole. Active and voluntary assimilation to British values, furthermore, was based on the personal affinity the Parsi developed in contact with things British. A set of semiotics was adopted by the Parsis in support of the affinity between things British and Parsi, and in praise of Parsi identity under colonial rule. At the same time, the assimilation to British values both competed and functioned alongside the Parsis' commitment to traditional identity.

The power of colonialism to shape the self-perceptions of the colonized is evident in contemporary Parsi representations of the community during colonial rule. The compatibility between colonial rule in India and the rise of the Parsis forms a staple motif in contemporary Parsi monographs. The historical and cultural overview of the Parsis and their relationship with the British offered in Parsi colonial writings remain useful and important in understanding the contemporary Parsis. The magnification of the Parsi community serves to shape the identity of the minority in the broader social environment, while reinforcing the sense, of identity within the community. Parsi self-attributes and accomplishments assume new significance under colonialism.[48] Contemporary Parsi narratives on

---

[47] T. M. Luhrmann, *The Good Parsi: The Fate of a Colonial Elite in Postcolonial Society* (Cambridge, Mass., 1996), contends that a virulent self-criticism, or trope of decay, has entered the present-day Parsi mindset, ostensibly as a result of the loss of identity as a colonial elite. Drawing on the literature on colonialism and gender, the author contends that this postcolonial trauma among the Parsis is most conspicuously reflected in the Parsis having internalized a gender-based colonial stereotype of the 'native' as the feminized other of the colonizer.

[48] The pre-eminent representative of this genre is Dosabhai Framji Karaka (1829-1902), *The British Raj Contrasted With Its Predecessors* (London, 1858),

the Parsis and British rule highlight the motivations behind the rise of the Parsi community to wealth, influence, and power in the nineteenth century. These narratives form a strong political argument on behalf of a new, educated, and urbanized Parsi up-and-coming elite, shaped in their perceptions and sensibilities by colonial rule. The desire to see Parsi achievement follow from the connection to the British and, in large measure, as dependent upon the connection is natural enough given the history of the community during the nineteenth century. Both contemporary traditionalist and reformist Parsis also shared this assessment. The first generation of Parsis to benefit from British contact, which included the *shetias*, found the stability and order the British presence brought to India worthy of praise. The second generation of Parsis, exemplified by the reformers, considered the benefit of British rule to lie in the intellectual and social influences it made possible.

The appreciation of the impact of British colonialism on the Parsis, as with that on Indian life in general, often disguises the complex set of processes to which British and Indian alike contributed. The British ability to aid and support Parsi identity is significant and complex. For example, the consolidation of British political power at Bombay indirectly contributed to the strengthening of Parsi identity. The British recognition of the authority of the Parsi Punchayet of Bombay in 1787, aimed to incorporate and socialize Parsi authority under colonialism. In recognizing a new urban Parsi mercantile elite as the leadership of the community, the British indirectly supported the strengthening of community authority and internal reforms to Parsi identity in the urban setting. Similarly, the perception of its obsolescence under colonialism, in part, contributed to the fall of the Punchayet. By mid-nineteenth century, a new generation of Parsi reformers portrayed the Punchayet as symbol of the class and caste authority of the shetias over the Parsis, and as the brake on social

The Parsees: Their History, Manners, Customs and Religion (London, 1858), *The History of the Parsis: Including Their Manners, Customs, Religion, and Present Position*, 2 vols. (London, 1884). Other major historical works that emerged during colonial rule include: the *Parsee Prakash*, a compilation of newspaper articles and notes of reference on the Parsis by Bomanjee Byramjee Patell and subsequently edited by Rustom Barjorji Paymaster, in seven volumes from 1888 to 1942; M. M. Murzban, *The Parsis*, 2 vols. (Bombay, 1917), offers a translation of the work of Delphine Menant's *Les Parsis* (Paris, 1898). The motif of noting accomplishments expression of cultural identity remains a characteristic of Parsi historical writing. See H. D. Darukhanawala, *Parsi Lustre on Indian Soil* (Bombay, 1939).

progress. The Parsis came to formulate judgements about their social evolution that were the product of a changing social and intellectual outlook within mid-nineteenth century colonialism.[49] The representation of India as an unchanging, unhistorical, static civilization dominated by caste and caste leaders, within a segment of European thought since the eighteenth century, influenced Indian reformers. Progress in nineteenth century India was interpreted as being led by a new intelligentsia that had been shaped by Western thought, and that championed new ideas on social and religious reform against the power of traditional hierarchies. This interpretation, however, misrepresented both the nature of leadership among the Parsis and the process involved in the Parsis' attempts to safeguard their identity throughout their history.[50] The Parsi reformers' outlook at mid-century reflected the extent to which the new, educated class of Parsis came to accept the framework of representations of Indian culture and institutions fashioned under colonialism and came to shape Parsi identity within these conditions.

The difficulties experienced by the Parsis with British colonialism also shaped the Parsis' efforts in preserving identity. At no time were the Parsis more hostile to the colonial environment than in the defence of their religious identity. This was most evident in the Parsis' resistance to the influences of the Christian missionaries during the 1830s. The growth and penetration of British power in India could equally test the strength of Parsi identity and compel change. British refusal to recognize the waning authority of the Parsi Punchayet from the mid-1830s, coupled to the reformers' attacks motivated the Parsis to re-examine the efficacy of the institution as a means of safeguarding identity. More problematically, by mid-century, the Parsis were in conflict with British legal culture in India. By 1824,

[49] See Ronald Inden, "Orientalist Constructions of India," *Modern Asian Studies*, 20, no. 3 (1986): 401-46; Rosalind O'Hanlon, "Cultures of rule, communities of resistance: gender, discourse and tradition in recent South Asian historiographies," in *Identity Consciousness and the Past*, ed. L. Seneviratne (Adelaide, 1988), 94-114; Gyan Prakash, "Writing Post-Orientalist Histories of the Third World: Indian Historiography Is Good to Think," in *Colonialism and Culture*, 353-88; R. O'Hanlon and D. Washbrook, "After Orientalism: Culture, Criticism and Politics in the Third World," *Comparative Studies of Society and History* 34, no. 1 (1992): 141-67.

[50] For a more critical view of the Parsi Punchayet, see Christine Dobbin, "The Parsi Punchayet in Bombay City in the Nineteenth Century," *Modern Asian Studies*, 4, no. 2 (1970): 149-64.

varying and conflicting sets of laws applied to the urban and provincial Parsi communities of Western India. The English law came to be applied to the Parsis of Bombay. Its unsuitability to their social requirements and circumstances shaped the Parsis' efforts to formulate and frame a Parsi law code at mid-century. The Parsis devised and composed a law code that took into account their traditions and customs while satisfying their legal requirements in contemporary British India. The creation of the Parsi law code further evinced the variegated nature of colonial domination and its ability to incorporate and assimilate Parsi identity within colonial culture. Colonial imperatives had adversely impacted on the practice of Parsi tradition, ultimately compelling Parsi tradition to accelerate its assimilation to contemporary British norms.

Parsi reaction in antagonism to British cultural influences, however, was unusual during the colonial era. The Parsi ability to actively assimilate and subsume British values and influences in support of identity distinguishes the cultural history of the community from mid-nineteenth century. The Westernization and Anglicization of Parsi social values and mores suggested a wholesale assimilation. In actuality, the process was consonant with the history of Parsi response to changes in the social milieu in benefit of Parsi identity. Amidst the great social changes of nineteenth century India, the Parsi ability to lead, promote and direct social change distinguishes Parsi agency in the colonial setting. In championing social change within the Parsi community, Parsis associated themselves with the new influences. The introduction of education in India has historically been attributed to Western influences. The Parsis were pioneers in the advancement of education in Bombay for themselves and in cooperation with other communities, prior to mid-century." The social and political connection between the British and Parsis favoured cooperation in the establishment of educational institutions beginning in

---

[51] The standard account of the British promotion of education in India remains, B. T. McCully, *English Education and the Origins of Indian Nationalism* (New York, 1940). See also Kenneth Ballhatchet, *Social Policy and Social Change in Western India* (London, 1957); Eric Stokes, *The English Utilitarians and India* (Oxford, 1959). Eckehard Kulke, *The Parsees in India: A Minority as Agent of Social Change* (Munich, 1974), attributes the necessity to reform the educational state of the Parsis to the confrontations with the Christian missionaries that exposed the poor state of Parsi knowledge. He utilizes a cross-disciplinary approach to analyze the social determinants that contributed to making the Parsis the effective agents of social change.

the first half of the nineteenth century while, from mid-century, the progress of education resulted in the rise of a new generation of Parsis prepared to lead the social advancement of the community. Both social advantage and cultural identification followed from the progress of Parsi education, as the Parsis were regarded as the most influential, literate, and progressive of communities. The ability on the part of the Parsis to make educational progress a marker of identity attests to the complexity of response to the introduction of British influences in India.

Transformations in Parsi religious tradition further shed light on the indigenous process of social change taking place within the colonial intellectual environment. To some extent, the Parsi response paralleled the general Indian response to colonial and European stimulus of Indian thought.[52] In the intellectual and cultural milieu of mid-nineteenth century colonial India, Western rationalist ideas combined with European scholarship into Indian civilization influenced the education and social activism of Indians. The discourse on social progress and religious reform that emerged within the Parsi community took place within the context of the tremendous influence of Western education and ideas upon the Parsis. The influence of contemporary Western scholarship largely shaped the direction and character of the Parsi reformers' investigations and the interpretation of their religion and history, as Parsi scholarship both emulated and acted in reaction to the Western gaze. An evolution of Parsi thought was underway by the latter nineteenth century that sought to place the Parsis' religious and social progress in the context of the new knowledge. Most significantly, a movement for religious reform arose among the Parsis that led to the introduction of heterodoxy within a conservative and hitherto unchanged religious tradition. An orthodox challenge in turn emerged. The reformulations of Parsi religious thought on the part of both reformist and orthodox movements attested to the habituation of Parsi thought to Western thought by the twentieth century. At the same time, the creativity of response by both reformers and orthodox reflected a much more compelling

[52] On the influence of Western ideas on Indian thought see J. N. Farquhar, *Modern Religious Movements in India* (London, 1929); C. H. Heismath, *Indian Nationalism and Hindu Social Reform* (Princeton, 1964); David Kopf, *British Orientalism and the Bengal Renaissance: The Dynamics of Indian Modernization, 1773-1835* (Berkeley, 1969); Kenneth W. Jones, *The New Cambridge History of India: Socio-Religious Reform Movements in British India* (Cambridge, 1989).

historical imperative at work than exclusively the subordination of Parsi thinking to contemporary trends. By the early twentieth century, a parallel process emerged in which the Parsis assimilated to a Western intellectual outlook, and adapted Western influences and ideas to the unique requirements of Parsi identity.

Summary

The history of the Parsis of India constitutes a history of efforts to preserve identity within a changing historical setting. Continuity underlies Parsi attempts to preserve and safeguard a sense of community identity. A historical pattern of response emerges that favours adaptability to the social environment, while refashioning influences within the social environment in support of the preservation, strengthening, and at times composition of a sense of group identity. In large measure, this entailed assimilation to the customs and ways of the social environment, in both pre-colonial and colonial times. This shaped the Parsi identity into a unique amalgam of Indian and Western characteristics added to a conservative religious practice. At times, the assimilation to the social environment posed the risk of succumbing to its influences and trends, once again, in pre-colonial and colonial times. At other times, the Parsis incorporated prevailing societal influences and trends as part of their identity as the active agents and pioneers of change. While outwardly Parsi conformity appeared as copy or imitation, and at times as garish imitation, it was as often internally congruent with some Parsi exigency. Changes in the social environment, consequently, could serve as the means around which to build cultural identity.

Whether in the adoption of the caste punchayet model, the fostering of social and political ties with the British, the ready adoption of Western education and other influences, the creation of a Parsi press, or the Parsis' entry into politics, the necessity to refashion mechanisms and influences to their requirements was felt by Parsis. The nature of the adaptations the Parsis made to their social environment, moreover, evinced certain ingenuity. The fragmented history of the Indian Zoroastrians on arriving in India, as well as their immediate exigencies had made it incumbent on the Parsis to periodically *compose* or shape new traditions for the community, as much as seek to preserve and safeguard what was believed to be an ancient legacy. The changes in Parsi ritual observances, the rise of the Parsi Punchayet, and the creation of the Parsi law code illustrate this process. It is fundamentally incorrect to see the history of the Parsis in India as solely the attempt to preserve an Iranian 'presence' on Indian soil. The history of the Parsis of India is that of the rise and creation of a unique Parsi/Indian community, defined by its religion and ancient heritage, but also shaped by the process of its adaptation to the milieu of India.

Adaptability on the part of the Parsis, however, did not preclude tensions within the Parsi identity. This was particularly so given that the pattern of historical adaptability in support of identity was not consciously perceived by the Parsis, often resulting in disagreement over the nature of identity and the course of action to safeguard it. By the middle of the nineteenth century, the structure of authority among the Parsis became diffused as competing centres of authority emerged that sought to shape Parsi identity from their perspectives. The vigour of these movements provided new understanding and appreciation of Parsi identity. Parsi participation and contribution to the Indian nationalist movement, moreover, owed to the rise of a broader sense of identity among educated reformers. At the same time, pluralism of thought and opinion among Parsis by the twentieth century introduced tensions and stalemate over authority within the community. The commitment to Parsi identity remained strong among reformers and traditionalists, while disagreement arose over the definition of that identity. Specifically, the issue of who could be called a Parsi and what constituted membership in the community was in dispute. In the absence of community consensus the Parsis turned to the British law courts as new centres of authority to settle issues relative to Parsi identity. The law courts were asked to rule on the definition of Parsi in two celebrated cases in 1906-08 and 1915-18, only to render decisions that did not end the discussion.

CHAPTER ONE

IDENTITY AND THE URBAN SETTING: THE MORAL AND MATERIAL SUPPORTS OF COMMUNITY

When the first Parsis arrived in Bombay in the mid-seventeenth century, Bombay was little more than a collection of fishing villages spread over seven unconnected islands surrounded by swamps.[1] On first coming to take possession of Bombay from the Portuguese, in September of 1662, as part of the dowry of the Infanta Catherine of Braganza to Charles II, Captain James Ley of the Royal Navy conveyed his disappointment at the sight of the paltry island.[2] By September of 1668, Bombay was once again transferred, this time from the Crown to the East India Company, on payment of a fee. As some of the first inhabitants, the Parsis had better gleaned the potential of Bombay, principally for their benefit, and had brought some order to the physical environment even before the final British take-over in February of 1665.[3] In 1665, the Parsi Kharshedji Pochaji Panday had provided the materials and men for the construction of the first fortifications of the town, while under Portuguese possession.[4] Within the next hundred and fifty years, Parsis would shape the familiar physical outline of Bombay and would become some of its principal inhabitants. The great impact the Parsis would have on making Bombay the premier city of Western India was paralleled by the powerful influence that urbanization would have on the history of the Parsi community. In the crucible of urban Bombay, the Parsis defined the nature of their community and shaped their responsibilities and obligations to one another.

---

[1] The archipelago of Bombay consists of seven islands that, at low tide, link to form four main islands. At the time of transfer, the British situated themselves at the southern tip of the archipelago facing the harbour. See James Douglas, *Bombay and Western India*, vol. 1 (Delhi, 1893); J. C. Masselos, "Changing Definitions of Bombay: City State to Capital City," in *Ports and Their Hinterlands in India (1700-1950)*, ed. Indu Banga (New Delhi, 1992), 273-316.

[2] M. D. David, *History of Bombay, 1661-1708* (Bombay 1973), 39.

[3] Ibid., 41-67.

[4] D. F. Karaka, *History of the Parsis*, 2 vols. (London, 1884), 2:48.

In his work *The Needs of Strangers*, the philosopher Michael Ignatieff ponders the relationship between the materially secure and the needy. Questions about human needs, he claims, are questions about human obligations. The pairing of the idea of need with the idea of duty and obligation binds humans beyond the demands of custom, habit, and historical inheritance. "The language of human needs is a basic way of speaking about this idea of a natural human identity.... A society in which strangers would feel common belonging and mutual responsibility to each other depends on trust, and trust reposes in turn on the idea that beneath difference there is identity."[5] From the time of the arrival of the first Parsis in Bombay the language of need, and the language of right that naturally derives from it, had come to be elaborated. Parsis felt the sense of dependence, materially, socially, religiously, and morally, as the parameters of their mutual needs and obligations began to take shape.

Many of the first Parsis to come to Bombay to make their fortune and name were the founders of great families closely connected with the development of the Parsi community. These Parsis, who would be honoured with titles and emoluments from the British, encouraged the arrival of other Parsis to Bombay. They would come to be regarded as the natural leaders of this incipient community, derive their prestige from their treatment of their less well-off brethren, providing employment, welfare, and leadership, while benefiting from the labour of those they employed and the respect due a benefactor. Whereas two generations previously the leaders of the Parsi community in provincial Gujarat had been the priests, the exigencies of the new setting worked to elevate those with material resources and contacts to the status of leaders. Dorabji Nanabhai is regarded as one of the earliest residents of Bombay; he successfully accommodated himself to the transition of power from the Portuguese to the British. In 1668, Dorabji was employed by the British to collect a body tax on the local inhabitants, which he managed to do without incident. Rustamji Dorabji (1667-1763) served the British following his father's death in 1688. In 1692, in the midst of a cholera epidemic that had decimated the British garrison in Bombay, Rustamji rallied the Koli fisherman and other residents of Bombay in the town's defence during an attack by the Muslim Sidi of Janjira. In

[5] Michael Ignatieff, *The Needs of Strangers: An Essay on Privacy, Solidarity, and the Politics of Being Human* (London, 1984), 27-8.

recognition of his services, the British honoured Rustmaji with the hereditary title of Patel or chief, and allowed him to collect taxes from the residents of Bombay. Rustamji's son, Cowasji Rustamji Patel (1744-99), played a prominent role in the development of Bombay and service to the Parsi community.[6] The Patel family was joined by the Banaji the Modi families as some of the first prominent Parsi inhabitants of Bombay in the late seventeenth century.

The ability to foresee the avenues to opportunity and wealth, to accommodate themselves to changing political realities, and the willingness to provide for their fellows commended the early Parsi inhabitants of Bombay as leaders. Consequently, enterprising Parsis assumed the role of leaders of both society and their community. Leadership bound the wealthy and influential Parsis of Bombay in obligation to the needs of their community. As early as 1669, application was made to the Governor for permission to erect the first *dakhma* or Tower of Silence on the land of Hirjibhai Vacha Modi, on the Pedder Road at Malabar Hill. The successful application was followed by its opening sometime between 1670 and 1675.[7] The *dakhma* of the Parsis in Bombay, like those in Gujarat, was essential to the Parsis' practice of exposure of the dead to vultures, and was located close to where Parsis settled. The site of the *dakhma* in Bombay initially consisted of a single, roofless circular structure containing a central well. As the Parsis settled in Bombay in greater numbers, the site would hold many more Towers.[8] At about the same

[6] B. B. Patell, *The Parsee Patells of Bombay: Their Services to the British Government* (Bombay, 1876), 5-7.

[7] Douglas, *Bombay and Western India*, 1:31, cites 1669 as the year permission was sought for the *dakhma's* construction. K. N. Seervai and B. B. Patell, "Gujarat Parsis from Their Earliest Settlement to the Present Time," in *Gazetteer of Bombay Presidency*, vol. 9, part 2, ed. J. M. Campbell (Bombay, 1899), 252, cite 1670 as the date (of opening) of the *dakhma*. David, *History of Bombay*, 136, cites 1673 as the year Governor Aungier granted the request for the site at Malabar Hill. Dr. John Fryer, in a letter written on January 16, 1675, describes the first *dakhma* of Bombay, or "Parsy tomb," as being lately reared. See R. B. Paymaster, *Early History of the Parsees in India* (Bombay, 1954), 48-9.

[8] At the time of Dr. Fryer's narrative, Hirji Vacha Modi's Tower of Silence was the only one in Bombay. By 1844, there were seven Towers of various conditions, of which two were reserved for Mancherji Jivanji Readymoney (1786), and the family of Dadibhai Nusserwanji Dadiseth (1798) respectively. The other Towers were built by Manockji Nowroji (1757), the Parsi Punchayet (1779), Framji Cowasji Banaji (1832), and Cavasji E. Bisni, known as Kapuskao's Tower (1844). The Parsis in locales where the population was small or migratory consecrated a cemetery, known as an *aramgah* or 'place of rest'. On a list of the Towers of Silence and

time, in 1673, Hirji Vacha Modi gave his name to the first *Ātash Ādarān* or Parsi fire-temple in the Fort district of Bombay, which survived until the fire of 1803. In 1709, Banaji Limji (*c.* 1654-1734) built the second Parsi fire-temple in Bombay. In 1783, the first *Ātash Bahrām* or cathedral fire-temple of the Parsis in Bombay was built through the charity of Dadibhai Nusserwanji Dadiseth. In accordance with Parsi custom, the *Ātash Bahrāms*, *Ātash Ādarāns*, and *Ātash Dādgāhs* bore the name of the individuals and families that undertook their consecration and construction for posterity.[9]

It has been remarked that the Parsis were early to appear but slow to settle in large numbers in Bombay.[10] The general population of Bombay remained largely migratory during its early history. The great influx of Parsis to Bombay, on a permanent basis, did not take place until the latter half of the eighteenth century. Albeit, the presence of both the *dakhma* and the fire-temple in Hirji Vacha's time suggests the importance that Bombay was assuming for the Parsis, as well as the commitment Hirji Vacha had assumed in erecting the edifices on behalf of the community. Hirji Vacha, who had come to Bombay from Surat, in order to erect either edifice would have had to successfully look after the accommodation of priests and their community in Bombay. The priests would have to have been fully initiated and qualified to perform special ceremonies for laying the foundation and consecration of the *dakhma*.[11] The importance Bombay had assumed for some Parsis was evident in the unusual and unprecedented act of Mancherji Jivanji Readymoney, the wealthy China trader, who had a *dakhma* built in Bombay in 1786, as his personal repository. Dadibhai Nusserwanji Dadiseth, who was also a

---

burial grounds in India and worldwide, see Seervai and Patell, "Gujarat Parsis," 252-4 (to 1898); and John R. Hinnells, "The Flowering of Zoroastrian Benevolence: Parsi Charities in the 19th and 20th Centuries," in *Papers in Honour of Professor Mary Boyce, Hommages et Opera Minora*, vol. 10 (Leiden, 1985), 294-6 (to 1905).

[9] R. E. Enthoven, ed., *The Tribes and Castes of Bombay* (Bombay, 1922), 461. There are two *Ātash Bahrām* (fire-temples) in Iran (Yazd and Tehran), and eight in India today. There are four in Bombay (consecrated in 1783, 1830, 1845 and 1897), two in Surat (1823), one in Navsari (1763), and one in Udwada (1742). For a list of the fire-temples in India and worldwide, see Seervai and Patell, "Gujarat Parsis," 247-51 (to 1898); and Hinnells, "Flowering of Zoroastrian Benevolence," 290-4 (to 1941); Marzban J. Giara, *Global Directory of Zoroastrian Fire Temples* (Bombay, 1998).

[10] Percival Spear, *The Nabobs* (Oxford, 1932), 74.

[11] The *Tānā* ceremony is performed to consecrate the foudation of a *dakhma*. See Modi, *Religious Ceremonies*, 245-52.

wealthy trader and the third generation of Dadiseth in Bombay whose family had come from Surat, similarly had a private *dakhma* built for his family in 1798.[12] Prior to the Parsis' settlement in Bombay, religious sites and functions were predominantly funded by subscriptions of the Parsis in local communities. The oldest fire-temples and *dakhmas* in Gujarat were built and maintained largely through subscription of the Parsis. As individual Parsis increasingly became wealthy, they assumed a greater share of the support of religious sites whether personally, by bequest following death, or through their heirs. For example, the Wadiaji and Banaji *Ātash Bahrāms* in Bombay were consecrated and built in 1830 and 1845 respectively, by the family heirs in memory of the family patriarchs at substantial expense. During the nineteenth century, as Parsi charity diversified to provide for various causes, the construction of religious buildings remained the conspicuous example of the investment Parsis made to their setting. While necessity dictated the establishment of the decent amenities of a community life, the long-term commitment to both Bombay and the interests of the Parsi community made for the social contract all civilized society demands.

The accommodation of Parsis in Bombay and their welfare and maintenance was part of a complex pattern of support practised among the Parsis. Rustam Manock of Surat was the greatest Parsi trader of his age and exemplar of Parsi benefactor. As a result of his trade and contacts that extended from the Mogul court to the European trading companies in the early eighteenth century, Rustam Manock had risen to a position of power and influence both among the merchants of Surat and within the Parsi community. His wealth and charity provided the Parsis of Surat with many amenities from bridges and roads, wells and water tanks, to rest centres and community residential areas or colonies within a town, known as a *wadi* or *pura*. A part of Surat where Parsis lived was known as Rustampura, named in Rustam's honour.[13] As one of Bombay's earliest Parsi set-

[12] See Karaka, *History of the Parsis*, 2:57n; J. G. Da Cunha, *The Origin of Bombay* (Bombay, 1900), 299.

[13] On Rustam Manock, see *Parsee Prakash*, 1:23; P. S. S. Pissurlencar, *Portuguese Records on Rustom Manock*, trans. S. B. D'Silva (Bombay, 1936); J. J. Modi, "Rustam Manock, the Broker of the English East India Company and the Persian Quisseh of Rustam Manock, A Study," in *Asiatic Papers*, vol. 4 (Bombay, 1929), 101-320; Jalbhai A. Seth, *Genealogy and Brief Account of the Seth Family* (in Gujarati) (Bombay, 1900); S. K. Hodivala, *History of the Seth Family* (in Gujarati) (Bombay, 1931).

tlers, the family of Rustam Manock aided the settlement of Parsis in Bombay. Rustam's son Nowroji Manockji purchased a considerable amount of land in Bombay.[14] And from the time of his arrival from Surat in 1730, Manockji Nowroji, the grandson of Rustam Manock, also had accommodated the arrival of Parsis in Bombay, settling them in a *wadi*. Manockji Nowroji's *wadi* was alongside a fire-temple he had built in 1732 that served as the centre for priests coming from Navsari. Manockji also made provision to build the second *dakhma* in Bombay following his death in 1748.[15]

The majority of Parsis from the eighteenth century had settled in the enclosed area of Bombay known as the Fort.[16] The Fort along with the original fortified area of the city known as the Castle, constituted Bombay Town or City. In 1811, the Parsi population of Bombay Town and Island was noted to be 10,042.[17] In 1812, the Parsi population was recorded to be 13,156, out of a resident population of 164,688 in Bombay Town and Island. In 1813, the first survey of the population of the Fort noted a population of 10,801 persons, 5,464 of which were Parsis.[18] By 1816, the Parsi population remained steady, while the number of Parsis living in the Fort was 9,153.[19] Generations of great Parsi families established their residences in the Fort. These prominent and wealthy Parsis of Bombay along with their counterparts in the other Indian communities were referred to as *shets* or *setts*, denoting their high social position, and as a class were referred to as *shetias*. The *shetias* also amassed great landholdings, and hereditary and commercial property throughout Bombay Island. In addition to the wealth generated from trade, the landholdings of the Parsi *shetias* in Bombay provided them with investment capital and rent.

Many of the landholdings of the Parsi *shets* were hereditary land grants from the British for services rendered. The Patel family had

---

[14] *Parsee Prakash*, 1:29 (obituary of Nowroji Manockji).

[15] Ibid., 36 (obituary of Manockji Nowroji); Karaka, *History of the Parsis*, 2:16-8; Seervai and Patell, "Gujarat Parsis," 199, 250; Enthoven, *Tribes and Castes*, 462.

[16] Letters of Jamsetjee Jejeebhoy to John Bax, Sec'y of Gov't, November 12, 1832, in General Department 1832 15/260:317, Department of Archives, Government of Maharashtra, Bombay (hereafter cited as G.D.); July 3, 1833, G.D. 1833 13/284:179.

[17] On the Parsi population in Bombay, see M. M. Murzban, *The Parsis*, 2 vols. (1917; reprint, Bombay, 1994), 1:165.

[18] *Gazetteer of Bombay City and Island*, vol. 1 (Bombay, 1909), 158-60.

[19] Murzban, *Parsis*, 1:166.

extensive land in Thana and Bassein, granted to them in reward for service to the British. Cowasji Rustamji Patel established a Parsi colony at Thana and held the right to issue passes to Parsis going there.[20] The Wadias were some of the first great landholders, and principal benefactors of Bombay and the Parsi community. Pestonjee Bomanjee Wadia (1758-1816), the China trader, owned palatial estates at Mazagon, Parel, and Breach Candy in Bombay. His residence at Parel, called 'Lal Baug' had grounds covering 100,000 square yards. In 1814, the report on land tenures in Bombay noted that Pestonjee owned the largest area among the inhabitants of the Fort of 15,598 square yards, worth Rs. 4,24,500, essentially making him the largest landowner in Bombay.[21] Pestonjee's brother Hormarjee Bomanjee Wadia (1766-1826), was a trader and broker for many British agency houses, and was head of the Parsi Punchayet of Bombay. He was one of the largest landholders in Bombay, and in 1808 was granted eight villages on Salsette Island by the Government of Bombay in exchange for land he held in the centre of the city. He resided at his estate at Parel, known as Lowjee Castle.[22]

The settlement of the great Parsi families in Bombay City, alongside the British, established an urban social elite and culture. With the exception of the merchant-prince Framji Cowasji Banaj (1767-1851), the great Parsi men did not aspire to the life of country landed grandees. Framji Cowasji Banaji was the great grandson of Banaji Limji, the founder of the Banaji family. Framji Cowasji invested his fortune from trade and commerce in real estate, and operated his own working estate known as Pavai, on Salsette Island, where he attempted to grow a wide variety of produce from sugar cane, tea, and cotton to silk worms.[23] The urbanized nature of the Parsi families' landholdings is significant as it was paralleled in the highly urbanized settlement of the Parsis in Bombay. The removal of greater numbers of Parsis to Bombay from provincial Gujarat followed economic opportunities and the pattern of patronage and charity avail-

---

[20] Patell, *Parsee Patells*, 18; Karaka, *History of the Parsis*, 2:53–t.

[21] Indian currency at this time contains units of pie, paisa (3 pie), anna (4 paise), rupee (16 annas), hajaar (1000 rupees), lakh (1,00,000 rupees), crore (100 lakhs). One rupee or Rs. 1 is equivalent to two shillings and a halfpenny.

[22] Francis Warden, *Report on the Landed Tenures of Bombay* (Bombay, 1814), 96-7; R. A. Wadia, *Scions of Lowjee Wadia* (Bombay, 1964), 98, 171-2.

[23] Karaka, *History of the Parsis*, 2:113-14; K. N. Banaji, *Memoirs of the Late Framji Cowasji Banaji* (Bombay, 1892), 33-57; D. E. Wacha, *Shells from the Sands of Bombay: My Recollections and Reminiscences, 1860-75* (Bombay, 1920), 456.

able in the new area of settlement. Many of the early Parsis of Bombay settled in the northern part of the Fort, not too distant from where the *shetias* resided, and close to where many of the first fire-temples were constructed. The early settlement of Parsis in Bombay, as a result of the agency of the wealthy families, would only be matched in the middle of the nineteenth century, at which time the settlement of large numbers of Parsis in *baugs* or residential colonies was made possible through the new wealth and prosperity of the commercial and industrial era. The pattern of settlement of the Parsis reaffirmed social and community ties and obligations, as well as formed a new sense of identity and loyalty tied to geography. Bombay had become the new home of the Parsis and its development the expression of the Parsis' influence in the new setting.

In this respect the duties and obligations felt by Parsis to the concept of the community, in many ways evident throughout the period since their arrival in India, were transferred to the more demanding confines of the urban setting. The Modis, Rustam Manockjis—whose descendants are known as Sett Khandans, Dadiseths, Wadias, and Banajis were only some of the earliest and most famous names to endow the Parsi community and Bombay with the largesse of their good fortune. The most essential and basic facilities of community life, such as a mortuary places and centres of worship, were followed by other public works such as the building of water tanks, land reclamation schemes, and the establishment of rest centres known as *dharamsalas*, essential to migrants especially in times of famine. In 1725, the Parsi merchant Bhikhaji Behramji Panday sank a well on the Esplanade for the use of both the Parsi and non-Parsi residents of Bombay, and which remains one of the oldest wells still existent.[24] In 1776, the construction of one of the first water tanks in Bombay at Khetwadi, was made possible through the charity of Cowasji Patel, and was maintained by the family up until 1834.[25] The Parsis also felt a sense of duty and obligation to aid the community during difficult circumstances. Drought and famine in Gujarat periodically witnessed the migration of Parsis to Bombay, where their co-religionists felt the obligation to provide assistance. During the great Gujarat famine and plague of 1790-91, Pestonjee Bomanjee Wadia, Nusserwanji Maneckji Wadia, and Dadibhai Nusserwanji Dadiseth pro-

---

[24] Karaka, *History of the Parsis*, 2:56.
[25] Patell, *Parsee Patells*, 19.

vided aid to thousands of Parsis settling in Bombay for a period of ten months, at a cost of Rs. 5,800 to each of the three men. A man of prolific charity, Pestonjee Bomanjee repeated his example on many similar occasions on behalf of the residents of Bombay and other Parsi centres, and was regarded as the most public-spirited man of his day.[26] Sorabji Manockji, another member of the Rustam Manock family, likewise followed Pestonjee Bomanjee's example.[27]

The sense of community felt by Parsis was not limited to the Parsi community. Liberality often translated for the Parsis into duty towards the greater community. Ratanji Manakji Enti (1733-1804) is reported to be the first Parsi to travel to Arabia in pursuit of trade. During the famine of 1790-91, Ratanji Manakji supervised the feeding of the poor of Gujarat on behalf of the Bombay Parsis. His insistence on accounting for the distribution of food by the acceptance of only new currency earned him his surname of Enti or 'obstinate,' and the name of new rupee or 'Entisahi' in his honour.[28] In her journal of a short residence in India of 1809, Maria Graham noted the extent of Parsi liberality, when during the famine of 1805-06 the Parsi merchant Ardeseer Dadee (1756-1810) arranged to feed 5,000 people for three months at his own expense.[29] Dadee's example was repeated in the decades to come by Parsis as their wealth increased, and they felt the need to elaborate on the idea of community. In May 1857, during a prolonged dry season, Eduljee Nusserwanjee Colabawalla supplied fresh water to the inhabitants of Colaba at his own expense.[30] During the Gujarat drought and famine of 1863-64, Cursetjee Furdoonjee Parekh (1812-96), the China trader, arranged to feed 3,000 people in Surat and Broach for three months, at a cost of almost Rs. 88,000. In addition, Parekh provided foodstuffs to the Portuguese authorities in Diu to feed the poor. Parekh was a generous philanthropist donating over Rs. 4,000,000 to public projects and humanitarian causes, and is best known for contributing Rs. 20,500 towards the building of the Flora Fountain in Bombay.[31] Parsi charity also extended across India, particularly as Parsis forged

---

[26] Wadia, *Scions of Lowjee Wadia*, 99; Karaka, *History of the Parsis*, 2:72, 77.

[27] Enthoven, *Tribes and Castes*, 465.

[28] Karaka, *History of the Parsis*, 2:37-8.

[29] Maria Graham, *Journal of a Residence in India* (Edinburgh, 1813), 44-5.

[30] *Bombay Times*, May 11, 1857.

[31] *Parsee Prakash*, 2:305, 561; H. D. Darukhanwala, *Parsi Lustre on Indian Soil* (Bombay, 1939), 90-1.

new trade and commercial opportunities. The members of the Vikaji family were revenue farmers for the Peshwa of Poona and later revenue and customs agents for the British between 1835 and 1845. In pursuit of the cotton trade between Bombay and the Deccan, they built roads and bridges through the Ghat Mountains. Vikaji Merji had fire-temples, *dakhmas*, and *dharamsalas* built in Tarapur, Belapur, Hyderabad, Sholapur, Aurangabad, and Secunderabad.[32]

Parsi charity furthermore was not limited to the confines of Bombay or India. Nasarvanji Kohiyar (*c.* 1717-97) utilized his wealth generated from trade and as dubash or agent for the Dutch at Surat, to provide for the Zoroastrians of Iran. He built and maintained a fire-temple for the Zoroastrians of Yazd, which contained a sacred fire brought from Surat. Kohiyar is also credited with reviving *Jamshedi Navroz* or the Spring Equinox festival among the Parsis.[33] From the beginning of the nineteenth century, as leading Parsis took account of events in Europe, Parsi charity towards non-Parsi objects outside India began. One of the earliest recorded donations by a Parsi was for Rs. 250, to provide famine relief in Ireland in 1822. This example was repeated twenty-five years later with Parsis giving over Rs. 10,000 in relief during the great potato famine.[34] The United Kingdom remained the overwhelming direction for Parsi charity to non-Parsi concerns outside India, with Parsi donations going to various causes from patriotic funds to educational and medical endowments. Parsi charity also found its way to continental Europe. The Parsi merchant-prince Jamsetjee Jejeebhoy (1783-1859) contributed some Rs. 6,000 towards fire relief in Hamburg in 1842. Jamsetjee Jejeebhoy was one of the greatest philanthropists of his age, who gave away Rs. 24,59,736 or over £245,000 towards public works and charities during his lifetime.[35]

The nature of Parsi charity was fundamentally born of the Zoroastrian life-affirming philosophy to contribute to the welfare of the world. The Zoroastrian credo to actively participate in the affairs of the world for the betterment of humanity encompasses the bestowal of charity, in innumerable forms, according to the ability and means

---

[32] Karaka, *History of the Parsis*, 2:124-30.

[33] Ibid, 2:38-9

[34] *Parsee Prakash*, 1:165, 474.

[35] Ibid., 397; *Bombay Times*, April 16, 1859; Jehangir R. P. Mody, *Jamsetjee Jejeebhoy the First Indian Knight and Baronet* (Bombay, 1959), 32-3.

of every Zoroastrian.[36] Both individual spiritual merit and social benefit derived from Parsi charity. Charity was practised among the Parsis prior to their arrival in Bombay, and was commented on by travellers to India from the earliest of contacts. In his *Voyage to Suratt* in the year 1689, the Reverend James Ovington offered one of the earliest European appraisals of the charitable nature of the Parsis:

> For they show a firm Affection to all of their own Sentiments in Religion, assist the Poor, and are very ready to provide for the Sustenance and Comfort of such as want it. Their universal kindness, either in employing such as are Needy and able to work, or bestowing a seasonable bounteous Charity to such as are infirm and miserable; leave no man destitute of Relief, nor suffer a Beggar in all their Tribe; and herein so far comply with their excellent Rule of Pythagoras, to enjoy a kind of Community among Friends.[37]

As the Parsis settled in Bombay, Parsi charity functioned to both aid that tenuous settlement and build the material foundations of community life that bound benefactors and beneficiaries in mutual support. The charity of the Parsi merchant, consequently, functioned alongside other traditional supports of community such as family, and religious and communal identity. The conspicuous character of Parsi charity, reflected in the naming of many charities after their patrons, also served to morally oblige the greater community in support of charity. During the nineteenth century, Parsi charity assumed a greater political significance under colonialism as it became an expression of the social and political power of philanthropic Parsi elites in British Indian society. The prolific Parsi charity towards British causes was a symbol of the affinity on many levels—social, cultural, and political—between the two communities. At the same time, as much as the Parsis came to operate within a society led by the British, the extension of charity to the British and others, was an expression of the community of values the Parsis had created in support of the improvement of the social condition and civic life.[38]

---

[36] On the spiritual merit of charity and Zoroastrianism, see *Saddar Nasr* 20, 29, 79, in B. N. Dhabhar, *Saddar Nasr and Saddar Bundehesh* (Bombay, 1909). See also M. N. Dhalla, *History of Zoroastrianism* (1938; reprint, Bombay, 1963), 75-80, 198.

[37] See Paymaster, *Early History of the Parsees*, 49-50.

[38] David L. White, "From Crisis to Philanthropy: The Dynamics of Eighteenth Century Parsi Philanthropy," *Modern Asian Studies 25*, no. 2 (1991): 303-20, notes the changing mechanics of Parsi charity as reflected in the practice by Rustam Manock in Surat, and his grandson Manockji Nowroji in Bombay.

The Economic Foundations of Community

In the discussion of the eleemosynary impulses of the Parsis, it should be noted that the prominent families in the early years of the growth of Bombay had, first and foremost, made their fortune and name through the singular desire to exploit (at times ruthlessly) the opportunities for trade, wealth, power, and influence acclaimed in that age. Charitableness found happy parallel in the personal ambition of the disciples of Croesus. Next to the uniqueness of their religion, the Parsis' commercial and economic success has characterized their history in India. The rise of Parsi economic power plays an essential role in the formation and evolution of Parsi identity. The rise of Parsi commercial wealth formed the basis of the economic, political, and social transformation of the Parsi community, and shaped the perceptions of the Parsis on the part of non-Parsis, and the self-perceptions of the Parsis.

The transformation of the economic and social state of the Parsis takes place in the changing economic setting of Western India, during the first half of the eighteenth century, in the period following the fracture and decline of the Mogul Empire and the rise of the European trading companies.[39] The contact between the Parsi merchants and traders of the provincial centres of Western India, and principally Surat, and the Europeans permitted both the accelerated rise of Parsi wealth and the consolidation of the European trading interests and factories in India. Among the merchant communities of Western India in the eighteenth century, the Parsis emerged as the premier, if latest, commercial group.

The rise of the Parsis to economic pre-eminence among the communities of Western India owed to factors economic, political, and cultural. The intimate knowledge the Parsis had of the social and cultural organization of Indian life, combined with an insightful understanding of the economic and developmental processes of Indian society and economy, advantage them in the changing economic set-

[39] Tapan Raychaudhuri, "The Eighteenth Century Background," in *The Cambridge Economic History of India*, vol. 2, c. *1700-1970*, ed. Dharma Kumar (Cambridge, 1983), 3-35; Ashin Das Gupta, *Indian Merchants and the Decline of Surat, 1700-1750* (Wiesbaden, 1979); K. N. Chaudhuri, *Trade and Civilization in the Indian Ocean: An Economic History from the Rise of Islam to 1750* (Cambridge, 1985); Holden Furber, *Bombay Presidency in the Mid-18th Century* (London, 1965); Pamela Nightingale, *Trade and Empire in Western India* (Cambridge, 1970).

ting. The economic conditions the Parsis faced in the eighteenth century were not essentially any different than those encountered by other Indian communities, and the Parsis operated within a dynamic and fluid economic and social environment alongside other enterprising Indians.[40] At the same time, throughout their history, the Parsis' ability to judge profit and loss, advantage and disadvantage, and react to both opportunity and adversity, ultimately benefited them. The rapidity with which Parsis took up the economic opportunities offered in cooperation with Europeans, and their ability to direct change to their advantage owed much to the process of assimilation, accommodation, adaptability, and agency the Parsis adhered to since their arrival in India. The Parsis benefited from their ability to foresee the rise of opportunity and adapt to the exigencies of the existing economic and political situation. Their versatility and adaptability were born of their historical accommodation to their social and cultural milieu, and the necessity to safeguard their personal interests, community, and identity as Parsis at all times and under all conditions. At times, this involved the necessity to risk new ventures and adjust to new situations, or forsake situations not to their benefit. The Parsis' removal to Bombay was a reaction to both impulses.

The social and political affinity Parsis developed with Europeans, and the British in particular, were initially an adjunct of the economic potentialities of cooperation both parties sensed from the beginning of their contact. The early British traders of the seventeenth and eighteenth centuries had entered a milieu in which commercial success was dependent on political and economic ties to other trading groups. Given the nature of their early commercial activities, cooperation between the Parsis and the British mutually benefited

[40] Various explanations have been posited to account for the rise of Parsi enterprise. Many have stressed the sociological reasons for the phenomenon alongside the economic ones, and often stress the Parsis' differences from India society, including the Parsis' lack of caste taboos in doing business with non-Parsis, their spirit of enterprise etc. See David L. White, "Parsis in the Commercial World of Western India, 1700-1750," *The Indian Economic and Social History Review* 24, no. 2 (1987): 183-203; Morris D. Morris, "The Growth of Large-Scale Industry to 1947," in *The Cambridge Economic History of India*, vol. 2, *c. 1757-1970*, 553-676; Ashin Das Gupta, "The Merchants of Surat, c. 1700-50," in *Elites in South Asia*, eds. E Leach and S. N. Mukherjee (Cambridge, 1970), 201-22; A. Guha, "The Comprador Role of Parsi Seths, 1750-1850," *Economic and Political Weekly* 5, no. 48 (November, 1970): 1933-8; Robert E. Kennedy, "The Protestant Ethic and the Parsis," *American Journal of Sociology* 68 (1962-63): 11-20; Eckehard Kulke, *The Parsees in India* (Munich, 1974), 78-9.

the two new trading entities. Other Indian communities, to varying degrees, shared this political and economic calculation and, in part, accounts for the relative differential advantage many Indian communities enjoyed in Western India under British colonialism. As British colonialism came to dominate India, the political nature of the relationship between British and Indians came to predominate the assessment of the relationship.

The Parsis of Western India had integrated themselves into the local society and functioned in a variety of occupations at the time of the arrival of the European traders and merchant-adventure companies. The Parsis had settled in all the major provincial centres, port cities, and port hinterlands of Western India.[41] The commercial world the Europeans entered was one of competition and rivalry among the major Indian traders and trading castes, which included Hindu Banias, Muslim Bohras, Armenians, and Parsis. By the eighteenth century, the three main commercial activities were: the procurement of goods, local and overseas trade, and financial brokerage. The Parsis were to varying degrees involved in all three activities, and attracted the attention of the Europeans. Parsis from the eighteenth century functioned as hawkers and traders, interpreters, contractors, and intermediaries providing British and European merchants and troops with fresh water, food, clothing, alcohol, boats, and various provisions and articles. Parsis also functioned as agents for British mercantile houses, guarantee brokers, and shipbuilders. The Parsi merchants, who came to Bombay from Surat, utilized their network of contacts to cooperate with Europeans to make themselves valuable.

Rustam Manock's network of commercial and political contacts, from suppliers in the hinterland to officials in the Mogul court, made him the premier Parsi broker-merchant of the early to mid-eighteenth century. Rustam was chief broker to both the Portuguese and British, gaining him a regular income and source of patronage that was also of benefit to the Parsi community. Both Nasarvanji Kohiyar and his son Kharshedji, a China trader, were agents for the Dutch and provided them with marine insurance. An individual such as Cowasji Rustamji Patel supplied the ships needed by the British to ferry

---

41 See comments of travellers, in Paymaster, *Early History of the Parsees*, 36 (Garcia Da Orta, 1534), 42-3 (Jean Albert de Mandelslo, 1638), 45 (Ogilby, 1670), 50 (Ovington, 1689); John H. Grose, *A Voyage to the East Indies*, vol. 1 (London, 1766), 125; James Forbes, *Oriental Memoirs*, vol. 1 (London, 1834), 110-12.

troops. The Modis, who were of priestly background and acted as community representatives in Gujarat, took their surname from their association with East India Factory in Surat as house stewards and supply agents. Nasarvanji Kavasji Petit (1769-1819), the founder of the family, came to Bombay from Surat in 1784, and was a supply agent and interpreter for the British, French, and Dutch trading companies. He took his surname from the nickname the French attached to him for his slight build. Hirji Jivanji, the second of three brothers who were known as Readymoney, was broker to Forbes & Co., the first mercantile house in India, and on his death in 1794, Hormarjee Bomanjee Wadia took his place. Hormarjee's son Bomanjee Hormarjee (1818-62) succeeded him as broker in turn. As brokers to Forbes & Co. and Bruce Fawcett & Co., the Wadia's were instrumental in financing crisis loans to the Government of Bombay between 1800 and 1805. By the nineteenth century, Parsi merchants controlled an extensive commercial enterprise in Bombay and Western India that encompassed every scale of business activity from the sale of European articles and luxuries, to the operation of a majority of the public establishments and hotels, to virtual control of the liquor trade. In 1720, Jamshedji Bhimjibhoy Patel started the first shop for the sale of British and local liquors in Bombay.[42]

The Parsis were also involved in the coastal and Indian Ocean export trade from Malabar to Goa, to ports in the Persian Gulf. Goods such as timber, food grains, pearls, calicoes, and cotton were traded, and by the latter eighteenth century muslins and silk were imported from Bengal and exported via Surat to the Gulf ports and as far as Istanbul. This activity involved Parsis and other Indians in close contact with Europeans as consignments were often freighted on each other's ships. The communications network Parsis and other Indians developed through this trade availed them to take advantage of political and economic developments, and make calculations in benefit of their fortunes. It was local Parsi and Muslim traders who helped sustain the enterprises of the early European private traders,

[42] Karaka, *History of the Parsis*, 2:9-11, 18, 38-40, 53, 55, 56, 60-5, 70-1, 75, 77, 253-9, 262; Wacha, *Shells*, 98, 211-12, 279-80, 626-7; Murzban, *Parsis*, 1:69; Enthoven, *Tribes and Castes*, 461; Delphine Menant, *The Parsis*, vol. 3, trans. Anthony D. Mango (Bombay, 1996), 241-2; R. A. Wadia, *A Forgotten Friend of India: Charles Forbes* 1st Bart. (Baroda, 1946), 14-5; idem, *Scions of Lowjee Wadia*, 163, 173; G. N. Madgaokar, *Mumbaiche Varnan* (in Marathi) (Bombay, 1863), 238; *Bombay Times*, March 29, 1859.

providing opportunities which otherwise were unavailable to those unconnected with a trading company.[43] By the nineteenth century, Parsi merchants and settlers followed alongside British troops on military campaigns expanding across British India. The firm of Jehangirji and Nasarvanji Jasavala sent their supply agents to set up shops for the British at Kabul during the Afghan Wars of 1838-42.[44]

The rise of Parsi wealth and influence in Bombay provides an insight into the rise of the British in Western India. If the military successes of the British in Bengal and Bihar had made retrenchment and economy a necessity for British imperialism during the eighteenth century, it was in Bombay and Western India that the concept of a commercial empire that included India proved its value. By the second half of the eighteenth century, the essential position of Bombay in the imperial trading system was established. The example of the lucrative network of private trade continued to commend the commercial value of Bombay to the East India Company, and encouraged the British to expend the effort to secure the Island and the west coast as an imperial possession. In trading with the commercial communities of India, the British traders found the capital, volume, and expertise that eventually saw them capture trade in Western India. The British domination of Western India clearly favoured the drift of the majority of Indian trading capital to them.[45]

The system of credit and capital investment available to traders and business-minded individuals exemplifies the complex network of imperial and colonial relations that was evolving in Western India from the mid-eighteenth century. This system tied a variety of Indian financiers, from grassroots moneylenders and bankers with links to the agrarian economy, to credit guarantors such as Parsis involved in internal and overseas trade. The high risk of credit brokerage may well have imposed a closer connection between contracting parties than other commercial enterprises. A new political atmosphere was merging where certain Indians, many of them Parsis, while benefiting from the opportunities of the British commercial presence

---

[43] Dilbagh Singh and Ashok B. Rajshirke, "The Merchants Communities in Surat: Trade, Trade Practices and Institutions in the Late Eighteenth Century," in *Ports and Their Hinterlands in India (1700-1950)*, 185-91. Nightingale, *Trade and Empire*, 18-21, cites the example of Francis Pym, who was able to join the East India Company after having conducted a modest private trade with local interests.

[44] *Parsee Prakash*, 1:401.

[45] Furber, *Bombay Presidency*, 64-5.

were socialized, and even subordinated, to private and broader public interests of British economic and political authority. At times, the travails associated with such contact may have appeared to outweigh the benefits for both parties. Rustam Manock and his sons encountered many difficulties in their dealings with the East India Company. Nowroji Manockji travelled to England in 1724, on the ship of Thomas Mathews, in order to secure the release of his brothers from detention in Bombay and Surat over a trade dispute.[46]

The advantages for the Parsis in cooperating with the British were not meagre. The early Parsis were considered so efficient at their trade that some British, as if in envy, deprecated their "persevering in the holy thirst for gold."[47] The ability to risk and benefit from the commercial, social, and political ties to the British, consequently, proved instrumental in the development of the Parsi community. The great Parsi *shetias*, those prominent men who would lead the community and come to control the Parsi Punchayet, constructed the power base of the community from the commercial wealth of the eighteenth century. The Parsis took advantage of the security offered by the British presence in Western India, to migrate and permanently settle in Bombay, thus facilitating the rise of Bombay as a major settlement. As Percival Spear remarks, "the Parsi shipbuilder rather than the English merchant was the true maker of Bombay."[48] The arrival in 1735 of Lowjee Nusserwanjee Wadia (*c.* 1700-74) by invitation as shipbuilder and later master builder to the British in Bombay from Surat, marked the beginnings of the ingress of large numbers of Parsis to Bombay.[49] In 1730, forty-six Parsi merchants were recorded as living in Bombay, and possibly 230 Parsis living in Bombay in total.[50] In 1780, the first census to record the number of Parsis in Bombay, taken by the Bombay Grain Committee, showed 3,087 Parsis out of a population of 33,444 individuals in Bombay.[51] By the turn of the century, Bombay was the centre of trade in West-

---

[46] Nowroji Rustam Manock was the first Parsi to go to England in 1724. See *Parsee Prakash*, 1:25-8; Karaka, *History of the Parsis*, 2:13-16; M. S. Commissariat, "The First Parsee in England (1724-25): Nowroji Rustom Manek of Surat and His Relations With the East India Company," in M. P. *Kharegat Memorial Volume*, vol. 1 (Bombay, 1953), 221-58; Das Gupta, *Indian Merchants*, 183-5.

[47] Walter Hamilton, *East-India Gazetteer*, vol. 1 (Delhi, 1828), 510.

[48] Spear, *Nabobs*, 71.

[49] *Parsee Prakash*, 1:32; Wadia, *Scions of Lowjee Wadia*, 1-2.

[50] White, "From Crisis to Philanthropy," 311-12.

[51] *Gazetteer of Bombay City and Island*, 1:156.

ern India and the Parsis were purported to be "the richest class of inhabitants."[52] By the 1830s, the brokers and contractors to the British were long considered community leaders.

Shipbuilding was an indigenous industry practised by certain Hindu castes, Muslims, and Parsis utilizing teak and other timber from the Konkan, Karwar, and Malabar, at the building docks of Daman, Surat, and Bombay. The Parsis had built a ship for the British as early as 1672 in Surat. In the eighteenth century, Parsis came to specialize in building ships that catered to European requirements. Shipbuilding remained *ad hoc* in character until the latter part of the eighteenth century, at which time entrepreneurial, managerial, design and industrial changes introduced by Parsi shipbuilders under British encouragement and patronage led to the development of large-scale manufacturing and labour organization. This represented the most advanced form of industrial organization for the time. Between 1736 and 1857, 267 crafts of various type and weight were built in Bombay. Four were over 2,000 tons each, and thirty over 1,000 tons each. At the beginning of the nineteenth century, there were six Parsi shipbuilding firms in Bombay, monopolizing all the docks.[53]

Parsi proficiency in shipbuilding highlighted the importance of technical innovation among successful Parsis. Parsi technical innovation formed another aspect of the Parsi ability to adapt for the preservation of identity. The Wadias were the premier Parsis to utilize their technical expertise and engineering skills in the service of the British to the benefit of their family and community. In 1833, Ardaseer Cursetjee Wadia (1808-77) along with an Indian blacksmith constructed the first private, Indian-built steamship in India, to the great interest of the East India Company, and in 1834 introduced for the first time gaslight in Bombay in his house, two decades before contracts were given to light Bombay streets. Ardaseer Cursetjee was one of the first Parsis to travel to Britain in 1839 for educational purposes, to study engineering.[54]

The arrival and settlement of the Parsis in Bombay underscored the value of securing Bombay and Western India in the trade with China for the British. The development of the trade with China was an essential component to the exploitation of the commercial poten-

---

[52] Graham, *Journal*, 37.

[53] V. D. Divekar, "Regional Economy (1757-1857)—Western India," in *The Cambridge Economic History of India*, vol. 2, *c. 1700-1970*, 350.

[54] See Wadia, *Scions of Lowjee Wadia*, 54-5; G.D. 1853 42/665:1-90.

tial of India. Prohibited from trading directly with Europe by the East India Company's monopoly, private traders that included Parsis supplied the trade between India and China to the benefit of both themselves and the Company. The Parsis' willingness to engage in the trans-shipping and 'country trade' between ports in the East set them apart from other Indians, and involved them in business with the Europeans. The European companies' interest principally lay in the trade between India and Europe, while they relied on local traders to supply goods and consignments from Eastern ports. The private country trade between India and China was made compatible with the interests of the East India Company by a series of financial devices employed by the Company to provide its treasury in Canton with funds without expending the resources of the Company in direct trade between India and China. Private traders deposited the proceeds of their sales in the Company's treasury in Canton and received bills assigned on Company or Indian government revenue.[55] With their access to ships and the resources of India, the Parsis were well suited to conduct the Eastern trade. The greatest Parsi profits, consequently, were made in the trade with China, principally in cotton, silk, and opium from the middle of the eighteenth to the nineteenth centuries. Hirji Jivanji is acknowledged to be the first Parsi to undertake the voyage to China in 1756.[56] By the 1830s, Parsi communities appeared in Canton, Amoy, and Shanghai, and the first Parsi burial ground outside India appeared in Macao in 1829.[57]

The Parsis were part of the emergence of a new trading pattern in the East. Prohibited from forming their own trading house in China and limited in the time they could stay in China by the East India Company's monopoly, the early Parsis involved in the China trade had to rely on the volume, quality, and efficient conduct of their trade to realize profits.[58] By the late eighteenth century, Parsis were involved in financing or owning ships for the China trade. The Banajis had early on established contacts with China and Burma through their trade in timber, silk, and opium. Banaji Limji came to Bombay from Bhagvadandi, near Surat in 1690. An employee of the

---

[55] Ashok V. Desai, "The Origins of Parsi Enterprise," *The Indian Economic and Social History Review* 5 (1968), 310; Michael Greenberg, *British Trade and the Opening of China, 1800-42* (Cambridge, 1951), 11-12, Ch. 5.

[57] Karaka, *History of the Parsis*, 2:57; Wacha, *Shells*, 412.

[56] Seervai and Patell, "Gujarat Parsis," 254.

[58] Greenberg, *British Trade*, Ch. 2, 20, 30, 33.

Company for a time, his foresight moved him to resign his commission and develop his own trade with Burma. The Bharda family, whose descendants are known as Damanwalla, was of priestly background from Tarapur in Gujarat. Beramji Bhikhaji Bharda and his sons Bhikhaji and Kavasji conducted the early opium trade from Daman to ports in Africa and China on their own ships. The Camas would build the basis of their wealth beginning with the China trade. Camaji Kuvarji (d. 1773) came to Bombay in 1735, and soon after his sons Mancherji and Edalji began the trade with the East. Jamsetjee Jejeebhoy made five trips to China and was the principal Parsi involved in the country trade between the ports of Bombay, Calcutta, Madras, and Canton, in the first decade of the nineteenth century. In 1814, Jamsetjee started his own merchant fleet, and in 1818 set up Jamsetjee Jejeebhoy & Co., renamed Jamsetjee Jejeebhoy Sons & Co. from 1836 to 1850.[59]

Jamsetjee Jejeebhoy is foremost example of Parsi who adapted himself to the cosmopolitan mixture of groups and interests taking shape in Western India in the early nineteenth century, to his benefit and that of the Parsi community. Jamsetjee Jejeebhoy became wealthy largely through the trade in opium. In association with family members and other Parsis, other Indian merchants, Chinese contacts, and through his dealings with European commercial houses in particular that of Jardine Matheson & Co. of Canton, Jamsetjee formed one important facet of an Indian trade network without having to leave India for China after 1807. Jamsetjee and associates were a diverse group that did not discriminate along religious or social lines, supported and aided one another, and remained as much friends as business associates. Jamsetjee and his Indian partners had established a network with Indian suppliers of opium in the Indian interior, which the British authority had been unable to co-opt for its own opium trade, and which saw a virtual monopoly of the Malwa crop shipped from Bombay by the 1830s.[60]

---

[59] Karaka, *History of the Parsis*, 2:44-6, 54-5, 59; Williamson Ramsay, *Memorandum on the Life and Public Charities of Jamsetjee Jejeebhoy* (London, 1855), 8; C. S. Nazir, *The First Parsee Baronet* (Bombay, 1866), 19-24; Wacha, *Shells*, 627; Mody, *Jamsetjee Jejeebhoy*, 32-3.

[60] Bombay Times, April 16, 1859; Jamsetjee Jejeebhoy (hereafter cited as J.J.) to William Jardine, August 6, 1831, Jamsetjee Jejeebhoy Manuscripts, 349:80, University of Bombay Library (hereafter cited as J.J. MSS); J.J. to John Romer, J.J. MSS, 359:44; J.J. Sons & Co. to Daniel & Co. and to Jardine Matheson & Co., on behalf of friends, December 24-25, 1838, J.J. MSS, 375:131-3; J.J. to De Vitre,

From the beginning of the nineteenth century, opium replaced cotton as the most profitable export item to China. From 1831, the opium trade by Indians provided the British authorities with steady revenue from the duty charged on the sale of opium passing through British territory to ports in India. The opium trade financed much of the private British firms' tea purchases in China. Parsis and other Indian merchants often bore the risks associated with the China trade. Politically and economically, it benefited the East India Company and the British agency houses to have Indians operate the opium trade, as the political embarrassment associated with engaging in a technically illegal trade was avoided. In addition, Indian merchants and shipowners bore the disadvantages of the costs of consignments, delays in credit remittance, and price fluctuations.[61] The Parsis benefited from the opium wars between the British and China, while also incurring the disadvantages associated with their trade. Parsi merchants lost shipments and were detained by the Chinese authorities.[62] Up to the 1860s, the major British and Parsi opium traders constituted an informal but tight oligopoly. Parsi merchants also become involved with American firms, consigning shipments of opium to them. Jamsetjee Jejeebhoy was the chief supplier for the American firm Augustine Heard & Co. From mid-century, Parsis penetrated markets deep in China, trading opium for silk.[63]

The Parsi traders treated the opium trade as a lucrative enterprise alongside the trade in other commodities. Moral reservations associated with the trade in opium, along with cultural and political questions concerning the penetration of colonialism into Asia, only entered the traders' calculations in as much as it affected their trade, if at all. The opium trade was so lucrative to some Parsi firms, such as P & D. N. Cama Co., that rewards were paid to police for the recov-

April 23, 1842, J.J. MSS, 369:120-1; Asiya Siddiqi, "The Business World of Jamsetjee Jejeebhoy," *The Indian Economic and Social History Review* 19, nos. 3 & 4 (1982): 301-23.

[61] J.J. to Capt. George Elliot, March 26, 1842, J.J. MSS, 369:94-6; J.J. to James Matheson, April 11, 1842, J.J. MSS, 369:115.

[62] J.J. to Capt. George Elliot, March 26, 1842, J.J. MSS, 369:94-6; J.J. to J. A. Smith, March 30, 1842, J.J. MSS, 369:101-2; J.J. to Sir Charles Forbes, May 21, 1842, J.J. MSS, 369:172; J.J. to Capt. Elliot, May 23, 1842, J.J. MSS, 369:180-1; Mody, *Jamsetjee Jejeebhoy*, 34; Darukhanawala, *Parsi Lustre*, 508-9.

[63] Stephen C. Lockwood, *Augustine Heard and Company*, 1858-1862 (Cambridge, Mass., 1971), 26-7; Yen-p'ing Hao, *The Commercial Revolution in Nineteenth Century China: The Rise of Sino-Western Mercantile Capitalism* (Berkeley, 1986), 61, 130-3.

ery of stolen opium stashes. British, Indian, American, and Chinese opium suppliers, traders and handlers adhered to the market imperative that conceived of China as a source of demand and India as a source of supply. For much of the nineteenth century, the trade in opium was freely conducted from India. The figures of opium sales and the profits of government were regularly quoted in the major newspapers. The revenue from the sales of opium for the year 1857, were quoted to have exceeded the most sanguine expectations of government, with the net proceeds totalling Rs. 3,51,54,460, up from the figure of Rs. 2,71,37,210 for 1856.[64] Outside commercial circles, the opium trade formed yet another topic of nineteenth century philosophical discussion. Questions surrounding the number of Chinese smoking opium, the number of fatalities that resulted from the addiction, and the role of Chinese traders and officials in the trade were routinely discussed in the English-medium press in India. In 1859, editorials in the *Bombay Times* contended that the question of suppressing the opium trade lay within the realm of the conscience, not legislation; and that suppression would be as mischievous and indefensible, as trenching upon liberties over which society has no legitimate control. The interests of morality, virtue, and religion, it was suggested, could best be served by the removal of government restrictions and the freer exercise of the trade.[65] By the 1850s, Indian Jews and Ismaili Khojas were also engaged in the opium trade, and overall commercial competition had increased.[66] By mid-century, most Parsi entrepreneurs had diversified their business ventures, as both the growing opprobrium reserved for the opium trade as well as the foresight to sense other business opportunities led Parsi energies being directed to pioneering new industries.

By 1855, Jamsetjee Jejeebhoy's commercial empire had effectively ended. His personal prestige and reputation, however, were never greater. The leading Parsi merchants of the first half of the nineteenth century had translated commercial success into the community prestige and influence that saw them rise to the leadership of the Parsi community. The Wadias provided three members to the Punchayet, and along with the families Shroff, Dadabhai, and Petit came to control the Punchayet. By 1832, Jamsetjee Jejeebhoy was

[64] *Bombay Times*, March 20, 1858.

[65] *Bombay Times*, April 5, November 2, 1859.

[66] Karaka, *History of the Parsis*, 2:257-9; Siddiqi, "Business World of Jamsetjee Jejeebhoy," 323.

the popular head of the Parsi community, and representative of the Indian community in Bombay. The contacts developed among the Parsi *shetias* were measure of the broader social ties forged among the leading individuals and families of Indian and British society in Bombay under the conditions of monopoly trade. The commercial ties of the eighteenth century had worked to socialize the leading citizens of Bombay to a common political culture led by the British, while the moral and material network within the Parsi community worked to socialize the Parsis to the leadership of the Parsi *shetias*.

Moral and Material Supports of Community in the Industrial Era

During the nineteenth century, the Parsis built on and consolidated the moral and material supports of community. The great Parsi merchant-princes of the eighteenth and early nineteenth centuries gave way to the rise of the great Parsi capital elites. The Parsi businessmen's progression into new enterprises and industries was logical if opportune. Parsi enterprise in the middle of the nineteenth century built on the expertise and resources of previous generations. The Parsi pioneers of the nineteenth century, consequently, were often the descendants of early *shetias* involved in brokerage and in trade. The Parsis' continued economic success was also aided by important prerequisites such as the innovation of joint-stock banking in Bombay, the development of new trading patterns and the opening of new markets, as well as by the intercommunity cooperation in Bombay under British political domination. The capital formations from trade provided for the rise of the banking and insurance industries in Parsi hands. The Parsis were some of the first Indians to join the new business organizations established by the British in Bombay. The Bombay Chamber of Commerce was formed in 1836, with ten of the original twenty-five members being Parsi. Members of the Wadia, Dadiseth, Banaji, and Readymoney families were all involved in the financial history of Bombay. Dadabhoy Pestonjee Wadia was the first Parsi and the only Indian member appointed to the new Bank of Bombay in 1836, and the Bank of Western India in 1842. In 1864, the Bombay Share Brokers' Association was formed under the Parsis Shapurji B. Bharucha (1845-1906), Byramji B. Kanga, R. M. Rutnagar and Nasarvanji Mancherji Cama, and was headed by the Jain Premchand Roychand (1831-1905). Competition ultimately spurred the rise of the banking industry in Bombay. In the context of the British domination of banking in India and the world financial system, the Parsis' entry into the financial world of Bombay formed the beginnings of a private economy in Indian hands.[67]

The cotton industry centred in Bombay was one of the first large-scale enterprises to emerge as a result of the rise of banking and changing trade patterns. Indian merchants' knowledge of sources of supply, brokerage, and the distribution and marketing of British cloth goods in India and abroad, placed them in an advantageous position to enter the cotton manufacturing and export trade. Both the American Civil War and the opening of the Suez Canal in the 1860s resulted in a cotton boom in Bombay and Western India. Cowasji Nanabhoy Davar (1814-73) is credited with opening the first steam powered press and cotton textile mill in India in 1854, at Tardeo in Bombay. Davar was the son of a Parsi merchant, was broker for two British firms, and operated his own firm that traded with China. Davar promoted four Bombay banks between 1846 and 1863, and participated in the formation of the Bombay Steam Navigation Company. Davar's initial attempt to finance a mill in 1851 was unsuccessful. It was only after the financial contribution of fifty of Bombay's leading businessmen, including a majority of Parsis, to the sum of Rs. 5,00,000 that Davar floated his mill.[68]

The difficulties in financing, technical expertise, and the management of labour necessary for large-scale cotton manufacturing, necessitated the cooperation of Bombay businessmen. The Parsis were familiar with the pattern of intercommunity cooperation since the early decades of Bombay, and they effectively exploited the opportunities for cooperation amidst the evolution of the economy in the nineteenth century. The Wadia, Petit, and Tata families were the largest Parsi business concerns associated with the textile industry and trade. In 1855, Manakji Nasarvanji Petit (1803-59), the son of N. K. Petit, began the Oriental Spinning and Weaving Company; the

[67] R. J. F. Sullivan, *One Hundred Years of Bombay, 1836-1936* (Bombay, 1937), 10. D. E. Wacha, *A Financial Chapter in the History of Bombay City* (Bombay, 1910); idem, *Shells*, 530-2; Wadia, *Scions of Lowjee Wadia*, 112-13; A. K. Bagchi, "European and Indian Entrepreneurs in India, 1900-30," in *Elites in South Asia*, 230-1; A. V. Desai, "Origins of Parsi Enterprise," 312.

[68] S. M. Rutnagur, *Bombay Industries: The Cotton Mills* (Bombay, 1927), 9-10; S. D. Mehta, *The Cotton Mills of India, 1854 to 1954* (Bombay, 1954), 13-15; Morris, "Large-Scale Industry," 574-5; Karaka, *History of the Parsis*, 2:247-8; A. V. Desai, "Origins of Parsi Enterprise," 312.

second mill established in Bombay, in cooperation with the Baghdadi Jewish businessman Elias D. Sassoon, the Kapol Bania Varjivandas Madhavdas (1817-96), and two Englishmen. M. N. Petit was a broker and China trader who soon followed the opening of the Oriental Mill with that of the Petit Mills, started in partnership with the Parsi Merwanji Framji Panday (1812-76).[69] Manakji's sons, Nasarvanji Manakji (1827-91) and Dinshaw Manakji Petit (1823-1901), followed his successful example in the cotton industry. D. M. Petit floated his first cotton mill in 1860, and followed it with four more by the end of the decade. By 1875, D. M. Petit was recognized as one of Bombay's wealthiest men and richest Parsis.[70] For over half a century, Parsis would dominate and pioneer advances in the cotton industry in India. In 1879, Nowrozjee Nusserwanjee Wadia (1849-99), who managed Petit Mills for D. M. Petit, founded the first of his mills, the Bombay Dyeing & Manufacturing Co. Ltd., pioneering the process of dyeing yarn and cloth in India.[71] The cotton mill industry in Bombay emerged as Western India's leading industry, dominated by an elite oligopoly of Indian firms. In 1874, there were 17 Indian-promoted mills to one British dominated project. Of the 95 mills established before 1914, Parsis promoted 34, Hindus 27, Europeans 15, Muslims 10, Jewish businessmen 4, with four listed as uncertain.[72] Bhatias, Khojas, and Jews also came to dominate the cotton mill industry during the economic boom of the 1880s.

Parsi involvement in the cotton mill industry also provided the opportunity to diversify into other economic pursuits. The strength of the Petit family in the cotton mill industry was only seriously challenged by the Parsi J. N. Tata. Jamsetjee Nusserwanjee Tata (1839-1904) was of priestly background from Navsari and the son of Nusserwanjee Tata (1822-86), a China trader who had become wealthy in large measure by supplying cotton to mills during the American Civil War. J. N. Tata was educated at Elphinstone College before going into the family business. He was familiar with the China trade and ventured to Britain to study the operations of the Manchester and Lancashire Mills. In 1869, Tata began his own climb to success, taking over an oil press factory and converting it to

69 Mehta, *Cotton Mills of India*, 21-2; Morris, "Large-Scale Industry," 581; Karaka, *History of the Parsis*, 2:248.

70 Karaka, *History of the Parsis*, 2:136-7.

71 Wadia, *Scions of Lowjee Wadia*, 244-5.

72 Morris, "Large-Scale Industry," 580.

cotton production, and subsequently selling it at profit to a Hindu broker. Tata's true business genius lay in seeking to innovate within the existing profitable cotton industry. By 1874, Tata made plans to build a large-scale cotton enterprise close to the source of supply, a ready market, and accessible communications and transportation lines necessary for distribution. In 1877, he opened his first major cotton mill, the Empress Mills in Nagpur. Like other Parsis before him, Tata believed technological advances were key to success, and introduced new spinning equipment to produce quality yarns capable of competing internationally. The creation of both the internationally renowned Swadeshi Mills, as well as India's first polytechnic university in Bangalore in 1909, by the Tata family on the vision of J. N. Tata, attests to the evolution of Indian industry and the movement for greater economic independence from Britain. Like other Parsis, Tata also felt the compulsion to diversify his industrial concern, venturing into iron and steel production. In 1907, three years following his death, the Tata Iron and Steel Company was created in Jamshedpur, a site in Bihar province named in his honour, and which was the foundation stone of one of modern India's greatest industrial conglomerates.[73] J. N. Tata is exemplar of the new modern entrepreneur. His business enterprise would set the standard for industrial growth, technical innovation, and economic self-sufficiency in India.

Tata's example was emulated by the other great Parsi enterprise to emerge in the twentieth century, the Godrej industrial empire. Ardeshar Burjorji Godrej (1867-1936) began his business empire repairing surgical instruments, but soon found his economic niche in the manufacture of cupboards, locks and safes, and steel house and office furniture. He diversified his business by manufacturing quality vegetable toilet soaps, and engaging in agricultural production. Under the direction of Ardeshar Burjorji's brother, Pirojshah, Godrej enterprises diversified into various industrial enterprises, ranking as one of modern India's largest private economic concerns.[74] Tata and Godrej exemplify the pattern of Parsi economic success in the twentieth century: to enter and dominate a particular field or industry while diversifying their economic base into other sectors.

---

[73] D. E. Wacha, *Life and Work of J. N. Tata* (Madras, 1915), 24; G. A. Natesan and Co., ed., *Famous Parsis* (Madras, 1930), 222; *A Short History of the 'Empress Mills,' Nagpur, Started Work 1st January, 1877, Golden Jubilee Volume* (Bombay, 1927); Mehta, *Cotton Mills of India*, 58.

[74] Darukhanawala, *Parsi Lustre*, 450-1.

The success of Parsi business by the twentieth century also owed to the commercial and trading patterns established by the early Parsi merchants at the beginning of the nineteenth century. The involvement of Parsis in the communications field was a necessary concomitant to their economic success. Prominent Parsis were now in the international trade of the industrial era. Jejeebhoy Dadabhai (1786-1849), the prominent banker and pioneer of steam navigation in Western India, created his own firm to trade with Europe, Africa, and China. The Petit family, pioneers of Western India's textile industry, established markets that extended to China, South Africa, and Iran. The Cama family established trading firms in London and Liverpool in 1855, and Paris in 1860.[75] Cowasji Dinshaw Adenwala (1827-1900) transformed the port of Aden into a facility capable of accommodating the steamer traffic of the time between the Indian Ocean and Europe, soon after his arrival in 1845. Cowasji and his family facilitated the settlement of Parsis and other Indians in Aden building a fire-temple in 1854, and providing extensive charitable works. Cowasji's son Hormusji Cowasji (1857-1939) expanded the family shipping firm establishing routes to East Africa by the last quarter of the century. H. C. Adenwala was an important member of the Parsi community and was knighted by the British in 1922.[76]

The establishment of Western India's railway system owed something to an ingenious and persistent Parsi, Jamsetjee Dorabjee Naegaumwalla. Jamsetjee Dorabjee (1804-82) had begun his career at the Bombay dockyards as a carpenter initially in the service of Jamsetjee Bomanjee Wadia, the master builder, and then the Bombay government. Jamsetjee became a contractor beginning with a project at the salt works at Sewree, before proceeding to construct many large projects in Bombay. Though previously inexperienced in railway construction, Jamsetjee tendered three bids to the Great Indian Peninsula Railway before being accepted to build a line from Bombay to Thana. His success in the operation led to other large contracts including the construction of the railway line into the Western Ghats. Jamsetjee Dorabjee's achievement in terms of both

[75]Natesan, *Famous Parsis*, 46, 66; Karaka, *History of the Parsis*, 2:132-3, 258; Darukhanawala, *Parsi Lustre*, 340-1; *Bombay Times*, April 9, 1860.

[76]See *Parsee Prakash*, 3:410, 796; C. H. Jhabvala, *Cowasjee Dinshaw Adenvala C.I.E.* (Bombay, 1920); A. N. Josh, *Life and Times of Sir Hormusjee C Dinshaw* (Bombay, 1939).

his technical and entrepreneurial skill is noteworthy given the existing monopoly on industrial contracts held by Europeans in India.[77]

The wealth of the industrial era now provided for the expansion and consolidation of the moral and material supports of the Parsis, as well as the improvement of Bombay civic society. Between 1820 and 1910, the greater part of the religious endowments of the Parsi community were built and/or consecrated: including at least one fire-temple, Tower of Silence or burial ground every year somewhere in India.[78] The greater part of the modern Parsi social infrastructure also took shape. From the 1830s to the 1930s, over 400 schools, libraries, hospitals and medical facilities were built and/or funded, principally for Parsis; with over 200 additional projects and funds going to various non-Parsi causes inside and outside India.[79] One of the more significant projects made possible through the Parsi charity of the nineteenth and early twentieth centuries, was the building of Parsi social housing. Both individual charity and charitable trusts provided for the construction of over forty *baugs* or housing colonies, and *dharamsalas* or rest centres from the 1830s to the 1930s. The building of the residential colonies reserved for Parsis constituted the largest social housing charitable enterprise among the Parsis since their settlement in Bombay.[80] From the middle of the twentieth century, another great wave of building Parsi social housing commenced. Also at this time, the majority of the social housing trust

---

[77] Karaka, *History of the Parsis*, 2:253-7; Bagchi, "Entrepreneurs," 226-7.

[78] Seervai and Patell, "Gujarat Parsis," 249-54; Hinnells, "Flowering of Zoroastrian Benevolence," 290-6.

[79] See tabulations in Hinnells, "Flowering of Zoroastrian Benevolence."

[80] The more well-known Parsi colonies in Bombay of the nineteenth century include: Allai Baug built by Jamsetjee Jejeebhoy in 1839, at a cost of Rs. 70,000; Cama Baug built by P. C. Cama in 1868, at a cost of Rs. 1,50,000; Merwan Baug known as the Parsi Sanitarium built by M. F. Panday in 1865, at a cost of Rs. 4,00,000; Albless Baug built by the Albless family in 1868, at a cost of Rs. 1,50,000, with the specific purpose of celebrating Parsi functions. Albless Baug was built by the Parsi contractor Jamasji Rattanji Mistry (1848-1920), who built much of the financial district of Bombay, and sites at Colaba and Marine Lines. Other major colonies built prior to World War II include: Navroz Baug (1908), Khareghat Colony (1912), Rustom Baug (1920), Dadar Colony (1925), Jer Baug (1928), Gamadia Colony (1936), Captain Colony (1938), and Cusrow Baug (pre-1939). See Da Cunha, *Origin of Bombay*, 300; Hinnells, "Flowering of Zoroastrian Benevolence," 296-7, 314-6; Darukhanawala, *Parsi Lustre*, 115. On social housing in the twentieth century, see the colonies run by the Punchayet, in Sapur F. Desai, *The History of the Bombay Parsi Punchayet, 1860-1960* (Bombay, 1977), 145-9; idem, *A Changing Social Structure* (Bombay, 1945), 32.

were supervised or amalgamated under the Parsi Punchayet of Bombay. Parsis contributed directly to the establishment of charities or through donations and bequests to Parsi charitable trusts, the largest being the Parsi Punchayet. From 1909 to 1939, Parsi charities showed a total annual income of over a million rupees, and reaching a one-year record of seven-and-a-half-million rupees in 1934.[81]

It was the conspicuous wealth and charity of the Parsi *shetias* and the new commercial and industrial elites that continued to capture the public imagination. To the old and great family names associated with Parsi charity like the Wadias, Banajis, and Jamsetjee Jejeebhoys, were added the names of members of the Camas, Readymoneys, Petits, and Tatas beginning from the middle of the nineteenth century. The conspicuous wealth was evident in the prolific construction of the new grand residences of the wealthy.[82] The number of Parsis that received hereditary and honorary titles from the British was a measure of the political significance that Parsi charity and the leadership of the Parsi philanthropists had assumed under colonialism. Eight Indians in the Bombay Presidency obtained hereditary baronets during British rule including three Parsis, three Jews, one Hindu, and one Muslim. The Parsis included Sir Jamsetjee Jejeebhoy in 1857, Sir Dinshaw Manakji Petit in 1890, and Sir Cowasjee Jehangir II (1853-1934) in 1908. By 1946, sixty-three Parsis were knighted.[83] From the fundamental Zoroastrian obligation to contribute to the welfare of the world, the Parsi leaders had advanced the moral and material foundations of the Parsi community in Bombay and Western India. Through their expanding largesse they underlined their pious ambitions and formulated a potent argument for their authority within the Parsi community. By the middle of the nineteenth century, the political control of the wealthy Parsi *shetias* over the Parsis effectively had ended. Despite the loss of their political control, however, the Parsi leaders' copious charity continued to be an expression of their participation in the civic life of Bombay and their continued relevance within the Parsi community. Parsi charity also became a potent symbolic marker of identity. The charitable persona of 'the Parsi community' was established as a result of the munificence of rich Parsis, as well as innumerable acts of

[81]Hinnells, "Flowering of Zoroastrian Benevolence," 298-9.

[82]Murzban, *Parsis*, 1:329.

[83]Sohrab K. H. Katrak, *Who Are the Parsees?* (Karachi, 1965), 288-93.

charity from average Parsis made possible through the new wealth of the nineteenth century. Significantly, while Parsi economic progress shaped the moral and material supports of community, the expanding cultural contacts with the British that resulted made for the easier assimilation of Parsi values to British culture. By mid-century, a new generation of educated Parsis prepared to extend Parsi influence beyond the economic realm.

Summary

The construction of the moral and material supports of the Parsis owed to factors economic, political, and cultural. The Parsis operated within variable economic and social milieus, necessitating social and economic innovation among them. These milieus included the mercantilist trading system of the eighteenth century, the rise of free trade, and a world credit system dominated by the British. The Parsis adhered to patterns of activity aimed to benefit the preservation of their sense of community and identity. From the association with the British, to the pursuit of specific economic activities and enterprises at specific periods in history, to the removal of the community to Bombay, to the provision of the moral and material infrastructure of community, to the diversification of Parsi energies from the economic to the social and educational realm, the Parsis evinced the ability to exploit opportunity, to adapt and innovate within their economic and social milieu, and to direct change in benefit of their community and identity. The economic benefit that accrued to Parsis in Bombay evinced the advantages for colonial subjects under an extractive imperial environment. At the same time, the Parsis had redefined the imperial encounter to benefit not only a small elite within the community but the larger community. The quest for economic advantage and pre-eminence on the part of Parsis, essentially, can be seen as an integral part of the quest to preserve identity, and the desire to remain economically, socially, and politically relevant as a community at any given time. It is not surprising, therefore, that the rise of the internal government of the Parsis should soon have followed the arrival and settlement of the Parsis in Bombay. The Parsis as a community began to construct not only the moral supports of community, but also the social, governmental, and ideological bonds of their society in Bombay.

CHAPTER TWO

IDENTITY AND THE INSTITUTION: A PUNCHAYET FOR THE PARSIS

The Rise of the Punchayet

The arrival of the Parsis in Bombay had begun a process of both building the moral supports of community life in the urban setting, and binding the new arrivals in support of Parsi identity. The increase in the numbers of Parsis from Gujarat to a growing and cosmopolitan Bombay imposed pressures on the cohesiveness of the incipient community that had to be addressed. The requirements of the Parsi community in Bombay inevitably had to take account of more than the availability of fire-temples and Towers of Silence. In the long run, a small community like the Parsis had to formulate and agree to, as a body, the rules that would define their social relations among themselves as well as the degree of enforcement of these rules. In the early years of the growth of Bombay, only the members of the prominent families had the recognized experience and authority to be regarded as leaders of community government. The Parsi *shetia* leaders formed the first informal and formal internal government of the Parsi community that came to be known as the Parsi Punchayet of Bombay. The Parsi Punchayet of Bombay was instrumental in defining and shaping Parsi identity in Bombay, and came to extend its authority over the Parsis of Western India. As the major centre of authority among the Parsis from the eighteenth century, the Punchayet shaped the sense of community and group identity, social norms, responsibilities, and obligations that attached to Parsi identity both in the urban setting and in general. At the zenith of the Punchayet's existence, a tacit social ideology emerged that came to represent the full desire of the Parsis to safeguard their identity as a people and community. Ultimately, both the rise of the Punchayet along with its decline owed to the historical process that sought to preserve and safeguard the sense of identity among the Parsis.

The date of the establishment of the first Parsi Punchayet of Bombay is not recorded. The process that witnessed leadership of the Parsi community in Bombay passing to the *shetias*, however, may well be said to have been under way before any formal Punchayet being constituted. The socio-economic ties formed between the prominent Parsis of Bombay would have encompassed discussion of the internal stability and order of their community. The emergence of the Parsi *shetias* as community leaders should not understate the significance of the development. In an essentially frontier setting, a wealthy, lay, commercially oriented leadership had emerged as the new centre of authority in the Parsi community. This new centre of authority would assume the responsibility for settling disputes within the community, safeguarding the political, social, and religious needs of the Parsis in Bombay, thereby regulating the nature of the community and Parsi identity. Little, however, is known of the first gatherings of the Parsi Punchayet of Bombay. Until the middle of the nineteenth century, when the Punchayet had lost the greater part of its authority over the Parsis of Bombay and India, the individual members only haphazardly kept the records of its proceedings. The first recognizable Punchayet in Bombay, *c.* 1725, included the five *akabars* or leaders: Banaji Limji as davar or 'head'; Jejeebhoy Jamshedji Modi, who was the grandson of Hirji Vacha Modi; and the sons of the broker Rustam Manock, Framji, Bomanji and Nowroji. The men were of varied backgrounds, though all from or near Surat; and brought to the early Punchayet and the community the qualities of sobriety, philanthropic benevolence, and negotiating acumen. All the men had experience dealing with the different European trading interests, and the sons of Rustam Manock had extensive dealings both fortunate and unfortunate with the East India Company.[1]

As a self-constituted body of five lay individuals all from a mercantile background, the first Punchayet in Bombay broke from the practice followed in Gujarat of having influential clerical representatives on a council of elders. The absence of clerical representatives from the Parsi priesthood on the Bombay council clearly represented the rise of a new class of leaders, exploiting its social base in favour of itself, as well as on behalf of the community. The new class of

[1] Sohrab P. Davar, *The History of the Parsi Punchayet of Bombay* (Bombay, 1949), 1.

individuals that had emerged was suited to managing the social and civil needs of the community, and had shaped the structure of Bombay Parsi society through its wealth and influence. With its commercial ties to the British and the opportunities for social intercourse such ties permitted, this small new class acted as the representative of the Parsi community to the British. The formal recognition of the authority of the Punchayet followed from its ability to demonstrate the social order and stability the British ruling power thought as requisite for the leadership of a community, and further enhanced the Parsi leaders' authority and social control over the community. As community life developed, the Punchayet assumed the responsibility for the settlement of a variety of disputes. As the sole authority for the Parsis in Bombay, the Punchayet was called on to adjudicate disputes and settle all social and religious questions for the community. The emergence of the first Parsi Punchayet of Bombay, consequently, reflected the reorientation of the leadership of the Parsi community in the new economic and political climate.

Prior to the reorganization of the Punchayet in 1787, the authority of the earliest of Punchayets was tacit and implied, not formally constituted. The earliest of Punchayets being self-constituted did not preclude the need for the Punchayet to secure the consent and cooperation of the Parsi community. As the community grew, that consent would have to be more formally sanctioned. One of the earliest recorded *anjumans* or community meetings of the Parsis of Bombay took place on April 16, 1749, when the Samast Anjuman of Parsis gathered to discuss a letter from the Navsari Zarthosti Anjuman regarding the disposition of the body of a deceased. The Navsari Anjuman had written that the feet of a deceased Parsi should be kept stretched before being taken to the *dakhma* or Tower of Silence. The Bombay Parsis had resolved in a general meeting to favour no one method, and communicated to Navsari their decision.[2] The nascent democratic nature of the Bombay Anjuman gathering and its refusal to pronounce definitively on the obsequies, suggest that both the political and social context in which the Parsis of Bombay deliberated were in the process of evolution.

The Parsi Punchayet of Bombay derived from the caste punchayet form of government and dispute settlement indigenous to

---

[2] *Parsee Prakash*, 1:38; R. E. Enthoven, ed., *The Tribes and Castes of Bombay*, vol. 3 (Delhi, 1922), 463.

India. Its roots among the Parsis stemmed from the cultural assimilation and adaptation the Parsis underwent after their arrival in India. The official call for the formation of punchayets in Bombay had owed something to the influence of the British on the Island. The creation of internal governmental structures for the communities in Bombay was part of the establishment of British authority on the Island. As President of Surat and second Governor of Bombay from 1670 to 1677, Gerald Aungier had devoted his efforts to bringing peace, order, and good profit to Bombay. He had drafted favourable terms for the settlement of Indians in Bombay that distinguished Bombay from the other European settlements in India with its cosmopolitan air and sense of racial tolerance. Most significantly, for the Parsis, the Indian inhabitants were granted the free exercise of their religion in Bombay.[3] Aungier was struck by the uniqueness of the Parsis from the other Indian communities. He observed the affinity of the religion of the Parsis to that of the Hebrews—monotheistic in conception and non-idolatrous in practice.[4]

The ability of the various communities to take up better representation for themselves while subservient to British authority was the chief goal behind Aungier's proposal for punchayets to the Surat Council in 1673.[5] The call for punchayets for the local communities in Bombay was part of the administration of justice in Bombay, and which included the maintenance of laws of the East India Company, and the establishment of courts of law.[6] The punchayets of Aungier's time were conceived as bodies to decide and arbitrate minor disputes and were to be restricted in their judicial powers to the decision of cases within their own caste or community, agreed to by those who sought arbitration. Having established the Court of Judicature at Bombay in 1672, Aungier was careful not to undermine its authority

[3] Understood as the Treaty with Neema Parrack as contained in George W. Forrest, ed., "Surat Letters," March 22, 1677, *Selections from the Letter, Despatches and Other State Papers Preserved in the Bombay Secretariat*, vol. 1 (Bombay, 1887), 112; Charles Fawcett, *The First Century of British Justice in India* (Oxford, 1934), 66.

[4] Colonel Henry Yule, ed., "Miscellaneous Papers," *The Diary of W. Hedges*, vol. 2, no. 75 (London, 1888), cccvi.

[5] Charles Fawcett, *The English Factories in India*, vol. 1 (Oxford, 1936), 81.

[6] On the evolution of legal institutions in Bombay, see Fawcett, *First Century of British Justice in India*; M. D. David, *History of Bombay, 1661-1708* (Bombay, 1973), 326-34; Erskine Perry, *Cases Illustrative of Oriental Life: Decided in H.M. Supreme Court at Bombay, The Application of English Law to India* (1853; reprint, New Delhi, 1988), 61-4

as the mightiest law court. Community disputes not agreed by litigants to be settled by the punchayets were left to the authority of the Court. In her description of the Parsis' "panchait" in 1809, Maria Graham noted how the little council remained cautious in its decisions lest it fall subject to the authority of British courts.[7] Eventually, as caste punchayets developed, the British and the Court recognized their increasing authority and social control over their communities. With the rapid settlement of Parsis in Bombay, the formal establishment of a punchayet would be the natural progression to the changes that had defined the community since its arrival in Bombay.

Governor Aungier's call for punchayets is significant in affixing the date of the first Parsi Punchayet of Bombay. Two sets of dates cited as those for the establishment of the first Parsi Punchayet in Bombay are between 1672 and 1675, and from 1725 to 1733.[8] The former would correspond to Aungier's request and the beginnings of the Parsis' settlement in Bombay. However, as British records relate that as of 1675 only the Portuguese Indian community had responded to the request, if the Parsis had formally sought to do so some clear note would have been made. Banaji Limji who became davar or head of the Punchayet is reported to have come to Bombay only in 1690, from Bhagvadandi.[9] From the five names of the members of the earliest recorded Punchayet, S. P. Davar determined that the first Punchayet could only have taken shape after 1725, when all five members were in Bombay, and no later than 1733, after which time the first of its members Nowroji Rustamji Manock, had died.[10] The latter period from 1725 to 1733, therefore, appears the more probable as the date of the establishment of the 'first' Parsi Punchayet of Bombay. The first gathering of the Punchayet gave formal effect to the process that was already under way and which witnessed leadership of the Parsi community passing to the wealthy and influential laymen. Both sets of dates, consequently, are compatible with the narrative to date and with one another. The earlier date,

---

[7] Maria Graham, *Journal of a Residence in India* (Edinburgh, 1813), 41.

[8] Sapur F. Desai, *The History of the Bombay Parsi Punchayet, 1860-1960* (Bombay, 1977), 3, cites the period 1672-75 as the date for the first Punchayet. J. R. B. Jeejeebhoy, "Communal Discipline Among the Bombay Parsees in Olden Times," in *M. P. Kharegat Memorial Volume*, vol. 1 (Bombay, 1953), 296, cites 1728 as the date that Banaji Limji established the first Punchayet.

[9] D. F. Karaka, *History of the Parsis*, 2 vols. (London, 1884), 2:4.

[10] Davar, *History of the Parsi Punchayet*, 2.

indeed preceding the Governor's call, may be said to represent the formation of social contact and community consciousness that was taking shape, while the latter represents that period in which the organization of the community takes more formal shape.

The Punchayet from 1733 to 1787, was a plutocratic body in which vacant seats were filled either by the sons of the original founders or among the wealthy families of Bombay. The son and grandsons of Banaji Limji are believed to have followed the latter as davar after his death in 1734. The maintenance of order and social peace among the Parsis of Bombay was the principal concern of the early Punchayet. The powers accorded to the punchayets from the time of Aungier by the Company had served the basic regulatory needs of the Parsis. By the latter half of the eighteenth century, it appears that the Parsi Punchayet was taking steps to strengthen its powers of internal government. This included the more stringent application of social control mechanisms including the appeal to corporal punishment. The earliest record of the Parsi Punchayet's communications with the British consists of a petition to Governor William Hornby in 1778, requesting the legal authority for the Punchayet to inflict physical punishment on the members of the Parsi community.[11] The British sought to balance the recognition of the authority of the Punchayet to mete out justice customary to the community and the government's overall jurisdiction, by setting a limit as to the severity of punishment to include beating offenders with shoes, but no other corporal punishment.[12]

At about the same time, the Punchayet took a substantial step to redefine the nature of the Parsi community. In June 1777, the Punchayet with the consent of the majority of the community passed a *bundobast* or ordinance proscribing marriage between *behdin* or lay females and *mōbads* or priests.[13] The Punchayet had passed this law in response to the practice among the priests, at their choosing, to marry their sons to laywomen while themselves prohibiting their daughters from marrying laymen. When in 1785 the regulation of

[11] Petition to the Hon. William Hornby Esq., in *Blue Pamphlets* of 1843 (Bombay, 1843), 56-7.

[12] Ibid., 57: Letter of William Hornby "To the Parsees not of the Priest Class," July 5, 1778.

[13] *Parsee Prakash*, 1:56. *Behdin* refers to the laity. *Āthornan* is the appropriate term for the clergy while *mōbad* is but one rung of priest. As the literature uses the term *mōbad* in regards to the dispute, I have observed the usage.

1777 was defied, with the betrothal of the baby daughter of Hormasji Behramji Patel to the son of the priest and watchmaker Behramji Nusserwanji Ghadially, the Punchayet convened an Anjuman or a public meeting of the Parsis, on October 27, 1785, to ostracize from the community all the offending parties involved. The communal discipline of the Parsis further dictated that all Parsis, laity and clergy alike, were bound to observe the ostracism of the offenders upon penalty. The determination of the Punchayet to see through its resolution was such that when the son of the priest Ghadially died, permission to consign his remains to the *dakhma* was withheld by the Punchayet.[14] The decision of the Punchayet and Anjuman was resented by the priestly class in Bombay who were unprepared to abide by the terms of the Bombay Parsis. This began the famous *behdin/ mōbad* dispute, which was large enough to capture the attention of the Bombay government. Faced with appeals from both sides among the Parsis, the government of R. H. Boddam appointed a committee of three to hear from the Parsis and propose some solution to the dispute.[15] At issue, was the ordinance passed by the Punchayet and disputed by the priests as inconsistent with the laws of their religion. Reporting soon after its establishment, the committee ruled in favour of the Punchayet finding that upon general principle the regulation of 1777 was proper and equitable, and "that the Parsees were full as competent to make one regulation as the Andearoos [priests] were to make the other."[16]

The *behdin/mōbad* dispute is significant in the early development of the Parsi Punchayet and the Parsi community of Bombay as it marks firstly, the assumption of the responsibility and direction of the Parsi community by the Parsi Punchayet of Bombay; and secondly, the socialization of the internal government of the Parsis to British power. By passing the ordinance prohibiting the intermarriage of laity and clergy in response to the practice of the clergy, the Bombay Punchayet had in fact assumed the caste authority over the Parsis. The Parsis had argued to the British committee that the regulation of the priests was no more than fifty years old, passed when the priests were at the height of their influence in Surat. In choosing

[14] Ibid., 65-6.

[15] Extract from the Minutes of Council, April 21, 1786, in *Blue Pamphlets of 1843*, 49.

[16] Ibid., 50-1: Report of the Committee Appointed for the Examination of Disputes Amongst the Parsees, May 1, 1786.

to pass its own resolution, however, the Parsi Punchayet of Bombay intended to assume the leadership of the community and the authority to regulate its customs and rules. The Punchayet had prevented the priests from establishing their own rules on marriage that aimed to set the priestly class apart from other Parsis in terms of status and economic advantage, and had affirmed its authority to make rules for the community in Bombay. Armed with the ability to ostracize individuals in breach of its resolutions within Bombay as well as the legal power to exercise corporal punishment, and backed by the Parsis of Bombay in support of its leadership, the Parsi Punchayet of Bombay could exercise authority over all the Parsis.

In acknowledging the right of the Punchayet to pass its resolution, the British committee favoured the class of Parsi society in Bombay that British officialdom had come to understand and deal with. The committee accepted the arguments of the Parsis of Bombay and found the regulation of the priests to be a "very unequal decree ... calculated for partial benefit and to enrich and aggrandize their own Caste."[17] The committee found the resolution of the priests to have been motivated less by religious concerns than economic ones designed to benefit the flow of dowries to them. The decision of the committee is the more revealing given its own difficulties in accessing Parsi custom and law. The British decision also appeared to go against the caste customs known to prevail in Bombay and parts of India, of taking daughters from other castes while refusing the females of one's caste to the males of another.[18] The committee found the evidence for what constituted Parsi custom to be ambiguous, yet favoured the decision of the Bombay Parsis in passing their resolution over the policy of the priests, which policy had some basis in the caste customs of other Indian communities.

The *behdin/mōbad* controversy marked the first time the British government was called on to adjudicate a dispute among the Parsis and the earliest instance that produced an official critique of the inner workings of the Parsi community. The committee had found the Parsis of Bombay and the clergy to have a poor knowledge of their laws and customs, which were either lost or incorrectly observed:

> It appears that the Parsees, at least those at Bombay, have lost much of their ancient knowledge and have abated in their rigid observance of

[17] Ibid.

[18] Enthoven, *Tribes and Castes*, 203.

> the Laws of their religion assuming and exercising great latitude of dispensation. Very few indeed even of their Priests can read their Law in the original language, and the translation into the language of India furnishes abundant matter of dispute and objection in the interpretation of the original Law.[19]

The committee's critique of the state of affairs within the Parsi community provided the government the opportunity to offer its recommendations to the Parsis and exercise its influence over them. While it accepted the right of the Punchayet to formulate regulations on behalf of the Parsis of Bombay, the committee acknowledged that the resolution passed by the Punchayet could only be effective as long as the Parsis were willing to be bound by it. To prevent future disputes and preserve peace and good order among the Parsis, the committee recommended the reconstitution of the Punchayet on a more equitable basis under the auspices of the government.[20]

On the recommendations of the three man committee, a Board of Consultation headed by Governor R. H. Boddam communicated to the head of the Punchayet the recommendation that a Punchayet of twelve be selected by the Governor from a list of twenty-four lay and clerical names returned by the Parsis. The new Punchayet of twelve would be accorded the powers to settle private disputes among Parsis, make regulations for the general benefit of the community, and exclude from the community persons offending against the rules and regulations of the Parsis. As measure of the authority the new Punchayet held, the family of Behramji Nusserwanji Ghadially and Hormasji Behramji Patel, whose children's betrothal had originally defied the resolution of the Punchayet in 1777, were urged by the Board to reconcile themselves to the decisions of the community.[21] The resolution of the Punchayet against the priests was eased and by 1830, *mōbads* were allowed to give their daughters in marriage to *behdins*, and the sons of priests were permitted to marry *behdin* females, provided the priests maintained the spirit of the agreement.[22]

The Parsi Punchayet of Bombay that came into being on January 1, 1787, had the legitimacy of both the formal sanction of govern-

---

[19] Report from the Committee Appointed for the Examination of Disputes Amongst the Parsees, May 1, 1786, in *Blue Pamphlets of 1843*, 50.

[20] Ibid., 51-2.

[21] Ibid., 53-6: Extract, Minutes from the Consultation, May 15, 1786, and Extract, Minutes from the Consultation, May 17, 1786. List of six Parsis and six Andearoos received and signed by Governor R. H. Boddam, January 1, 1787.

[22] Jeejeebhoy, "Communal Discipline," 313.

ment and the confidence of the Parsi community whose official leadership it had now become. The new Punchayet that emerged in 1787, however, remained an elite body and was composed principally of the leading members of the Parsi community who had been members of previous Punchayets. Five of the six laymen and two of the six priests approved by the Governor for the Punchayet on January 1, were among the twenty individuals who had taken part in the last general meeting held by the Bombay Zarthosti Anjuman on October 27, 1785. The elite composition of the Punchayet reflected the nature of Anjuman meetings of the late eighteenth century, which were attended by the most prominent of Parsi residents of Bombay. Despite the elite nature of the Punchayet, the role and importance of the Anjuman or general body of Parsis had also come to be recognized by both government and the Parsis. With the reconstitution of the Punchayet on a more legitimate basis, both its role and that of the Anjuman would come to be elaborated by the Parsis. In his history and critique of the Punchayet, the social reformer Manockjee Cursetjee Shroff (1808-87) noted the changes in the Punchayet following its reconstitution. The Punchayet published and promulgated its rules and dictates known as *bundobasts*, which were approved by the Anjuman of the Parsis. The Anjuman was convened by sending round a crier, "heralding forth in every street, nook, and corner inhabited by the Parsees in Bombay—at such an hour—and in such a Church (always in a place of their public worship), the general assembly of the caste will be met; stating its business to be then and there brought on for decision."[23]

From a dispute among the Parsis had emerged an institution that confirmed the change in the social state of the Parsis since their arrival in Bombay; and which would be instrumental in shaping the identity of the Parsis in the next half century. The reorganization of the Punchayet had clarified the grounds upon which future Punchayet legitimacy would rest. The moral authority of the Punchayet owed less to the balance of laity and clergy achieved in its composition than to the process by which it composed itself. The Punchayet's success in meeting future challenges whether for leadership

[23] Manockjee Cursetjee, Letter No. 1, November 9, 1844, in *The Parsee Panchayet, Its Rise, Its Fall and the Causes That Led to the Same: Being a Series of Letters in the Bombay Times of 1844-45, Under the Signature of Q. in the Corner, Published at the Request of Some Gentlemen of the Parsee Community and With the Permission of the Author* (Bombay, 1860), 1.

or against its authority, would largely depend on its own ability to lead and represent the interests of the majority of Parsis. The British government had in large part acknowledged this fact in the dispute between the Parsis and the priests. Government also insisted that the Punchayet could only avoid future disputes by being seen to represent the interests of the majority of Parsis, starting with its composition. In 1787, it had served the interests of both British and Parsis to have the Punchayet formally sanctioned by the government. In supporting the Punchayet, the British both encouraged the political socialization of the Parsi leadership to their authority, while inadvertently they had facilitated the process in support of Parsi identity that the new Punchayet would contribute to.

The Punchayet at its Height

In the years after its reconstitution the Punchayet took steps to consolidate its authority. The Punchayet took measures to make Bombay more independent of the ecclesiastical jurisdiction of Navsari, which was the centre of Parsi priestly authority. Prior to the reconstitution of the Punchayet, the Bombay Parsis relied on priests sent from Navsari to perform certain religious ceremonies. In 1740, the first priest arrived in Bombay from Navsari under a formal agreement between the two communities. In 1750, a request was made for two priests qualified to perform the *Tānā* ceremony, a requisite to lay the foundation of the *dakhma.* Relations between the Bombay Parsis and the priests of Navsari continued to be difficult as the latter resisted the growing power of the former. In 1755, a memorial to the Punchayet containing the signatures of seventy-seven Parsis complained about the four Navsari priests in Bombay who refused to train other priests.[24] The Bombay Parsis continued to be under the religious authority of Navsari in 1777, when permission was obtained to construct a *chotra* or emergency ossuary to expose and inter the Parsi dead, during a cholera epidemic in Bombay.[25] As recognition of its new authority following its reconstitution, the Punchayet gained the consent of the Navsari priests to have important religious ceremonies performed in Bombay, free of their permission. In 1791, the Bombay community obtained its own *varasyo* or white bull, essential in the

[24] Enthoven, *Tribes and Castes*, 463-5.
[25] Desai, *History of the Bombay Parsi Punchayet*, 45.

performance of certain Parsi rites, and in the same year the first *Nīrangdin* ceremony, consecrating the *gōmēz* or bull's urine, was performed in Bombay.[26] With the growth of the religious endowments and institutions of the Parsis in Bombay in the decades to come, largely under the control and management by the Parsi Punchayet, the Bombay community came to exercise as much control over the religious life of the Parsis of India as it did over their social and political affairs.

The power the new Punchayet had assumed was evident in the actions it now undertook to address issues of fundamental importance to the Parsis. At the Anjuman meeting of February 19, 1791, steps were taken to deal with the issue of bigamy among the Parsis. This was the first occasion that the Parsi Punchayet of Bombay sought to pronounce on an important social issue such as marriage among Parsis. The Anjuman resolution stated that no one whose wife is living can take another, and whosoever leaves his wife without cause was to be considered a sinner by the Parsis. Permission to marry a second time could be granted to both wife and husband by the Punchayet where circumstances permitted such as in a case of sterility and infertility, a husband's impotency, or a wife's adultery, provided the case was proved.[27] On March 8, 1794, the Punchayet also made provision to permit a wife to remarry if a husband was absent for a period of ten years without her consent provided she obtained the consent of the Punchayet.[28] In 1811, a wife was given permission to remarry as her husband was absent for eight years and believed to have been lost in war near Hyderabad.[29] Whereas the Parsi priesthood held the right of solemnization of the Parsi matrimonial union, the Anjuman resolution of 1791 effectively gave to the Punchayet the right and authority of the disposition of that union.

The Anjuman resolution of 1791 was largely an attempt by the Parsis of Bombay to gain control over an issue that had its roots in the rural setting. The nature of the Parsi marriage bond, involving by definition the marriage solely between two Parsis, was an essential element of the definition of Parsi identity. The need to better define the Parsi marriage bond came to preoccupy the Parsis from the time of the reconstitution of the Punchayet. The necessity to distinguish

---

[26] *Parsee Prakash*, 1:870.

[27] Ibid.

[28] Ibid., 875.

[29] Ibid., 887.

the Parsi matrimonial union from that of other communities had historically been important to the Parsis. This implied that the Parsis of India were endogamous, marrying within the community. At the same time, the Parsis were not unaffected by both the social pressures within and the cultural practices outside the Parsi community, of the Indian setting, which could lead to such practices as bigamy, infant marriage, and interfaith liaisons. With the urbanization of the Parsis, the new affluence, mobility, and cosmopolitan contacts imposed new pressures on the Parsi matrimonial union. The rise of the Punchayet offered the Parsis the ability to better define and safeguard the matrimonial union. In outlawing bigamy and stating those cases where a Parsi could remarry, the Parsi Punchayet had distinguished the Parsis from the polygamous Indian communities around them. The nature of the provisions on marriage and the authority exercised by the Punchayet and Anjuman in framing them, suggested that Parsi tradition was being reshaped in the new setting and under the new possibilities of community government.

In 1791, the Punchayet began to assert its authority and adjudicate marital cases. The Punchayet, furthermore, withstood challenges to its decisions, and authority and right to govern the community from those Parsis who sought to appeal over the Punchayet to the civil authorities. One particular case is noteworthy involving a Parsi liquor shopkeeper guilty of bigamy. Framji Cooverji complained to the Governor's Council that he, his wife and his parents had been put 'out of caste,' and the Parsis prohibited from patronizing his shop by Pestonjee Bomanjee Wadia, on his own initiative, as a member of the Punchayet. Framji Cooverji noted the arbitrary nature of the decision, as he had been singled out while the Punchayet did not punish other Parsis who acted similarly. When the Governor's Council sent the minutes of the complaint to the Punchayet, the Parsis held an Anjuman meeting at Banaji Limji fire-temple in 1793, at which time the entire assembly confirmed the appropriateness of Pestonjee Bomanjee's actions. Pestonjee Bomanjee had acted with the tacit consent and approval of the Parsis against Framji Cooverji and his relations, for having breached the resolution of 1791 without the consent of the Punchayet.[30] The scrutiny that Pestonjee Bomanjee's actions were subjected to by the greater Anjuman suggests that a level of public overview had emerged in the dealings of the Punchayet since 1787.

[30] Ibid., 873; Davar, *History of the Parsi Punchayet*, 27.

At the same time, the ability of Punchayet members to act on behalf of the Parsis independent of the explicit approval of the Anjuman was also confirmed.

The importance that Punchayet members had assumed revealed the opportunity for decisive leadership available to the Parsis,and the vulnerability of the institutional organization. The next challenge to face the Punchayet was not from outside but from within. Within the span of twenty years following the reconstitution of the Punchayet, its authority was eroded as standards fell. Neither government nor the Parsis filled vacancies on the Punchayet, and the sons of former members replaced their deceased fathers without the formal consent of the community.[31] The prescribed formality by which a new member of the Punchayet was chosen, usually on the death of a member, was for the Punchayet and Anjuman of Bombay to recognize the installation of a new member on the third day of mourning following the death of the deceased Punchayet member. On this third day, the *Uthamnā* ceremony in memory of the departed was held, to commemorate the name of the departed and enumerate the individual's benefactions in life and by offering donations to charity in the name of the departed. Throughout the early history of the Punchayet its moral authority and ability to act were periodically damaged by the incursion of nepotistic and class interests. The pattern had been set. As long as the members of the Punchayet acted in conformity with the interests of the majority of Parsis, including what they believed in good faith to be the interests of the majority of Parsis, the Punchayet was a formidable tool of social control and community cohesiveness.

In 1818, the Parsis undertook to restore the authority of the Punchayet. A period of nearly twenty years began in which the Punchayet was at the height of its power and influence. A public meeting of the Parsis was held at Dadiseth fire-temple on the March 4, 1818, where a new Punchayet was chosen. An additional six lay officers were added to form for the first time a Punchayet of eighteen, exclusively elected and chosen by the Parsis. Rules regarding the future conduct of the Punchayet were also enacted, including procedures for the convening of public meetings to decide and observe the operations of Punchayet justice. The procedures included the settling of

[31] Graham, Journal, 41; Karaka, *History of the Parsis*, 1:224.

minor disputes between Parsis by as few as two Punchayet members, who could add to their numbers where they thought proper. Their decision when accepted by the litigants would be approved by the larger Punchayet and binding on the parties. A complainant who was dissatisfied with the decision of two or four Punchayet members could, as a form of appeal, request a settlement before a Punchayet of ten or twelve, or the whole Punchayet of eighteen. Where a complainant was still dissatisfied with a decision, provision was made to assemble a whole Punchayet of eighteen and as large as twenty-four, in the presence of the general assembly of the Parsis. In the event of the Punchayet being divided over a dispute, the decision of the majority of those assembled would be considered as final and binding on the parties involved.[32] The decision to permit an open and accessible form of dispute settlement by the Parsis served not only to add legitimacy to the dispensing of justice among the Parsis, but also sought to bind the community to the interests of its members.

The new Punchayet enacted a series of regulations unanimously approved by the public assemblage. Many of the regulations reaffirmed the authority the Punchayet had assumed since 1791, and upheld the standards of the community. Certain social ills and practices believed deleterious to the cohesion of the Parsi community and practised by the Parsis were given the full attention of the reinvigorated Punchayet. Laws against bigamy and infant marriage as well as ordinances regulating the customs and habits of the Parsis were enacted. The regulation against bigamy and other marriage rules were re-enacted in 1818. In reserving to itself the sole authority to adjudicate matrimonial disputes between Parsis, the Punchayet manifestly declared itself the authoritative regulator of the Parsi caste. Its authority, furthermore, was backed by the power to censure and put 'out of caste' all those "wearing the 'badge of Zardost,'" i.e., all Zoroastrians in Bombay.[33] Since the first resolution against bigamy in 1791, the authority of the Punchayet had gradually come to be extended over the Parsis of Western India, with notifications of judgements against Parsis being circulated to all the towns Parsis inhabited. When in 1811, a Parsi went to Surat to remarry without the permission of the Punchayet of Bombay, the Punchayet sent notifications to the towns of Gujarat including the principal centres of

[32] Cursetjee, *Parsee Panchayet*, 4: Letter No. 2, November 1844.

[33] Ibid., 5-6.

Surat, Broach, Navsari, Bulsar, Gandevi, and Udwada warning the Parsis of the breach of the Punchayet's resolution against bigamy.[34]

The Punchayet also demanded accountability and responsibility from the members of the community. The Punchayet appropriated to itself the right to hear the merits of individual appeals and forbade the unilateral actions of parties who did not desire to involve the Punchayet in their affairs, including convenient understands between spouses. In setting the terms for the settlement of marital disputes, the Punchayet maintained the distinction of marriage as much a social act as a private union. Consequently, whether a first wife gave her consent to allow her husband to take a second wife, or in writing absolved the husband from the marriage vows, unless adjudicated by the Punchayet the terms were unacceptable by the standards of the community.[35] Permission to remarry had been granted since 1791, on limited grounds; though divorce in the strict sense of a separation by law, where the marriage bond is dissolved (divorce a *vinculò a matrimoni*) did not exist. A form of formal separation was permitted, although a couple remained married until permission was requested to remarry by one of the parties.[36] Where leave was given to remarry the Punchayet demanded proper provision for the first wife by the husband, including of her "food, clothing, place of abode, her jewels, and for the funeral and other expenses after her death."[37] Provision was also made to deposit money with the Pun1chayet for the maintenance of a first wife by a husband who had been given permission to remarry.

The Punchayet had been fit to ensure the welfare of the first wife since it passed its first resolution against bigamy and began adjudicating marital disputes in 1791. In 1792, Cursetjee Manockjee Shroff

---

[34] *Parsee Prakash*, 1:887.

[35] Cursetjee, *Parsee Panchayet*, 6: Letter No. 2.

[36] Both J. R. B. Jeejeebhoy and S. P. Davar employ the word 'divorce' to describe the permission given to Parsis to remarry from the Resolution of February 19, 1791. As the Parsis deem themselves to practice monogamy, the term divorce may be used; though in the strictest sense this form of 'divorce' is better described as a divorce *a mensa et thoro*, from bed and board, akin to a formal separation, where a couple is separated but still married. This construction is more in line with the wording of the Resolution, which granted permission to 'remarry' on specific grounds, as well as the nature of dispute settlement practised by the Punchayet. On a definition of these terms, see Framjee A. Rana, *Parsi Law: Embodying the Law of Marriage and Divorce and Inheritance and Succession, Applicable to Parsis in British India* (Bombay, 1934), 9.

[37] Cursetjee, *Parsee Panchayet*, 5: Letter No. 2.

(1764-1845) asked to remarry on the ground that he had no children by his first wife, and was not likely to. He was granted leave to remarry by the Punchayet upon giving assurances that he would provide for his first wife. Cursetjee Manockjee continued to provide for his first wife under his roof alongside his second wife and five children.[38] In 1811, the Punchayet gave permission for a Parsi to remarry given his wife's feeble-mindedness. He had to provide her with Rs. 200 and regularly see to her other needs. Upon meeting these terms, the wife also gave her consent to the separation. In 1812, a Parsi was ordered by the Punchayet to provide his first wife with an annuity of Rs. 90, plus Rs. 336 in cash, as compensation for the maintenance he had not provided for the past seven years during which he had been living in bigamy.[39]

Moreover, the Parsis did not consider leave to remarry automatic or perfunctory, whatever the character and circumstances of a spouse. Infertility on the part of a wife was not sufficient cause to permit a husband to take a second wife, even where he provided for her maintenance, until his wife had passed the age of childbearing. The Punchayet also adjudicated instances of breaches of promise to marry, and could compel parents and children to acknowledge betrothals on pain of penalty.[40] In 1804, an Anjuman meeting was held at Dadiseth fire-temple at which time a woman from Surat was ordered to have her daughter married within a month or else be dealt with severely. The Punchayet upheld the betrothal, which had been some eight to nine years in the making and agreed to by the father of the girl.[41] The regulations adopted in 1818 were clearly meant to illustrate that a breach in the obligations and responsibilities Parsis had entered into with one another were to be regarded as a breach of the authority of the Punchayet. Bigamy, adultery, desertions of wives by husbands, and other marital problems were believed by the Punchayet and the Parsis to be particularly deleterious to the small community. In designing its regulations the Punchayet sought to regulate the community norms within the framework of social peace and social justice.

The Punchayet also developed mechanisms to pressure and discipline both offenders and the general community into the observance

---

[38] *Parsee Prakash*, 1:871.

[39] Ibid., 887.

[40] Cursetjee, *Parsee Panchayet*, 6: Letter No. 2.

[42] *Parsee Prakash*, 1:884; Davar, *History of the Parsi Punchayet*, 28.

of its regulations. Not only had the authority and influence of the Parsi Punchayet of Bombay come to be extended to all the Parsi communities of Western India by the nineteenth century, but also its authority bound all Parsis to observe and support its decisions and judgements against offenders. Excommunication, or putting an offender 'out of caste,' was the most severe penalty the Punchayet and community could impose, and involved as much a comprehensive social ostracism as a religious penalty. Social ostracism was a custom the Parsis adopted from the Indian social milieu. Being put out of caste effectively debarred an interdicted Parsi from attending all religious rites, ceremonies, and festivals at any fire-temple, or having the benefit of funeral rites performed by a priest at a *dakhma*. In a small community like that of the Parsis, being put out of caste effectively stripped one of any identity as a Parsi. The comprehensive nature of social ostracism within the Parsi community was such that any Parsi who associated with or provided succour to a Parsi who had been put out of caste, whether he or she be a parent, spouse, or other relative, a priest, or a corpse-bearer was liable to penalty or punishment from the Punchayet.

The famous case of Jamsetjee Byramjee Laskari or Luskuree, serves as the model for Punchayet disciplinary justice. Laskari was of priestly background, but had become wealthy as a trader. Convinced he was immune from the authority of the Punchayet by virtue of his wealth and connections, while in Surat, Laskari took for himself a second wife during the lifetime of his first. Upon returning to Bombay, Laskari and his new wife were expeditiously put out of caste by a public meeting of the Parsis at Dadiseth fire-temple in 1818. Upon learning of his excommunication, however, Laskari displayed the worst of his disposition by assaulting the priest sent to advise his family of his excommunication. A suit filed in front of a magistrate in the Petty Sessions by the Punchayet, however, soon elicited a different response from Laskari. He feigned contrition, once again, miscalculating on the response of the Punchayet. Having circumvented the rules of the community in committing bigamy, believing himself to have been above the justice of the average Parsi, and having compounded his miscalculations by letting his spleen get the better of him, Laskari proved the perfect example for Punchayet justice.

Determined to see this proud knee bend, the Punchayet convened a public meeting at Dadiseth fire-temple on April 10, 1818, at which time Laskari's punishment was decided. In the presence of the public congregated for the purpose, Laskari was commanded to strike himself over the face with his shoe five times; to beseech pardon from the priest he had assaulted, while having a *putka* or haltered cloth round his neck; and to recompense the Punchayet for the legal costs associated with taking him to court. When on the June 16, the Anjuman was assembled for the display a certain leniency was elicited for Laskari given his contrition, as he had rather to scratch his nose with his shoe than beat himself. Laskari was also commanded to pay the Punchayet's expenses totalling Rs. 225 for having had to hire a solicitor and a barrister. On July 2, Laskari's written apology to both the priest he had assaulted and the Punchayet was read. Both he and his wife beseeched the pardon of the community whilst having a *putka* round their necks and swore never to flaunt the propriety of the community upon threat of such punishment as the Punchayet should see fit to impose. Having sought pardon and having been ordered to pay an additional Rs. 2,000 for the maintenance of his first wife, Andearoo Jamsetjee Byramjee Laskari and his second wife were forgiven and readmitted to the community.[42]

In committing a wanton act against all the proprieties of the Parsis so soon after their determination to pass resolutions against harmful behaviour, Laskari had made his name one of the most discussed in Bombay and had invited society to execrate him. The example made of Jamsetjee Byramjee Laskari and his second wife had served the purposes of social control within the Parsi community. The severity of punishment and the depth of contrition exacted from Laskari were meant to serve as both example and deterrent to other Parsis, and lent legitimacy to the process of readmission and redemption in the eyes of the Parsis. While the Laskari case stands as the model for Punchayet discipline and social control, given the momentum the Punchayet maintained in the succeeding years, it may well be said that the case of Laskari was less exceptional than the standard the Punchayet set for itself and the Parsi community. As Manockjee Cursetjee observed in the 1840s, the Laskari case stood as "one of the hundreds of decisions which the late Parsee Punchyat [*sic*] came to without partiality, without favour, and in all cases where individuals, whether rich or poor, transgressed the Rules of the caste."[43]

[42]Cursetjee, *Parsee Panchayet*, 8-9: Letter No. 3, November 19, 1844.

[43]Ibid., 9.

While shaming and punishment served the purposes of open justice and deterrence, redemption and rehabilitation had also to be available if social cohesion was to achieve its full aim. The readmission of Laskari and his second wife served this purpose. It is worth noting that the Punchayet did not annul the second marriage as, in a situation where a religious ceremony was properly conducted, the Parsis did not invalidate the ceremony but sought to make right the situation that existed. In 1792, the Punchayet had annulled a bigamous second marriage, where it was found that only one priest had officiated at the ceremony, rendering it improper. In that case, the second wife was forced to break her bangles, as if to signify widowhood.[44] The Parsis believed it in the interest of the community to never forsake a member altogether. Like the other Indian communities, the Parsis favoured the readmission of contrite wrongdoers to the community by the caste Punchayet. Unlike other Indian communities and castes, however, the Parsis imposed more severe social and religious penalties against wrongdoers, believing such measures vital for the discipline and cohesion of the minority community.[45] The Parsis favoured the emulation of practices of the indigenous social environment that benefited their community cohesiveness, while at the same time adapting the practices to their requirements. The right to readmit an excommunicated Parsi to the community was reserved to the Punchayet. In 1825, Framjee Homjee was readmitted to the Parsi community twelve years after being excommunicated for having committed bigamy, and during which time his child was denied consignment to the *dakhma*.[46]

The Punchayet regarded infant marriage as another practice particularly harmful to the social fabric of the Parsi community: "There have been instances where nuptial ceremonies of infants have been performed while sitting on their mother's laps, having sugar plums administered to them in order to keep them quiet and from crying during the performance of the ceremony by their priests!!"[47] The Punchayet saw fit to outlaw this practice believing it not only to have

[44] *Parsee Prakash*, 1:872.

[45] A money fine was often the prescribed penalty for various transgressions in Indian society in Western India. See N. K. Wagle, "Government, the Jāti, and the Individual: Rights, Discipline and Control in the Pune Kotwal Papers, 1766-94," *Contributions to Indian Sociology* 34 (2000), pp. 321-60.

[46] Jeejeebhoy, "Communal Discipline," 315.

[47] Cursetjee, *Parsee Panchayet*, 17: Letter No. 7, December 22, 1844.

been against the interests of the children, but equally the cause of future strife between husbands and wives often leading to bigamy. Zoroastrianism enjoined every Zoroastrian to marry and provided the religious justification for early marriage. The Zoroastrians of Iran had their own marriage customs that included consanguineous marriage, and the Parsis also maintained the practice of marriage between close kin.[48] Infant marriage among the provincial Parsis was part of a socio-religious custom the Parsis were historically familiar with, but one that the Parsis rationalized as borrowed largely from the Indian social environment. In recording her impressions of the Parsis, Maria Graham noted how many poor Parsis settled their children's marriages at five or six years of age, in conformity to the Hindu custom.[49] The practice was part of a socio-economic pattern that tied families together as much as children and which involved, at times, elaborate ceremonies. The reliance on *joshis* or astrologers, the presentation of large dowries and gifts, and the holding of ostentatious nuptials by the families engaging in infant marriage all were the subject of the Punchayet's attention. On October 18, 1823, some nineteen *bundobasts* or regulations the Punchayet had made since 1818, against practices deemed harmful to the Parsi identity, were published in the Gujarati newspapers.[50]

The actions of the Punchayet against bigamy and infant marriage aimed to replace one social pattern with another. The Punchayet redefined Parsi marriage away from those inimical customs derived from the traditional Indian social environment, and socialized the Parsis to a pattern that favoured the cohesiveness and uniqueness of the Parsi identity. The marriage ceremony of the Parsis in part derives from Indian custom, though the rituals and mores of the Parsis distinguishes it from the Hindu bond. The Indian Zoroastrians had composed their own marriage ceremony, adding the Indian form known as the *Āshirvād*, to that which they had imported from Iran. Unlike in the Hindu ceremony, in the Parsi ceremony fire is not a central element. The central religious part of the ceremony that binds the couple and is performed by the priests is Iranian in origin.[51] The

---

[48]Jamsheed K. Choksy, *Purity and Pollution in Zoroastrianism: Triumph Over Evil* (Austin, 1989), 89-90.

[49]Graham, *Journal*, 41.

[50] Cursetjee, *Parsee Panchayet*, 18: Letter No. 7.

[51]Remarks of Nowrozjee Furdoonjee and Sorabjee Shapoorjee, Secretaries to the Managing Committee, Parsi Law Association, February 28, 1862, in Judicial

Parsis, furthermore, placed no prohibitions against widow and widower remarriages as did the Hindus. The Punchayet through its regulations and reforms recognized the definition of marriage and family to be an integral step in the definition of social and political community. In spite of the efforts of the Punchayet, the practice of infant marriage remained difficult to eradicate altogether. Its eradication while enforced through the power of coercion during the time of the Punchayet and the force of law after 1865, still encountered the obstacle of social custom. Despite the tremendous progress of education among the Parsis, and the compilation of a Parsi law code by the mid-nineteenth century, ambiguity remained over the legitimacy of infant marriage.[52]

The admission of non-Parsis to the Parsi community was another question that preoccupied the Parsis in their attempts to better define the Parsi identity. Over the course of their history in India, as the Parsis became strictly endogamous they did not proselytize other communities. The question of admitting non-Parsis into the community remained an issue of such importance and debate that the Parsis had appealed to the Zoroastrian priests of Iran as to their opinions on the subject, as part of the *Rivāyat* correspondence. The Iranians in their response to the Parsis' missives did not oppose the conversion of 'slaves' or 'servants' to Zoroastrianism provided the correct ceremonies were performed, the candidates were of good faith, and no harm came to the community.[53] The opinions of the Iranian priests while seeming to expose a divide between the two Zoroastrian communities over the admission of *juddīns* or non-Zoroastrians to the faith reflected an academic response coupled to lack of knowledge of the Parsis' cultural evolution.

The evidence regarding the extent to which the Parsis converted or admitted Indians into the community, particularly prior to their arrival in Bombay, is difficult to assess. It appears that at the time of the first correspondence between the Parsis and Iranian Zoroastrians,

---

Department 1863 20/143:303-7, Department of Archives, Government of Maharashtra, Bombay (hereafter cited as J.D.); J. J. Modi, *The Religious Ceremonies and Customs of the Parsees* (Bombay, 1922), 15-46; Enthoven, *Tribes and Castes*, 205-8.

[52] On the personal law of the Parsis, *see* Chapter Five.

[53] B. N. Dhabhar, *The Persian Rivayats of Hormazyar Framarz and Others* (Bombay, 1932), xxxi, 275-6. See also M. N. Dhalla, History of Zoroastrianism (1938; reprint, Bombay, 1963), 474-6.

in the fifteenth century, the Parsis continued to convert the locals. Changa Asa, who was a great lay leader of the Parsis in Gujarat, and who is credited with initiating the contact with Iran, is held to have followed the practice of the medieval Parsis in converting Hindus to increase the size of the community.[54] Parsi tradition, as represented by the *Qisseh-i Sanjan*, on the other hand, abjured proselytism as it went against the compact the Parsis were believed to have entered into on arrival in India with the Raja of Sanjan not to convert locals and proselytize their religion. Whatever the facts behind this interpretation of the history of the Parsis, the date of the narrative, composed in 1599, suggests that the Parsis may only have ended the practice of selectively admitting non-Parsis to the Parsi community by the seventeenth century. By the nineteenth century, however, for many Parsis the question of admitting Indians to their community raised as many social as religious questions. The Parsis had so conformed to the Indian milieu and, at the same time, so adapted to their new prosperity that a sense of ethnic pride and exclusivity of identity had emerged strong enough to make the admission of Indians to the Parsi community objectionable.[55]

The issue appears to have gained urgency for the Bombay Parsis in the nineteenth century as the new prosperity of the community and the social mobility of the urban setting put the Parsis in greater contact with other communities than at any other time in their history. For the most part, the caste customs of the other Indian communities, in addition to the sensibilities of the Parsis, militated against conversions. The issue for the Parsis during the era of Punchayet authority remained one of how to deal with the private actions of Parsis introducing non-Parsis into the Zoroastrian fold. The Punchayet was forced to deal with the issue of Parsi men who had taken non-Parsi women as their mistresses, and sought to raise the children of the union as Parsis. The private and clandestine investing of illegitimate children with the *sudra* and *kustī* or shirt and thread cord worn by the initiated Zoroastrian, preoccupied the community and risked the reputation of the Punchayet over the issue. Where the admonitions by the Punchayet to individual Parsis to desist from such practices

---

[54]K. N. Seervai and B. B. Patell, "Gujarat Parsis from Their Earliest Settlement to the Present Time," in *Gazetteer of Bombay Presidency*, vol. 9, part 2, ed. J. M Campbell (Bombay, 1899), 189.

[55]Delphine Menant, "Social Evolution Among Parsis," *Journal of the Iranian Association* (January 1921): 265-70.

were not heeded, or felt by many not to have been consistently or forcefully enough stated, the fairness and firmness of the Punchayet soon became the issue. In 1818, the Punchayet demonstrated its own difficulty over the issue when it sanctioned the admission of the illegitimate daughter of a Parsi father to the fold while, at the same time, declaring that without its permission none other than the children of Parsi parents could be regarded as Parsi. The issue of selective admissions of individuals to the Parsi fold divided the Punchayet as some members decried the absence of a consistent policy.[56]

In 1830, the Punchayet sought to provide leadership on the issue by devising rules on the admission of non-Parsis to the community. At the Anjuman meeting of August 11, 1830, the Punchayet stated that from this date onwards, the admission of non-Parsi children to the community was to be stopped, and no one who was not a Parsi was to be invested with the *sudra* and *kustī*. The Punchayet did not retroactively enforce its decision, and accepted the presence of children born illegitimately to Parsi men to the community up to the date of the Anjuman meeting. However, it laid out rules to inform and warn Parsis as to the conduct expected from them henceforth. It warned all priests not to initiate non-Parsis upon penalty of being defrocked and put out of caste. It cautioned the members of any family that admitted a non-Parsi in their midst that they would be put out of caste. The Punchayet made it incumbent on Parsis to prove that illegitimate children accepted to the community were accepted before the date of the Anjuman resolution. Parsis were advised to take a hand in observing the conduct of their fellows so that misconduct did not occur, and the Punchayet placed the onus on all Parsis, including third parties, to inform the Punchayet where a Parsi had acted against the standards of the community. The Punchayet prepared notifications of its ruling to be distributed to all the Indian Zarthosti Anjumans. The Punchayet's resolution applied to areas outside Bombay and India, and other jurisdictions were asked to report Parsis who had breached the rules of the community.[57]

The Punchayet sought to address a difficult issue for the Parsis in putting forward its resolution. It sought to formulate rules of conduct to inform the Parsis as to their obligations as members of the com-

[56] Karaka, *History of the Parsis*, 1:168-9; Jeejeebhoy, "Communal Discipline," 304: Gujarati Circular to the Punchayet of December 10, 1828.

[57] *Parsee Prakash*, 1:897-8.

munity, as well as to be seen to be providing leadership. To some degree, however, the acceptance and admission of children of Parsi men by non-Parsi women from illegitimate liaisons to the community, involved a difficulty for the Parsis that struck at the heart of their community and religious identity, and which was not easily resolved through the passage of rules. While the Parsis sought to safeguard and distinguish the nature of their community by stating their opposition to the admission of non-Parsis, the Parsis were also loath to altogether forsake children who were born of Parsis. In the same way that the Punchayet did not forsake wayward Parsis who had been put out of caste and permitted their readmission where advisable, so too, the Punchayet (undoubtedly reflecting tensions within the community) felt the need to weigh the circumstances of each admission. Where a priest performed the *Navjote* or confirmation ceremony of a non-Parsi child, the Punchayet and the Parsis of the early nineteenth century were particularly pained to dismiss definitively the case and shun the child.

The Punchayet and the Parsis, nevertheless, did not abide the covert initiation of illegitimate half-Parsi children into the community. The Punchayet sought to uphold its resolution and in 1836, the Punchayet put out of caste three Parsi priests for having performed the *Navjote* ceremony of illegitimate children without its sanction.[58] The sensitive issue of the admission of individuals to the Parsi community involved a variety of issues social, economic, in addition to religious and spiritual. The issue remained beyond the power of social control on its own to address. Throughout the history of the Parsi community, up to the present-day, the question of community membership would be determined less by any central authority than by the mood of the community, the situations that face individual Parsis, and the response of institutions and organizations to the different currents of opinion in the community.

Other regulations were passed from 1818 to 1823 that aimed to proscribe customs and petty social rituals commonplace in Indian society. All manner of superstitions practised by Parsis not deemed uniquely Zoroastrian were to be expunged. The frequenting of places of worship other than Zoroastrian, as well as the performing of rites, vows, or ceremonies appertaining to Hindus and Muslims, were all to be outlawed. The Punchayet specified those holidays and holy

[58]Jeejeebhoy, "Communal Discipline," 304: The meetings of June 23, 28, 1836.

days observed by the Hindus and Muslims, as well as the places where these rites were performed, to be avoided by the Parsis.[59] Regulations were passed against superfluous ceremonies some Parsis insisted on performing at weddings and funerals. As early as 1796, the Punchayet had begun to regulate the Parsis' social ceremonies. At the Anjuman meeting of June 5, the Punchayet had proscribed the use of meat at marriages and other festive functions where food was consecrated, as it was felt the killing of animals was inauspicious on such occasions.[60] After 1818, the Punchayet passed regulations limiting the expense, extent, and duration of all the practices. The Punchayet was meticulous in the scrutiny it gave to the customs of the Parsis, to the point that it decreed a limit to the number of guests to be invited to a function, and the menu and quantity of food to be served, to the pound.[61] The length of the mourning period after a funeral was limited: "That on the death of an infant, the meeting of the women should be as short as possible; on that of a child from 1 to 7 years of age, they should meet but for three days; and on the death of anyone above that age, to meet ten days, and ten days only."[62] In a practical sense, the Punchayet hoped to counter the most conspicuously extravagant tendencies that arose during these occasions, and which it believed enervated the community of both its resources and its morale. The impression of these practices within and without the community was a further consideration. The image of priests chasing after Parsis to perform superfluous ceremonies only to collect a gratuity for their services, often to the material disadvantage of the pious; or the giving of lavish food offerings and gifts on special ceremonial days, including those days reserved for remembering the dead; or the unrestrained grief of Parsi women almost vying for attention in their bereavement, all appalled the Punchayet.

It is of particular note that the injunctions of the Punchayet were often enacted with reference to the actions of the women in the Parsi community. The situation of women in Parsi society was relatively liberal compared to that of women in Hindu and Muslim society. Parsi women were not compelled to veil or screen themselves off from everyday society, and as married, widowed, or single women

[59] Cursetjee, *Parsee Panchayet,* 11-12: Letter No. 4, November 26, 1844, pertaining to the Anjuman meeting of November 4, 1819.

[60] *Parsee Prakash,* 1:878.

[61] Cursetjee, *Parsee Panchayet,* 15-6: Letter No. 6, December 9, 1844.

[62] Ibid., 16.

enjoyed rights and protections unavailable to Hindu and Muslim women. Nevertheless, in a patriarchal society, the Parsis and the Punchayet imposed on those believed most closely associated with maintaining community standards the onus of responsibility, barely masked through compulsion. Women served as the visible symbol or measure of the inner health of the community to the community itself and to other communities. The sense of self-responsibility on the part of Parsis reflected the self-perception of the community. The Punchayet felt obliged to safeguard both the perception and theactual state of the community. A consensus emerged as to the use of strong coercive measures to force conformity. At the Anjuman meeting of June 5, 1796, the Punchayet had passed one of its first restrictions on the conduct of women in banning Parsi women from singing in public on festive occasions. This form of conduct was believed unbecoming Parsis and more in the fashion of Hindu women of the streets.[63]

In 1819, the Punchayet felt obliged to state that many of the social evils that prevailed among the Parsis were a result of the way the "women of our caste, now-a-days, go about in an extremely unguarded manner."[64] The Punchayet noted that too often it was Parsi women who had taken up superstitious practices such as the wearing of amulets, charms, threads and other periapts, obtained from conjurers and necromancers, and had introduced their husbands and families to such practices. It was stated, consequently, that it was the responsibility and obligation of all Parsis to observe the resolutions of the Punchayet and aid in their observation where they knew the resolutions to have been breached, upon penalty of themselves being publicly disgraced. To assist women to better observe the rules of the community a curfew was invoked, from sunset to sunrise, during which time no woman was to conduct any business outside her home upon penalty of being seized in public and detained. If a woman was unavoidably detained at a relation's house after sunset, it was incumbent on her and those around her to have her accompanied home by a servant with a lighted lantern. Whereas in the early days of Bombay a sense of trust had united the incipient community in responsibility over its members, by the early nineteenth century, a web

---

[63] *Parsee Prakash*, 1:879.

[64] Cursetjee, *Parsee Panchayet*, 10-12: Letter No. 4.

of measures linked the community to the sense of its obligations. While not forsaken, the sense of trust now reposed in the onus of each Parsi towards being Parsi.

The enforcement authority of the community often fell to the unique figures of the *nasāsālārs* or corpse-bearers, whose chief function was to collect and dispatch the dead to the *dakhma*. The relationship of the *nasāsālārs*, as with that of the *āthornans* or priests, to the Parsi community is shaped by their specialized role and function in Parsi society. In Zoroastrian theology, dead matter is associated with evil, and any contact with dead matter or anything associated with dead matter by a Parsi, after a certain time, is regarded as a form of pollution. The role of the *nasāsālārs* is to ensure that no contamination of the living occurs during the disposal of the dead. The *nasāsālārs* consequently maintained a distance from other Parsis, often living in separate areas in towns; and took part in the functions of the community only after observing rules of commensality and undergoing purification ceremonies.

The *nasāsālārs* had been authorized to act on behalf of the Punchayet by the meeting of November 4, 1819, and their power to shame and coerce Parsis to follow the community's norms was formidable. Their duties included acting as sentries and watchmen outside the Fort-Gates and areas around which the Parsis settled, seizing and detaining any woman during the curfew set for women, placing women in the *nasā khānā* or Parsi mortuary for any length of time as punishment, or shaving the heads of women who were in breach of community standards as a mark of disgrace.[65] The role of the *nasāsālārs*, however, extended beyond their function as nominal police. They functioned as heralds and criers of messages to the community, who announced the convening of Punchayet and Anjuman meetings and the resolutions that stemmed from the meetings. In assigning to the *nasāsālārs* the task of carrying out the punishment of Parsis when necessary, the Punchayet had made them as much the instruments suited to deter Parsis from acting against the community's standards as the instruments to punish the breach of those standards. The regulations against the actions of women and the role assigned to the *nasāsālārs* marked the evolution of the Punchayet's efforts to force compliance of its dictates. Since the petition in 1778

---

[65] Ibid., 10-11.

to Governor Hornby asking permission to beat Parsis with the shoe, the Punchayet had co-opted for itself the use of coercive powers. In 1792, the Punchayet had begun to flex its authority over wayward Parsis, including women, and maintain community standards as much as adjudicate disputes. At the Anjuman meeting of October 24, 1792, the Punchayet granted leave to remarry to a carpenter and decreed that his adulterous and errant wife be restricted to her home with her head shaven.[66] In a similar case in 1794, the Punchayet decreed that an adulteress return to her village in Sumali, upon penalty of having her head shaven and being driven out of Bombay. She was to report to the *patel* or chief of her village, and to be provided a stipend of Rs. 4 a month for her maintenance while restricted to her home in the company of proper guardians.[67]

The passage of the resolutions of 1818-19 was a measure of the seriousness of the Punchayet's commitment to enforce community standards and warn Parsis of its intentions. The Punchayet had effectively involved all Parsis in the task of social control over the members of the community, and had delegated the enforcement of its dictates to select individuals. The employment of coercive measures to keep Parsis in line reflected a certain community consciousness that was strengthened with the rise of a powerful Punchayet. It is significant that the Parsis were particularly concerned with the regulation of those features of community life that affected the cohesiveness of the community. It was over such issues as marriage, gender duties, and religious observance that the Parsis came to define the features of their social, cultural, and religious identity. With the eventual demise of the power of the Punchayet, by the middle of the nineteenth century, it was over the same issues that a new generation of Parsis expended its energies.

Many of the practices the Parsis had engaged in prior to the reforms went against the basic spirit of Zoroastrianism as a religion of moderation. The detail the Punchayet gave to its resolutions was equally a measure of the enhanced role the institution had assumed in safeguarding Parsi identity. Having assumed the responsibility to adjudicate Parsi social relations as well as to regulate the customs of the Parsis, the Punchayet had started a process of composing trad-

66 *Parsee Prakash*, 1:872.

67 Ibid., 875.

ition among the Parsis. It had become the vehicle of social control by redefining the parameters of social control. The Punchayet went far towards the composition of new conventions in support of Parsi identity. While many of the reforms by the Punchayet were consistent with the Zoroastrian value system, given the fragmentation of the history of Zoroastrianism and that of the Parsis, the Parsis' endeavours to redefine and reshape their identity owed as much to their immediate needs as to an appeal to the ways of the past.

The actions of the Punchayet from 1791 to the 1830s reflected the strength of community consciousness that had taken shape, and the desire among the Parsis for conformity of conduct and lifestyle. The consensus reflected the Parsis' common membership in their community and the desire to safeguard and define their identity within that community. The consensus the Parsis reached was largely shaped by the necessity and opportunity to refashion a new culture of opinion in support of the Parsi identity in the urban setting. In adopting the punchayet model and adapting that model to their special requirements in Bombay, the capability to shape identity was enhanced. The emergence of the Parsi Punchayet of Bombay as an effective instrument of social control and social cohesiveness formed part of the continuity of historical process in support of identity the Parsis had adhered to over the centuries. While the historical forces that shaped the Parsis' actions in support of identity were not necessarily perceptible to them, the support the Punchayet garnered among Parsis was a measure of both the commitment of the Parsis to safeguarding their identity in Bombay, and the success of the Punchayet in that aim. Representative of the will of the community, the Punchayet could proceed to carry out seemingly intrusive and draconian measures:

> The resolutions of the late Punchyat [*sic*] were not considered as mere 'idle words;' nor were they made to apply to individual cases, but to the whole Parsee community; and were consequently by the whole community respected ... because the parties knew them to have been passed by the Punchyat at their general assembly, and to have been conscientiously given.[68]

While throughout its history the Punchayet remained an elite body, by the early nineteenth century, the dialogue between Punchayet and

[68]Cursetjee, *Parsee Panchayet*, 12: Letter No. 4.

community underpinned Punchayet authority. Ultimately, the authority and legitimacy of the Punchayet depended upon the Parsis' confidence in the institution. At the height of its influence, the interests of the Punchayet and the Parsis had come to coincide.

The Punchayet could never have been effective without the existence of an audience inclined towards its message and willing to endure its dictates. For a time, the welfare of the community had become linked to the probity of the Punchayet, while the success of the Punchayet could no less be a reflection of the state of the community. Inevitably, the process that had made for the rise of the Punchayet also made for the decline in its power and authority. As greater numbers of Parsis no longer viewed the Punchayet as an effective institution, and as a plurality of opinion emerged as regards the best means to safeguard Parsi identity, alternate means to safeguard identity were sought. The theme of identity in the process of accommodation and adaptation had defined the Parsis in India. How to utilize change for the benefit of Parsi identity remained the goal.

The Decline of the Punchayet

The rise of the Punchayet evinced the determination of the Parsis to reinterpret the nature of their social progress since coming to Bombay. In a period of twenty years, the Parsis had established the means for the achievement of order and government that had fostered a sense of identity and even political community. Traditions were reinterpreted establishing conventions of conduct that went far in forming new sets of tradition. Faith was placed in the rituals of authority to safeguard the precious sense of identity, allocating freedoms and obligations guided by a central institution. Yet, an institution is only partially instructive of the values of a people. The trust placed in an institution as the bulwark of order and guidance offers multitudinous possibilities of action, but equally risks undermining the very set of relationships between people it is entrusted with safeguarding with the institution's decline.

By 1836, the Parsi Punchayet's ability to maintain the faith of the community in its actions had seriously come into question in some quarters. The ostensible problem was the unpopular conduct of some of the Punchayet members. "All was peace and harmony," notes the commentator, "so long as the then Punchyat [*sic*] acted upon the principles laid down by their '*Bundobasts*'."[69] However, a schism soon formed between the old and new members. From 1818 to 1820, during the height of Punchayet authority, Framji Nanabhoy Davar had been *davar* or head and chief dispenser of justice of the Punchayet. In 1820, Jehangir Framji Davar succeeded his father, and formally held the title of *davar* until his death in 1854. Jehangir Framji's ineffectual performance as head moved the Punchayet to recognize Hormarjee Bomanjee Wadia as de facto head of the Punchayet until his death in 1826. From 1826 to 1836, Nowrojee Jamsetjee Wadia (1774-1860) presided as head of the Punchayet, though he was not formally recognized as such. In October 1830, the last election on record of a member to the Punchayet was made.[70] When by 1830, individuals unconfirmed by the Anjuman took their seats in the Punchayet one irregularity compounded another. The old practices of partiality between litigants, class-justice, nepotism, delays in decision-making, all seemed to return to the proceedings of the Punchayet. Bigamy and interfaith liaisons were no longer vigilantly opposed, and the lack of faith in the Punchayet reduced the urgency for Anjuman meetings.

In 1830, the case of the wife of Fardoon Navaub illustrated the dilemma aptly. The young woman was abandoned by her eighty-year-old husband and ill served by the Punchayet. She was compelled to petition the judges of the Supreme Court of Bombay with the aid of the Attorney of Paupers in order to force her errant husband to make suitable provision for her welfare. The attention of the Parsis was brought to the case when an Englishman came to address the plight of the woman, and hold up the state of the existing Punchayet to the Parsis: "The whole of the Parsee caste ought to combine to do her this justice.... The wholesome and salutary effects of the Punchyat's [*sic*] decision are now perverted, I am afraid, to purposes unworthy the character of a tribunal so many years revered and respected by all [the] caste."[71] The unfavourable commentary from outside the community galvanized many Parsis in their displeasure and disgust with the Punchayet. The Fardoon Navaub case once more exposed the vulnerability of the Parsis in regulating community matters, as some forty years after the Parsis' earliest attempts in

---

[69] Ibid., 2: Letter No. 1, November 9, 1844.

[70] *Parsee Prakash*, 1:897.

[71] See letter of Englishman, in Cursetjee, *Parsee Panchayet*, 20-1: Letter No. 8, January 7, 1845.

Bombay to adjudicate family disputes, they had been unable to settle a dispute between husband and wife without embarrassment to the community and an appeal to the English law. With the waning of the authority of the Punchayet by the 1830s, appeals to the English law by Parsis dissatisfied with Punchayet justice once again raised the question of how best to safeguard and adjudicate questions relative to the Parsi identity. By 1836, protests and resignations within the Punchayet effectively marked the point at which the age of Punchayet authority was over.

Nowrojee Jamsetjee Wadia was the first to resign from the Punchayet. His resignation letter to his colleagues dated June 8, 1836, noted his inability to continue to perform his duties on behalf of the Parsis given the decline in the standards of the Punchayet and community.[72] His resignation letter was published in the Gujarati newspaper the *Samachar* on June 16, 1836. The editorial of the *Samachar* accompanying Wadia's resignation notification warned of the precarious situation the Parsis had placed themselves in with the downfall of their institution:

> That another, and equally upright, member of the Punchyat [*sic*] is also going to throw up his office; and when such leading members will tear themselves away, one after another from this body, it is impossible to prognosticate what might not befall the Parsee community![73]

The specific grievance precipitating Nowrojee Jamsetjee Wadia's resignation was the almost wilful inclination on the part of some Punchayet members to dispense with administering impartial justice in favour of delivering convenient and selective adjudications. In 1836, the Punchayet member Ardaseer Hormarjee Wadia took a second wife during the lifetime of his first over the objections of a split Punchayet and a hostile Parsi public opinion. The *Bombay Gazette* of June 11, 1836 described Ardaseer Hormarjee as a "gay Lothario" who had better "look before he leap," as bigamy was against the rules of the Parsi caste and a crime in English law punishable by seven or more years transportation.[74] Ardaseer Hormarjee, however, went on to marry his second wife with the encouragement of Punchayet members.

---

[72] Ibid., 25: Letter No. 11, March 6, 1845.

[73] Ibid., 24: Letter No. 10, February 4, 1845.

[74] Ibid., 32: Letter No. 13, April 22, 1845.

The division that had formed between the old and the newly made members of the Punchayet distinguished the history of the institution from the 1830s. Both the appointment of Punchayet members and the decisions of the Punchayet came to be problematic as the Parsis divided over the norms the community adhered to and how to enforce them. As the consensus among the Parsis on the function of the Punchayet declined, the probity of the institution also declined. While some members gave way to personal motivations in the conduct of Punchayet affairs, others acted in reaction to the vicissitudes of the Punchayet, adopting new approaches to leadership for the welfare of Punchayet and community. The idea of the Sir Jamsetjee Jejeebhoy Parsi Benevolent Institution was put forward between 1842 and 1849, in commemoration of Jamsetjee Jejeebhoy becoming the first Indian knight. It was conceived of as a philanthropic and educational institution on behalf of poor Parsis, and as a form of substitute Punchayet overseen by government.[75]

Jamsetjee Jejeebhoy had joined the Punchayet in 1823, and as a traditionalist he was not intent on seeing the demise of the Punchayet, and lamented its deterioration. Jamsetjee Jejeebhoy, however, symbolized the change a segment of Parsi opinion was undergoing. His contact with the British, in particular, offered him an insight into new approaches to leadership and means to safeguard the concerns of the Parsis. In the atmosphere of the 1830s, however, the division in outlook between Parsis over the future of the Punchayet augured less for its reconfiguration than its decline.

Nowrojee Jamsetjee Wadia's resignation was the spark that led to the immediate crisis in the Punchayet in 1836. Other leading members of the community and Bombay society followed his departure. Framji Cowasji Banaji was the scion of one of the first great families of Bombay, and was a leading businessman and philanthropist of the early nineteenth century. On resigning from the Punchayet, Framji Cowasji laid bare the sins of the institution before the Parsis. In addition to turning a blind eye to the sin and crime of bigamy among the Parsis, Framji Cowasji blamed the Punchayet for permitting all the sins of the Parsis, once so vigorously outlawed, to reappear:

---

[75] Letter from Sir Jamsetjee Jejeebhoy to Sir George Arthur, the Governor and President in Council, February 14, 1844, in *Correspondence, Deed, Bye-Laws etc., Relating to 'Sir Jamsetjee Jejeebhoy's Parsee Benevolent Institution,' Established in Bombay, 1849* (Bombay, 1840), 22.

> We have of late failed in our objects in establishing any beneficial rules for our community. We have caused more evil than good for our people. You require not to be told the extent to which evil deeds are prevalent among us.... You will take no notice of, much less punish, such [immoral] individuals.... And this because all the dread (hitherto felt) on the part of the males and females among the Zoroastrians has vanished, because you gentlemen of the Punchayet, have not brought and will not bring, such offenders to punishment. You are cognizant of their offences, but will make no arrangement to put a stop to this growing evil, the influence of which is every day increasing among us.[76]

Framji Cowasji went on to list many instances where the Punchayet had been oblivious to the wanton actions of Parsis who transgressed the community's norms, and less than impartial and consistent in its rulings against others. The growing tendency among the Parsis to resort to their own devices to settle their disputes particularly worried Framji Cowasji:

> Much of the Punchayet's business being kept in arrears, the poor people at last go tired of running after us, and ruining themselves by the delay.... Thus when the leaders of the Punchayet will not administer fair and impartial justice to those who represent their grievances to you where are they to go to? To whom are they then to apply? Veritably, under such circumstances, they are forced to act independently of the Punchyat [*sic*], and it will be impossible for the Punchyat to punish them for defying its authority.[77]

Framji Cowasji also alluded to the potential harm that could befall the Parsis with the decline in leadership given the ambiguity of Parsi custom under English law in India. In 1811, a British court accepted as tradition the right of an illegitimate Parsi to inherit his father's entire estate. The Parsis presented evidence that it was Parsi tradition for an illegitimate Parsi son to receive only life maintenance, and reversed the decision on appeal. Framji Cowasji believed that without an effective Punchayet Parsi custom would undergo change unsuitable to the Parsis. The latter case is significant as it was cited as one of the instances where the difficulty in determining law and usage among the Parsis induced the British to submit the Parsis of Bombay to the English law.[78]

---

[76] Cursetjee, *Parsee Panchayet*, 26: Letter No. 11.

[77] Ibid., 29.

[78] Ibid., 27-8. See also Report into the usages recognized as laws by the Parsee Community of India, and into the necessity of special legislation in connection with

Cursetjee Manockjee followed Framji Cowasji in resigning from the Punchayet. Cursetjee Manockjee had joined the Punchayet in 1818, and his refusal to countenance the actions of the Punchayet in 1836 was a measure of his great displeasure with the existing Punchayet and his belief that an effective institution was recklessly being torn asunder.[79] The critique of the Punchayet by his son, the reformer Manockjee Cursetjee, attests to the impact the decline of the Punchayet had on a generation of Parsis. The vehemence on the part of some at the degeneration of the Punchayet evinced the magnitude of the loss for the Parsis. The decline of the Punchayet in fact reflected both the weakness of the institution and the tremendous changes that were affecting Parsis by the 1830s. The delinquent Punchayet members had invariably contributed to the downfall of the institution. The norms of the Punchayet, however, had really only been an extension of the norms the Parsis had adhered to and sought to adhere to. The peccadilloes of the Punchayet members and their inability to uphold community standards reflected the tension persistent in the general community in rising to the challenge. Moreover, during the course of the nineteenth century, many Parsis were influenced by education and new ideas, which affected their self-perceptions, disinclining them to be subject to the dictates of a flawed institution. With the availability of alternative means to resolve issues of concern to Parsis, including the British law courts, the role of the old Punchayet was reassessed. For many Parsis, the Punchayet no longer offered the most effective means of safeguarding community interests. Between 1791 and 1836, the Parsis had utilized the Punchayet to redefine aspects of their identity and community; now once again, a reassessment of their situation would have to be essayed this time without the aid of the Punchayet. By mid-century, the reassessment of the Punchayet's role in safeguarding Parsi interests led to revisionism of its history on the part of those Parsis who represented a new centre of authority in the Parsi community.

With the rise of a new generation of reform-minded Parsis, the movement to safeguard the interests of the Parsis went beyond the

---

them, October 13, 1862, para. 4, in J.D. 1863 20/143:215-29. See Chapter Five.

[79] See *Obituary Notices of the Late Cursetjee Manackjee, Esq., As They Appeared in All the Native and English Newspapers of Bombay* (Bombay, 1845).

preoccupation with the Parsi Punchayet. From the mid-1850s, the rationale for a Punchayet was debated in the press:

> Under the lamentable circumstances, would it not look wise or speak well of the people, if the highly respected and venerable members of the body, when having confidence in their bad sense, bad laws, and incompetency to govern the educated present generation, give up the institution at once, or the Government of the country adopt a more serious measure if they think that there is, as there is, no necessity for the Punchayet amongst the civilized people like the Parsee of the present generation.[80]

The reinterpretation of the role of the Punchayet by contemporary reformist Parsis largely focused on the imperfect nature of the institution. The Punchayet leaders' periodic tendency to fall short of the community's expectations—permitting class and nepotistic interests to influence Punchayet decisions, becoming inconsistent in their rulings, and filling vacancies on a hereditary basis, often unapproved by the community—reflected on the integrity of the institution. This tendency represented a feature of the institutional method, though not its hallmark. In greater part, the problem of the interpretation of the Punchayet lay in the impression of its anachronism in an age of tremendous change for the Parsis. The social, intellectual, and political atmosphere among the Parsis had changed by mid-century to make the Punchayet unsuitable as the sole or chief means of safeguarding Parsi identity, as it had been a generation previously. The Parsis' need to avail themselves of new models and means of safeguarding identity reflected the fact that the Punchayet model had served its purpose, rather than it had never worked. By mid-century a split along traditionalist and reformist lines emerged within the Parsi community on the fate of the Punchayet.

Denouement

The reassessment of the role of the Punchayet in fact had begun prior to mid-century. The disillusionment with the Punchayet was complete with the diminution of Anjuman meetings. By the late 1830s, less than half of the thirteen members of the Punchayet bothered to attend meetings even though the size of the Punchayet had been

[80] *Bombay Standard*, August 24, 1859.

increased to thirty-six in 1836, to offset absences. Repeated attempts to hold Anjumans of the Parsis, including over important matters, came to naught.[81] With the Punchayet's business falling into arrears many Parsis increasingly acted independently. When the Punchayet did move itself to act, it often went to extremes, completely out of step with the times. On September 8, 1858, for example, the Punchayet passed a resolution reaffirming its authority to excommunicate and ostracize both wayward Parsis and those who gave them succour. When in the same year a Parsi woman committed bigamy, she and her second husband were excommunicated, and her deceased father's body was refused all obsequies till the couple were made outcasts by the family.[82] In 1860, the Punchayet's refusal to consign the remains of the daughter of an excommunicated Parsi to the *dakhma* created a scandal. When the family and supporters of the deceased physically forced the *dakhma* authorities to accept the corpse, aided by sympathetic priests who performed the necessary rites, the authority of the Punchayet to act in any capacity without the authority of the entire community became a matter of open debate.[83] The last great gathering of the Congress of the Parsis was for the eulogy of Sir Jamsetjee Jejeebhoy on May 12, 1859.[84] By July, however, the legitimacy of the Punchayet to call further Anjuman meetings was itself in question. So great was the opposition to recognizing the legitimacy of the Punchayet by the Parsi reformers, that on the occasion to mark the end of the Great Indian Mutiny of 1857, on July 28, 1859, the Parsis were forced to hold thanksgiving celebrations at two separate fire-temples: one convened by the Punchayet leaders and the other by the reformers.[85]

The past effectiveness of the Punchayet continued to maintain the faith of some Parsis in the institutional method of safeguarding identity. During the 1830s and 1840s, attempts were made to reconstitute the Punchayet by the Punchayet leaders through appeals to govern-

[81] Davar, *History of the Parsi Punchayet*, 52-4, 65-70. In 1840, the Senior Magistrate of Police advised the Parsis to agree on a suitable means of autopsy for Parsis, which the authorities could utilize in any inquiry into violent deaths. The Anjuman meeting of April 28, 1840 produced only fifteen witnesses, rendering the exercise futile. It was only after subsequent meetings that the Parsis agreed to place no impracticable formal objection to post-mortem inquiries into violent deaths.

[82] Jeejeebhoy, "Communal Discipline," 303.

[83] *Bombay Gazette*, February 9, 11, 15, 1860.

[84] *Bombay Times*, May 14, 1859.

[85] *Bombay Times*, July 30, 1850.

ment. All the attempts came to naught as a legally constituted Punchayet was felt to be both at odds with the evolving power of British justice and law in India, and unable to gain the confidence of the Parsi community. The necessity for a legally recognized Punchayet that could command the regard of the Parsis was now coupled with attempts to seek a redefinition of the status of their personal law. While the idea of a Punchayet remained, it no longer was the priority of the Parsis as the necessity for a Parsi code of laws came to take precedence.

Despite the end of the era of an all-powerful Parsi Punchayet, the idea of an institution able to guide the discussion of issues of importance to the Parsis remained relevant. In 1865, the Punchayet was effectively discharged of any remaining legally recognized social and religious responsibilities with the passage of the Parsi Laws as regards interstate succession and inheritance, and marriage and divorce by the Indian government based upon proposals by the Parsis. By an interesting twist of fate, the new Parsi Laws established separate matrimonial courts for the Parsis that were conceived on the Punchayet model. After 1865, the Parsi Punchayet was transformed into the chief custodian of the Parsi community's properties and trusts, and functioned as charitable institution on behalf of the Parsis. While for much of its history the Parsi Punchayet of Bombay was the leading institution of the Parsis, dispensing social justice and regulating community matters, it was also the guardian and custodian of the properties and funds of the Parsi community. Select Punchayet members had administered the donations, bequests, properties and funds left to the Parsi community in a semi-formal manner as trustees since the time of the first *davar* Banaji Limji in 1820.[86] Through charitable bequests and steady management, by the latter part of the century, the funds of the Punchayet totalled some twenty-two lakhs of rupees or Rs. 22,00,000.[87]

The strength of the Punchayet had always resided in the approval it had received from the community; so much so, that most of the Punchayet's *bundobasts* had not been constructed with an eye to being codified as substantive law. The Congresses of the Parsis had been the living constitution of the community, so to speak. Their periodical convocations had established the regulations and customs

[86] *Parsee Prakash*, 1:175.

[87] Karaka, *History of the Parsis*, 1:241-2.

that prevailed among the Parsis to the satisfaction of the majority of Parsis. The British government had tacitly recognized this fact throughout the history of the Punchayet, and this was confirmed in the lack of support government gave to the Punchayet with the waning of community support. The decline in the authority of the Punchayet, then, was due to factors both institutional and social coming together by the 1830s. These included the irregularities of the Punchayet leaders, a changing social outlook that made the Punchayet's actions in safeguarding identity appear harsh and outdated to Parsis, and social contacts and changes that encouraged both traditionalists and reformers to observe alternative ways to safeguard the Parsi identity. Among these contacts and changes included the greater co-operation between Parsis and British, the influence of Western education, and the recourse to legal and legislative channels.

The decline of the old Punchayet had not meant the decline in the *raison d'être* of the Parsi community. Rather, it made for the diffusion of efforts of the Parsis into other fields of social and political activity. The Punchayet was divested of the function of social control and transformed itself into an effective vehicle, perhaps the central institution, of social welfare and charity among the Parsis after 1860. The necessity to better define and safeguard the Parsi identity continued to be felt in different ways, through a variety of institutions and movements, and over the broad spectrum of opinion and action within the Parsi community.

CHAPTER THREE

THE CHALLENGE TO IDENTITY: THE PARSI BOYS' CONVERSION CASE

On May 1, 1839, Dhanjibhai Nauroji, a Parsi boy claiming to be sixteen years old, was baptized a Christian at the Mission School of the Reverend Doctor John Wilson at Fort. A day later a second boy of eighteen, Hormusji Pestonji, was similarly baptized. In his narrative of the events surrounding his conversion, written many decades following the event, Dhanjibhai Nauroji described the atmosphere on the appointed day: "The newspapers gave warning that Dhanji was today about to leave the religion of his fathers, and enter that of strangers. They violently denounced the baptism, and the Parsis moved heaven and earth to prevent it."[1] So agitated was the Parsi community of Bombay at the news of the conversions that the leadership of the Parsi Punchayet in cooperation with Heerjeebhoy Dadabhoy, the uncle and guardian of Dhanjibhai, sought the return of Dhanjibhai on a writ of habeas corpus and the prosecution of Dr. Wilson before the Supreme Court of Judicature at Bombay.

The Parsi boys' conversion case would put the Parsis in confrontation with the colonial environment over the fundamental issue of Parsi religious identity. As a result of the row over the conversions, and the ensuing court case, many assumptions that the Parsis had come to believe over the previous hundred years came into question. Their knowledge of their religion and their seeming invulnerability to religious criticism from other faiths, their ability to protect and regulate their community with the aid and cooperation of British justice, and the very notion of what constituted success and progress for the community were now matters of debate. The Parsi boys' conversion case would come at the end of a difficult decade for the Parsis in which traditional authority was in decline, and the best means to safeguard and shape identity was increasingly debated. The Parsi

---

[1] Dhanjibhai Nauroji, *From Zoroaster to Christ: An Autobiographical Sketch of The Rev. Dhanjibhai Nauroji the First Modern Convert to Christianity From the Zoroastrian Religion* (London, 1909), 47.

boys' conversion case was a precedent in the response of Indians to colonialism. It also marked a major step in the Parsis' transition from insular community to colonial elite.

The circumstances of the case were that Dhanjibhai Nauroji had come to Bombay from Gujarat to live with his uncle five years earlier following the death of his father, and had been placed in the General Assembly's Institution to obtain an English education. Heerjeebhoy Dadabhoy claimed that he had become aware of Dhanjibhai's desire to convert on the eve of the baptism on April 30, and was prevented from gaining access to Dhanjibhai by Dr. Wilson to prevent the conversion. In seeking to obtain the habeas corpus, Heerjeebhoy charged Dr. Wilson with breaching the terms and understanding under which Dhanjibhai had been placed in his care, and had withheld Dhanjibhai in order to convert him to Christianity. Heerjeebhoy stated his belief:

> That undue and improper means have been used by the said Reverend Dr. Wilson, to convert and seduce the said Dhunjeebhoy Nowrojee from the religious faith of his ancestors and family, and that the commencement and progress of such conversion have been purposely and fraudulently kept from the knowledge of this deponent, and of the family and Parsee friends of the said Dhunjeebhoy Nowrojee.[2]

Based on Heerjeebhoy's application a writ of habeas corpus was granted on May 3, ordering Dr. Wilson to produce Dhanjibhai Nauroji before the Court on May 6. In so doing, the Court further permitted a reply to the writ by Dr. Wilson to be heard in camera on May 6. The case was further continued by Acting Justice John Wither Awdry, permitting both Heerjeebhoy Dadabhoy and Dr. Wilson to file further affidavits and present witness testimony. Affidavits were filed on the May 11, and the cause was continued on May 16, for a final heating in open court and judgement. From May 6 until a final judgement in the case, Dhanjibhai was at liberty to go where he pleased.

In their respective testimonies, both Heerjeebhoy Dadabhoy and Dr. Wilson characterized their motives to have been in the best interests of Dhanjibhai. Both parties, however, sought to defend their role inside and outside the courthouse. For Heerjeebhoy, the conversion of his nephew had placed him in an embarrassing position in terms

---

[2] Quoted from the *Oriental Christian Spectator*, June 1839, 212 (hereafter cited as *OCS*).

of his standing in the Parsi community. His testimony was an attempt to exonerate his role and assuage the passions of the Parsis incensed at his carelessness in permitting the conversion. Heerjeebhoy was particularly sensitive to any imputation that he had been derelict in supervising his nephew's upbringing. As the course of the trial wore on, however, Heerjeebhoy's testimony resembled more a deposition of denials than a recitation of responsibility, and belied the bit part the chief protagonist against Dr. Wilson came to play in the conversion controversy. As figurehead in the prosecution of Dr. Wilson, the ineffectual Heerjeebhoy Dadabhoy masked the tremendous importance the Parsi community and its leadership placed on the conversion of the Parsi boys.

In his defence, Dr. Wilson described the history of his work and the relationship between himself and Dhanjibhai. Dr. Wilson and his wife Margaret had arrived in India in 1829, and had started an English school at their residence at Ambrolie in Bombay in 1832, with the support of the Scottish Missionary Society. The mission school aimed to provide education to the children of respectable parents, and combined instruction in Christianity and general education. When Dr. Wilson's school first started, the attendance included 45 Hindu and 3 Parsi boys. In 1834, the attendance included 37 Hindus, 9 Parsis, and 4 Muslims. By 1837, there were 216 boys in the school division and 14 in the upper division.[3] In 1835, the mission was transferred to the Church of Scotland and became known as the General Assembly's Institution at Military Square in the Fort area of Bombay. Rules and regulations regarding the management of the school were drawn up and public notice had been given in the newspapers of Bombay that in addition to secular education, the precepts and doctrines of Christianity would be taught. Dr. Wilson believed this fact to have been understood by the Indian community of Bombay when, shortly after the Institution's opening, Dhanjibhai Nauroji became a pupil. Dhanjibhai was described as showing great interest in Christianity from the moment of his admission to Dr. Wilson's school. Dhanjibhai had faithfully studied the Scriptures and gave every indication of converting. Furthermore, no illegal restraint was exercised over Dhanjibhai. Dr. Wilson claimed that Dhanjibhai had resided at his residences at Malabar Hill and Ambrolie since April

3 *OCS*, August 1834, 203; M. D. David, *John Wilson and His Institution* (Bombay, 1975), 26-7; *OCS*, November 1837, 523.

19, of his own free will, and with the consent of Heerjeebhoy Dadabhoy.[4]

Dr. Wilson's defence, no less than Heerjeebhoy's, concerned itself with Dr. Wilson's standing within his own community. From 1813, restrictions on missionary societies' activities in India had been removed. During the 1820s and 1830s, foreign Bible societies had taken an aggressive role in India seeking to preach freely and open schools. The Age of Mission Schools in India had begun and would last until 1854, when a more organized and formalized structure of educational development would emerge. The imparting of education to Indians seemed a natural and essential assumption of missionary activity to a segment of the missionary community in India in the 1820s and 1830s. With the expansion of urban centres and the growth of commercial activity, the belief was that Indians would be willing to take advantage of English-medium education in particular. Not only would English-medium education draw in large numbers of well-placed Indians, but also would eventually provide a steady stream of preachers and teachers. The growth of both mission schools that provided education to students at lower levels and the establishment of central institutions of higher learning across India during this period encouraged missionary educational activities.[5] The Parsis may not have appreciated this point when they consigned the educational welfare of their children to missionary schools providing English-medium education, but the spread of literacy was an essential concomitant to the teaching of Christianity. Heerjeebhoy Dadabhoy in placing Dhanjibhai in Dr. Wilson's Institution had sought to take advantage of the availability of an English education for his nephew without regard to who was providing it.

The focus on education as part of missionary activity and English-medium education in particular, however, had not been universally welcomed in missionary circles. The expansion of private

[4] *OCS*, June 1839, 213-14; George Smith, *The Life of John Wilson* (London, 1879), 75-6.

[5] Kenneth Ingham, *Reformers, in India, 1793-1833: An Account of the Work of Christian Missionaries on Behalf of Social Reform* (Cambridge, 1967), 55-83; M. D. David, "Histoy of the Church in India," in *Asia and Christianity*, ed. M. D. David (Bombay, 1985), 162-73; idem, "The British Colonialism in South Asia and Christianity," in *Western Colonialism and Asia and Christianity*, ed. M. D. David (Bombay, 1988), 83-91; P. J. Marshall, "The Moral Swing to the East: British Humanitarianism, India and the West Indies," in *The East India Company, 1784-1834*, ed. C. H. Philips (Oxford, 1961), 69-93.

schools was an ambitious undertaking financially, and was never believed to provide rewards commensurate with the effort. The bias in evangelical circles, including the Scottish churches, had been in favour of traditional evangelism and proselytism. The focus on educational activity and the running of schools had marked a departure from tradition and, consequently, had to be constantly justified by its advocates in India.[6] Throughout the 1830s, the advocates of English-medium education in India were forced to come up with ways to placate metropolitan criticism. The conversion controversy presented then Reverend Wilson with a timely opportunity to assuage the misgivings of the more traditional missionaries and the metropolitan critics in the Church of Scotland. Wilson's writings and commentaries on the religious beliefs and practices of the various communities he encountered in India, including his examinations of Parsi writings, had for some time provided him with the vehicle with which to inform and enthuse the missionary community about the need for education among the peoples of India. Wilson's scholarship on the Parsi religion was part of his ongoing critique of the religions of India. Wilson had engaged the Brahman community in debate from 1830 to 1834, and the Muslim community since 1831, in his new publication the *Oriental Christian Spectator.*[7] The *Oriental Christian Spectator* had been started by Wilson in 1830, as a periodical containing works and commentaries on Indian religions and life from the missionary perspective, and continued until 1862. It often repeated the indictment of Eastern communities prevalent in contemporary Western literature. By engaging Indians, Wilson believed he had opened a discussion between the Christian and Indian communities that had not taken place previously, while he was confident of besting the latter.[8]

Wilson's interest in Oriental studies was never far removed from his missionary pursuits. Wilson's inquiries into the religion of the Parsis put him in conflict with them from 1831 till the conversion

---

[6] By 1890, missionary policy in India was reversed with greater emphasis going to evangelization and vernacular education, especially of the lower castes. See M. Rose Greenfield, *Education versus Evangelization* (Amritsar, 1888), 3-16; D. Mackichan, *The Missionary Ideal in the Scottish Churches* (London, 1927), Ch. 7; J. M. Mitchell, *In Western India* (Edinburgh, 1899), 60; *The Missionary Controversy: Discussion, Evidence and Report 1890* (London, 1890), 4.

[7] *OCS*, June 1830, 186-95.

[8] Smith, *Life of John Wilson*, 62-8; Norman Daniel, *Islam and the West: The Making of an Image* (Edinburgh, 1960).

controversy; with increasing attention being paid to Wilson by individual Parsis, the Parsi press, and the Parsi Punchayet. In his earlier writings, Wilson had questioned the accuracy and authenticity of Zoroastrian scriptures, and had impugned both the character of the prophet Zarathustra and the Zoroastrian value system.[9] Wilson's allusions to the religion of the Parsis in 1831 were meant as the prelude to the discussion that was anticipated, and the Parsis took the bait. The editor of the newspaper *Bombay Samachar* questioned the advisability of Wilson and the missionaries' attempts to promote Christianity by impugning the religion of Indians.[10] The Parsi editor Nowroji Dorabji Chandaru (1807-59) took up the cudgels against Wilson under the sobriquet of 'Nauroz Goosequill,' subsequently adjusted to 'Swanquill,' in editorials in the newspaper the *Hulkaru and Vartman*. Nowroji Dorabji upheld the value of all religions, and questioned Wilson's attacks on the prophet Zarathustra and Zoroastrianism's tenets, all the while confident that the conversion of a Parsi could not be dreamt of." In his exposition of Zoroastrianism, however, Nowroji Dorabji exposed the weakness of the Parsis' knowledge of their religion. When Nowroji Dorabji denied the place of the Cosmogony within the Zoroastrian scriptures and questioned the authenticity of the religious work the *Bundahishn*, the disapprobation of the Parsis was brought down upon him, including that of the high priest Dastur Edulji Dorabji, who had provided the Parsis with a Gujarati translation of the *Bundahishn*.[12] The division within the Parsi ranks and the spectacle of the champions of the Parsi tradition quarrelling over the content of that tradition provided grist for Wilson's mill.

Wilson's criticism of the religion of the Parsis proved worthwhile. In 1833, Wilson began the debate with the Parsis in earnest with the publication of his critique of the Zoroastrian text the *Vendīdād*. The 'Lecture on the *Vendidad Sade*' consisted of a series of discourses in which Zoroastrianism's claim to being divine revelation, monotheistic, ethical, and offering salvation was questioned and impugned.[13] In 1839, Wilson delivered his 'Sermon on The Doctrine of Jehovah,'

[9] *OCS*, July 1831, 235, August 1831, 271.

[10] *OCS*, September 1831, 332-5.

[11] *OCS*, October 1831, 381-4.

[12] Ibid., 385-6.

[13] John Wilson, *A Lecture on the Vendidad Sade of the Parsis Delivered at Bombay On the 19th and 26th June 1833* (Bombay, 1833), 39, 47.

and in 1843 published his work *The Parsi Religion*, putting forward his interpretation of the history of Zoroastrianism. Wilson's debate with the Parsis established his reputation within the Christian community, gained him the attention of the Indian community, and had introduced him as a significant player in the controversy over educational policy in Western India. In January 1836, Wilson took his place as the President of the Bombay Branch of the Royal Asiatic Society, and in May 1836 the University of Edinburgh invested the Reverend Wilson with the honorary title of Doctor of Divinity.[14]

The Parsis found it difficult to meet the challenge put to them by Dr. Wilson on an intellectual and scholarly basis alone. Between 1840 and 1841, attempts were made by the Parsis to address the points put forward by Dr. Wilson, including on the urging of the Parsi Punchayet. The polemic nature of these works written in Gujarati attacked both Dr. Wilson and the threat posed by Christian theology and conversion.[15] Dr. Wilson deprecated all the attempts as relying on faulty and inaccurate translations of original texts, or incapable of meeting the arguments put forward by him.[16] The motivations behind Dr. Wilson's own scholarship had rendered the Parsis' replies both suspect and unreliable from the outset. As with much of the European scholarly approach to the Orient since the eighteenth century, Dr. Wilson's inquiries into the texts, languages, and civilizations of the East aimed to ideologically characterize the East in contrast to the West, as to reveal and advance knowledge. The scholarship of Dr. Wilson did not elicit the merits of a comparative analysis of religious systems as much as it aimed to expose the defects of the Zoroastrian religious outlook. Scholarly inquiry was equally subordinated to the purpose and design of Dr. Wilson's evangelical activities in India. The injection of Dr. Wilson into the religious debate in the 1830s essentially rendered the poor calibre of Parsi knowledge somewhat a moot point. The scholarly and polemical encounters with Dr. Wilson exposed to the Parsis their own sense of inadequacy as regarded the knowledge of their religion and tradition. Ultimately,

---

[14] *Bombay Gazette*, August 23, 1839; John Wilson, *The Doctrine of Jehovah* (Edinburgh, 1847); Smith, *Life of John Wilson*, 132.

[15] See Smith, *Life of John Wilson*, 226. Nowrozjee Furdoonjee (1817-85) started the magazine *Rahnuma-i Zarthushti* in 1842, as a guide for Zoroastrians against the missionaries.

[16] *OCS*, July 1842, 333-9; Smith, *Life of John Wilson*, 131.

while Dr. Wilson pricked the apathy of the Parsis as to their invulnerability from the scrutiny and criticism of other religions, the power of the Parsis' social bonds would work to discount his message and impact. Community solidarity united to turn a deaf ear to the Christian missionaries.

No publicity was more infectious in providing support for the missionary cause than that of a good conversion. The baptisms of Dhanjibhai Nauroji and Hormasji Pestonji, and the possible conversion of a third Parsi Framji Bomanji, presented Dr. Wilson with the tangible result of his goal of education, evangelization, and proselytism. The background of the Parsi converts as members of an influential community bestowed prestige on Dr. Wilson's accomplishment, and provided a visible return on missionary investment in the urban setting. Three youths, from a community that had boasted the conversion of a Parsi was not to be dreamt of, had freely consented to become Christians. The propaganda value of conversions, nevertheless, belied the fact that they were rare. Dr. Wilson had exposed the vulnerability of the religion of the Parsis to Western scholarship, and had caused concern and controversy in the Parsi community, yet the foundations of his policy were no less vulnerable. While Dr. Wilson could tout a victory in the conversion of one, two, five Indians, whether Muslim, Brahman, Catholic Armenian or Parsi, the very factors that made the conversion of a Parsi a coveted goal also worked to ensure that it was rare.[17] The Bombay Parsis as members of a moneyed and increasingly powerful community had placed their children in institutions emphasizing English schooling, anxious to take advantage of the social and economic opportunities English education offered. At the same time, they remained ever scrupulous to protect and safeguard what defined them as a community.

Prior to the actual appearance and testimony of the Parsis incourt, their influence had been felt. Dr. Wilson had stated that the chief reason the matter had come to court was a result of the pressure brought to bear on Heerjeebhoy by the Parsis to do so. Dr. Wilson claimed Heerjeebhoy had confessed to his nephew and him his desire not go to court, and his apprehension that he "would be turned out of caste, and loose his situation and his life," if he did not do so.[18]

---

[17] On Wilson's progress in baptizing Indians, see Smith, *Life of John Wilson*, 134-5

[18] *OCS*, June 1839, 222, 229.

One of the reasons Dr. Wilson used for not returning Dhanjibhai to the Parsis was his belief that Dhanjibhai would be harmed if he were to do so. Heerjeebhoy denied such a confession, or that any harm would come to his nephew; however, it is conceivable that Herjeebhoy's actions and testimony were motivated by fear.[19]

The combination of the tactics of the missionaries and the social response it elicited from traditional Indian society accounted for the paucity of converts in the early part of the century. It is wholly consistent with the history of Christian missions in India that the fervour with which they carried out their task provoked opposition. Their tactics as often repelled than attracted potential converts. Their denunciations of Indian religious practices and theology while aiming to expose the false beliefs of Indians, too often resembled harangues rather than homilies. By condemning what they did not want to understand, they raised barriers of resentment against themselves and Christianity, and awakened traditional societal mechanisms that favoured social cohesion and control, including the recourse to occasional violence.[20] In the case of Dr. Wilson, his criticism of the Parsis elicited a sense of solidarity from them that he was not altogether able to appreciate. The strength of the social bonds that Dr. Wilson dismissed as unimportant in any commitment to one's religion, proved a potent force in determining the prospect of any conversion among the Parsis. This was also the case among the members of other Indian communities whose social and ethnic identity could not be divorced from their religious identity. Dr. Wilson's efforts to convert Parsis worked directly against the historical efforts of the Parsis to safeguard and distinguish their social, ethnic, and religious identity from all the other communities around them. With the conversion of a Parsi, what to that time had been a nuisance was seen to be a threat to the community as a whole.

---

[19] Ibid., 230.

[20] On the missionaries and Indians, see E. Daniel Potts, *British Baptist Missionaries in India, 1793-1837: The History of Serampore and Its Missions* (Cambridge, 1967), 207-44; Duncan B. Forrester, *Caste and Christianity: Attitudes and Policies on Caste of Anglo-Saxon Protestant Missions in India* (London, 1980); Penelope Carson, "Missionaries, Bureaucrats and the People of India, 1793-1833," in *Orientalism, Evangelicalism and the Military Cantonment in Early Nineteenth-Century India: A Historiographical Overview*, ed. Nancy G. Cassels (Lewiston, 1981), 125-55; Sundararaj Manickam, *Studies in Missionary History: Reflections on a Culture-Contact* (Madras, 1988).

The intemperance on the part of many Parsis over conversions would certainly have been a cause of concern for Heerjeebhoy Dadabhoy. Indeed, he was wise to expect it from a community accustomed to displays of corporal punishment against those who breached community standards, including standards that imposed sanctions against the relations of an offender. Heerjeebhoy's guilt in the eyes of the Parsis lay not in any crime but the carelessness of having permitted Dhanjibhai to convert. While the Parsis had met the challenge of Dr. Wilson's criticism of their religion over the course of a decade, the precedent of the conversions presented the Parsis with a threat from outside the community, aided unwittingly by the ineffectual Heerjeebhoy Dadabhoy. The day set for the final hearing of the case on the May 16, vividly put on display the hot-blooded nature of the Parsis as Dhanjibhai described the tumult that ensued on arriving at the courthouse:

> When our carriage reached the Court House numbers of Parsis sprang forward and surrounded us; some seized the wheels of the carriage; some laid hold of the horses; and one violently wrenched open the carriage window, and began to try and drag me out. On seeing this some of the gentlemen who were with us quickly got out of their carriages and ran to our assistance. The police constables hastened up also, and saved us from the violence that was threatened. The British soldiers of the 18th Irish Regiment were there too, all on the *qui vive* to charge the mob, but the commanding officer saw that things were not quite so bad as to need that. When we reached the verandah of the Court, the crowd was so thick that we could not get to the staircase. Two constables, one on either side, took me by the hand. The others pushed the people back with their fists. It was with the utmost difficulty that we succeeded in reaching the room where the trial was to be held.[21]

Other Parsis had sought to quiet the crowd.[22] The leaders of the Parsi community who came to court, however, were perhaps less concerned over the spectacle on the courthouse steps than with the challenge to the community's legal authority to govern itself under English law.

Describing the scene at the courthouse on May 16, 1839, the day reserved for the second hearing of the case, Dhanjibhai writes that "at 11 o'clock the Judge took his seat, and then the twelve heads of the Parsi Punchayet, wild with excitement, made their appearance

[21] Nauroji, *From Zoroaster to Christ,* 51-2.
[22] *Bombay Times,* May 3, 1839.

also. The Judge gave these gentlemen seats of honour with himself."[23] A case involving the religious faith and the personal conscience of a teenager had invited the interest of the leadership of the Parsi community. Despite the honour bestowed on the Parsi elders in court, the case of the Parsi boys' conversion would expose the ambiguity of the Parsi community's standing under British justice. The Parsis had also sought the prosecution of Dr. Wilson. The circumstances of the case and the situation the Parsi community found itself in by 1839, however, made the Parsis feel that they and their leadership were actually on trial or, at least, under scrutiny. The reputation of Dr. Wilson, the scrutiny under which the Parsi religion had been put, the taunts from the Christian press, and the legal situation of the Parsis of Bombay under the jurisdiction of the English law, placed a heavy burden on their case. Affidavits of eminent Parsi trustees and Justices of the Peace were read in court and were intended to show the solidarity of the Parsi community led by the Punchayet in opposing the conversions.[24] The claim both legal and moral of a Parsi boy professing to be of age to determine his own fate, however, put the weight of English common law against the tradition and rights that had governed the Parsi community to that time.

In their testimony before the court, members of the Parsi Punchayet noted the history of the Parsis' customs and traditions of internal government that had been adhered to by the community for close to a century. They believed these customs to have been recognized and guaranteed by the Government of Bombay and the British government in the East Indies that adhered to the principle of noninterference in the religion and customs of native communities. The Parsis' strategy was to present their case as involving the right of a guardian over his ward (a parent over his child), and by extension the right of a community to protect its members. The Parsis maintained that they were the injured party in the whole episode. The Parsis had placed great faith in the efficacy and integrity of English educational institutions in placing their children in them, with the belief that a proper general education would be provided, and confident that their private religious beliefs would not be interfered with. If anyone had harmed Dhanjibhai and others, the Parsis implied, it was Dr. Wilson who had corrupted the youth of Bombay, and had estranged and

[23] Nauroji, *From Zoroaster to Christ*, 52.

[24] *OCS*, June 1839, 233.

alienated them from their religion, family, and friends. The Parsi elders maintained that an injustice had been done to their community, and unless Dhanjibhai was returned to his uncle it would be as if "a great and unexpected inroad has been made upon their privileges as hitherto believed to be secured and guaranteed to them by the British laws."[25] Confident in the strength of their social bonds, the Parsis were undisturbed by and indeed oblivious to the incongruity evident in their interaction with the Christian missionaries. With their appeal, a legal case had been turned into a case of political import.

In bringing their case to court, the members of the Punchayet and the Parsis were confident of the favourable hearing they could expect from a British Indian court. The conversion case did not constitute a precedent in the history of the Parsi community under English law. Since 1787, the authority of the Parsi Punchayet had been recognized under English law, with a history of judgements in its favour. The Parsis maintained that the rules and customs of their community were for Parsis alone to determine. In asking a British court to recognize the authority of their tradition, the members of the Punchayet did not ask for the approbation of English law to the content of that tradition, but the acknowledgement that its disposition was a matter for the Parsis alone to decide. The Parsis' response to the episode of the conversion of two Parsis was representative of the cultural norms that had come to inform their social, cultural, and religious thought over the previous century, including the evolution of a level of social cohesion. The Parsis had shaped their community in Bombay to the requirements of their identity. The need to safeguard identity witnessed the creation of rules and obligations applicable to members of the community and to the leadership. The presence of the Punchayet leaders in court reflected the importance the Parsis placed in their traditions. The Parsi leadership in this respect appeared before the court not as the beneficiaries of privilege and caste authority, as Dr. Wilson saw them to be, but as the representatives of the Parsis and their traditions before the court. Under British colonialism, the Parsis had gained the ability to better regulate their community. The limitations of that ability would now be exposed in a British court.

The conversion case compelled both the Punchayet and the Parsis to defend the very content of Parsi tradition as relating to its coherency and appropriateness under English law. The Parsis' proposition

[25] Ibid., 233-5.

that the case of Dhanjibhai should be approached with sensitivity to the collective interests of the Parsi community by British justice imposed on the Parsis' case the burden of proof that the traditions they asked the court to acknowledge firstly, did not conflict with the welfare of Dhanjibhai and, secondly, existed in a sufficiently coherent and consistent a manner so as to permit a British court to favourably adjudicate. The Parsis at the courthouse had demonstrated the depth of their opposition to the conversion of Dhanjibhai. However, the ability to precisely define their traditions and establish what stood as law before a British court presented the Parsis with a difficulty.

The Parsis' difficulties in the conversion case were foreshadowed from the beginning of the British government's reform of the system of law in western India in the early part of the century. The British desire to incorporate the codes of law and traditions of Indians into a more rationalized codified system disadvantaged the Parsis. The lack of extant religious and legal codes among the Parsis imposed on them a particular burden.[26] As Governor of Bombay from 1819 to 1827, Mountstuart Elphinstone (1779-1859) had commented on the essential stability the Punchayet system provided Indian society as part of his plan to retain the system, while at the same time he affirmed his faith in the relative superiority of British norms and institutions.[27] The British difficulty in determining and adjudicating Parsi tradition and law witnessed the Parsis of Bombay being subject to the application of English law from 1824. At the same time, the Parsis of the Mofussil (provincial district) were still governed by customary law, in so far as it could be ascertained. Along with the difficulties of the Parsi Punchayet from the 1830s, the status of Parsi tradition and law under colonialism remained problematic. The legal status of the Parsi community would remain unresolved until mid-century.[28]

In the absence of a tangible record of their community's traditions and customs perusable by a court, the Parsis in the conversion case had made an appeal on the basis of religious toleration. Such an appeal, however, the court was obliged to apply equally. Unable to present their cultural norms in a manner suitable to British legal custom,

---

[26] R. D. Choksey, *Mountstuart Elphinstone the Indian Years, 1796-1827* (Bombay, 1971), 424.

[27] Edward Colebrooke, "Memoir of the Honourable Mountstuart Elphinstone," *Journal of the Royal Asiatic Society of Great Britain and Ireland* 18 (1861): 281-4.

[28] On the evolution of Parsi law, *see* Chapter Five.

they were left to argue on a point of British tradition equally applicable to the other side. The point was not lost on the defence, as Mr. Campbell maintained that the same religious liberty and toleration claimed by the Parsis must be available to Dhanjibhai. Moreover, with what must have been incidental pleasure, Mr. Campbell further questioned the very basis upon which the Parsis could make any claim to the observance of custom by the court or, for that matter, themselves:

> But it is pretended that there is some peculiarity in the Parsi law which is to control the decision in this case.... My Lord, What is Parsi law? Since I have been in Bombay, I have never been able to discover it; and I have never met with any man who had.... At one time, as it suits their purpose, they adopt a custom analogous to Hindu law, at another time they adopt a custom analogous to English law. I think I may insist, that the Parsis have no law, by which any decision can be formed regarding this case.[29]

Portraying the Parsis as capricious and selective in the presentation of their evidence, as incapable of presenting compelling evidence for the precedence of their tradition, and suspect in their motives, the defence claimed the Punchayet members' abiding goal to be the reconversion of Dhanjibhai and the preservation of their prestige.[30] The defence concluded its case by stating that only English law could and should decide the liberty of both Dhanjibhai and Dr. Wilson.

The indictment of the Punchayet by the defence was severe and in keeping with the beliefs and cultural outlook of some in the European community, not least of all the missionaries, in regards to the leadership of Indian communities. The belief that caste leaders maintained a monopoly of power over their respective communities through the interpretation of all tradition was an axiom of missionary belief.[31] The Parsis' critics, like those who visit the land of El Dorado, refused to appreciate the native wisdom and comfort in never leaving one's valley. Notwithstanding the indictment of the Punchayet by the defence, the Punchayet leaders' calculation in seeking the prosecution of Dr. Wilson had depended on the support and weight of community sentiment behind it. Ironically, in accusing the Punchayet members of violent intentions towards Dhanjibhai and the desire to reconvert him, the defence had unintentionally acknowl-

[29] *OCS*, June 1839, 225-6.
[30] Ibid., 259-60.
[31] Forrester, *Caste and Christianity*, 26; Potts, *Baptist Missionaries*, 223.

edged the coincidence of interests between Parsi leadership and community. The symbolism of a reconversion was undoubtedly a powerful incentive in demanding the habeas corpus. Dhanjibhai's conduct had greatly upset the Parsis, as he had renounced and forsaken the religion of his birth, and committed sacrilege indeprecating its symbols. Dhanjibhai's personal beliefs and wishes were also consistently downplayed by the Parsis, and represented as misguided and ill-informed.[32] Traditional society's ability to stoop to conquer functioned as a form of social control. It is speculation whether the row over the conversion of Dhanjibhai Nauroji prevented other Parsi conversions: the dramatic spectacle of the court case performing a function of social control. The episode of the conversion reached its nadir with Jamsetjee Jejeebhoy's offer to Dhanjibhai of a lakh of rupees to reconvert. Dhanjibhai in his autobiography also wrote that the Parsis continued to persecute his friends Hormusji and Framji for some time after the trial.[33]

In closing its case, the prosecution reiterated the concerns of the Parsis. Mr. Howard contended that the consistency of the Parsis' beliefs was clear:

> What the Parsis deposed to as to their own customs, must be taken as matter of fact, and could not be displaced by the learning of any European gentleman.... It could not be supposed, that a Native would deliberately send his child to a school to be untaught his own religion, to be made an outcast of, to be alienated from his own family. It was not in the minds of a people, who clung to their religious usages with such tenacity, to suppose the possibility of a conversion.[34]

Mr. Montriou further asked his lordship to contemplate, Christian bias aside, his own feelings if the situation were reversed and his child placed in a school professing non-interference in religion, "is suddenly discovered to be a Parsi. Put the case in this form and we can better understand the reason the Parsis have to feel aggrieved."[35] The prosecution's remarks were more than just a reminder of the necessity for religious neutrality on the part of the law. They encapsulated the cultural understanding that informed the Parsis' actions, and upon which the Indian community sought to form an accommodation with British colonialism. The truth of the Parsis' social trad-

---

[32] *OCS*, June 1839, 216, 220, 249.

[33] Nauroji, *From Zoroaster to Christ*, 55-6, 61-3.

[34] *OCS*, June 1839, 261.

[35] Ibid., 264.

ition rested on those internal rationalizations that had given the tradition its shape and meaning: the desire and need to safeguard an identity in the midst of change. The prosecution conveyed the protean truth about the nature of Parsi tradition and law. Asked to reveal itself directly, it could take on an array of beguiling shapes, resting on age-old practice and ritual observance, seemingly irrational and superstitious to the uninitiated or, for that matter, even to the initiated like Dhanjibhai.

In his judgement, Justice J. W. Awdry felt that he could not grant the habeas corpus. The case for Justice Awdry had resolved itself into the simple question of whether granting the writ and returning Dhanjibhai to the custody of his uncle contrary to his wishes was in the best interests of the boy given the evidence presented. Justice Awdry felt that sufficient doubt existed as to Heerjeebhoy Dadabhoy's motives in applying for the writ to warrant its refusal. Justice Awdry found Heerjeebhoy Dadabhoy's claim for custody to be ambiguous and lacking in parental feeling. Justice Awdry also ruled that illegal restraint had not been exercised over Dhanjibhai, and Dr. Wilson was cleared of any charges. Justice Awdry further ruled that Dhanjibhai, while not legally of age to be considered free from paternal control, was of sufficient age to choose for himself and exercise his own discretion where and with whom he would go. Asked to do so in court Dhanjibhai chose to go with Dr. Wilson. In 1842, Dhanjibhai would leave with Dr. Wilson for Europe.[36]

The judgement in the conversion case had an enormous effect on the Parsi and Indian communities of Bombay. The judgement began a process of reassessment within the Parsi community as to the best means to safeguard its interests. Describing the moment the verdict was announced, Dhanjibhai noted that: "At this the leaders of the Punchayet in a great rage noisily pushed back their chairs, and rudely left the Court. The people saw that the decision was distasteful to them, and raised menacing shouts."[37] Whatever the license employed in Dhanjibhai's account, the concern the verdict created in the community as a whole was as palpable as the reaction of the Punchayet members depicted. The indignation the leadership of the Parsis may have shown only masked the unease the Parsis must have initially felt at the adverse judgement. With the end of the trial, a three-sided

[36] Ibid., 265-6; *OCS*, January 1843, 36-7.

[37] Nauroji, *From Zoroaster to Christ*, 53.

response emerged among the Parsis that included: political agitation, intercommunity cooperation, and educational reform. Towards the end of 1839, the Parsis sought to test the weight of their political influence with a petition to government styled the 'Anti-Conversion Memorial,' containing 2,115 signatures. The Memorial called on the Bombay government to move the Legislative Council of India and subsequently the Imperial Parliament to provide: redress in law for a case of conversion, to prohibit further missionary incursions into India, to set twenty-one as the legal age of majority for children to decide their religious rights, and to disadvantage those who convert in terms of their rights of inheritance and parental authority.

The petition of the Parsis and other Indians evinced the tremendous political significance that underlay the conversion case. Given the tenor of the times, however, it was not well received. The Government of Bombay politely rebuffed the Parsis' ambitious gambit, citing its commitment to the policy of strict religious neutrality. Others in the European community took the Memorial as an unseemly attempt by the Indian community to influence government, if not threaten a breach of law following the verdict. The English language press noted the weakness of the Parsis in putting forward a political argument from a toleration question.[38] The petitioning of government for redress of grievances was a pattern the Parsis were well familiar with and had employed under British colonialism. The political rebuff offered by government damaged the perception among Parsis that some form of special relationship existed between the two communities. The Parsi boys' conversion case exposed the limits of the Parsis' ability to demand political concessions by right, and influenced the Parsis in coming years to take the initiative in defining their place in Indian law.

The conversion case moved the Parsis to reassess their relationship with the other communities of Bombay. The Bombay trial had forged a sense of unity among Indians disturbed over the issue of Christian conversions. The inchoate unity was based more on the perceived sense of impediment than on any political nationalism, yet it began the process by which the Parsis forged ties with other communities. The Parsis' grand remonstrance to the Legislative Council

[38] Wilson, *The Doctrine of Jehovah*, 150-3, Appendix: Proceedings Adopted by the Parsi Community Subsequent to the Prosecution in Her Majesty's Supreme Court of Bombay; *Madras Spectator*, May 18, 1839 in *OCS*, June 1839, 286; Bombay Gazette, June 28, 1839.

and Imperial Parliament included among its signatories the names of Hindus and Muslims, and formed one aspect of the communities' attempts to show their united displeasure. The Memorial of the Indians of Bombay while ineffective had not gone unnoticed in the Christian press. Behind the editorial gibes, a note of concern was felt by the Christian community at the strange religious confederation of "Parsees, Hindoos, and Mahommedans, uniting for mutual defence against the proselytism of Christians."[39]

The withdrawal of Indian children from mission schools formed the more tangible and immediate reaction to the conversion case. Community leaders actively promoted both the withdrawal of Indian children from mission schools and the potential establishment of opposition Indian schools. Pamphlets in Marathi and Gujarati called on Indians not to send their children to mission schools, warning of the social turmoil that the insidious teachings of the missionaries would bring.[40] The decision seems to have had an effect as following the trial Dhanjibhai noted the drop in the numbers of Indian pupils in Dr. Wilson's school alone, from 500 to between 60 and 70.[41] While the renunciation of English education had never been suggested, the essential value of an English education not having changed, the impetus for educational reform among Indians had begun. By 1842, the Parsis were discussing the creation of a Parsi-run school and in 1849, Sir Jamsetjee Jejeebhoy put his lakhs to better use with the opening of his Parsi Benevolent Institution, offering an independent Parsi educational system favourable to Western education.

The conversion case was also a precedent in the relations between the Indian community, missionaries and the law. It was the first legal challenge by an Indian community to Christian proselytism in Bombay, and was the catalyst in other communities' resistance to conversions in court. In 1843, the Reverend Robert Nesbit converted a Brahman youth to Christianity. The converted youth Narayan Sheshadri continued to reside with the Reverend Nesbit, as did his twelve-year-old brother Shripat. The conversion gained the attention of the Marathi Hindu community of Bombay and its leadership. Calls went out to boycott mission schools, and the Brahmans removed half of some 223 pupils in the Church of Scotland schools in

[39] *Friend of India*, May 30, 1839, in *OCS*, June 1839, 287.
[40] Ibid., 280-1.
[41] Nauroji, *From Zoroaster to Christ*, 59; *OCS*, February 1840, 57.

Bombay.[42] The father of the boys made a protest to both the Police Magistrate and the law courts seeking the return of the younger boy, Shripat. The Supreme Court of Bombay ruled in favour of the father, upholding the right of a parent over a minor child, reversing an earlier judgement, and ordered Shripat returned to him.[43]

The legal challenge of Indian communities to Christian conversions, however, was tempered by the evolution of the law in India. The decision of the Supreme Court of Bombay in 1843 would conflict with a decision in a similar case involving the custody of children some years later in the Supreme Court of Calcutta. The Supreme Court of Calcutta refused to make an order of habeas corpus and give up a boy of fourteen to his father, on the principle that a writ of habeas corpus was only intended to prevent illegal restraint. Where illegal restraint did not exist and a child was of an age to choose for himself, the Court allowed him to exercise his own discretion where he would go.[44] As both the Parsi boys' conversion case and the case in the Supreme Court of Calcutta demonstrated, the amalgam of British and Indian legal traditions was redounding to favour the former. For practical as well as political reasons, a new Western-oriented concept of legality was emerging in India.[45] The judgement in the Parsi conversion case potentially threatened the advances the Parsis had made to protect and safeguard their traditions under British colonialism. The advancement in the education of their children in British institutions was problematic given the introduction of Christian religious teaching, and the lack of extant Parsi religious and legal codes further imperilled the protection of Parsi tradition under British justice. Without the authority of written sources and precedents, the British could regard the propositions of the Parsis as against the principles upon which British laws were founded.

The conversion case came at the end of a decade of difficulties and adjustments between the Parsis and British colonialism. The last

---

[42] *OCS*, December 1843, 597-613.

[43] Ibid., 207; 'The Queen *v.* Rev. Robert Nesbitt: The Bramin Converts Case,' November 3, 1843, in Erskine Perry, *Cases Illustrative of Oriental Life* (1853; reprint, New Delhi, 1988), 103-9.

[44] Perry, *Cases Illustrative of Oriental Life*, 107.

[45] Jorg Fisch, *Cheap Lives and Dear Limbs: The British Transformation of the Bengal Criminal Law, 1769-1817* (Wiesbaden, 1983), 3-7, notes the dominance of English law and principles in the evolution of criminal law in India.

great occurrence of disorder among the Parsis of Bombay was in June 1832. Relations between Parsis and the authorities deteriorated ostensibly over a matter of religion. From June 6 to 7, 1832, the Parsis of Bombay organized a strike in protest of the British government's policy to capture and dispose of nuisance pariah dogs without owners. The Parsis protested the killing of creatures they had reverence for, and utilized their power and influence in Bombay in furtherance of their protest. The shops in the bazaars closed, the Bombay port facility was paralysed, and a general strike enveloped Bombay Town and Island that greatly inconvenienced the European inhabitants of Bombay and denied them their supplies and sustenance. The strike culminated in a mob scene and riot at police headquarters in Bombay that was put down by British troops.[46] The riot was largely confined to the lower orders among the Parsis and other communities, with the Parsi elite and leadership both unaware of the planned strike and somewhat powerless to control events. The strike and riot had caused a rupture between British and Parsis that both the British and the Parsi leadership were eager to repair. The steadfastness of the Parsis in protection of their religious identity, including in antagonism to colonialism, presents a unique contrast to their overall socialization as a loyal colonial community.

Summary

The initial crisis of confidence the Parsis felt following the conversion case gradually gave way to a better understanding of where their interests as a community lay. The consensus to defend and protect Parsi identity remained strong during the conversion case. Following the case the Parsis came to reassess the best means by which to protect that identity. The Parsis emerged from the episode with a desire to broaden their horizons beyond the community and avail themselves of new opportunities in benefit of identity. The intercommunity ties forged amidst the crisis of the conversions, most profoundly, came to be regarded as part of the interests of the Parsis. The sense of common threat gave way to a more mature sense of communality and mutuality of interest. In particular, the push for educational advancement among the communities of Bombay be-

[46] Jesse S. Palsetia, "Mad Dogs and Parsis: The Bombay Dog Riots of 1832," *Journal of the Royal Asiatic Society*, series 3, vol. 11, part 1 (2001), pp. 13-30.

came a priority. Mid-century witnessed cooperation across community and caste lines and social reform within community and caste identities. All the Indian communities of Bombay shared the desire for social progress, to varying degrees, and the push for social reform by one community spurred the desire for reform among the other communities.

The commitment to religious identity continued to remain strong among the Parsis. The Parsis remained the most impervious to the direct influences of Christian missions among Indian communities. While Parsis came to appreciate the religious message of Christianity, no movement ever arose among the Parsis that consciously or inadvertently imitated Christian influences, such as the Brahmo Samaj. Conversions continued to take place following those of Dhanjibhai Nauroji and Hormasji Pestonji; however, the majority of Parsis had come to discount them. In part, this was due to a certain resignation at the inability to influence the outcome legally where a Parsi was of legal age to choose his religious faith.[47] In large part, it was due to the nature of the conversions: almost all the conversions involved Parsis converting in order to take religious orders. Whether this was a matter of purely personal conscience and conviction on the part of those converted, or demonstrated the pressure the Parsis could exert to make conversion untenable for anyone other than those contemplating a clerical life, it is difficult to say. Some converts were bitter at the treatment they received at the hands of the Parsis.[48] From mid-century, Parsi reformers were concerned with the movement for religious reform. They utilized Western education, training, and scholarship on behalf of religious reform and the strengthening of Parsi identity. Traditionalists and reformers alike came to regard Christian conversions within the community as anachronistic and as an "old game played over again."[49] They noted the hypocrisy of Christian missionary attempts to angle for converts when Christian values were in a poor state in Europe. Other Parsis aimed to counter Christian propaganda in new publications based on Western rationalist philosophy.[50] After mid-century, the social re-

[47] Perry, *Cases Illustrative of Oriental Life*, 97; D. E. Wacha, *Shells from the Sands of Bombay* (Bombay, 1920), 649.

[48] Nauroji, *From Zoroaster to Christ*, 63; *Bombay Times*, December 15, 1859.

[49] *Rast Goftar*, October 9, 1864.

[50] *Bombay Times*, December 22, 1856.

former Dinsha E. Wacha noted that the missionaries' contacts with the Parsis were largely over.[51]

The case of the Parsi boys' conversions had posed a challenge to the Parsis at a timely moment in the history of their efforts to safeguard identity. It had come during the waning of traditional authority, and as internal tensions had begun to make Parsis reassess the model by which to safeguard their interests. The confrontations between the Christian missionaries and the Parsis in the 1830s, consequently, provided the circumstances surrounding the Parsis' reassessment of their interests, not necessarily the cause behind it.[52] The debates with Dr. Wilson and the court case in 1839 intensified the internal debate over social change already in progress. The Parsis had met the challenge from the missionaries on one level, while desirous to address the question of their social evolution raised by the debates with the missionaries. The Parsis' faith in the British had only momentarily been disturbed as a result of the conversion case, though, significantly enough, over the one issue that could disturb that faith: the Parsis' commitment to their religious identity.

With the new found self-confidence and assertiveness that developed by the second half of the nineteenth century, it is therefore little surprise that the Parsis interpreted the episode of the Parsi boys' conversion with a sense of nostalgia. The Parsis had reconciled themselves to the missionaries as one more community within Bombay civic society. The Parsis also reconciled themselves with Dr. Wilson, and noted his passing in 1876, as an eminent citizen of Bombay. The Parsi journalist, poet, and social reformer Behramji M. Malabari (1853-1912), whom Dr. Wilson had befriended and tutored, wrote the poem 'Wilson Virah,' in his memory.[53] Dhanjibhai Nauroji who compared his and his friends' travails at the hands of the Parsis to those of St. Paul among the Romans, noted in his autobiography the mutual respect between himself and the Parsis that eventually came out of the episode of the Parsi boys' conversion. In 1846, Dhanjibhai was ordained by the Free Presbyterian Church of

---

[51] Wacha, *Shells*, 652.

[52] Eckehard Kulke, *The Parsees in India* (Munich, 1974), lays the incentive for educational and religious reform among the Parsis on the confrontations with the Christian missionaries.

[53] Dayaram Gidumal, *The Life-Work of B. M. Malabari* (Bombay, 1888); J. J. Modi, *A Glimpse Into the History and Work of the Zarthoshti Din-ni Khol Karnari Mandli* (Bombay, 1922), 172.

Edinburgh, and returned to lecture and tour in India as a missionary following his ordination.[54] The one time outcast while devoted to his God and wishing His truth on the Parsis could still reflect that:

> I was born a Parsi and I am still a Parsi of the Parsis.... I am one with my brethren according to the flesh. Whatever touches them touches me. Their joy and sorrow are mine. I love them, and if need be, I am ready to lay down my life for them. The bitter feeling that arose amongst them at the time of my baptism has long since passed away. We are now great friends, and when I meet my Parsi friends we greet each other with warm hand-shake. I am proud to belong to a race which stands foremost by reason of many high qualities among the races of the East.[55]

[54] *Bombay Times*, July 25, 1857.
[55] Nauroji, *From Zoroaster to Christ*, 84-5.

CHAPTER FOUR

IDENTITY AND SOCIAL REFORM

1. *Education and the Parsis*

The controversy of the conversion of the Parsi boys had not dampened the great enthusiasm the Parsis held for things Western, including the desire to emulate and adopt British intellectual and educational values in their social progress. On the occasion of the first Convocation at the newly founded University of Bombay on April 28, 1862, Sir Henry Bartle Frere, Chancellor of the University, urged the new graduates, Hindus and Parsis, to appreciate the sacred trust confided to them for the benefit of their countrymen as the new representatives of their communities.[1] The awakening of many Indians to the value of education and the potential it offered for the improvement of Indian society had long preceded the Chancellor's words. A leading few among the Parsis had early on gauged the potential offered by education in augmenting and broadening or even changing the power base of the community. The exploitation of educational opportunities was the most conspicuous aspect of a re-evaluation of the Parsis' social progress. The debates with the missionaries and the effect of Western influences had moved the Parsis to question not only the nature of their social progress but the means by which they could direct the progress and modernization of the community. From mid-century, the call for social reform among the Parsis encompassed a re-evaluation of all the internal rationalizations whether social, religious, or political that had sustained the Parsis in the protection of their identity over the previous hundred years. A plurality of outlooks and opinions emerged, which challenged the consensus over how best to safeguard Parsi identity that had been fashioned since the Parsis arrived in Bombay. The plurality of opinion, in turn, shaped Parsi self-perceptions offering new opportunities and challenges to the social progress of the community.

[1] *Bombay Times*, April 28, 1862.

Contributions of the Shetias

The initial involvement of the Parsis in the rise of educational institutions in Bombay was part of the effort of the prominent and enlightened citizens of Bombay to form an organization on behalf of education in Bombay City. This effort preceded the work of the missionaries in establishing schools, which had begun in the late 1820s; and operated parallel to the work of government in devising an educational policy for Bombay and Western India. In 1815, the Society for Promoting the Education of the Poor was established as a school for needy and half-caste Europeans, and was familiarly known as the Bombay Education Society. In August 1820, at a meeting of the subscribers of the Education Society, a special committee of Europeans and Indians was formed to raise funds and prepare plans for a scheme for Indian education. The new Native School and School Book Committee's task was to assist and improve Indian schools, and help to establish and support any further schools, primarily by providing suitable books of instruction for use in both English and the local vernaculars. The establishment of the Committee was part of the process underway to promote education among Indians, and was indirectly supported by government officials and influential Englishmen such as Governor Mountstuart Elphinstone, the President of the Bombay Education Society. In addition to the three official members on the managing committee, four prominent individuals were chosen to sit on the committee as directors from each of the four principal communities of Bombay: British, Parsi, Hindu, and Muslim.[2]

The desire to better distinguish educational efforts on behalf of Indians from that of Europeans led in August 1822 to the discontinuation of the Native School Book and School Committee as a branch of the Education Society, and the creation of the Bombay Native School Book and School Society, as a separate society. The Society was a timely amalgam of private and government interests on behalf of education in Bombay. Government provided the degree of regularity and permanence necessary for the success of an organized system by establishing schools, while the Education Society trained teachers, and the Native Society supervised and organized

---

First Report of the Bombay Native School Book and School Society (Bombay, 1824), 2-3.

the printing and distribution of books. An annual grant of Rs. 6,000 from the government was also provided to the Society.[3]

The work of the Bombay Native School Book and School Society had attracted the prominent Parsi, Hindu and Muslim citizens of Bombay. Of the twelve Indian members to serve on the managing committee of the Society in 1822, the four Parsis included Jamsetjee Jejeebhoy, Framji Cowasji Banaji, Mulla Firoze, and Hormusji Dhunjibhoy. In 1827, when the Bombay Native School Book and School Society changed its name to the Bombay Native Education Society, the number of Parsis on the managing committee remained the same with Kaikhusroo Sorabjee replacing Hormusji Dhunjibhoy.[4] In the same year, Jamsetjee Jejeebhoy made his first benefaction in support of education in Bombay with a donation of Rs. 11,000 to the Native Education Society.[5] In 1839, on the eve of the Parsi boys' conversion case, eight Parsis were associated with the management and direction of the Bombay Native Education Society out of some fifty individuals involved in the Society's affairs.[6]

The enthusiasm of the *shetias* or rich Parsi leaders for the encouragement of education in Bombay is an interesting phenomenon. The influential Parsis associated with the Bombay Native Education Society were not themselves educated men in the modern sense. Both Jamsetjee Jejeebhoy and Framji Cowasji Banaji had no formal schooling, merely the education afforded by the cut and thrust of a lifetime in commerce and trade. Both merchant-princes received some Gujarati tuition, and were sufficiently literate to converse and write in English and Indian vernaculars, as a result of their business dealings with individuals from different communities, and both possessed knowledge of book-keeping. The heirs of Lowjee Wadia were privately tutored in English by European teachers, though they took no interest in the support of educational schemes.[7] Most of the rich

[3] Ibid., 5; Kenneth Ballhatchet, *Social Policy and Social Change in Western India, 1817-1830* (Oxford, 1957), 261; B. T. McCully, *English Education and the Origins of Indian Nationalism* (New York, 1940), 105.

[4] *Fourth Report of the Proceedings of the Bombay Native Education Society, 1827* (Bombay, 1828), 3.

[5] Jehangir R. P. Mody, *Jamsetjee Jejeebhoy the First Indian Knight and Baronet, 1783-1859* (Bombay, 1959), p. 131.

[6] *Twelfth Report of the Proceedings of the United Institution of the Elphinstone College, and School of the Native Education Society, 1839* (Bombay, 1840), 5-6.

[7] Williamson Ramsay, *Memorandum of the Life and Public Charities of Jamsetjee Jejeebhoy* (London, 1855), 6; D. E. Wacha, *Shells from the Sands of*

Parsi families of Bombay in the first half of the nineteenth century were opposed to sending their children, specifically their sons, to the new schools that were emerging in Bombay. The preference remained to have sons rejoin the family business after a basic education; the successful adaptation of the uneducated father probably reenforced the practicality of such a course.[8]

The involvement of men like Jamsetjee Jejeebhoy and Framji Cowasji Banaji in educational efforts reflected as much a desire to participate in the leadership of Bombay society alongside the British as an appreciation of the value of an education for Parsis and other Indians. The small number of Parsis associated with educational efforts in Bombay reflected a political culture that viewed the support for education as an elite undertaking in the promotion of a civic culture. The opportunity for contact with the British cooperation over schemes for education afforded was not lost on these men. The close commercial ties Parsis and British shared had translated into a mutually advantageous social and cultural cooperation.[9]

The social contacts had fostered a sense of trust between the parties, at all times coloured by the particular interests of each of them. Jamsetjee Jejeebhoy enjoyed the friendship and confidence of Governor Mountstuart Elphinstone, and Framji Cowasji Banaji was no less regarded as a trusted and eminent citizen.[10] The cooperation between British and Indians formed part of the emerging political culture of collaboration that served the interests of many parties in India. Significantly, in fostering such close links with non-Zoroastrians it was the great *shets* of the community who broke the uneasy prejudice among the Parsis in mixing with other communities, and validated the new spirit of secular intercourse with the Europeans. After mid-century, the fortunes of many of the *shetias* of the late eighteenth and early nineteenth century were in relative decline. Faced with a new industrial age, and the natural downturns in the economy, the interests of the great families were served in forging new sources

---

Bombay (Bombay, 1920), 281, 456; C. M. C., *Framjee Cowasjee Banajee: A Memoir* (Bombay, 1922), 6-7; Maria Graham, *Journal of a Residence in India* (Edinburgh, 1813), 44.

[8] D. F. Karaka, *History of the Parsis*, 2 vols. (London, 1884), 1:301; Dosabhai Framjee, *The Parsees: Their Manners, Customs, and Religion* (London, 1858), 215-19.

[9] Wacha, *Shells*, 685.

[10] Ibid., 763; Karaka, *History of the Parsis*, 2:113; G. A. Natesan and Co., ed., *Famous Parsis* (Madras, 1930), 30.

of influence and power beyond the economic realm. In the late 1820s, Jamsetjee Jejeebhoy, Framji Cowasji Banaji, and the Saraswat Brahman Jagannath Shankarshet (1802-65) successfully petitioned Parliament for the right of Indians to sit on Grand Juries, leading in 1834 to thirteen Indians being appointed JPs.[11] The advantage afforded the government in co-opting the Indian elite into its political system of rule was also manifold. The active participation of this class in any scheme for education aided this process. Both the political socialization of the *shetias*, as well as the creation of a new elite class of interpreters, teachers, and good Indian gentlemen, remained the goal of British policy from the early part of the century.[12] While the great *shets* and their families might be slow to see the advantages of the new education for themselves, their involvement in and association with the establishment of educational institutions in Bombay was an important aspect in the rise of the institutions on behalf of Indians.

Through their efforts on the Bombay Native Education Society, the influential Indian citizens of Bombay aided the spread of education. In 1830, there were fifty-six Society schools, each containing about 60 boys, amounting overall to 3,000 boys under a course of education. In the Central School in Bombay, 250 boys had been through a course of study in the English language. Fifty had left it with a competent knowledge of the language, and an acquaintance with geography, mathematics, and geometry. Vernacular education was also offered to 945 boys in the Marathi school, and 427 boys in the Gujarati school, both in Bombay. Parsi students predominated in the BNES schools, particularly the Central English School.[13]

The Indian elite's contribution to educational efforts in Bombay was also evident in the establishment of college classes and professorships in 1827. The Bombay Native Education Society led by Jamsetjee Jejeebhoy, Framji Cowasji Banaji, and Mahoodas Runchodas raised funds to establish professorships in honour of the retiring Governor Elphinstone. The Society collected Rs. 2,15,000, with the

---

[11] K. N. Banaji, *Memoirs of the Late Framji Cowasji Banaji* (Bombay, 1892), 23-4.

[12] *Report of the Board of Education, 1850-51* (Bombay, 1852), 5; Edward Colebrooke, "Memoir of the Honourable Mountstuart Elphinstone," *The Journal of the Royal Asiatic Society of Great Britain and Ireland* 18 (1861): 301.

[13] *Fourth Report of the Proceedings... 1827*, 21-2; *Sixth Report of the Bombay Native Education Society*, 1830 (Bombay, 1831), 1.

Parsi contribution to this total being over Rs. 30,000. Subsequent donations from the public amounted to some Rs. 4,43,900, with Rs. 17,000 being donated by the Maharaja of Satara. With an additional grant from the Government of Bombay, Elphinstone College was founded and three professors were sent for, from Europe. Elphinstone's immediate successor, Governor Sir John Malcolm, acknowledged the significance of the efforts of the leading Indian inhabitants of Bombay to education.[14]

The material contributions of the leading citizens of Bombay, including the Parsi *shetias,* to the spread of education in Bombay marked the evolution of the *shetias*' role from community leaders to civic leaders, and may be said to have been an extension of the charitable and leadership role they had always maintained within their own communities. The benefaction in memory of Elphinstone was one of many in honour of the leaders of Bombay government and society that the leading Indian citizens of Bombay had undertaken, and which redound to the benefit of education in Bombay. Others benefactions included the establishment of the Clare Scholarship in 1835, and the Sir James Rivett-Carnac Scholarship for medical students in 1841. Jamsetjee Jejeebhoy and his family took a particular interest on behalf of educational charitable endowments, and sought to involve the other leading Indians alongside government in the civic improvement of Bombay. The most significant results of Jamsetjee Jejeebhoy's efforts were the establishment of the Sir Jamsetjee Jejeebhoy Hospital in 1845, and contributions to the Grant Medical College and College scholarships; the creation of the Sir Jamsetjee Jejeebhoy School of Art in 1857, as India's first professional school of design; and the Deccan College in Poona, funded by the second Jamsetjee Jejeebhoy (1811-77) in 1864.[15]

One of the more prominent names associated with the progress of education in Bombay was Cowasjee Jehangir. Cowasjee Jehangir Readymoney (1859-1915) was a descendant of one of Bombay's earliest Parsi families. Having begun his rise to wealth as a godown

---

[14] *Fourth Report of the Proceedings ... 1827*, 8, 28-32; *Twelfth Report of the Proceedings ... 1839*, 47-53; Ramsay, *Memorandum*, 131; Karaka, *History of the Parsis*, 2:283-4; *University of Bombay (1857-1957) Centenary Souvenir* (Bombay, 1957), 32.

[15] Jamsetjee Jejeebhoy to James Parish, March 19, 1838, J.J. MSS, 357:l-5ff; *Bombay Times*, April 16, 1859; *Bombay Times*, May 26, 1857; *Bombay Times*, Novembers, 1859.

keeper, Cowasjee's business acumen saw him rise to the status of merchant-prince. He was the second Parsi knighted by the Queen in 1872. Among his many charitable donations, that totalled some fifteen lakhs or Rs. 15,00,000 during his lifetime, Cowasjee provided for the first permanent building that became the Elphinstone College, situated originally in Byculla. In April 1863, Cowasjee offered Rs. 1,00,000 in a proposal in cooperation with the Government of Bombay for the erection of a building to form the centre of the newly amalgamated University of Bombay, and by August had paid the sum. Cowasjee's financial contribution on behalf of the University was matched and raised by Bombay's most successful businessman of the time, Premchand Roychund. Premchand offered two lakhs in August 1864, subsequently raised to four lakhs, on news of Cowasjee's offer. Cowasjee Jehangir and Premchand Roychund's benefactions on behalf of the University saw the erection of its principal buildings—the Cowasjee Jehangir Hall (1875) and the University Library and Rajabai Clock Tower (1878).[16]

By 1840, a coordinated educational system in Bombay City had emerged. The Bombay Native Education Society and the Elphinstone College were amalgamated to form the Elphinstone Native Education Institution, renamed the Elphinstone Institution in 1845. Of the twenty Indian members associated with the joint operations of the Institution, the Parsis included Jamsetjee Jejeebhoy, Framji Cowasji Banaji, Bomanjee Hormarjee Wadia, Rustomjee Kaikobadjee, Dadabhoy Pestonjee Wadia, Cursetjee Jamsetjee Jejeebhoy, Dosabhoy Sorabjee, and Manockjee Cursetjee and Nowrozjee Furdoonjee, both of whom were prominent reformers.[17] Most significantly, the Board of Education was formed headed by Sir Erskine Perry, Chief Justice of the Supreme Court of Bombay, and included Framji Cowasji as a member until his death in 1850, at which time he was replaced by Bomanjee Hormarjee Wadia. At the time of the creation of the Board of Education, the Elphinstone Institution had 550 pupils, and by 1850, the number had risen to 916. The total number of pupils receiving education under government in the Bombay Presidency in 1840 was 5,941 in 97 vernacular and English

[16] *The Times of India*, October 23, 1863; J. Cowasjee Jehanghier, *Life of Sir Cowasjee Jehanghier Readymoney* (Bombay, 1890), 41-50; D. E. Wacha, *A Financial Chapter in the History of Bombay City* (Bombay, 1910), 47-51, 202-3; idem, *Premchand Roychund: His Early Life and Career* (Bombay, 1913), 144-5.

[17] *Twelfth Report of the Proceedings ... 1839*, 5-6.

schools. By 1850, the total number of pupils receiving similar education was 12,712 in 185 schools.[18]

The contribution of the Parsi *shetias* to the formation of educational opportunities in Bombay had largely consisted in lending their prestige, largesse, and political connections to various schemes. Their efforts, however, were also significant in the establishment of schools for Parsis, and the popularizing of education within the Parsi community. The efforts of both traditionalist and reformist Parsis would prove essential to the widespread adoption of education, and the inculcation of the value of education among the Parsis. Ironically, the prejudice among the wealthy commercial class against education was only lessened with the rise of a new generation and class of Parsis that took advantage of educational institutions. The centre of gravity of Parsi influence and power was shifting to the educated. As Dosabhai Framji Karaka noted, the wealthy:

> ... had to realise the fact that, if they did not leave their sons a better legacy than gold, they would be unable to keep their place in society, while the educated and enlightened members, although belonging to the middle and less wealthy classes, would take precedence over them in everyway.[19]

The desire of the wealthy Parsi leaders to augment the power base of the community through the support of education, and the desire on the part of a new generation of Parsis for the intellectual and material benefits associated with education, worked to shape both Parsi educational efforts from the 1840s, and the progress of social reform from mid-century.

Independent Parsi Schools

The first schools for Parsis had owed their creation to the efforts of Jamsetjee Jejeebhoy and the traditionalist Parsis. In 1831, N. M. Pouchana had funded an English school for Parsi boys at Bazaargate in Bombay; and three years later N. D. Gai had started evening classes for boys.[20] In 1836, Jamsetjee Jejeebhoy, Jeejeebhoy Dadabhai, and Framji Cowasji Banaji each contributed Rs. 3,000 to establish the Parsi Benevolent School for teaching Gujarati and religious

[18] *Report of the Board of Education, 1850-51*, 7-8.

[19] Karaka, *History of the Parsis*, 1:301.

[20] *Parsee Prakash*, 1:136, 266.

literature.[21] In 1844, Dadabhoy Pestonjee Wadia, Bomanjee Hormarjee Wadia, and others started an English school for Parsis under the direction of Henry Hinton.[22] The Sir Jamsetjee Jejeebhoy Parsi Benevolent Institution was established in 1849, and marked a turning point in the efforts of an indigenous community to foster educational opportunity within its own ranks. The conversion controversy of the two Parsi boys of 1839, had given impetus to the efforts of one such as Jamsetjee Jejeebhoy to 'rescue' Parsis from the dubious mercy of the Christian missionaries in their education. The proposal for the Sir Jamsetjee Jejeebhoy Parsi Benevolent Institution had emerged to mark Jamsetjee Jejeebhoy being conferred the first Indian knightood in 1842. The Parsis undertook to subscribe to a fund for the translation of books into Gujarati for the community in the name of Jamsetjee Jejeebhoy to the value of Rs. 15,000. The offer had moved Jamsetjee to the extent that he created a fund, the interest of which would be applied towards a scheme to relieve the distress of the poor of Bombay and the towns of Gujarat, and provide education for their children. Sir Jamsetjee and Lady Avabai offered the sum of Rs. 3,00,000 to the scheme, along with shares from the Bank of Bengal. The total amount offered for the trust by Jamsetjee came to Rs. 4,44,000 or over £44,000, with the Parsi Punchayet providing bank shares and capital in the amount of Rs. 2,45,000, in support of the scheme. A deed of settlement and by-laws was signed between Jamsetjee, the Punchayet, and the government and provided for a committee or Punchayet of twelve individuals to run and oversee the operations of the Institution.[23]

The majority of the funds of the Sir J.J.P.B. Institution were utilized for education, with a little less than a quarter being reserved to assist the indigent, disabled, aged, and disadvantaged in regards to marriage, health and funeral expenses, both in Bombay and in parts of Gujarat. The majority of the funds were allocated towards schools in Bombay and Gujarat. The Central English School opened on October 17, 1849, in Bombay, later to be referred to as Sir Jamsetjee

---

[21] Ibid., 294; Banaji, *Memoirs*, 24; Natesan, *Famous Parsis*, 83; Mody, *Jamsetjee Jejeebhoy*, 131.

[22] R. A. Wadia, *Scions of Lowjee Wadia* (Bombay, 1964), 113.

[23] *Correspondence, Deed, Bye-Laws, etc., Relating to 'Sir Jamsetjee Jejeebhoy's Parsee Benevolent Institution,' Established in Bombay in 1849* (Bombay, 1849), 1-15, 18-23, 85-102; Bombay Times, April 16, 1859; Ramsay, *Memorandum*, 31; Mody, *Jamsetjee Jejeebhoy*, 135.

Jejeebhoy Fort Boys' School. It was soon followed by three more boys' schools in Bombay, the second English boys' school located in Surat, and seven or more Gujarati vernacular boys' schools in the Gujarat towns of Navsari, Broach, Tarapur, Billimora, Bulsar, and Udwada. Provision was also made for vernacular girls' schools in Bombay, two of which were opened by 1850, followed shortly by a third. Vernacular girls' classes were added to the schools in Surat, Navsari, Tarapur, and Billimora; all of which added a novel character to the scheme for education among the Parsis, and in Western India.[24] In the towns that did not initially provide education to girls, attempts were ongoing to provide funds. In Broach, for example, where some 60 Parsi boys attended the Sir J.J.P.B. Institution school, Nowrojee Byramjee, the Deputy Collector, offered to maintain a girls' schools at his own expense, in an effort to move the Parsis of Broach to take action.[25] By 1860, there were some eighteen schools run by the educational department of the Sir J.J.P.B. Institution containing 2,000 Parsi youths of both genders, of which the schools in Bombay accommodated 430 boys and 485 girls, followed closely behind by Surat with 420 boys and 90 girls.[26] By 1864, the Central School prepared students for matriculation examinations for entry to the University of Bombay that had opened in 1857.

As a charitable institution, the Sir J.J.P.B. Institution had as its principal aim to communicate knowledge and instil an indispensable desire for self-improvement in its pupils. As a practical point, it also aimed to help prepare students to find respectable and useful employment, or progress to education at a higher level. By 1860, about 50 men from the Institution obtained employment every year. The government noted its gratification at the ability of the Institution's English school to compete with the very limited number of English schools in obtaining University scholarships.[27] With the growth of other Parsi schools alongside the Sir J.J.P.B. Institution, the inculcation of the value of education spread among the Parsis, and basic literacy became the norm. Consequently, whether the Parsi followed the course of higher education or returned to business or the working

[24] *Bombay Times*, April 9, 1860.
[25] *Bombay Times*, March 21, 1857.
[26] *Bombay Times*, April 9, 1860.
[27] *Bombay Times*, November 2, 1859, April 9, 1860.

world, education had become a requisite and marker of identity among the Parsis.

Jamsetjee Jejeebhoy hoped to provide the teaching of Zoroastrianism in the Institution schools on a par with the teachings of Christianity taught in the missionary schools. However, as Jamsetjee had intended the government to hold the funds of the Institution as trustee, the opposition of the government to funding religious instruction prohibited the Sir J.J.P.B. Institution schools from exclusively teaching Zoroastrianism. The intention of government to prohibit any compulsory introduction of religious education into schools it was associated with, however, did not preclude the teaching of moral and religious principles. Furthermore, as the Institution was principally, though not exclusively, intended for Parsis, the cultural and psychological atmosphere of a Parsi school went far in promoting the sense of community solidarity and affinity, with or without rigorous religious instruction.

Jamsetjee Jejeebhoy's efforts to provide schools in Gujarat also symbolized the sense of obligation and responsibility the Parsis continued to feel for the Mofussil or provincial community. All the Parsis had migrated to Bombay from the provincial setting and the connection felt to that milieu remained more than sentimental. The creation of provincial schools that emphasized vernacular education in Gujarati was aimed to avert the potential loss of traditional learning and identity. At the same time, the want of material opportunities in Gujarat, and the impossibility of obtaining higher education outside Bombay, facilitated the deruralization of Parsis. The creation of Parsi schools in provincial areas was important in providing that Parsis settling in Bombay had a basic education.

The provision for girls' education by the Sir J.J.P.B. Institution also marked a significant accomplishment, particularly on the part of more traditionalist Parsis. The education of Parsi girls in schools was largely left to the missionaries, prior to the Parsis' involvement in 1849. Margaret Wilson had begun to supervise the six girls' schools run by the Scottish missionaries after her arrival in Bombay. In 1832, she opened the Bombay Ladies' School for Destitute Native Girls, with twenty-nine girls in attendance, including Parsi girls.[28] In her reminiscences on her stay in India, the Viscountess Falkland noted the beginning of Parsi-run education in Bombay, including that for

[28] *OCS*, August 1834, 273-4.

girls: "I once attended an examination of a Parsee school, at Sir Jamsetjee Jeejeebhoy's house.... The little girls sat in rows on benches, and from the variegated colours of their drapery and glittering jewels, they looked like parterres of the gayest possible flowers."[29] At a time when general education was still limited to being provided in government-run or missionary schools, the novel experience touring Parsi-run schools for girls and boys provided to Lady Falkland was a conspicuous expression of the Parsi commitment to education.

Among the Indian communities in Bombay and Western India, the creation of schools and the spread of education were most conspicuous among the Parsis. By 1852, the Parsis led in the number of students attending schools run by the Elphinstone Institution in Bombay: with 493 Parsis enrolled in lower level schools compared to 267 students from the various Hindu communities.[30] The quality of education in the schools run by the Sir J.J.P.B. Institution and the Parsi Punchayet also appears to have met the standards for education set by the Board of Education. The exception being that better maps were required in the schools, and the Gujarati texts printed by the Punchayet press were not of as good a quality as those obtained in the government seminaries.[31] Attempts were made to remedy this situation, for example, by the Parsi residents of Broach who raised funds for better facilities and equipment for students, and provided prizes to students as incentive for academic achievement.[32]

In Bombay City, the Parsis, members of the small Bohra community, and other Gujarati trading classes of Western India were among the growing lower and middle classes of society that exploited the new educational opportunities. These trading communities were joined by the Brahmans, particularly castes of the Marathi Brahmans, who partook of educational opportunities both at higher and lower levels as a means of overcoming the dislocation of their leadership role in Western India following the British conquests of their territories. By the latter quarter of the century, the Brahman castes would come to predominate higher educational places. At 6.8 per cent to 5.8 per cent of the population of Bombay City and Island between 1864 and 1891, the Parsis continued to maintain a steady

[29] The Viscountess Falkland, *Chow-Chow: A Journal Kept in India, Egypt and Syria*, vol. 1 (London, 1857), 51.

[30] *Annual Report of the Elphinstone Institution*, 1852 (Bombay, 1853), 48-50.

[31] *Bombay Times*, February 25, 1857.

[32] *Bombay Times*, March 21, 1857.

percentage of the college going population. As the numbers from other communities increased in educational institutions, the percentage of Parsis decreased.[33] In 1870, Parsis composed 34 per cent of the students at Elphinstone College, equal to the percentage of Brahman students. In 1882 and 1885, the percentage of Parsis at Elphinstone remained steady at 26 per cent and 28 per cent respectively, while the Brahman population fluctuated. By the 1880s, the Parsis were regarded as the most literate community in Bombay.[34]

Contributions of the Parsi Reformers

The rise to prominence of a new educated class of Indians, particularly in Western India, is the unique feature of the spread of education in India. It was this group that went to the institutions of higher education that had been established with the aid of the *shetia* members of their own communities, and who gave effect to the educational changes by championing the cause of social progress and reform within their respective communities. The new class of reformers that emerged from the Elphinstone College and Institution, the Grant Medical School, and the Government Law School shared a collective identity as reformers both during the course of their educational experiences and once beginning their careers. The reformers held themselves out as a new and 'young class,' educationally and generationally distinct from their elders, both in general terms and

[33] In 1864, the Parsis totalled 49,201 individuals or 6 per cent of the population of Bombay City and Island. In 1872, the Parsis totalled 44,091 individuals or 6.8 per cent of the population of Bombay. In 1881, the Parsis accounted for 48,597 individuals or 6.7 per cent of the population of Bombay. In 1891, the Parsi population was in relative decline to the growing population of Bombay, and stood at 47,458 individuals or 5.8 per cent. On population and Census figures, see The *Gazetteer of the Bombay City and Island*, vol. 1 (Bombay, 1909), 158-64; Christine Dobbin, *Urban Leadership in Western India* (Oxford, 1972), 8, 153; Eckehard Kulke, *The Parsees in India* (Munich, 1974), 35; J. C. Masselos, *Towards Nationalism* (Bombay, 1974), 6; idem, "Changing Definitions of Bombay: City State to Capital City," in *Ports and Their Hinterlands in India (1700-1950)*, ed. Indu Banga (New Delhi, 1992), 293; Karaka, *History of the Parsis*, 1:92; K. N. Seervai and B. B. Patell, "Gujarat Parsis from Their Earliest Settlement to the Present Time," in *Gazetteer of the Bombay Presidency*, vol. 9, part 2, ed. J. M. Campbell (Bombay, 1899), 183.

[34] Dobbin, *Urban Leadership*, 35, 162. The Census of India of 1911 represents that the Parsis continued to show the highest figures of literacy with 74 per cent of the population of 51,000 individuals as literate. Some 13,477 Parsis were recorded as unable to read and write a letter. See *Parsee Prakash*, 5:21.

within their caste communities.[35] The careers of the Parsis, as with that of the other Indian reformers, were varied, although most were clearly to be designated as professionals. Prominent Parsi reformers like Nowrozjee Furdoonjee and Dadabhai Naoroji were both assistant professors at Elphinstone College, and Manockjee Cursetjee was Judge of the High Court. Sorabjee Shapoorjee Bengallee (1831-93) had a varied career in business and journalism, and with Kharshedji Rustomji Cama, who came from a privileged background, shared the reputation of being a scholar.

The educational interests of the Indian reformers and philosophers were first piqued in the salons of the Elphinstone Institution where they banded together to form groups and societies to discuss various academic and intellectual issues, as well as investigate the need for social reform. The close contact forged within the urban environment of Bombay and the institutional setting of the colleges encouraged a sense of corporate identity and group cooperation, while at the same time the compartmentalized nature of the Bombay social structure rendered unified social and political activity over specific issues more difficult. The initial contact between reformers of divergent sectarian backgrounds, consequently, was principally over intellectual and academic interests. The interests of the reformers eventually branched out into forming societies devoted to reforms whether educational, social, or religious in character within their own caste communities, while maintaining the sense of corporate identity, cooperation and solidarity among all Indian reformers. The reform agenda of the educated worked for the improvement of society through the dissemination of learning and education, and the transformation of the customs and practices of Indians through the implementation of specific social and religious reforms within their caste communities consistent with the new learning.

The Students' Literary and Scientific Society established on June 13, 1848, was one of the first manifestations of the reformers' sense of united identity and social obligation. The Society was formed principally through the efforts of Professors Patton, Green, and Reid

[35] Dadabhai Naoroji, *The Manners and Customs of the Parsees: Paper Read Before the Liverpool Philomatic Society* (London, 1862), 22. This class would be derogatorily referred to as 'Young Bombay' by their opponents for their inexperience and radical program, akin to the Young Bengal movement, but would co-opt the epithet as part of their identity.

of the Elphinstone Institution, and initially confined its membership to academics and students currently or at one time associated with the Elphinstone Institution. At its commencement, it had twenty-four original members. In 1853, membership was extended to include all educated individuals from the various communities of Bombay City, but not the *shetias* or individuals involved in commerce.[36] The new educated class was particularly involved in the promotion of literacy as well as the encouragement of the growth of educated opinion in Bombay. From 1845 to 1857, the educated class and its supporters established and funded no less than nine libraries throughout Bombay Island, and twelve in the Mofussil, with collections in vernaculars and English literature. The Students' Literary and Scientific Society maintained its own library, which in 1852 was amalgamated with the Native General Library, established in 1845 by the Military Board Office. The Library became one of Bombay's premier collections and was subsequently transferred to the new Framji Cowasji Institute in 1864.[37] At the annual meeting of the Native General Library for 1858, Mr. C. Beyts captured the spirit of the reformers in stating that: "In a truly catholic spirit, [the Library] holds out its advantages to all alike—it knows of no sectarianism—Christian, Hindu, Parsi, Mahomedan, Jew—all may come, without let or hindrance, to slake their thirst at the fount of knowledge."[38] A culture of educated opinion had emerged that was non-communal in character and had at heart the application of the new learning to the scrutiny of Indian life.

The Students' Literary and Scientific Society had also taken on the task of operating schools. The opening of schools for girls was the most novel and enlightened example of the Society's commitment to the cause of educational reform in Bombay. The idea of female education was one among many subjects on the condition of females in India discussed by the reformers at the second meeting of

---

[36] *Students' Literary and Scientific Society Proceedings, 1853* (Bombay, 1853), 1-7 (hereafter cited as *S.L.S.S.*); N. S. Bengallee, *The Life of Sorabjee Shapoorjee Bengallee C.I.E.* (Bombay, no date), 18.

[37] *S.L.S.S., Proceedings, 1854-55* (Bombay, 1856), 4-5; *Bombay Times*, March 4, 1858; *A Brief Account of the Framjee Cowasjee Testimonial and the Principal Correspondence Relating to the Framjee Cowasjee Institute* (Bombay, 1871); C. M. C. *The Framjee Cowasjee Institute: Its Origin, Its Work and Its Future* (Bombay, 1917), 30-1.

[38] *Bombay Times*, January 31, 1859.

the Society in August 1849.[39] On October 21, 1849, the Society opened six schools in Bombay for the education of 24 Hindu and 44 Parsi girls. The hours of instruction were at first from 7 to 10 a.m. as the work of teaching was wholly performed by volunteer tutors: members of the Society, all of whom were otherwise employed during the day, either as teachers or instructors in the Elphinstone Institution. Initially in this way, three Hindu Marathi schools were conducted for five months, and three Parsi Gujarati schools for eight months. At the close of 1850, there were 308 girls on the attendance rolls, comprising 105 Hindus and 203 Parsis. By June of 1851, a school was opened outside the Fort, for Gujarati Hindu girls, by the Hindu Buddhi-Vardhak Sabha, and was followed by a second school for the same class in 1854 within the Fort, with support from the Bania merchant Mangaldas Nathubhai (1832-90) at Rs. 200 a year. Regular classes soon followed with paid masters appointed to teach during the usual school hours, from 9 a.m. to 5 p.m. In 1851, a fourth Parsi school was also opened in the Mazagon area of Bombay, making in all nine schools for girls. In 1852, the attendance was 545 girls; and by 1855, there was an attendance of 1,087 children of both genders in the schools, including 740 girls comprising 178 Marathi-speaking Hindus, 87 Gujarati-speaking Hindus, and 475 Gujarati-speaking Parsis. By February 1856, the Society ran sixteen schools with 1,132 pupils, of which nine schools contained 654 girls.[40]

On July 4, 1857, the Society decided to transfer the management of the Parsi Girls' Schools to a provisional committee of Parsis that would undertake their future support. On March 23, 1858, the Parsi Girls' School Association was formed. The decision of the Parsis to manage their own girls' schools primarily aimed to rescue female education from a lack of funding within the Society, and appeal directly to public-spirited Parsis and the community as a whole to better maintain the schools for Parsi girls. The Parsi Girls' School Fund at the date of transfer was Rs. 9,000. By 1858, Rs. 14,763 in donations and Rs. 1,744 in annual subscriptions were raised, creating a fund of some Rs. 25,000.[41]

---

[39] *S.L.S.S., Proceedings, 1854-55*, 8.

[40] *S.L.S.S., Proceedings, 1853*, 9, 26-7; *S.L.S.S., Proceedings, 1854-55*, 11-13; *S.L.S.S., Proceedings, 1855-56* (Bombay, 1856), 43; *Bombay Times*, July 25, 1856, November 15, 20, 1858.

[41] *S.L.S.S.. Proceedings, 1856-57* (Bombay, 1860), 2; *Bombay Times*, March 31, 1858, March 10, 1859.

Notwithstanding the reformers' high hopes, the financial situation of the Parsi Girls' School Association remained tenuous in the years following its creation. At the end of 1859, the funds amounted to Rs. 37,786. Receipts for the year had amounted to over Rs. 5,800, and expenses and disbursements to Rs. 5,882. In 1860, the receipts totalled Rs. 5,256 while the expenditure amounted to Rs. 6,442. The disbursements in the last two years having exceeded income necessitated expenditure from the fund.[42] There were four schools maintained by the Association: the largest of the schools in Fort with 394 girls; one in Chunden Wady, which was conducted by a Parsi lady, with 118 girls; one in Mirza Mohla with 88 girls; and one in Mazagon with 62 girls in attendance.[43] Despite the periodic shortfalls in the yearly receipts and expenditures of the Association, it was a measure of the Parsis' commitment that the scheme for female education endured and, for many reformers, suggested its expansion.

If the steady growth of a system of Parsi education involved the growing recognition of the Parsi community's need to broaden the opportunities for advancement, the creation of the Parsi Girls' School Association indicated the intent to guide that advancement along a progressive course. In seconding the creation of the Association in March 1858, Nowrozjee Furdoonjee, the Secretary of the Parsi Girls' School Association, reflected on the logic of the course the Parsis had taken:

> Gentlemen, it is needless for me to dilate at length on the necessity, I may say, the duty of educating from childhood the female portion of our community, in imparting instruction in useful knowledge. Our ladies ought to be qualified properly to discharge their domestic and social duties, and increase the happiness of all the members of their families' previous training in reading, writing, and other acquirements, which adorn and dignify the sex. Our countrymen have already experienced the advantages of education, imparted to the male portion. Equal, nay, greater advantages will accrue from the dissemination of education amongst the female portion.... It is therefore clearly our duty to use our utmost efforts to promote the diffusion of female education and to establish well-regulated seminaries on a good and firm basis, seminaries in which Parsee girls might acquire all the accomplishments that are necessary to make them enlightened, useful, agreeable, and virtuous members of society.[44]

---

[42] *Bombay Times*, June 30, 1860, April 11, 1861.
[43] *Bombay Times*, April 2, 1859, June 30, 1860.
[44] *Bombay Times*, March 31, 1858.

For Nowrozjee Furdoonjee and the reformist Parsis the education of females was the reasonable corollary to the education of Parsi boys; and for a select few, as part of the greater goal of the emancipation of women in Indian society. Precisely those who had always regarded education as a liberating force to be encouraged and not dreaded led the push for the educational emancipation of women. The generation of Parsis who had taken to the opportunities offered by the Elphinstone Schools came to regard the adoption of female education as a necessary concomitant to the social and moral advancement of the community.

The enthusiasm for female education, however, was not universally shared. While the leading *shetias* of the community recognized the practical advantages of education for new generations of male Parsis for their advancement in Indian society, the rationale behind female education was problematic.[45] So pervasive was the initial opposition to the idea of female education by conservative and traditionalist Parsis that the progressive *shetias* educated their own daughters at home in deference to public opinion. Jamsetjee Jejeebhoy had his daughter Pirojbai educated privately at home, as did Framji Cowasji Banaji.[46] In 1842, Jamsetjee and other prominent Parsis desirous to educate their daughters in schools were chastened by the open hostility encountered by Meheribai Hormusjee Cursetjee, who was the first Parsi to send her daughter Dosabai to an English school for girls.[47]

The barriers to female education clearly demonstrated to progressive Parsis the necessity to emancipate Parsi women from the nature of their existence. The effort on behalf of female education consequently coincided with efforts to enhance the public profile of Parsi women. By mid-century, the role of Parsi women in society was in transition. Progressive Parsis challenged those practices that excluded females from their visible participation in society. For example, Hormusjee Bapoonjee Viccajee drove about with his wife in an open carriage in Surat, and sat with her on the balcony of their residence. Other Parsis, including members of the families Cama, Wadia, and Manockjee Cursetjee, followed his example.[48] Increasingly, Parsi women were seen venturing out on to the maidans or the

45 *S.L.S.S., Proceedings, 1854-55*, 17.

46 *OCS*, October 1837, 471.

47 Dosabai Cowasjee Jessawalla, *The Story of My Life* (Bombay, 1911), 41-2.

48 *Bombay Times*, October 13, 1858, May 24, 1861.

public spaces of Bombay usually in groups, and to special events; all of which led to excited comment in the newspapers as to the inevitable breakdown of public barriers for Indian women.[49] In taking up the cause of female education in the face of public opposition, the Parsi reformers demonstrated the leadership role they were assuming in influencing the social and cultural milieu of Bombay. They also evinced the leadership role they were assuming in both guiding Parsi public opinion and challenging the control of the traditional leaders over the community. The reformers had begun the process whereby the authority in the Parsi community was accelerated away from the traditionalists and any central institution, to more diffuse pockets of opinion and authority, thereby redefining the very nature of authority and social control in the community.

While traditionalist opinion remained cool to the idea of female education, nothing succeeds like example in India. It was the perseverance of the reformers in starting schools for girls and personally teaching in and operating them that commended their efforts to many Parsis within the community, including wealthy Parsi patrons, and ensured their survival. One of the first major donations in support came shortly after the girls' schools of the Students' Literary and Scientific Society opened. Kharshedji Nasarvanji Cama (1816-85), his father Nasarvanji Mancherji and his brother Dhunjibhoy Nasarvanji donated Rs. 4,800 to the managing committee of the Students' Literary and Scientific Society. The donation made it possible to extend the school hours in the Gujarati schools from initially three hours a day to a full day; and had made it possible to operate the schools for a period of two years, after which time, it was believed, the schools could attract public contributions.[50] The Cama name would often be associated, both morally and financially, with supporting the cause of reform. Among the many public bequests he made on his death in 1859, Dhunjibhoy Nasarvanji Cama left Rs. 10,000 in support of the Parsi Girls' School Association.[51]

The reformers' commitment to female education was such that in addition to their time, financial contributions were also forthcoming. Sorabjee Shapurjee Bengallee underwrote the expenses of several

[49] Wacha, *Shells*, 83 6; *Bombay Times*, February 1, 1858.

[50] *S.L.S.S., Proceedings, 1854-55*, 10-11; *S.L.S.S., Proceedings, 1856-57* (Bombay, 1860), 2; *S.L.S.S., Proceedings, 1858-59* (Bombay, 1860), 8-9; *Bombay Times*, November 15, 1858.

[51] *Bombay Times*, June 24, 27, 1859.

schools in Bombay and Gujarat, at a cost of thousands of rupees. The reformers' example moved the more wealthy Parsis to contribute their resources. In 1865, Sir Cowasjee Jehangir Readymoney underwrote the expenses of a girls' school at Khetwadi, in Bombay, which Sorabjee had supported for six years; and in 1882, Nusservanji Ratanji Tata underwrote the expenses for a girls' school in Navsari, which Sorabjee had also supported for many years. A man of modest means, Sorabjee Shapurjee Bengallee contributed Rs. 66,787, earned in investments, towards the completion of a school in Bombay in 1885, named in honour of his mother Bai Bhikaijee Shapurjee Bengallee.[52]

The contributions to Parsi schools reflected the impact the progressive idea of education had on the Parsis, and the desire on the part of the community to put their rising economic strength behind educational advancement. Attempts were also made to popularize the idea of education for girls by progressive Parsis. Annual exhibitions of the Parsi girls' schools were held by the Parsi Girls' School Association, at which time as many as 500 girls assembled to receive prizes from prominent Parsis for their educational accomplishments.[53] As a result of the efforts of the reformers, what had originally been proposed as a transfer of the management of the schools from the Students' Literary and Scientific Society to the Parsi Girls' School Association for a period of three years, was permanently under Parsi control. The success of the Association prompted Nowrozjee Furdoonjee to dare to suggest that the Parsi girls' schools would be kept up and maintained for hundreds of years.[54]

The remarks of Nowrozjee Furdoonjee on behalf of female education also reflected the affinity with Western attitudes towards the liberation of women formed by progressive Parsis. Indeed, reformist Parsi attitudes paralleled contemporary radical British attitudes on gender and progress, if not their entire agenda.[55] For many Parsis, the desire to lift women from the ignorance and intellectual lethargy they believed custom and tradition had cast them into reflected their own dissatisfaction with the moral character of their community life

[52] Bengallee, *Life of Sorabjee Shapoorjee Bengallee*, 19-20.

[53] *Bombay Times*, April 2, 1859, June 30, 1860, April 11, 1861, 55

[54] *Bombay Times*, March 31, 1858.

[55] See remarks of John Stuart Mill, Parliamentary Reform—Representation of the People Bill, Clause 4 (Occupation Franchise for Voters in Counties), May 20, 1867, *Hansard's Parliamentary Debates*, 3d ser., vol. 187 (1867), cols. 817-29.

and its effects on them. The education of girls and women was a barometer of the overall standard of community life that Parsis increasingly wanted. Whereas in the days of the Punchayet in the 1820s, the reflection of Parsi values forced strict constraints on the actions of women, twenty years later the education of women on a par with men was held by some to be the appropriate community standard. The apparent inconsistency of a community advancing in every way except the progress in women's conditions was also an intellectual contradiction reformers and new generations of Parsis were unwilling to accept. In a letter to the *Bombay Times*, K. R. Colah lamented the attitude of many Parsis to the situation of women, in terms J. S. Mill could have appreciated:

> It is surprising that, with all the talked-of energy of the Parsees, they are unable to understand and appreciate the blessings of female education, or seem content to give their daughters only the elements of knowledge.... Such rudimentary knowledge will not suffice to make their homes happy, will never place females in a position to enjoy their rights and their privileges and, will never raise them from mental degradation.... This excellent mode of argument ... will reflect the shame on the Parsee community, and particularly that portion of it which pretends to enlightenment and civilization.[56]

The educational progress of Parsi women consequently formed the yardstick for the prodigious pace of both modernization and Westernization among the Parsis. If women in some way continued to be the representation of the character of the community, their education corresponded to the desires and intentions of a growing segment of the Parsi community. The efforts of the Parsis on behalf of educating women would in fact produce some of India's first professional women. For example, Cornelia Sorabji was the first female advocate in India, and Perin Jamsetjee Mistri was the first female architect in India.[57] Heralded as the "glad harbinger of a bright dawn," the rapid pace of female emancipation, as for many in the West, became the conspicuous example of the Parsi community's resolve to remove the encrusted conservatism of the past.[58] The contradiction of what by present standards would be essentially a paternalistic outlook did not register with those pushing for the vindication of the rights of

---

[56] *Bombay Times*, May 5, 1860.

[57] See *Parsiana*, March 1991; H. D. Darukhanawala, *Parsi Lustre on Indian Soil* (Bombay, 1939), 387.

[58] Wacha, *Shells*, 688-9.

women and other rapid reform. The push for female emancipation led by men composes an interesting study in the evolution from traditional to modernist outlooks. The reformers in championing the education of women, whatever their gender, in championing the autonomy and essential worth of the human being, had effectively crossed the line from traditionalists to modernists, if somewhat oblivious to the new world they were creating.

By 1860, the proposal to introduce general English education into the schools, including for females, was openly debated among Parsis. English had increasingly become an important medium of expression for Parsis, and the principal language of expression among an elite. In 1858, the report of the Native General Library noted the decided preference educated Indians, and in particular Parsis, had for English novels and literature, with books on Oriental literature being in least request.[59] For some Parsi reformers the education of Parsi males and females in the vernacular, and particularly in the Gujarati of the Parsis, was wholly inadequate in terms of a proper education.[60] The reformer Bomanjee Cursetjee addressed many letters to the *shetias* of the community supporting English education for Parsi females. Bomanjee Cursetjee noted that the education of Parsi women, no more than Parsi men, could not proceed in a language that had no literature, and preferred that education should be in the tongue spoken by nearly the whole world. It was only through an English education, furthermore, that he believed that females among the Parsis could most effectively exert their civilizing influence on all of the Parsis.[61] His efforts, however, were opposed by Parsis who regarded the introduction of English education to females as both a chimera, given the need to remedy defects in the existing programs of the Parsi Girls' Schools, as well as absurd and cruel by Parsis sympathetic to educating girls, but doubtful as to the logic in providing an education which the social situation of females prevented them the benefits of enjoying.[62]

---

[59] *Bombay Times*, January 31, 1858.

[60] In 1859, the failure of all the Parsi students matriculating for degrees at the University of Bombay, nearly half of 128 candidates, was attributed to the unusual nature of the Parsis' Gujarati being incompatible with the test paper in Sanskritized Gujarati. See *Bombay Times*, November 2, 24, 1859. The *Rast Goftar*, November 20, 1859, blamed the failures on the incompetence of the supervision provided.

[61] *Bombay Times*, August 30, 31, 1859.

[62] *Bombay Times*, September 1, 2, 1859.

The promotion of English education among Parsi girls and women in Bombay owed its efforts to the Parsi reformers, and in particular to the figure of Manockjee Cursetjee. Manockjee Cursetjee was the son of Cursetjee Manockjee Shroff, the member of the Parsi Punchayet from 1818 to 1845. Manockjee Cursetjee's critique of the Parsi Punchayet in the *Bombay Times* from 1844 to 1845, had begun the reformist challenge to the traditionalist beliefs of the Parsis as regarded their social progress. Manockjee's public career began as assistant collector at the Bombay Customs after which he rose to the Bench, first as a Judge of the Court of Requests, and afterwards of the Bombay Small Causes Court. Among his public accomplishments, Manockjee was a member of the Royal Geographical Society, the first Indian non-resident Fellow of the Royal Asiatic Society in 1835, member of the Bombay Branch of the Royal Asiatic Society in 1839, and the first Indian member of a Masonic lodge in 1842. Despite having been rejected for initial membership in both the B.B.R.A.S. and Masonic lodges in India, it was as often in spite of such prejudice that Manockjee and other Anglophile Parsis expressed their appreciation for European ways and worked to facilitate the entry of other Indians into the societies.[63]

Manockjee Cursetjee's commitment to female education began in 1845 with the education of his daughters Cooverbai, Aimai, and Serenbai, in the vernacular and English under a governess. In educating his daughters in English, Manockjee followed the pioneering example of his cousin, Meheribai Hormusjee Cursetjee, who in 1842 was the first Parsi to send her daughter Dosabai to an English school run by Mrs. Ward. The Parsis' consternation at the actions of Meheribai led to calls for her excommunication.[64] In educating his daughters and introducing them to society and the world, Manockjee an-

---

[63] Manockjee Cursetjee, *On the Admission of Natives to Offices of Trust and Emolument Hitherto Exclusively Held by Europeans*, nos. 1-14 (Bombay, 1850), 1-9; idem, *On the Admission or Otherwise of the Natives Into Literary Institutions*, nos. 1-17 (Bombay, 1850), 1-14; *Parsee Prakash*, 1:277. Manockjee was admitted to the Masonic lodge in Paris in 1842, though he was twice rejected for admission to Masonic lodges in India. In 1843-44, Manockjee opened the Lodge Rising Star of Western India that admitted Parsis and Indians, and included all the prominent Parsis both reformist and conservative of the time as members. D. F. Wadia, *History of Lodge Rising Star of Western India No. 342 S.C.* (Bombay, 1912).

[64] *Parsee Prakash*, 4:32 (obituary); Jessawalla, *Story of My Life*, 32-3; Letter No. 24, in A Few Out of the Many Letters and Extracts of Letters, Addressed to *Manockjee Cursetjee Esq., and to Others Regarding Him; Also Selections from the Newspapers of the Day* (Bombay, 1849), 11.

swered the doubts of those who believed that it was folly to educate Parsi women in English while they had no freedom of social intercourse. Manockjee treated his daughters to the company of Bombay society, and in 1862 he took his two younger daughters to Europe with him to expose them directly to Western culture and civilization. Manockjee's sojourns with his daughters placed him among a select but growing group of Parsis who ventured abroad with their female relations, since Kavasji Rastamji Banaji had taken his wife to Calcutta with him in 1838.[65] For Manockjee, the education of women was not a prelude to an early marriage and preparation for necessarily being a wife and mother, as it was for most Parsis. Rather, it aimed to lay a foundation for self-instruction and the building of moral character as a whole. For Manockjee, the education of Indians in English schools and their exposure to English culture and values was as important to their moral improvement as to their educational advancement. Education, consequently, was the means to the Anglicization of Indians and, in Manockjee's view, the moral regeneration of India.[66]

The first English school for girls was started by Manockjee in 1859, in his house 'Villa Byculla,' with a dozen girls, and superintended by a paid English governess and Manockjee's daughters as her assistants. Manockjee's efforts earned him the praise of progressive opinion including that of J. D. Bethune, founder of the first Native Female School in Calcutta, Governor Elphinstone, as well as from an influential and wealthy Parsi like K. N. Cama.[67] In 1863, Manockjee undertook plans to obtain a permanent building for the school, contributing Rs. 5,000 on behalf of a fund for the new institution. With subscriptions and a grant of land free from the Government of Bombay, the Alexandra Native Girls' English Institution opened in 1863, named in honour of H.R.H. the Princess of Wales, Princess Alexandra of Denmark. The Institution was the first of its kind in India providing a liberal education with studies in artistic refinements. For many years the Institution suffered financial problems despite Manockjee's ingenious efforts to raise funds, including holding a charity bazaar under royal patronage in 1870. It was only by the 1880s that the Institution was placed on a viable financial

[65] M. M. Murzban, *The Parsis*, 2 vols. (1917; reprint, Bombay, 1994), 2:339-40.

[66] Manockjee Cursetjee, *A Few Passing Ideas for the Benefit of India and Indians* (London, 1862), ii, 12, 27, 51.

[67] Ibid., 11.

course. Manockjee personally contributed in total sum Rs. 25,000 in support of the Institution.[68] The Institution clearly reflected the commitment of Manockjee Cursetjee and a segment of Parsi society in support of English education. It also represented a view of modernization within the Parsi community as dependent on the adoption of Western and British values.

The efforts to provide English education to females ran parallel to those on behalf of establishing schools for Parsi boys and girls, but were not always regarded as necessarily complimentary to the latter. The inevitability of providing all Parsis, including females, with an English education was not readily acknowledged. Even the *Rast Goftar*, which was the first reformist newspaper among the Parsis, could not support Manockjee's singular views on English education for females. The *Rast Goftar* believed forsaking vernacular female education in favour of English education to be eminently liberal, yet fundamentally in error. The *Rast Goftar* noted both the residual cultural hostility of Indian society and the practical difficulties associated with schemes for female English education, including the want of English schoolmistresses, as apt to render the scheme impractical. The *Rast Goftar* further believed that the more important principle and goal of supporting the overall education of Parsis and Indians, which included females and begun by the reformers years earlier, would likely be impeded by the drive for English education.[69] The philosophy and program of Manockjee Cursetjee reflected the diversity of thought and opinion that was emerging among the Parsi reformers over the course and pace of educational reform specifically and social reform in general. Manockjee Cursetjee was unusual for the depth of his admiration for things British, as was recognized by the reformers themselves.[70] The rapid pace and prodigious extent to which some reformers sought to introduce reforms relative to others anticipated the tension and discord that was to come over Parsi identity and change.

---

[68] *The Times of India*, July 23, 1863; *Oriental Review*, March 19, 1903; Karaka, *History of the Parsis*, 1:324-8.

[69] *Rast Goftar*, February 8, 1863.

[70] *A Few Out of the Many Letters and Extracts of Letters, Addressed to Manockjee Cursetjee Esq.*, 1-2, 5-10; Letter of Nowrozjee Furdoonjee to Kaikhusrow Hormusjee, Sec. to the Parsi Law Commission, April 28, 1862, in J.D. 1863 20/143:321.

Parsi Anglophilism

The rapid and inexorable Anglicization of Parsi manners reflected the coalescence of Parsi and British values from mid-century. The depth of Anglophilism among Parsis, particularly among the educated and well-to-do, reflected the new cultural imprint that indelibly marked the Parsi character and identity. The zest for things British was reflected in a host of cultural forms the Parsis made their own. In music, sport, literature, and the desire for Western consumer goods, the Parsis adopted British taste, style, ideals, and sensibilities. The love of Western music, particularly classical music, was evident in the growing number of Parsi ladies who took violin and piano tuition, the patronage of music, and the large Parsi audiences that attended celebrated concerts in Bombay.[71] The opening of Parsi sport centres or gymkhanas, and the games Parsi men partook of reflected the cultivation of a gentlemanly taste in sports. The Bombay gymkhana opened in 1875, designed to amalgamate the various sports clubs for Europeans. The Hindu Gymkhana of Bombay opened in 1878. The Parsi Gymkhana of Bombay opened in 1888, and within twenty years a succession of Parsi Gymkhanas and athletic institutes opened across India through the donations and sponsorship of Parsis. Parsis had taken to such sports as swimming, boxing, wrestling, fencing, marksmanship, and hunting during the last quarter of the nineteenth century, and by the twentieth century were active in setting records in tennis and racket sports, and popular new sports such as cycling, roller skating, motor sports, and aeronautics. Parsi women were also equally daring in their competition. Lady Meherbai Dorab Tata played in tennis competitions in Britain and Europe in her sari, to the delight and astonishment of her audience; and Lady Serenbai Petit was the first Indian woman to fly a plane solo in 1929. Well-to-do Parsi women qualified for licences as pilots at the new aero clubs in India, and a select few competed alongside Parsi men in setting solo flight long distance records.[72]

While historically India also shaped British sporting tastes, the transmission of cultural values through sport was evident in the type and nature of the sports Parsis adopted. Well-to-do Parsis emulated

---

[71] Karaka, *History of the Parsis*, 1:329; *Bombay Times*, October 24, 1856.

[72] See multiple references in H. D. Darkhanawala, *Parsis and Sport* (Bombay, 1935).

the sporting habits of British elite culture and lifestyle. In 1845, Jamsetjee Jejeebhoy had sent a gift of four high bred Arab horses to Queen Victoria. Stables were often run by Parsis and it was a Parsi firm that imported horses from Arabia. In 1883, three gentlemen became the first Parsis to own racehorses, encouraging interest in equestrian sports among Parsis. Polo playing among very rich Parsis reflected the British enthusiasm for the sport learned in India. Sir Dinshaw Petit, the third Baronet, was the first individual to import his own team from Britain in 1933.[73]

The British influence on the Parsis was not limited to the sporting entertainments of the elite of Parsi society, as competitive sports, particularly team sports, reflected the general Parsi emulation of both British sporting values and British social values about physical and moral progress. The Parsi enthusiasm for sport on the British model was perhaps best symbolized in the commitment to the game of cricket. The Parsi shock for cricket reflected both the love of the sport coupled to its association with British social tastes. The Parsi interest in cricket was evident well before mid-nineteenth century, when the early Parsi players took part in matches dressed in traditional Indian *bandis* or pyjama suits, along with handkerchiefs tied on their heads in the Parsi style to protect them from the sun. The Oriental Cricket Club for Parsis was started in Bombay in 1848, and renamed the Zoroastrian Cricket Club in 1850. Two Parsi cricket tours went to Britain in 1886 and 1888, by then fully accoutred in traditional English cricket dress. The Parsi team did not fare particularly well, losing on both occasions; however, the aim of learning and participating in the premier British sport and national game alongside the British formed the major accomplishment of the tours. By the twentieth century, Parsi women also shared the interest in cricket, as amateur competitions were organized between Parsi men and women.[74]

The reflection of British taste was also evident in the copious accumulation of the latest British consumer goods by Parsis that their economic prosperity during the nineteenth and twentieth centuries

---

[73] Jamsetjee Jejeebhoy to David Jardine, March 15, 1845, J.J. MSS, 354; *Bombay Times*, March 29, 1859; Darukhanawala, *Parsis and Sport*, 16-17.

[74] See Darukhanawala, *Parsis and Sport*; M. K. Patel, *History of Parsi Cricket* (Bombay, 1892); J. M. F. Patel, *Stray Thoughts on Indian Cricket* (Bombay, 1905); Murzban, *Parsis*, 2:326a; J. A. Managan, *The Games Ethic and Imperialism: Aspects of the Diffusion of an Ideal* (New York, 1986), Ch. 5.

made possible. In 1809, Maria Graham described the opulent lifestyle enjoyed by the Parsi merchant-princes, as Bombay's wealthiest inhabitants and principal landholders. The Parsi *shetias* had partaken of every European luxury desirable, from their own carriages and horses, to the consumption of European liquors, to owning multiple homes, in addition to those "they let to the British."[75] In 1838, the *Asiatic Journal* noted the houses of Parsi merchants to be filled with European furniture, as befit persons in whose hands was the greater portion of the wealth of Bombay.[76] By the last quarter of the nineteenth century, a Parsi middle class had emerged. Parsi-run businesses made a steady profit in the importation and distribution of both British goods and Western-style goods in India from furniture, clothing, personal items, to vintage spirits and motor cars, as was attested to in the advertisements of the Bombay papers, and the pubication of a Parsi Trade Directory in the twentieth century.[77]

The process of Anglicization among the Parsis and contact with things British was also accelerated by the highly urbanized nature of the Parsi community of India. Parsi merchants had ventured across India, since the eighteenth century, establishing themselves as shopkeepers dealing in European articles. In 1861, "several educated Parsees in the city of Surat," had banded together to form a joint-stock company specifically aimed to introduce among the Parsis of Surat European luxury items and comforts of life, which the Parsis of Bombay had hitherto enjoyed. A particular luxury enjoyed by Parsis during the nineteenth century was the consumption of aerated water, as the new consortium was eager to import a soda water machine to Surat as soon as possible.[78]

To some extent, it may be said that the emulation of British cultural sensibilities and values was consistent with the process of assimilation and adaptation to the social environment the Parsis historically adhered to. The Parsi response was also not unusual among either Indians or other people under colonialism. The Parsis had prospered with their contact with the British, inordinately than im-

---

[75] Graham, *Journal*, 72.

[76] As reffered to in Mary Carter, "The Parsis in Bombay," *The Empire Review* 53 (1931): 129-31.

[77] *Bombay Times*, July 21, 1856, October 24, 1856; Darukhanawala *Parsi Lustre*, 605.

[78] *Bombay Times*, March 4, 1861.

plied by their numbers, and it was not unusual consequently that the British cultural model became a standard and exemplar for the Parsi desire for progress. Furthermore, British culture found an affinity with Parsis, both well-to-do and less well off, that did not purely correspond to calculations of material advancement under colonialism. In his *History of England*, Part I, in Gujarati, Jehangir Burjorjee, the then editor of the Parsi-run *Rast Goftar* newspaper, reflected his love of his subject matter, described by a reviewer as possessing an originality that is *a priori* in its favour.[79] Beyond the aping of British manners and the stereotype of colonial elites modelling themselves on the colonizers, however, the Parsi response is significant for the depth and level of its consequence for Parsi identity. The imprint of British culture on the Parsis was as profound as the Parsis' assimilation to the social influences of India in the centuries following their arrival. Indeed, the British cultural model was consistent with the Parsis' view of their future social progress.

To some extent, it may be said that those who championed rapid social reform, Westernization and Anglicization, were somewhat oblivious to the consequences to the Parsi identity. The accelerated process of Anglicization, particularly among an elite but also among Parsi society as a whole, invariably coloured Parsi self-perceptions of their social, cultural, and historical evolution and identity. The British cultural model was represented as consistent with Zoroastrian values, and at the same time stood as both ideal and aspiration of the Parsi future. The rapid cultural assimilation to British values, however, increasingly overshadowed other aspects of Parsi identity. The Anglicized education of Parsis, particularly of elite Parsi women, often outranked the value inherent in a proper general Indian education. The development of the social graces, as typified in the English girls' school, became the standard by which women were regarded as educated. The importance of Gujarati in providing a practical common language, and as an important source of cultural identity was increasingly less valued in juxtaposition to English by the Parsis in their, at times, uncritical emulation of British values, as the century progressed. Whereas in the first half of the century, the community sought to eradicate deleterious practices and influences of Indian society on Parsi women, the process of assimilation by the 1860s

[79] *Bombay Times*, April 1, 1861.

was such that the active and conscious Anglicization of the manners of refined Parsi women was encouraged and promoted.

The apish emulation of British style was not altogether unnoticed by some Parsis, whose gift for self-parody was unparalleled. Manockjee Cursetjee was a favourite target of the Parsi-run press for his Anglophilism. On one occasion, the Parsi-run *Bombay Chabook* newspaper urged the Parsis not to invite Manockjee to their parties as Manockjee had given up wearing the traditional Parsi suit, known as the *jama* and *pichoree.*[80] The pace of Anglicization by the latter nineteenth century was such that neither elements of the press nor the opposition to the education of women concerned themselves over the adoption of basically 'foreign' customs, so valued were British ways. The Parsis could ignore the potential risks associated with social change as long as they remained the agents of change, as in many respects they were in regards to economic advancement and educational progress. Self-criticism in the early decades of reform continued to serve the promotion of advancement. As the process matured, both the pace of advancement and the nature of self-criticism increasingly formed part of the debate.

2. *The Reform of Religion*

The enthusiasm with which Indians had taken to education attested to the high value that had come to be ascribed to the ideals and rationale of European thought. The speculation and questioning that the new knowledge spurred in the men of the Elphinstone Institution and other schools, guided and channelled by British teachers and scholars, would take a course unforeseen by the British, and at times astonishing to many Indians. Many Indians took to the ideals of humanism, rationalism, and liberalism to question the basis of their own beliefs and standards, and fashioned a response as engrossing to the Westerner as to the Indian.[81] As pioneers in the growth of education in Western India, the Parsis were as much the agents of social change as its beneficiaries. The exposure to the learning of Europe produced a response among Parsis both compelling in the depth of

---

[80] *Bombay Times*, April 9, 1857.

[81] See David Kopf, *British Orientalism and the Bengal Renaissance* (Los Angeles, 1969).

absorption of Western ways, and novel in its challenge to the established order.

The impact of Western rationalism and other contemporaneous thought had a tremendous effect on the Parsis, other influences, including contact with the missionaries, never did. With the introduction of the new learning and the opportunities it opened during the nineteenth century, the Parsis were offered the means to rationalize their religion in the service of their social advancement. The rejuvenation of Zoroastrianism appeared an essential task for the educated Parsi reformers. The creation of the Rahnumai Mazdayasnan Sabha or Religious Reform Association in 1851 witnessed the attempt by the reformers to re-examine and regenerate the religious tradition of the Parsis. Nowrozjee Furdoonjee started the Sabha and was its first president. Nowrozjee Furdoonjee was also the editor of the conservative Parsi-Gujarati language newspaper the *Jam-e-Jamshed* during the debates with the missionaries in the 1830s, and the first Indian assistant teacher at the Elphinstone Institution.[82] The Sabha also included a young Dadabhai Naoroji as its secretary, and was supported financially by K. N. Cama. The Sabha marked the departure of the Parsis from the intercommunity contacts with the other Elphinstonians, such as on the Gujarati Dnyan Prasarak Mandli (Society) established to discuss questions relevant to the Gujarati Parsi and Hindu students at Elphinstone, and towards a concentration on the social, cultural, and intellectual needs of the present generation of Parsis. The focus on social and religious reform concentrated the energies of the educated Indian reformers towards specific issues relevant and relative to their individual caste communities in Bombay. The creation of the Sabha and the goal of the reformers to champion and lead the cause of religious reform within their own community, at the same time, was intended to compliment the common purpose and sense of corporate identity and solidarity among the educated class of Bombay over the cause of social reform in general. The radical improvement in the social and religious conditions within a particular caste community was seen as the advancement of social progress as a whole by the reformers.

By working for reform within the confines of their community, the Parsi reformers reinforced the sense of Parsi group identity. This

[82] Wacha, *Shells*, 648.

allowed for greater cooperation between reformers and other Parsis over issues of concern to the community, including with prominent progressive Parsi *shetias* and traditionalists like M. N. Petit and Framjee Nasserwanjee Patel (1804-92). The reformers of the Rahnumai Mazdayasnan Sabha in part drew on the frustrations and uncertainties felt by generations of Parsis at the state of their religious knowledge and practices. The movement for comprehensive religious reform ostensibly reflected the general Parsi concern to strengthen Parsi identity. Unlike the traditionalists, however, who also were concerned for the Parsi identity, the new generation of reformers re-interpreted Zoroastrianism in a way that rejected all that did not meet the test of their rationalist view of the world. The emergence of the reformers reflected in educational and generational transition within the Parsi community. Thereas previous generations of Parsis employed the strength of social compulsion to safeguard and shape Parsi identity, the reformers appealed to the power of critical thinking. What previous generations held as traditional in belief the new reformers denounced as superstition and ignorance. The outlook, agenda, and approach of the Parsi reformers, consequently, marked a qualitative departure in Parsi efforts to safeguard and shape identity, and would ultimately contribute to the divide among the Parsis over the nature and pace of social reform.

The rise of the reformers marked the emergence of a modernist outlook among a segment of the Parsis in both their impression of themselves and their program of reform. The impulse of the reformers to see themselves as a new class, as much conceptually as socially, and different from all the other generations that preceded it, was evidence of the new outlook. D. E. Wacha described the reformers as "a rare professional class in those days and highly respected," while the *Rast Goftar* noted their "perseverance, and a noble self-regard of their own interests."[83] The unique contribution of the new generation of reformers at mid-nineteenth century was utilizing the new education and Western scholarship as the medium through which to effect a redefinition of identity among the Parsis. At the heart of the reformers' efforts was the desire to recapture what was regarded as the pristine nature of their religion, made evident by the scholarship into Zoroastrianism. Through their works and reasearches

[83]Ibid., 271; *Rast Goftar*, February 8, 1863.

the reformers brought about a new understanding of Zoroastrianism and the heritage of the Parsis that worked to shape how a generation of Parsis saw and defined itself.

The reformers' agenda of religious reform stemmed from their reinterpretation of the Zarathustrian achievement. The reformers regarded Zoroastrianism as a historically founded world religion that propounded a unique ethical monotheism, activist in its moral outlook while essentially voluntary in its commitment. The reformers' understanding of Zoroastrianism gave precedence exclusively to the originality of Zarathustra and his writings. The *Gāthās* constitute the only religious source directly attributable to Zarathustra. For the reformers, the *Gāthās* became the chief if not sole source of appreciating Zoroastrianism. This approach largely fragmented the Zarathustrian contribution from the larger heritage of Zoroastrianism, which the majority of Parsis espoused. The religious vision of Zarathustra, in fact, forms a complicated reinterpretation of inherited Iranian religious ideas. The contribution of Zarathustra to ancient religion was both revolutionary in its conceptualization and innovative in aspects of its observance. The religion of Zarathustra was an expression of the evolving socio-religious state of the Iranian peoples during the second millennium B.C.E.

The pantheon of the ancient Iranians and Indo-Aryans included a number of deities, which were often personifications of natural phenomena, or of social norms and institutions. The most prominent feature of ancient Iranian religion in the time of Zarathustra was the evolution of dualism. The dualism of ancient Iran at its most basic was expressed in terms of the opposition of truth (Avestan *asha*) and falsehood (*druj*) in the cosmos. A cosmological dichotomy of order and chaos emerged that came to define all aspects of myth and life. The Iranian pantheon was divided between gods and demons essentially, as symbolized by the *ahuras* and *daēvas* respectively. Under the ancient Iranian priestly class of magi, of which Zarathustra was a member, a dualistic ideology came to define the Iranian religious perspective. The pantheon of Indo-Aryan gods was simplified and reversed among the Iranians. The *ahuras* and *daēvas* emerged in contradistinction to the Vedic *asuras* and *baghas*. Early Zoroastrianism represents an original attempt to unify the diverse nature of early Iranian dualism. Under Zarathustra, Ahura Mazdā rose as principal deity and head of the *ahuras*, and symbolized truth, order, and beneficence.

A transformation in the significance of ritual also occurred under Zarathustra. Religious observance was expressed in traditional forms, though under Zarathustra the meaning had changed. The worship of the gods was performed through the central ritual called *yasna*, which in Zarathustra's time composed a religious, social, and cultural rite and festival of communion between god and man. As a priest or *zautar* (Vedic *hotar*), Zarathustra carried out the *yasna* that involved the invocation of Ahura Mazdā and his divine attributes through the medium of the fire-ritual, and included the recitation of songs, and ritual offerings, specifically of plants (*hauma*), and debatably animals. The *Gāthās* of Zarathustra expressed the hymns of praise and songs of devotion to Ahura Mazdā composed and recited on the ritual occasions. The *Gāthās* of Zarathustra reflected the continuity with an ancient tradition of divine communion through song, and the unique personal and ethical connection Zarathustra had made with ritual observance. Most significantly, the dualism of Zarathustra was marked by a strong ethical conception of humans' place in the universe. Human nature in Zoroastrianism was held to be essentially good, and humans shared with divinity the power to change the fate of the universe through their individual ethical choices in life.[84]

Notwithstanding the reformers' enthusiasm for Western scholarship, they were oblivious to the difficulties and problems associated with the attempts to characterize Zoroastrianism. The nature of the 'innovation' and 'revelation' of Zarathustra, and the connection between Zarathustra and modern Zoroastrianism continues to be debated. The modern understanding of ancient Iranian religion is dependent upon the available sources, both textual and material. The sources on historical Zoroastrianism, both indigenous and foreign, range from Achaemenian royal inscriptions and Zoroastrian religious texts, to Greek and ancient Indian Vedic literature respectively. The *Avestā* forms] the principal source of knowledge of ancient Iranian

[84] On the nature of early Zoroastrianism, see Ilya Gershevitch, "Zoroaster's Own Contribution," *Journal of Near Eastern Studies* 23 (1964): 12-38; Gherardo Gnoli, *Zoroaster's Time and Homeland: A Study on the Origins of Mazdaism and Related Problems* (Naples, 1980); Mary Boyce, *History of Zoroastrianism*, vol. 1, *The Early Period* (Leiden, 1975), Ch. 1; idem, *Zoroastrianism: Its Antiquity and Constant Vigour* (Costa Mesa, 1992), Chs. 1-4; Helmut Humbach, *The Heritage of Zarathustra: A New Translation of the Gāthās* (Heidelberg, 1994); *The New Enclyclopaedia Britannica*, 15th ed., s.v. "Middle Eastern Religions."

religion, and is a collection of a variety of texts composed by different authors over the course of Zoroastrianism's development. The extant text of the *Avestā* represents a fragment of the work compiled in the Sasanian period. The *Gāthās* constitute some seventeen songs or quasi-philosophical invocations, are the oldest part of the *Avestā*, and form part of the Zoroastrian liturgy. The *Gāthās* were originally oral works in an unrecorded Eastern Iranian language later referred to as Gāthic Avestan or Old Avestan, from the texts from which they derive; and closely resemble the language of the Indian RigVeda (second millennium B.C.E.). It is from the evidence of the *Gāthās* that the period of Zarathustra's life may be fixed between 1200 and 1000 B.C.E. Zoroastrianism as practised among the Parsis had come to be shaped by the long evolution of the religion since the time of Zarathustra. The Parsis held to the concept of a God of Good represented by the figure of Ahura Mazdā who was aided by beneficent spirits or divine manifestations of God, and who was in conflict with the lesser entity of Evil, the Lie, and Darkness, represented by the figure of Angra Mainyu or Ahriman. The Parsi reformers unequivocally represented Zoroastrianism as monotheistic to both Parsis and the world. They would affect the perception of the religion among Parsis, if not its traditional practice.[85]

The Rahnumai Mazdayasnan Sabha had begun to discuss the nature of Zoroastrianism and work towards its reform by means of public addresses and discourses, and distributing circulars and pamphlets. The reformers' view of Zoroastrianism departed from the Parsis' traditional observance of the religion, and was evident in their philosophy and agenda. The philosophy of the reformers gave precedence to the *Gāthās* of Zarathustra, attacked the inordinate and perfunctory ritualism among Parsis associated with the latter Zoroastrian period, and came to interpret Zoroastrianism as monotheistic. The reformers' agenda included: simplifying Parsi religious practices

---

[85] On the evolution of Zoroastrianism and its historiography, see A. V. W. Jackson, *Zoroaster the Prophet of Ancient Iran* (New York, 1899); Jacques Duchesne-Guillemin, *Religion of Ancient Iran*, trans. K. M. JamaspAsa (Bombay, 1973); Ilya Gershevitch, "Approaches to Zoroaster's Gathas," *Iran* 33 (1995): 1-29; Gherardo Gnoli, *The Idea of Iran: An Essay on its Origin* (Rome, 1989), 129-83; Mary Boyce, *Textual Sources for the Study of Zoroastrianism* (Manchester, 1984); Shaul Shaked, *Dualism in Transformation: Varieties of Religion in Sasanian Iran* (London, 1994); Albert de Jong, *Traditions of the Magi: Zoroastrianism in Greek and Latin Literature* (Leiden, 1997).

and rituals, as they believed rituals were neither justified in Zoroastrian religious literature nor consistent with the spirit of the message of Zarathustra; reforms to the prayers of the Parsis, including their translation into the vernacular as part of liturgy; changes to the Parsi calendar; and providing better education to priests. From their researches, the reformers came to appreciate the religion of Zarathustra anew, and sought to commend reforms to Zoroastrianism among Parsis through an educative approach. Dadabhai Naoroji denounced what he regarded as the ritual and folk practices of the Parsis, as for example the use of *nīrang* or consecrated bull's urine as an antiseptic in purificatory ritual, as unbecoming the religion.[86] Both Kharshedji Rustomji Cama and Sorabjee Shapoorjee Bengallee squarely laid the blame for the religious ignorance of the community on the priests.[87]

K. R. Cama had emerged as the pre-eminent religious reformer among the Parsis at mid-century. A member of one of Bombay's oldest and wealthiest families, K. R. Cama had studied Avestan and Pahlavi in Europe during the 1850s, and had returned to India in 1859 ready to utilize his Iranist studies in benefit of the Parsis. Cama's criticism of the priesthood bore testimony to the critical methodology he had adopted. At a lecture delivered by a Parsi priest on 'Zoroastrianism as a species of deism' in 1861, Cama criticized the priesthood for the level of scholarship it brought to intellectual discussions:

> In our days of civilisation, learning and knowledge, the Dustoor and his supporters (whoever they be) cannot so easily enchain the rising youthful minds—minds whose motto is, 'Your reasons, reasons, reasons.' Either you do worship, or you do not worship fire. If you do, then you are downright idolaters. If you do not, then you make yourselves liable of being charged with a gross and culpable inconsistency of religious belief. Here, then, are the two horns of the dilemma. Choose either, but let us by all means have a candid and open statement of your belief.[88]

To improve the state of the Parsi priesthood in 1861, Cama started a private class for priests in Avestan and Pahlavi at his residence in Bombay. By 1864, he had enlisted the support of priests and other Parsis concerned with the state of Parsi religious knowledge to open

86 Naoroji, *Manners and Customs*, 21.

87 *Bombay Times*, July 20, 1857; Bengallee, *Life of Sorabjee Shapoorjee Bengallee*, 21.

88 *Bombay Times*, March 16, 1861.

the Zarthoshti Din-ni Khol-Karnari Mandli or Society for Furthering Research on Zoroastrianism. The Society aimed to further Iranist studies, and bring together both scholars and non-academics.[89]

Significantly, the outlook of the reformers paralleled the progression of Western views on the religion of the Parsis. The reformers' general understanding of Zoroastrianism followed the growth in scholarship in religious studies over the past century, and reflected the presuppositions and beliefs of Western religious scholars. The reformers took account of the latest philological researches, which in the nineteenth century were seen as key to understanding the ancient texts, and followed the latest debates over the nature of Zoroastrianism. The most significant debate in nineteenth century research into Zoroastrianism was whether to regard the religion as monotheistic. Since the eighteenth century when European contact with the Parsis began, the perception within Enlightenment scholarship was to regard Zoroastrianism as a dualism. The earliest European scholarly attempt to study Zoroastrianism began with the work of the Oxford professor of Arabic and Latin, Thomas Hyde, in 1700. Hyde represented Zoroastrianism a moral or ethical dualism, and greatly influenced the Western perception of the religion.[90] In 1758, the Frenchman Abraham-Hyacinthe Anquetil Du Perron, 23, employed at the Bibliotheque du Roi in Paris, was the first European scholar to meet with the Parsis of Surat, including the priests, observe their practices and obtain valuable Zoroastrian manuscripts. He procured copies of the *Vendīdād Sade*, *Vendīdād* in Pahlavi (Middle Persian) and Zend (Middle Persian Interpretation or Exegesis), and a volume of Yasna (liturgy) and *Yashts Sade* in Zend and Sanskrit. Du Perron's appreciation of Zoroastrianism led him to see the religion as a dualism.[91] By the middle of the nineteenth century, with the accumulation of the textual sources on Zoroastrianism, the debate over the nature of

[89] J. J. Modi, *A Glimpse Into the History and Work of the Zarthoshti Din-ni Khol-Karnari Mandli* (Bombay, 1922), 10. Other seminaries at mid-century included: the Mulla Firoze Madressa (1854), and the Sir Jamsetjee Jejeebhoy Madressa (1863).

[90] Jacques Duchesne-Guillemin, *The Western Response to Zoroaster* (Oxford, 1958), 1-19; P. J. Marshall, *The Great Map of Mankind: British Perceptions of the World in the Age of Enlightenment* (London, 1982), 12.

[91] *Parsee Prakash*, 1:23; K. E. Kanga, trans., *Extracts from the Narrative of Mons. Anquetil Du Perron's Travels in India* (Bombay, 1876); J. J. Modi, *Anquetil du Perron and Dastur Darab* (Bombay, 1916); Arthur Waley, "Anquetil-Duperron and Sir William Jones," *History Today* (January 1952): 23-33.

Zoroastrianism grew. The writings of Zarathustra were considered of particular importance, and it was from them that a new generation of scholars sought to trace the evolution of the religion.[92] The German Iranist Martin Haug was the first to articulate Zoroastrianism as a monotheistic religion in lectures and writings while in India from 1859 to 1866. The interpretation of Zarathustra offered by Haug placed Zarathustra in the company of the other great religious prophets who had reformed pre-existing traditions to create a new world faith. From a philological analysis of the *Gāthās*, Haug characterized Zarathustra as a great reformer and "civilizing instructor" to the Eastern Iranian tribes and peoples. Zarathustra had championed a great reform of the older Vedic religious forms practised by the Aryan peoples in India and Iran that ostensibly dispensed with polytheistic forms, and refashioned Zoroastrianism to resemble an ethical monotheism. Ahura Mazdā was declared the supreme godhead, from which emanated the twin sources of good and evil; and from which humanity was to actively choose the path to follow in life. Haug's praise of Zarathustra as "one of the greatest men who ever lived and as one of the benefactors of mankind," and his denunciation of the system Zarathustra encountered, also gave to Haug's scholarship a strong value judgement, and that would characterize the subsequent debate over the nature of Zoroastrianism.[93]

---

[92]The understanding of Zoroastrianism has been affected by the evolution, transformation, and fragmentation of the religion and its sources during its long history. During the first Persian Empire of the Achaemenids (c. 550-330 B.C.E.), the religion came to be adopted alongside other religious forms by the different tribes and peoples of Iran. The conquest of the Persian Empire in 330 B.C.E., by Alexander of Macedon destroyed many of the textual sources on Zoroastrianism. Zoroastrianism survived the Macedonian conquest and the periods of Seleucid (*c.* 312-140 B.C.E.) and Parthian (*c.* 141 B.C.E.-224 C.E.) rule. During the Sasanian Empire (*c.* 224-651 C.E.) Zoroastrianism revived as the state religion. All the extant religious sources at that time were canonized and committed to writing, coalescing the various traditions over the centuries into a larger tradition; a tradition that was distinguished by conservatism and ritualism. With the fall of the Sasanian Empire in 651 C.E., to the Muslim Arabs, Zoroastrianism became a minority religion surviving from generation to generation among its followers until the Parsis settled in India. See Mary Boyce, *History of Zoroastrianism*, 3 vols. (1975, 1982, 1991); Ehsan Yarshater, ed., *The Cambridge History of Iran: The Seleucid, Parthian, and Sasanian Periods* 3 (2) (Cambridge, 1983); Martin Schwartz, "The Religion of Achaemenian Iran," in *The Cambridge History of Iran*, vol. 2, ed. Ilya Gershevitch (Cambridge, 1985), 664-97.

[93] Report on "Lecture on Origin of Parsee Religion," by Martin Haug to the United Service Institution, Poona, in *Bombay Times*, March 28, 1861; Martin Haug,

The lectures and writings of Haug had a tremendous influence on the Parsi reformers who clung to them as a vindication of Zoroastrianism from the 'taint' of dualism. The Parsi reformers' emulation of the West largely informed their response to Zoroastrianism and the Parsi heritage. The compulsion to defend Zoroastrianism from the charge of being a dualism represented a reaction to the comparison of Zoroastrianism with the Judaeo-Christian religious tradition. The early Parsi reformers adhered to the judgement prevalent in nineteenth century Western circles that viewed monotheism as the most advanced stage of religious theology. Haug's message also found accord with those Parsis long dissatisfied with traditional observance and worship. The call to simplify and reform the observances and rituals of the Parsis found validation in the interpretation of Zoroastrianism associated with Haug. The reformers' reliance on the early European scholarship into Zoroastrianism, however, ignored the limitations of this analysis. Haug's interpretation, based strictly on a philological approach, essentially was unfamiliar with the religious literature on Zoroastrianism subsequent to the writings of Zarathustra, was indifferent to the religious practices of the Parsis as relevant to the nature of Zoroastrianism, and freely interpreted the legacy of Zarathustra with contemporary Western presuppositions in mind.[94] The reformers were also dismissive of the efforts the Parsis had made to preserve their heritage, including the priesthood, and that had benefited the evolution of Western scholarship.[95] The works of Haug and the Parsi reformers had elevated anew the religious legacy of the Parsis only to disturb what had always been the traditional approach to the Parsis' religion, as the Parsis were assumed to have convoluted the religious message and practice of the prophet they so venerated.[96] Subsequent scholarship into the secondary Zoroastrian

---

Essays on the Sacred Language, Writings and Religion of the Parsis (London, 1884), 300.

[94] Mary Boyce, "The Continuity of the Zoroastrian Quest," in Man's *Religious Quest*, ed. W. Foy (London, 1978), 603-19; idem, *Zoroastrians: Their Religious Beliefs and Practices* (London, 1979), 202-3; Firoze K. Kotwal, "The Authenticity of the Parsi Priestly Tradition," *Journal of the K. R. Cama Oriental Institute* 45 (1979): 24-33; Edward Said, *Orientalism* (New York, 1985), 132.

[95] On the impressions of the Parsi priesthood, and its efforts on behalf of maintaining Parsi tradition, see Graham, *Journal*, 36-7; William Ouseley, *Travels in the East More Particularly Persia* (London, 1813), 98-9; Mario Vitalone, *The Persian Revayat 'Ithoter': Zoroastrian Rituals in the Eighteenth Century* (Naples, 1996), 14-16.

[96] *Bombay Times*, March 28, 1861.

texts would both challenge the Haug interpretation of Zoroastrianism and reveal the complexity of characterizing the nature and evolution of Zoroastrianism. Towards the end of the nineteenth century, translations of the Pahlavi literature by E. W. West, and of the *Avestā* by James Darmesteter, began the process of examining all the literature associated with Zoroastrianism in the debate over its evolution. Both men consulted with the Parsis and re-examined the new literature in light of the Parsis' practices.

The movement for religious reform remained a potent force within the Parsi community affecting the perception of the religion among the Parsis. The early movement for religious reform was a measure of the extent to which the Parsis had taken to the introduction of education by mid-century. As the scholarship into Zoroastrianism progressed and matured, particularly in the twentieth century, competing assessments of the exact nature of Zoroastrianism emerged among the Parsis, and a plurality of opinion emerged between reformers, traditionalists and orthodox as to the necessity and extent of religious reform among the Parsis.

Continuity and Discontinuity

The rise of the Parsi reformers at mid-century had marked a fundamental change in the perception of community and social progress among a segment of the Parsis. At the same time, the reform movement conformed to the pattern of cultural adaptation and accommodation characteristic of the history of the Parsis in India. The reform movement of the Parsis continued the process of redefining the Parsi identity in relation to the Parsis' surroundings. It strengthened identity from within the community by confirming the uniqueness of Parsi identity, while also accommodating identity to contemporary social influences. The new scholarship into Zoroastrianism exposed for the reformers the uniqueness of the religion of the Parsis, while offering them the ability to reshape Parsi identity in the contemporary milieu. A century previously, the Parsis had utilized the Punchayet and its mechanisms to shape community identity and accommodate themselves to the new social milieu of Bombay under British rule. By mid-nineteenth century, the Parsi reformers through the power of their education emerged as a new centre of authority within the Parsi community.

The emergence of the reformers as a new centre of authority within the Parsi community disguised the similarity of historical response between reformers and previous generations of Parsis over Parsi identity. The characterizations of the Parsis and their religion by the reformers, moreover, reflected the extent of their assimilation and socialization to the contemporary Western intellectual milieu, and how British and Western traits and values came to overwhelmingly influence and colour Parsi perceptions of their identity. The reformers adhered to the idea of the Parsis as more resembling genuine Europeans than any other caste in India.[97] The exposition of Zoroastrianism as a monotheistic, non-idolatrous, tolerant, and ethical religion, inferentially in contrast to the European perception of Hinduism or Islam, on the part of the reformers, illustrated a historical imperative at work.[98] From mid-century, a new generation of educated Parsi reformers came to represent themselves and their religious heritage within and without the Parsi community. K. R. Cama revealed what he held to be the unique nature of the religion to an audience of Parsis and non-Parsis. Similarly, Dadabhai Naoroji utilized the interest in the history of the Parsis to promote understanding of the culture of Indians as a whole among the British, while working for political reform in Britain.[99]

In representing themselves as a new class and generation, the Parsi reformers confirmed the social evolution the Parsis had undergone over the course of a century. The strength of the reformers lay in the articulation of the general dissatisfaction with the state of knowledge in the community, and the rationale behind its amelioration in the new cultural setting of mid-century India. Their leadership as well as moral authority emanated from their own successful educational elevation. Fundamentally, however, the reformers continued

---

[97] Walter Hamilton, *East-India Gazetteer,* vol. 1 (Delhi, 1828), 610.

[98] Zoroastrianism's historical influence on the Judaeo-Christian tradition is significant and compelling. On the Zoroastrian influence on Judaism, see John R. Hinnells, "Zoroastrian Influence on the Judaeo-Christian Tradition," *Journal of the K. R. Cama Oriental Institute* 45 (1976): 1-23. A comparison of the two traditions is provided in Jacob Neusner, *Judaism and Zoroastrianism at the Dusk of Late Antiquity: How Two Ancient Faiths Wrote Down Their Great Traditions* (Atlanta, 1993).

[99] See K. R. Cama, *A Discourse on the Mithraic Worshp and Rites and Mysteries Connected With It: Delivered at the Freemasons' Jamshedi Naoroz Festival, Scottish Masonic Hall* (Bombay, 1876); Naoroji, *Manners and Customs,* 21-3.

the historical pattern of strengthening the sense of Parsi identity while adapting in response to contemporary influences. Both the novelty of their approach and the constraints of their outlook, it may be argued, shaped the movement for social and religious reform into a formidable social phenomenon.

The mutuality of interests among reformers and other Parsis was in evidence at various times at mid-century over issues that related to safeguarding Parsi identity. The concern for the fate of the Zoroastrians of Iran was an issue that united Parsi efforts at mid-century. The Zoroastrian community of Iran had retained for the Parsis wonderment over the centuries. The Parsis' fascination for the ancient Iranian past belied the tremendous transformation the Parsis of India had undergone in the nineteenth century in relation to their ancestral land. The Parsis had welcomed waves of Iranians coming to India over the centuries, where the latter had come to be known as Iranis within the Parsi tradition. By the middle of the nineteenth century, the reversal in the fortunes of the two communities moved the Parsis to seek aid and redress for their co-religionists in Iran. In 1853, the Society for the Amelioration of the Condition of the Zoroastrians in Persia was established along with a relief Fund, under the leadership of M. F. Panday. Merwanji Framji Panday was a pioneer of the cotton industry in Bombay, and member of a prominent family whose mother and relations were refugees from the persecution in Iran. In 1854, the businessman Manekji Limji Hataria (1813-90) went to Iran as emissary of the Parsis and the Persian Zoroastrian Amelioration Society to report on the condition of the Iranian Zoroastrians. During an eventful stay principally near the centres of Yazd and Kerman, Hataria noted the debilitating restrictions and covert persecution that the Zoroastrian community of Iran was subject to. Providing material funds when and where he could to relieve the distress of his fellow Zarthosti in Iran, Hataria thereupon returned to Bombay with the knowledge of what the new world needed to come to the aid of the old.[100]

The Persian Zoroastrian Amelioration Society was a unique manifestation over a common cause as it combined the leadership energies of reformers such as Nowrozjee Furdoonjee, Dadabhai Naoroji and K. N. Cama, and conservative Parsis such as M. N. Petit, the

[100] Mary Boyce, "Manekji Limji Hataria in Iran," in *K. R. Cama Oriental Institute Golden Jubilee Volume* (Bombay, 1969), 19-31.

Society's president, Rustom N. Wadia (1876-1919), and Muncherjee M. Bhownaggree (1851-1933) alike, and was supported by all the Parsis. Determined to bring about material change in the condition of the Iranians, the Society pursued a strategy to utilize the capital and influence of the Parsis in the cause. In addition to providing material relief and reconstruction for the Iranians, the Society was dedicated to removing all forms of persecution visited on them, including the invidious Islamic *jaziya* or head tax on the Zoroastrians. From 1857 to 1882, a campaign was waged by the Parsis that including sending deputations to Iran. In 1857, M. L. Hataria secured an audience before the Shah of Persia through the auspices of Sir Henry Rawlinson, the British Ambassador at Teheran, which resulted in a reduction in the tax. In 1873, reformers and *shetias* such as Nowrozjee Furdoonjee, Dadabhai Naoroji, Ardaseer Cursetjee Wadia and Dr. Rastamji Kavasji Bahadur met in London to present the Shah with a gold leaf memorial. It was not until 1882 that a second petition by the Parsis secured a royal *firman* abolishing the tax.[101]

The efforts of the Parsis on behalf of the Iranian Zoroastrians marked a historic change in the relationship between the diaspora and ancestral communities. The Bombay Parsis had effectively assumed the leadership of the world Zoroastrian community as they had over the Parsis of India two centuries earlier. The efforts on behalf of the Iranians equally highlighted how far the Parsis had progressed from their co-religionists, and their past. By dint of their wealth, power and influence, and education the Parsis found more in cooperation with their British friends in support of the Iranians than in the pathetic existence of the latter. The efforts of the Persian Zoroastrian Amelioration Society were led by many reformers, though supported and in sympathetic alliance with all levels of Parsi society. The efforts of the Parsis on behalf of the Iranians underscored the ability of the Parsis of India to unite to bring about change well outside their geographical confines. Yet, the same energies and passions that could unite in a cause continued to divide over a cause.

As much as the reform movement may be said to have been consistent with the process of adaptation and accommodation the Parsis had historically adhered to, the reform movement equally represented discontinuity in that process. The works and the philosophy of

---

[101] *Parsee Prakash*, 1:659-62; Karaka, *History of the Parsis*, 1:71-81; Murzban, *Parsis*, 1:132-4.

the reformers exposed a gulf between Parsis over how to regard their heritage and its future disposition. The religious reform movement had in fact introduced heterodoxy to the Parsi religious tradition. This in turn witnessed the rise of a traditionalist and orthodox reaction to change. The tendency toward schism was a periodical feature in Parsi history; however, past disputes had not fundamentally come to affect Parsi identity.[102] The consequences of the agenda of the reformers on the Parsi community were more profound. For the first time, orthodoxy and heterodoxy of religious outlook and identity among the Parsis emerged as a result of the movement for religious reform. Both orthodox and heterodox outlooks existed within the one Parsi tradition, introducing a tension to Parsi identity. 'Orthodoxy' came to define a segment of opinion, and a minority of articulated opinion among the Parsis. While all Parsis were of one mind in identifying themselves as Parsi, the exact definition and nature of that identity became a matter of debate. By the twentieth century, various religious perspectives ranging from reformist, progressive, traditionalist, conservative, orthodox and ultra-orthodox outlooks, philosophies, and ideologies distinguished the debate over identity within the Parsi community.

The emergence of a heterodox religious outlook within the Parsi community, coexisting alongside traditional and orthodox outlooks, reflected the extent to which the reform movement had come to challenge traditional authority without being able to completely supplant it. In the past, heterodoxy had been either expunged from the community, or had voluntarily removed itself from the religious concerns of the community through disinterest and disaffection. The educational and social abilities of the Parsi reformers of the nineteenth century afforded heterodoxy the ability to remain in the community and effect reappraisals within it. On the other hand, the heterodox nature of the reformers prevented them from defining the

[102] The *behdin/mōbad* dispute of the eighteenth century was the last time a schism had emerged. It had been resolved largely by the process of material change initiated with the arrival of the Parsis in Bombay. See Chapter One. The greatest dispute among the Parsis arose over the Parsi calendar. The division of the commuity into *Qadimi* and *Rasmi* or *Shāhānshāhi* sects became permanent. However, with the exception of the observance of the Parsi New Year at different times, and some differences in the marriage ritual between the two sects, the dispute had not irreparably divided the Parsi community. See Introduction.

community exclusively. It was a measure of the commitment of the reformers to Parsi identity that they remained active in the interests of the Parsi community. To some extent, the reformist and orthodox philosophies were removed from the regular religious concerns and activities of the majority of Parsis, while, at the same time, their presence exacerbated contentious issues within the community without being able to bring about a resolution.

The education and scholarship of the reformers consequently had both encouraged and constrained their authority within the Parsi community. Their research and scholarship on Zoroastrianism made the movement for religious reform imperative, while their scholarly perspectives equally limited the extent to which they could claim the adherence of the entire community. The reformers' achievement lay in initiating a much needed and valuable investigation of Zoroastrianism among the Parsis. The early movement for religious reform, moreover, sought to revive the spiritual character of the religion of the Parsis. To make the religion intelligible, relevant, and spiritually satisfying to the adherent and the observer composed an enterprise in the best spirit of the greatest religious reformer of the Parsis, Zarathustra himself. The understanding of Zoroastrianism the reformers contributed to remains the basic perception of the religion as adhered to by progressive Parsis today, and has in some form affected every Parsi.

The movement for religious reform, however, demanded changes to the religion of the Parsis that had as much to do with conforming to the reformers' social view of themselves as modernists as it did with purifying religion in the name of faith. The risks and ironies inherent in any such enterprise escaped the reformers. The same spirit that sought to utilize scholarship in the true imitation of Zarathustra was oblivious to the potential difficulties in basing a viable theology on the very philosophical and esoteric works of Zarathustra alone; and this was made evident with the progression of scholarship on the works of Zarathustra. The same spirit that sought to reform the prayers and liturgy of the Parsis away from the Avestan language, which is unintelligible to Parsis, obscured the genius of the Zarathustrian innovation in reforming the ancient and sacred Vedic tongue. By the twentieth century, as reformist thought broadened under the influence of modernity, a segment of reformist thought tended toward outright agnosticism. As J. H. Moulton noted, the creed of the reformers aimed to satisfy the intellect but paid insufficient attention to the needs of the heart.[103]

While the reformers were not devoid of heart, their philosophy at times was more consonant with an intellectual pursuit than a religious quest that addressed the religious needs of the average Parsi. Religion within the limits of reason alone might have appealed to the intellectual cousins of Kant, but only added further disunity to a religious tradition distinguished by historical fragmentation. The rise of other philosophies within the reformist ranks such as Unitarianism and Freemasonry seems to attest to the possibility that Zoroastrianism, including in its most pristine interpretation, was not altogether a sufficient worldview for some reformers. Having reduced God to an idea like any other, religion as a way of life becomes but one philosophy of life.

Perhaps the complete diffusion of control over religious outlook among the Parsis can be seen in the effects the agenda of the reformers had on orthodoxy. The creation of the Sabha of the reformers had produced an orthodox response in the creation of the Rahe Rastnumai Zarathustrian Sabha or the True Zoroastrian Way, started by Mancherji Hormasji Cama (1815-94). The Sabha's newspaper was the *Suryodaya* or Sunrise, of 1863.[104] While the orthodox initially did not dispute the efficacy of the new learning, and encouraged the advancement of education, they strenuously objected to the use the reformers put it to. The advocates of orthodoxy centred their arguments on an appeal essentially to tradition. In the observance of traditional theology, liturgy, ritual, and practice of the religion, the orthodox believed Zoroastrianism as adhered to by the Parsis over the centuries to have preserved the identity of the Parsis. The arguments of the reformers, however, in addition to making it incumbent on the orthodox to explain their stance, moved them to entertain various ideological and intellectual movements in defence of their stance. The spread of Theosophical ideas among the orthodox by the late nineteenth century illustrates this phenomenon.

The Theosophical Society was started in New York City in 1875, under the direction of Colonel Olcott and Madame H. P. Blavatsky. By the 1880s, many Parsis were drawn to the appeal of the Society with its claim to being able to open hidden, gnostic truths, and the

---

[103] J. H. Moulton, *The Treasure of the Magi* (London, 1917), 175.

[104] Kulke, *The Parsees in India*, 96.

esoteric meaning of life, including through the teachings of Zoroaster. In actuality, the Theosophists proposed an eclectic mix of Hindu and Buddhist philosophies, which included a belief in transmigration, reincarnation, yoga, and various mystical practices. The Theosophists attracted those Parsis who believed Theosophy offered a sympathetic view of the teachings of Zoroaster based on Western scholarship, while less literal and rationalist in its vision of the world than that of the reformers. In opposition to the "dry-as-dust grammarians" among the philologists, Theosophy exalted the use of ritual and ceremony, and employed allegory and fanciful reinterpretations of Zoroastrian texts and history that appealed to orthodox Parsis.[105]

The agenda of the Theosophists owed more to a mystical than scholarly appreciation of Zoroastrianism. Theosophy presented a muscular philosophy that eclectically drew on the points of other faiths and systems. The progress and appeal of Theosophical ideas to some Parsis, including a segment of the orthodox community, evinced the change religious opinion among the Parsis had undergone. The orthodox accepted the arguments of a movement outside the community and essentially outside the tradition, while unwilling to accept the proposals of the Parsi reformers. Orthodox Zoroastrian values defended by Theosophy included: the faith in the mystical and magically efficacious power of prayer in Avestan; a defence of dualism that was couched in the language of pseudo-scholarship; as well as a defence of one of the oldest folk practices of the Parsis, of isolating women during their period, so as to prevent ritual pollution.[106] The adherence to Theosophy on the part of some Parsis continued the debate among the Parsis over the nature of Zoroastrianism. While for some Parsis Theosophy complimented basic Zoroastrian beliefs and practices, for other Parsis it represented a system very much against the fundamental nature of Zoroastrianism.

The plurality of religious opinion that emerged within the Parsi community by mid-nineteenth century, then, marked a change in the character of the community and the identity of the Parsis. Without having completely transformed traditional religious opinion, the reformers effected a change in the basic perception of the religion of

---

[105]H. P. Blavatsky, "Zoroaster in 'History' and Zarathustra in the Secret Records," in H. P. Blavatsky: *Collected Writings, 1881-82*, vol. 3 (Wheaton, Ill., 1968), 449-57; M. N. Dhalla, *History of Zoroastrianism* (1938; reprint Bombay, 1963), 504.

[106]Dhalla, *History of Zoroastrianism*, 502-5.

the Parsis within the community, unprecedented in so short a time. A true plurality of opinion and outlook emerged within what had been an insular, minority community. The Parsis' dilemma in part lies in their self-perceptions, the result of their history in India. With the dislocation of tradition from Iran to India, the one constant in the history of the Parsis in India has been their ability to adapt. The Parsis have had to define themselves in juxtaposition to their social environment for so long, while safeguarding the sense of their exclusiveness that Parsi identity has taken on different layers. The experiences of the Parsis in the British period added yet another, and more weighty, layer to that identity. Throughout their history, the Parsis' desire to preserve their identity has been coupled to the need to expand the capacities of the whole environment. Having turned historical adversity into the virtue of directing social change to their advantage, the Parsis have relied on change, of varying degrees, to define themselves.

Amidst divisions among the Parsis, the mutuality of concern for Parsi identity underlies Parsi actions. Orthodox and reformist segments of the community each claim a part of the definition of what it is to be called Parsi, and recognize the contributions of the other to Parsi identity. The orthodox must acknowledge the achievements of those Parsis who have so changed and shaped the modern Parsi community, and the reformers can no less abandon the heritage passed down to them. While the intensity of language and debate has often obscured their affinities, the mutuality of interest and concern between reformers and orthodox has historically and will continue to be evinced over many issues of concern to the Parsis of India.

3. *The Growth of Parsi Opinion*

The Parsi-run Press

The growth of intellectual opinion in the nineteenth century, and the contest for reform among the Parsis was in large measure conducted in the press of the day. As with the drive for economic power and the rise of educational institutions, the creation of a newspaper press owed much to the efforts of the Parsis themselves. The rise of a vernacular press among the Parsis owed to the need to shape opinion in support of cultural identity. From mid-century, the press formed the vehicle through which a plurality of opinion within the Parsi community emerged and shaped the Parsis' cultural outlook. The credit for establishing the earliest printing press in India goes to the Portuguese in the middle of the sixteenth century. In 1678, the Kapol Bania Bhimji Parrack introduced the first printing press in Western India with the aid of European printers. In 1778, Rustom Caresajee started his own press, and in 1780 printed the first English calendar in Bombay, crediting the Parsis with establishing the first indigenous printing press in Western India.[107]

While paralleling the establishment of educational opportunities and institutions, the beginnings of the newspaper press in Western India marked the development of a culture of opinion independent of the realm of the academies. The early press appealed to educated opinion and drew on the talents of the newly educated, but was early on shaped by its own needs and constraints. The Parsis' need for a printed calendar gave a cultural consistency to the symbols and iconography of traditional Parsi society. As with economic development and educational progress, then, in the acquisition of the tools of printing lay the answer to the Parsis' need to control their social environment in the service of their identity. If, however, printing was utilized in support of traditional life, the rapid rise of the vernacular press equally responded to the need to channel the rapid pace of social change in their favour. In 1797, B. J. Chapgar moulded the first Gujarati type and by 1812, Fardoonji Marzban (1787-1840) set up his Parsi printing press. Marzban's press produced a Parsi calendar in Gujarati script two years later, and a *Khorda Avestā* prayer book in Gujarati script some years after that. By 1822, Fardoonji established the *Bombay Samachar* signalling the Parsis' entry into vernacular journalism.[108]

The *Bombay Samachar* was the first vernacular journal in the Bombay Presidency and only the second vernacular paper to be published in India. It appeared some thirty years following the first attempt at English-medium newspaper journalism in Bombay in 1789, and some nine years after the beginning of the first English-medium newspaper in India in Calcutta. In 1832, Bal Shastri Gangadhar Jambhekar started the first Anglo-Marathi newspaper the *Bombay*

[107] J. R. B. Jeejeebhoy, "A Historical Survey of Bombay Journalism," in *Jam-e-Jamshed Centenary Volume* (Bombay, 1932), 274.

[108] Ibid., 279.

Durpan, and in 1840 started the Marathi language monthly *Dig Durshan*.[109] By 1849, there were five Parsi-run Gujarati papers in existence. The Parsi-run vernacular press in Gujarati had begun as an attempt to provide a practical and useful organ for the benefit of Bombay Indian society parallel to British standards of public discourse. The rapid rise of a Parsi-run press reflected the ability of Parsis to absorb those standards and make them their own. The *Samachar* represented the perfect mix of independent indigenous action and British intellectual influence in Indian society. It began its existence as a weekly, at a subscription of two rupees a month. The *Samachar* provided a readable mix of world and Indian digest, commercial, legal, and social news, and advertisements and announcements to Bombay society. Often referred to as the merchants' paper, the *Samachar* utilized the most basic and innocuous of subject matter to instruct and guide Indian reading opinion. The paper's declared aim was to foster and build up a thoughtful reading public, highlighting the new responsibility that journalism felt itself called on to perform: "With a view, therefore, to secure in the near future for our readers as easy comprehension of some such topics as our people are at present generally ignorant of, we propose from the very beginning to trace their spring and fountain."[110] Its style was a reflection of its perceived role in the life of the city.

The *Samachar* was equally committed to utilizing the vernacular medium to the benefit of as large a Gujarat-reading Indian public as possible. The *Samachar* reflected, in a literary medium, the positive social changes the cosmopolitan mixture of elements had made for the growth and prosperity of Bombay society. The *Samachar* standardized the Gujarati in its columns to be intelligible to both Parsis and Hindus, unfamiliar with the idiomatic nature of each other's Gujarati.[111] Despite being a Parsi-run newspaper, the *Samachar* avoided any staunch political or communal opinion. A clear intellectual outlook, however, was evident in the high regard for British values as well as the journalist's commitment to the concept of the freedom of the press, from the first edition of July 1, 1822.[112] The ambiguous relationship between the vernacular press and the British

---

[109] J. C. Masselos, *Towards Nationalism* (Bombay, 1974), 31.

[110] R. P. Karkaha, "Article II—The Oldest Paper in India: The Bombay Samachar," *Calcutta Review* 106 (1898): 224.

[111] Ibid., 225.

[112] Ibid., 224, 229.

authority also revealed the steady commitment of the early editors to their metier.[113] In the first ten years of his stewardship, Fardoonji Marzban had formulated a journal of opinion loyal in its affiliation and independent in expressing the concerns of its readership. In championing the freedom of the press, the Parsi-run press had evinced the suitability of an independent press to India. Indeed, the professionalism of the *Samachar* commended the *Bombay Times* to recommend a survey of the vernacular papers by the English language Bombay press.[114] Ironically, for all the British qualms over the rise of the early press, particularly the vernacular press, it was the inward eye of criticism that emerged and not a widespread criticism of government. Meeting the needs of its reading audience, the *Samachar* became one of India's oldest newspapers. In executing rather modest measures, the *Samachar* made a novel statement in regards to the role of the press in the intellectual climate of early nineteenth century Bombay, and the role of the Parsis in Bombay society.

The Parsis had begun to express their opinions in print soon after the beginnings of a newspaper press in Bombay. When some of the early reforms of the Punchayet were canvassed and later promulgated in the first decades of the nineteenth century, exchanges of opinion appeared in print in the second English-medium paper in Bombay, the *Bombay Courier*.[115] The inception of the *Samachar* provided opportunity to express Parsi opinion in Gujarati. As an emerging leader of opinion in the Parsi community, Fardoonji Marzban supported the gradual progress of reform among the Parsis. Of priestly background, Mobad Fardoonji supported the elimination of superstitious and non-Zoroastrian practices among the Parsis, and advocated the improvement of religious education in the *Samachar*. The *Samachar* sought to reflect the changes in early nineteenth century Parsi life, while not being overwhelmed by them. The *Samachar* sought to foster consensus within the Parsi community as to the need to periodically update tradition in the service of a strong

---

[113] B. M Sankhdher, *Press, Politics, and Public Opinion in India: Dynamics of Modernization and Social Transformation* (New Delhi, 1984), 109; R. P. Karkaria, "Article III—The Revival of the Native Press of Western India: The *Rast Goftar*," *Calcutta Review* 107 (1898): 226.

[114] *Bombay Times*, January 7, 20, 1857.

[115] J. R. B. Jeejeebhoy, "Communal Discipline Among the Bombay Parsees in Olden Times," in *M. P. Kharegat Memorial Volume*, vol. 1 (Bombay, 1953), 298.

community.[116] In the 1830s, Fardoonji Marzban supported the reform of the Parsi Punchayet in the interests of the institution and the Parsis.[117] By the 1830s, other vernacular newspapers controlled and dominated by the Parsis were quickly evolving a more distinct opinion, often dedicated less in support of traditional society and more to the cause of social satire and criticism.

In 1830, Nowroji Dorabji Chandaru started the weekly *Mumbai Vartman*, which in 1832 became the *Hulkaru and Vartman*, and in 1833 became the *Chabook* or 'Whip'. The *Chabook* exposed the peccadilloes of the Parsis, especially the upper classes. Less a reformist journal than a tabloid with a gift for cynicism, its comment was unequalled among the Parsis at the time. Its emergence reflected the decline of traditional deference and the rise of ambivalence and angst of public opinion amidst changes in society. Nowroji Dorabji was also the creator of the *Bombay Free Press* in 1835. Under Nowroji Dorabji, the *Chabook* was an unflinching opponent of the Parsi Punchayet of the time, which afforded the paper an unceasing theme for sarcasm and abuse. Nowroji Dorabji often characterized the Punchayet as remarkable more for the imbecility of its members than for their exertions for the good of the community.[118] The *Chabook*, however, was equally vigilant in opposing hypocrisy and corruption of any kind that aimed to disadvantage the people. Nowroji exposed one of Bombay's largest criminal cliques in 1843, known as the Bunder Gang. For twenty years, this conspiracy of some 300 persons had amassed a fortune through crime, principally through the burning of ships to collect the insurance.[119] The *Chabook* was also keen to expose the prejudice of Europeans against Indians. In 1857, the *Chabook* chided a Mr. Herbert, the Session Judge of Surat, for ordering a Parsi by the name of Rustomjee Hormusjee to divest himself of his shoes when appearing before the court. The *Chabook* traced back the 'shoe question' to 1822, when the sons of the Punchayet leader Bomanjee Hormarjee Wadia were the first Indians to be subject to this invidious custom, by no less than the Judges of the Sudder Adawlut Court in Surat, upon whom the Parsis were paying a courtesy call. Lord Elphinstone banned the custom though it per-

[116] *Bombay Samachar One Hundred and Fifty Years, 1882-1972* (in Gujarati) (Bombay, 1972), 31.

[117] Manockjee Cursetjee, *The Parsee Panchayet* (Bombay, 1860), 24-5.

[118] *Bombay Times*, February 5, 1857, May 30, 1859.

[119] J.D. 1843 81/935:20-5; *Bombay Times*, May 30, 1959.

sisted, with even the editor of the *Chabook* on an occasion suffering the contumely.[120] The *Chabook* also joined with the other Parsi-run papers of the time in opposing Christian proselytism. The *Chabook* was of the opinion that all converts should be examined as to their true motives in becoming Christians.[121] While the editorial opinion of the *Chabook* was renowned for its point and vigour, like the *Samachar*, the *Chabook* opposed lending itself to any staunch ideological position. While the *Chabook* often lampooned the Parsi aristocracy, under Nowroji it opposed the Parsi reformers and changes to the customs of the Parsis. The *Chabook* described the reformers as infidel highwaymen, and mercilessly attacked the Manockjee Cursetjee for his Anglophilism.[122]

The *Chabook's* policy to expose corruption, hypocrisy, and pretentiousness of conduct corresponded with the growing sentiment of the age to hold up the leaders of society and the Parsi community to scrutiny. The emboldening of the press reflected the emergence of new journalists espousing new ideas.[123] The rise of the writer's own sensibility corresponded with the modern view of artistic identity emerging that was replacing the dependence on patronage, and which reached its natural evolution in the rise of the critic. The *Chabook* provided the early newspaper audience of Bombay with a mixture of principle and parody. The early papers of Bombay like the *Samachar* and the *Chabook* sought to create an audience out of the reading public, rather than necessarily represent an ideology. The public's taste for variety, however, equally made papers such as the *Chabook* fair game for satire. When in 1860 a Parsi editor of the *Chabook* who was married eloped with a married Parsi woman, the Bombay Parsis were provided with ample titillation from a press ready to hoist the *Chabook* on its own petard.[124] The brash entertainment value provided in a newspaper like the *Chabook* aided in the formation of a new genre by mid-century, particularly among the Parsis, dedicated to self-parody and mass appeal.

Traditionalist opinion among the Parsis was reflected in the *Jam-e-Jamshed* or 'Cup of Jamshed,' started by the Parsi Punchayet in 1832, originally as a weekly, under its first publisher Pestonjee

[120] *Bombay Times*, January 7, 1859.
[121] *Bombay Times*, February 5, 1857.
[122] *Bombay Times*, April 9, 1857.
[123] Sankhdher, *Press, Politics, and Public Opinion*, 108.
[124] *Bombay Times*, August 2, 1860.

Maneckjee Motiwalla (1808-58). Its early pages were graced by the writings of men who were later regarded as reformers such as Nowrozjee Furdoonjee, Khaikhosru Naoroji Kabraji (1842-1904), and Dosabhai Framji Karaka. During the course of the century, the paper helped shape conservative thought which developed into a distinct philosophy of conservatism. On the centenary of the *Jam-e-Jamshed*, as accolades from friend and foe poured forth, the paper had long since comfortably settled into its role as the voice of respectable conservatism. The longevity of the paper attested to the influence it had continued to have over generations of readers. Sir Jehangir Coyajee noted how for a century the *Jame* had kept the banner of Liberalism flying: "That Liberalism might indeed seem to be the heritage of the Parsi community which the *Jame* has so well served. Well and faithfully has that journal guarded that heritage."[125]

The social philosophy of community that emerged among the Parsis during the first half of the nineteenth century, though perhaps unarticulated as such at the time, formed the basic conservative temperament and desire for security, safety, and peace. This conservatism of mind and temperament represented man's 'natural' disposition against any substantial change in his social situation, and acquiescence in conformity to the standards of the group. This conservatism came to distinguish between change, as the natural transformations in society and reform, as the deliberate transformation of values and institutions by a select group. Parsis had always sought to direct social change in the interest of preserving identity. The emergence of reformism, on the other hand, in the opinion of the Parsi conservative threatened the stability of the community and group identity. With the rise of the reformers (the philosophical radicals of the Parsis) to the forefront of attention, Parsi conservatism had been pushed to the background while, like orthodoxy, for the first time emerging as a philosophical label. As a conservative organ, the *Jame* articulated the consensus of conservative thought among Parsis that upheld the values of moderation, constitutionalism (the intellectual's law and order), and traditionalism, with a large dose of Tory paternalism in the form of philanthropy and noblesse oblige. The sound-ness of the policy of conservatism practised by Parsi traditionalists was believed self-evident, and stood as the measure of social reform: "For it

---

[125]Jehangir C. Coyajee, "An Appreciation," in *Jam-e-Jamshed Centenary Volume*, 11.

upholds the best traditions of the community, advocates a gradual evolution towards healthy progress, and strongly condemns a precipitous advance with all its attendant evils."[126] The Parsi conservative placed his faith in the existing society and, like all genuine conservatives, felt no need to write manifestos, as he believed he lived in the best of all possible worlds.

Notwithstanding the emergence of the *Jame* as the valuable vessel of conservative opinion in the eyes of many Parsis and, indeed, basking in the afterglow of that sentiment at its centenary, at times the *Jame's* quest to remain the voice of the Parsi majority put it on the defensive. As reform redefined many aspects of traditional Parsi society and religion on the basis of utility, Parsi conservatives and the *Jame* were unsure of their response. Initially, the mutuality of the goal between reformers and traditionalists to revitalize Parsi life and strengthen Parsi identity appealed to the *Jame* editors. However, as wholesale reforms were advocated by the reformers to such things as the calendar, rituals and prayers, accompanied by a full assault on the priests and other pillars of traditional life, traditional Parsi opinion felt constrained to offer proposals beyond a defence of existing society. It is an interesting parallel that precisely at the time that an articulated and distinctive conservative identity was emerging, the strength of its influence was under tremendous pressure from the new progressivism. Much of the history of the *Jame* in the nineteenth century is the attempt to remain the relevant voice of Parsis in opposition to change.

In seeking to remain relevant, however, the *Jame* at times was more often pushed by public sentiment than leading public opinion. In the battle for public loyalties, the accusation of pandering to mob opinion was something the reformers were prepared to use against conservatism. In April of 1891, a public sensation arose as to the guilt of the Parsi Maneckji Aslaji and two Khoja youths, when two Parsi women fell to their deaths from the top of Rajabai Clock Tower at the University of Bombay.[127] When the High Court of Bombay acquitted Aslaji three months later, the vernacular press, and the traditionalist Parsi press in particular, was singled out for its role in encouraging the feelings of the public to get the better of its

---

[126] Kaikhosru N. Chandabhoy, "The Jame and the Parsis," in *Jam-e-Jamshed Centenary Volume*, 151.

[127] See D. E. Wacha to Dadabhai Naoroji, July 17, 1891, in *Dadabhai Naoroji Correspondence*, vol. 2, part 1, no. 153, ed. R. P. Patwardhan (Bombay, 1977), 252.

judgement. In an address to the editor of the *Jam-e-Jamshed*, Sorabjee Shapoorjee Bengallee noted that:

> No wonder it is that on hearing such a version, the minds of the Parsis were enraged and a wild outcry was the result, but the entire blame rests on the heads of those who played upon their feelings by giving currency from day to day to fictitious reports. Especially you and other Editors of the Parsi newspapers have clearly rendered yourselves deserving of high censure for believing such baseless allegations to be true and circulating them. I beseech you in all humility that you, journalists, should desist from misguiding your fellow men and take steps to prevent a further rise of feeling by putting an end to this agitation.... Though it is desirable on many occasions to keep well with the community, it does not become the leaders to lose all public courage and submit to the senseless noise and din of an agitated public and allow themselves to be dragged by rather than lead it aright to all communal matters.[128]

A ubiquitous social reformer who was largely self-educated, Bengallee was active in journalism having begun his own monthly magazines the *Jagat Mitra* in 1850, and the *Jagat Premi* in 1851 on Persian history and other subjects. In 1857, Bengallee started the magazine *Stri Bodh* especially written for women, with the financial support of the Parsi lady Dosabai Framji Cama.[129]

The indictment of the *Jame* by the reformers formed part of the general polemic over social reform taking place within the Parsi community from mid-century, and which saw both the evolution of newspaper opinion and the rise of new journals reflective of social trends. The bitterest diatribes against the reformers appeared in journals devoted exclusively to an orthodox Parsi point of view such as *Suryodaya* and the *Satya Mitra* of 1874, started by Muncherjee K. Mansukh (1823-1902).[130] In 1914, the ideological war over social reform among the Parsis reached a nadir when a charge of libel was laid against the proprietor, and the editor and publisher of the *Jam-e-Jamshed.* Jehangir B. Marzban (1848-1928) and his son Pirojsha J. Marzban (1876-1933) were found liable for having maligned Parsis attending the second Zoroastrian Conference in 1911. In its assault upon the reformers and the Zoroastrian Conference, the *Jame* had abandoned the liberal standards of the journalist in favour of the language of the partisan. The court had sensed this in ruling the *Jame*

---

[128]Bengallee, *Life of Sorabjee Shapoorjee Bengallee*, 66-7.

[129]Ibid., 7, 9.

[130]Jeejeebhoy, "Historical Survey of Bombay Journalism," 282

articles as defamatory, and far exceeding "the limits of fair and legitimate criticism."[131] In an attempt to remain ahead of the progressives, lead and rally conservative public opinion, the *Jame* had become a victim of its own tactics. For much of its history, however, to the present day the *Jame* has been a novel and popular expression of the views of a cross-section of Parsi society.

Parsi Theatre

The success of the Gujarati language press in terms of circulation and subscribers among the Parsis owed much to the educational and social changes underway through the course of the century. Both the Parsis' high literacy and interest in partaking of new cultural mediums sustained interest in the press. The fascination with new cultural mediums also saw the rise of Parsi theatre by mid-century. Theatre in Bombay had a fleeting existence since the late eighteenth century, with productions from Europe periodically performing in the city at improvised venues. It was in 1844 that the first public theatre house in Bombay appeared. The Grant Road Theatre was made possible by the donation of a piece of land in the heart of the city by Jagannath Shankarshet, followed by subscriptions for its erection.[132] It was not until the 1860s during a period of economic prosperity that public theatre took flight. As early as the 1850s, the Parsis developed both English language and Parsi-Gujarati vernacular theatre. During the 1850s, the Parsi students of the Elphinstone College started an amateur dramatic company known as the Elphinstone Dramatic Club, which specialized in English language drama, including Shakespearean plays.[133]

It was vernacular theatre, however, that initially captured the attention of the Parsi public. "Thespis gave birth to a child of high promise and forehead fair," the *Bombay Times* noted of the first public theatrical performance among the Parsis, on October 29,

---

[131] See Navajbai Dorabji Contractor, "Jehangir B. Marzban," in *Jam-e-Jamshed Centenary Volume*, 163; Darukanawala, *Parsi Lustre*, 298-301; *Jam-e-Jamshed* Defamation Case, Full Text of Judgement, reprinted in *Journal of the Iranian Association* 4, no. 4 (July 1915): 132, 135.

[132] Chairman Bombay Theatrical Company to J. G. Lumsden, Sec. to Gov't, January 25, 1853, in G.D. 1853 15/264:111-14; Wacha, *Shells*, 341-50.

[133] Ibid., 354-5.

1853, by the Parsi Theatrical Company.[134] The evening's performance included a play entitled 'Barjor' about a hero from Persian history, and a farce entitled 'The Marriage of Nagursha,' concerning the pitfalls surrounding child betrothals among the Parsis. Other drama companies of the 1850s included the Parsi Corps Dramatique and the Zoroastrian Theatrical Club. The Parsi productions were performed at the premises of the Grant Road Theatre on Saturday evenings, and an evening's performance usually included a dramatic work such as a Shakespearean play, in vernacular parody, followed by a farce.[135] The Parsi productions were it appears exclusively performed by male actors, with occasionally an inexperienced actor in female attire inadvertently referring to cast members in the masculine article.[136] The Parsi dramatic companies, however, sought to encourage the attendance of Indian females, with the Parsi Theatrical Company tailoring a performance specifically for the amusement and edification of Parsi ladies. One evening's selection included Shakespeare's 'Taming of the Shrew,' followed by the farce the 'Magicians,' in which was exposed the wily tricks practised on Indian females by Brahmans and Hindu astrologers.[137]

The choice of subject matter by the new medium reflected long-held Parsi concerns. From the number of people that attended Parsi theatre productions to the sustained bursts of applause that greeted the actors, the *Bombay Times* could not but note, "the Zoroastrian community feel an unabated interest in dramatic entertainments."[138] Both acclaim and critical reviews, however, accompanied a night's performance as theatre among the Parsis came to be a regular feature of Bombay cultural life.[139] Even the traditionalist Parsi press accepted theatre as a legitimate form of expression among the Parsis, with the *Jam-e-Jamshed* offering a critical assessment of a night's performance:

> We confess that there was much of instruction in the forcible language with which the young baronet moralised upon the fair Venetia, and his moral expressions, delivered as they were, in a manner most eloquent and emphatic, created an astounding effect upon the hearts of the

[134] *Bombay Times*, February 23, 1857.

[135] *Bombay Times*, November 30, 1858, April 9, 1859.

[136] *Bombay Times*, September 15, 1857.

[137] *Bombay Times*, April 28, 1858.

[138] *Bombay Times*, December 9, 1857.

[139] *Bombay Times*, September 15, 1857, March 16, 1858, November 30, 1858.

> whole circle of observers.... Let no one conclude from the criticisms we have entered into that the performance was less worthy in itself. Notwithstanding all the faults we have found, we are of opinion that it must have been both amusing and instructive to the audience to a certain extent.[140]

Dramas, *nataks* or skits and farces, had captured the imagination of Indians, particularly Parsis who led the genius for self-parody.[141] The earthy, irreverent, self-parodying joviality that distinguishes a part of the Parsi character was born of a mixture of influences that included the Zoroastrian life-affirming outlook, the Parsi sense of their minority position in India, and finally a fascination for British cultural forms. The educated 'sophisticates' among the Parsis were well suited to exploiting the democratization of social tastes, while innovating a new genre.[142] The farces performed in Parsi theatre were particularly well received by audiences for their creativity in exposing the hypocrisy of everyday life among Parsis and other Indians. Parsi theatre was a natural outgrowth of the Parsi gift for satire that had taken root in the Parsi-run journals, and a unique expression of Parsi life in the urban setting. In 1854, the *Parsee Punch* appeared dedicated predominantly to publishing novelty items including cartoons, off-coloured humour, and social satire. The *Parsee Punch* was started by Dadabhoy Soheri, and from 1858 changed its name to *Hindi Punch*, in an attempt to broaden the appeal of social satire. The paper continued to be published by Parsis until the 1930s.[143]

The continuing Parsi fascination for theatre would by the early decades of the twentieth century witness the rise of some of India's first films and talkies produced by Parsis, in the first movie theatres built and operated by Parsis. In 1902, Jamsetji Framji Madan (1856-1923) launched a projection show in a tent in Calcutta. This was one of the earliest film picture shows in India since the Lumiére Brothers of France had staged their 'cinematographe,' or French version of Edison's 'kinetoscope' projection show, in Bombay in 1896. Born in Bombay, J. F. Madan had started his career in the theatre industry as a prop boy in Calcutta. Madan and his sons would control a film and theatre empire across India, which at its height included 126 theatres

[140] *Bombay Times*, December 31, 1859.

[141] Wacha, *Shells*, 355.

[142] In the twentieth century, Adi Marzban (1914-87), poet, playwright, and editor of the *Jam-e-Jamshed*, was the premier practitioner of Parsi humour.

[143] Jeejeebhoy, "Historical Survey of Bombay Journalism," 282.

in 1931. Madan brought largely foreign films to Indian audiences as well as produced indigenous films in its studios, and was the first Indian production company to release sound films. The Madan film empire essentially ended by the early 1930s, just as the Indian film industry, and in particular the Bombay talkies, came into being.[144]

Parsis were actively involved in the rise of the modern film industry in India. J.B.H.Wadia was a scion of the Wadia family of Parsi shipwrights of the eighteenth century. He was educated at Elphinstone College, graduating with a Master of Arts and a law degree. Jamshed and his brother Homi founded probably the most successful Parsi-run film production company, Wadia Movietone, which had a ship as its logo in tribute to the Wadia family heritage. Wadia Movietone specialized in Indian stunt and action films in Hindi, Tamil, and Telugu, as well as documentary and newsreel production in cooperation with government. The Hindi film *Hunterwali* of 1935, depicting the exploits of a female Robin Hood, was typical of the genre and success of the company. By the mid-1830s, Minerva Movietone was founded by the actor Sohrab Modi. Educated at the University of Bombay, he first worked as a film projector operator before entering into acting roles in 1914. Like Wadia Movietone, Minerva Movietone specialized in dramatic and historical films, and in 1940 produced the epic Hindi film *Sikander*, depicting Alexander of Macedon's military campaign in India.[145] The rise of a Parsi-run film industry marked the conjunction of the educational, artistic, and business talents of the Parsis, and contributed to the development of a unique cultural medium in India.

Rise of Communal Tensions

The Parsis of the nineteenth century, however, had taken to a genre that was not universally popular among all the communities of India. One evening's theatrical performance included an original work by a young Parsi entitled 'Two Wives Better Than One,' which was intended to reveal the "voluptuousness and immoralities of a Mussul-

[144] Firoze Rangoonwalla, *Seventy-five Years of Indian Cinema* (New Delhi, 1975), 9-14; Erik Barnouw and S. Krishnaswamy, *Indian Film* (Oxford, 1980), 7-8, 64-6.

[145] Rangoonwalla, *Indian Cinema*, 82-3; Barnouw and Krishnaswamy, *Indian Film*, 110-11.

man harem."[146] Such subject matter was bound to raise the ire of those Muslims not altogether enamoured with the gaudy folk. Communal tensions at mid-century, which were largely attributable to the uneven pace of social progress among Indian communities, made the hyperbole of the vernacular press the pretext for communal disaffection and jealousies.

The *Samachar Darpan* run by the Parsi Nowroji Gae was the fourth Gujarati paper to emerge in Bombay in 1849, and the first to publish daily.[147] The *Chitra Gnyan Darpan* or 'Mirror of Pictorial Knowledge' followed it a year later, and was the first illustrated weekly journal in India. Under two Parsi editors, Jehangir H. Punthaki and Behramji Cursetji Gandhi (1829-86) until its demise in 1854, the Chitra gained great notoriety for its lithographed illustrations, particularly in October 1851, when it reproduced an image of the Prophet Mohammed, along with a history of the leader. Angered by the likeness of the Prophet appearing in public print, and doubly incensed by the somewhat blurred depiction, the Muslims rioted against the Parsis whom they blamed for the deliberate insult.[148] Beginning a period of tension in the modern history of the two communities, which witnessed riots in Bombay and parts of Gujarat against the Parsis again in 1857 and in 1874, it was in the press that the Parsis found the only effective means to voice their feelings, including at times their sense of isolation and community resolve.

In 1857, two Parsis were murdered including a Parsi high priest in Broach in Gujarat, during riots that occurred at the time of the Great Mutiny of 1857. On February 13, 1874, a more violent rendition of the situation in 1851 occurred, as parallel once again held good to the pretext following the publication in June 1873 of a book entitled *Famous Prophets and Communities*, containing an article on the life of Mohammed by the Parsi Rustomji Hormusji Jalbhoy. On each occasion, the Parsis felt the full measure of their minority position. Assaulting Parsis, looting homes and shops, and desecrating fire-temples and Towers of Silence, the Muslims perpetrated their outrages at times in front of an indifferent police, local administration, and Bombay government. On all three occasions, the riots were clearly premeditated, with riots in 1851 and 1874 occurring follow-

[146] *Bombay Times*, March 17, 1860.
[147] Karkaria, "The Rast Goftar," 235.
[148] J.D. 1852 25:52-70, 233-35.

ing Friday prayers at the mosque. Religious frenzy became the pretext and guise under which communal competition and heightened communal awareness were expressed. In 1851, riots followed three weeks after the publication of the article in the *Chitra Gnyan Darpan*; and in 1874, riots followed some nine months after Jalbhoy's book was released, and despite the withdrawal of the book by the author in an effort to assuage tensions. During the Broach riot in May of 1857, the Parsis believed that the three most influential Muslim officials in the area, the foujdar, the qazi, and the moulvi, were aware of plans to target Parsis.[149] In 1874, the trust of the Parsis in the British was severely tested as both the Commissioner of Police for Bombay, J. H. Souter, and the Governor of Bombay, Sir Phillip Wodehouse, held the Parsis equally worthy of blame for the riots. Petitions by the Parsis warning the government of potential trouble and requesting protection were unheeded. J. H. Souter was particularly felt to be prejudiced against the Parsis in voicing his lack of concern for their welfare, and in refusing to expeditiously call for military assistance.[150]

Something of a turning point in the modern relations between the two communities, as well as the Parsis' relationship with the public authorities, the Parsi/Muslim Riots of 1874, as those of 1851 and 1857, galvanized the Parsi community in its anger at the course of events, and its protest against the conduct of the police and the government. The leading Parsis of Bombay including traditionalists and reformers alike supported a Memorial to the Marquis of Salisbury, the Secretary of State for India, containing the signatures of 8,452 Parsis asking for an inquiry into the origins of the riot and the conduct of the authorities.[151] The Secretary of State for India in reply to the Memorial downplayed the Parsis' concerns, including the necessity for an inquiry, and largely supported the actions and response of the British officials during the riots.[152]

---

[149] *Bombay Times*, May 20, 21, 23, 29, 1857, June 11, 24, 1857.

[150] Humble Petition of Principle Parsee Inhabitants Residing in Bombay to H.E. Sir Philip Wodehouse, February 13, 1874, in J.D. 1874 110/291:47-54; *Parsee Prakash*, 2:468-84.

[151] *Parsee Prakash*, 2:485-91: "Memorial of the Parsee Inhabitants of the City of Bombay, April 13, 1874"; "Parsi-Mohammedan Riots, 1874—Mr. Pherozeshah's Experience 14th February, and Protest Meeting of 12th April," in *Some Unpublished Later Speeches and Writings of the Hon. Sir Pherozeshah Mehta*, ed. J.R.B. Jeeieebhoy (Bombay, 1918), 4-8.

[152] *Parsee Prakash*, 2:492-3.

The Diversification of Opinion

The Parsi/Muslim Riots of 1851 were the catalyst for the creation of probably the greatest Parsi-run reformist newspaper, the *Rast Goftar* or 'Herald of Truth'. The riots of 1851 had left many Parsis questioning the ineffectual response of the traditional *shetia* leadership of the community; some of whom it was believed had taken shelter and had done nothing to stop the rioting. Progressive Parsi opinion had coalesced in the shape of the new newspaper to criticize those within the Parsi community who, it was felt, no longer provided the leadership necessary at a time of great social change. The *shetias* had become the symbol of all that the reformers saw as the entrenched conservatism within the Parsi community.[153] Notwithstanding its timely beginning, the newspaper was the natural expression in a literary and social sense to the movement for reform begun by the educated Parsis. Many of the early patrons, proprietors, editors, and contributors were from educational institutions and members of the Rahnumai Mazdayasnan Sabha. Dadabhai Naoroji was founder and first editor of the *Rast Goftar* from 1851 to August 1852. Edulji Nasarvanji Prussia and Jehangir Burjorji Vacha succeeded him. From January 1858, S. S. Bengallee was editor for two years without remuneration. During its seventy year existence, the *Rast Goftar* at various times was edited and contributed to by the Parsis Nowrozjee Furdoonjee, Kharshedji Rustomji Cama, Dosabhai Framji Karaka, Nanabhoy Rustamji Ranina (1832-1900), Ardesar Framji Moos (1827-95), Cowasji Edulji Khumbata (1830-1916), and Pestonji Jehangir Taleyarkhan (1831-1914).[154]

The *Rast Goftar* began as a fortnightly on November 15, 1851, and from February 1, 1852 became a weekly appearing every Sunday morning. The *Rast Goftar* suffered a loss of Rs. 1,000 a year till 1857.[155] It was only with the substantial aid and liberality of the progressive *shetia* K. N. Cama that the paper was able to remain financially viable. K. N. Cama was a member of the Rahnumai Mazdayasnan Sabha, and had contributed to Nowroji Gae's *Samachar Darpan*. In 1858, the paper was converted into a joint-stock concern

[153] *Rast Goftar*, January 9, 1859.

[154] Karkaria, "The Rast Goftar," 242; Bengallee, *Life of Sorabjee Shapoorjee Bengallee*, 14.

[155] Karkaria, "The Rast Goftar," 239-40; S. C. Sanial, "History of the Press in India X. Bombay—IV," *Calcutta Review* (1910): 353n.

increasing its circulation from 432 to 852. In 1861, the Hindu social reformer Karsondas Mulji (1832-71) became proprietor of the *Rast Goftar* following the amalgamation of the paper with the *Satya Prakash.* On September 8, 1869, the paper was sold to Behramji F. Marzban and Merwanji F. Marzban, of whom the latter was its owner into the twentieth century.[156]

In addition to championing the cause of reform against conservatism within the Parsi community, the *Rast Goftar* reflected the concerns relevant to Indian social reformers. It was a staunch defender of the Indian community against European prejudice.[157] In 1858, English columns appeared with the stated object of providing the Indian community in general and the educated classes in particular, with more reliable data than otherwise available. The *Rast Goftar's* specific aim was to defend Indians against charges of disloyalty during the Great Mutiny of 1857. This was the first occasion that English columns appeared in a Gujarati paper, and the quality of the first columns edited by Cowasji Edulji Khumbata appeared to catch the attention of the English editor of the *Bombay Times,* who with bemused condescension remarked that he could hardly believe the columns to have been written by an Indian.[158] The *Rast Goftar,* in fact, was somewhat late among the Indian press to come to the defence of Indians following the Mutiny. The Parsi-run press as a whole had taken exception to any imputation that the Parsi community in particular had not unanimously opposed the Muslim-led Mutiny. For some in the European community, the Mutiny heightened their general dissatisfaction with the Indian-run press, to the point of describing its role as disloyal. The *Bombay Times* under the editorship of Dr. George Buist, in particular, came in for criticism. The *Bombay Times* began in 1838, and in 1859 was amalgamated with the *Standard* into *The Times of India.* The *Bombay Times* from its beginnings had displayed a negative bias towards Indians, including the Parsis during the case of the Parsi boys' conversions in 1839.

In December 1857, the Parsi editors of the *Samachar,* the *Samachar Durpan,* the *Parsee Punch,* the *Jam-e-Jamshed,* and the *Parsee Friend,* signed a letter of protest to the *Bombay Times* asking its editor to acknowledge his error, and exonerate the members of the

---

[156] Sanial, "History of the Press," 252n.

[157] *Rast Goftar,* April 3, 10, October 30, November 6, 1859, May 21, 1865.

[157] Sanial,"History of the Press," 253; *Bombay Times,* February 25, 1858.

Indian press and public from accusations of disloyalty unjustly preferred against them. The Parsi editors noted that an examination of the press by the censor would reveal the Indian press' utter abhorrence for the violence and destruction of the Mutiny. They also noted their duty to oppose:

> ... as impolitic and unjust, the conduct of a portion of the English Press and British-born inhabitants of this country, who, like yourself, express vindictive and blood-thirsty feelings, make no distinction between the rebels and the loyal Indians, indulge freely in wholesale vituperation, and seek to wreak vengeance against whole nations, whose utter extermination they in their unreasoning exasperation, recommend.[159]

The fourteen Indian proprietors of the *Bombay Times*, including six Parsis, then met to dismiss Buist as editor, and publicly announce their decision.[160] The proposal and final decision of the proprietors to dismiss Buist, however, only appeared to confirm the prevailing cultural divide between Europeans and Indians. It garnered ridicule and rebuke from Buist, as to the lack of understanding among Indians of liberal traditions, and gained him public sympathy.[161] Notwithstanding the public reaction, the Parsi literary establishment was prepared to use the clout they had assumed by mid-century in opposition to European prejudice.

The criticism of the Indian community during the Mutiny largely obscured the depth of loyalty to British rule among Indians, and particularly Parsis, before and after the Mutiny. In this respect, educated Indian opinion expressed a greater sense of political community in India than did British opinion. Even the *Rast Goftar's* attempts to unite Parsi opinion against government decisions, in the months following the Mutiny, were chastised by Parsis as mischievous and as misrepresenting the motives of the rulers.[162] The Parsis' avowals of loyalty, as may be imagined, were profuse. The concern for safety was such that many Parsis openly advocated the establishment of a Parsi militia to be utilized by the British army.[163] The *Jam-e-Jamshed* went so far as to report any rumours of rebellion among the Muslim

[159] *Bombay Times*, December 19, 1857.

[160] *Bombay Times*, December 28, 1857, January 6, 1858.

[161] *Bombay Times*, December 10, 11, 19, 29, 1857.

[162] *Bombay Times*, November 2, 1859.

[163] *Bombay Times*, June 18, July 15, 1857.

sepoys of Bombay.[164] The Parsi Punchayet had sent out printed circulars calling a public meeting at the seashore and at one of their fire-temples to offer prayers and ceremonies following the quelling of the rebellion.[165] The Parsis had joined with the other Indian communities of Bombay and India in officially celebrating the end of the rebellion in 1859. On the latter occasion, loyalty to the British was evinced in the midst of internal community disputes that led to reformers and traditionalists holding celebrations in separate fire-temples.[166]

The activity of the Parsi-run press during the Mutiny was measure of the growth of political opinion among Parsis and other Indians. The appearance and disappearance of English columns in the *Rast Goftar* were a barometer of the changes in policy and viewpoint of the paper. From 1865 until 1887, the columns were discontinued. By the late 1870s, a split in the reform movement occurred as extra-community issues principally involving politics divided Parsis. The Parsi-run press had always carried the news of the day and major issues of concern beyond the Parsi community, including paying attention to Bombay municipal politics. The evolution of journalism into nationalist political discourse, however, crossed a barrier for many of the old-line reformers. The *Rast Goftar* under its new publisher and editor Kaikhosru Naoroji Kabraji remained devoted to the social concerns of Parsis and other Indians, while other prominent Parsis associated with social reform were reaching more towards political identity. Kabraji joined the paper in 1861, relieving the Hindu social reformer Karsondas Mulji, and edited the paper until 1902. Kabraji continued editing the paper in the traditional spirit of social reform dedicated to the improvement of social outlooks and conditions, and the focus on cultural issues.[167] In 1888, the English columns were revived for a year following the Golden Jubilee of 1887, S. C. Sanial suggests, with the object to criticize the Indian National Congress formed in Bombay in 1885.[168] The *Rast Goftar* opposed the participation of the Parsis in nationalist politics, and parted company with Dadabhai Naoroji and other Parsis involved in the early nationalist movement like Pherozeshah Mehta and Dinsha

---

164 *Bombay Times*, June 2, 1857.

165 *Bombay Times*, July 22, 1857.

166 *Bombay Times*, August 5, 1859.

167 Wacha, *Shells*, 356.

168 Sanial, "History of the Press," 353n.

Wacha. By the 1890s, the *Rast Goftar* turned its opposition to Parsi involvement in nationalist politics into support for imperialism.[169]

For Parsis like Dadabhai Naoroji, Pherozeshah Mehta, and Dinsha Wacha, the progression of reformist energies into nationalist politics was wholly consistent with the idea of social reform. The education of greater numbers of Indians, the Westernization of attitudes, and the growing capacity of Indians in the public arena, by the last quarter of the nineteenth century, had all augured for the political maturation of Indian reformist opinion. The uniting of reformist political opinion on behalf of pan-Indian issues, furthermore, was seen as the fulfilment of the corporatist reformist vision enunciated a half-century earlier. While Parsis like Kabraji and Naoroji split over the course of reform, the Parsi Behramji M. Malabari attempted to unite more traditional reformist goals, such as the emancipation of women and education of Indians, with political propaganda and agitation. Largely self-educated, Malabari was a journalist, poet, and social reformer whose energies were directed outside the Parsi community. His efforts on behalf of ending both the practice of child marriage and enforced widowhood among the Hindus earned him both praise and contempt.[170] Malabari gained the support of prominent Hindus such as Karsondas Mulji, Bhau Daji, and Narayan Daji, and of fellow Parsis like K. R. Cama and S. S. Bengallee, but was opposed by Hindu nationalists such as Bal Gangadhar Tilak, who did not believe in the reform of Hindu social traditions, especially by non-Hindus. Like the political agitation of Naoroji and Wacha, the social agitation of Malabari reflected the diversification of reformist thought. Whereas the nationalist Parsis essentially sought to build and join in a new coalition on behalf of political reform in the interests of Indians, including Parsis, Malabari stands as an example of a Parsi who transcended strictly communal interests on behalf of social reform. He worked to change the social traditions of other communities, despite both the opposition from outside his own ethnic community, and the movement for political conformity among Indians.

The division over the path reform should take and the rise of the nationalist cause among some Parsis worked to further diversify

---

[169] See Chapter Six.

[170] See B. M. Malabari, *The Indian Problem* (Bombay, 1864); idem, *An Appeal to the Daughters of India* (London, 1890); idem, *The Indian Eye on English Life: Or Rambles of a Pilgrim Reformer* (Bombay, 1895); Dayaram Gidumal, *The Life and Life-Work of B. M. Malabari* (Bombay, 1888).

journalistic opinion. The evolution of public opinion, particularly reformist opinion, toward political representation marked the eventual decline in the relevance of a paper like the *Rast Goftar*, and witnessed the rise of new newspapers. The rise of Parsi-run papers espousing political allegiances signified the emergence of a true plurality of opinion in the Parsi community by the latter part of the century. In 1880, Malabari bought the fledgling *Indian Spectator*, making it the leading voice of social reform in the changing political atmosphere of the late nineteenth century. In 1882, the Anglo-Gujarati *Kaiser-i-Hind* was started by the Parsi Framji Cowasji Mehta, and edited by the Parsi Pherozeshah Meherji, as the organ of the Indian National Congress. Pherozeshah Mehta's *Advocate of India* appeared in 1886 and *Bombay Chronicle* between 1913 and 1915. Dadabhai Naoroji's monthly periodical *The Voice of India* of 1883-84, brought the grievances of India to the British public.[171]

Summary

By the middle of the nineteenth century, the Parsis were in the process of the transformation of their social outlook and state. Both traditionalists and a new generation of reformers had come to see the advantages in adopting new social influences. Primary among these was the recognition of the value of education. The improvement in Parsi vernacular and English language education was seen as essential to strengthening cultural identity among the Parsis. Indeed, the attainment of an education was incorporated as part of the Parsi identity. The education of a Parsi became an integral characteristic of his/her identity as a Parsi. The impact of British values on the Parsis, in general, also was overwhelmingly well received as it conformed to the pattern of accommodating and incorporating positive influences in support of Parsi identity. The incorporation of Western values into the value system of the Parsis permitted of the Parsis' assimilation to modernity.

The Parsi intelligentsia formed the major group associated with the transmission of Western values. The Parsi intelligentsia shared the desire for educational advancement, as well as general social reform alongside the other Indian educated groups in Bombay. The

[171] Jeejeebhoy, "Historical Survey of Bombay Journalism," 278.

Parsi reformers had conformed to the pattern in Bombay of initiating specific social reforms within their caste community. The Parsi agents for the transmission of new ideas worked within the confines of community and caste that tended to reinforce the strength of Parsi identity. Significantly, while the appreciation of Western culture and academic influences shaped the knowledge of the Parsi reformers' own culture and religion, the reformers adhered to the process of directing change in support of identity that the Parsis had historically followed. Eventually, the broadened definitions of Parsi identity the reformers had contributed to shaping led to tensions within the Parsi community, as the plurality of thought contributed to heterodoxy of religious thought within a conservative religious tradition. The Parsi reformers sought to safeguard Parsi identity, while reinterpreting much of the nature and character of that identity. Aided by the Parsi press, the plurality of opinion and outlook over issues relative to Parsi identity became a permanent characteristic of Parsi identity. Plurality of opinion and outlook within the Parsi community also meant that over certain issues and problems relative to Parsi identity, the Parsis would find it difficult to reach consensus on solutions.

At mid-century, however, the cause of social reform remained an important issue for the Parsis, as the place of Parsi tradition in English law once again emerged as the major concern. The fight for the Parsi Laws of 1865 concentrated the energies of Parsis, both progressive and conservative, and marked the major achievement at mid-century in resolving the legal status of the Parsis in Indian law.

CHAPTER FIVE

IDENTITY AND THE LAW

1. *Laws for the Community: The Parsi Laws*

By the middle of the nineteenth century, the Parsis of India were in need of a legal framework by which to regulate their most basic social affairs. The guiding authority of the Parsi Punchayet had become problematic as it faced both the questioning of its legitimacy from inside and pressures from outside the Parsi community. In 1838, the old Punchayet's fate was effectively decided when the Legislative Council of India denied its application to reconstitute itself and re-establish its authority over the Parsis.[1] The government's own finding reflected the lack of consensus among the Parsis as to reviving the old Punchayet. The demise of the old Punchayet left the Parsis subject to a variety of legal applications, including the English law, the law of ascertaining usages and customs, various litigious suits, and at times no law at all. It was with a desire to remedy the situation that the push for a law code in regards to intestate inheritance and succession, and marriage and divorce arose in the middle of the nineteenth century, and came to form the Parsi Laws of 1865.

Notwithstanding the Parsis' economic power, their relationship with the British, and the tremendous change in their social condition by the middle of the nineteenth century, the necessity of a law code to safeguard identity came to preoccupy the Parsi reform agenda. The history of the Parsi Laws of 1865 illustrates, as with the rise of the Punchayet, the Parsis' need to compose a tradition in support of their identity. In large measure, the Parsi Laws of 1865 would be the natural corollary to the changes the Parsis were undergoing economically, educationally, and philosophically. The political and educational influence of the Parsis would help to facilitate the enactment

[1] Petition of November 21, 1838, to Rt. Hon. Lord Auckland, Governor General of India, in *Blue Pamphlets of 1843* (Bombay, 1843), 22-8. Also contained in J.D. 1863 20/143:351-7.

of the Parsi Laws. The enactment of the Parsi Laws would resolve a major aspect of the Parsis' place in Indian law, and would also reflect the evolution of thought the Parsis had undergone in defining their social relations during the course of the century. At the same time, the Parsi Laws would open more deliberately than at any other time the question of the definition of Parsi identity. Whereas external legal safeguards secured aspects of the Parsis' communal identity, internal disputes over the rights of a Parsi within the community, and particularly over the issue of accepting converts, would arise out of the process undertaken to create the Parsi Laws in the Parsi Punchayet Case of 1906-08.

The need to enact a code of laws for the Parsis corresponds with the history of British attempts to establish a system of law for India. Since the latter part of the eighteenth century, when the British took over the financial, legal, and administrative rule of Bengal, the proposition on the part of British colonialism was not to disturb the civil laws of Indians, particularly as regarded their personal laws, while incorporating them into a more rationalized system. The exigencies of economy, power and capability of the British, as well as both philosophic design and the inadvertence of circumstances would shape the evolution of law in India. The establishment of courts of law across India, as well as the introduction of British legal culture in the form of English law and precedent intended to give unity and certainty to the system of law in India, ultimately contributed to the evolution of a new legal culture from the interaction of Eastern and Western cultures, dominated by the British.[2]

The evolution of law under British colonialism posed particular problems for communities other than Hindus and Muslims. While the decision to observe the civil laws and usages of Indians was extended to the Parsis, the scale of its implementation was increasingly limited by 1827. The 'laws' of the Parsis were not like the laws of Hindus or Muslims. No religious law or extant body of codes existed among the Parsis that could stand as substantive Parsi law. The Parsis' customary usages and practices had evolved to meet their social

[2] On the history and evolution of law in India, see George Claus Rankin, *Background to Indian Law* (Cambridge, 1946); J. Duncan M. Derrett, *Religion, Law and State in India* (London, 1968); idem, *History of Indian Law* (Leiden, 1973); B. N. Pandey, *The Introduction of English Law into India* (London, 1967); U. C. Sarkar, *Epochs in Hindu Legal History* (Hoshiarpur, 1958), 377; Lloyd and Suzanne Rudolph, *The Modernity of Tradition* (Chicago, 1967), Ch. 3.

and religious requirements from time to time, but did not compose a body of legal norms uniformly applicable to the entire community. In large part, the greatest concern was occasioned when legal challenges and disputes arose which threatened to disturb the complacence of the community concerning their legal status. In the Gheestas' inheritance case of 1811, Sir James Mackintosh of the Recorder's Court (created 1797) admitted the illegitimate son of a Parsi who had died without leaving a will to the inheritance, on evidence that it was the usage and custom of the Parsis to recognize the religiously confirmed child of a Parsi. While the decision was reversed by Sir John Newbold, the new Recorder, upon further evidence by concerned Parsis that an illegitimate son was entitled to life maintenance only, the incident had raised a serious doubt as to the reliability of adjudicating matters in a British court between the Parsis of Bombay, based on the appeal to usage and custom.[3] The dispute was one of the earliest cases to come before a British court in Bombay in regards to Parsi intestate inheritance, and had arisen prior to the Punchayet's reforms to outlaw bigamy and illegitimacy in 1818.[4] The existence of a strong Punchayet able to adjudicate community disputes, however, only masked the latent weakness of the Parsis in not having codified laws under British colonialism.

In the Charter of 1823, which established the Supreme Court of Bombay, the Parsis of Bombay were excluded from the benefit of appealing to their laws and usages in regards to contract, inheritance and succession in the fashion of the Hindus and Muslims. The difficulty in ascertaining the law of usages and customs among the Parsis of Bombay had induced the authorities to apply English civil law to the Parsis in the urban setting. Even a staunch friend of the Parsis such as Erskine Perry, later Judge of the Supreme Court, observed that as regards the Parsis "there is a discreditable doubt as to what the law is."[5] The Parsis of the Mofussil (provincial district), however, remained subject to having law administered to them in accordance with such usages and customs, as the litigants in a suit were able to prove before a court as binding on the Parsi community.

[3] Report into the usages recognized as law by the Parsee Community of India, and into the necessity of special legislation in connection with them, October 13, 1862, para. 4, in J.D. 1863 20/143:215-29.

[4] Manockjee Cursetjee, *The Parsee Panchayet* (Bombay, 1860), 27-8.

[5] Quoted from Rankin, *Background to Indian Law*, 23.

This system of substantive law was confirmed by the provisions of Regulation IV of the Code of 1827 (section 26 and 27, Clause 2). Regulation IV provided where there was an absence of Acts of Parliament and Regulations of Government applicable to any case the usages and customs of the country in which the suit arose or if none such appeared the law of the defendant shall govern a decision. Where a doubt arose as to the usages or customs to be applied, the court was to ascertain the law to be applied by examining persons versed in such law, or the heads of the sects and castes.[6] Where no customary law could be deduced, the Mofussil Parsis were subject to the rules of 'justice, equity and good conscience' as applied by a British judge. This expression was construed to mean the rules of English law applicable to Indian society and circumstances.[7] Consequently, from 1824, a dual system of substantive law prevailed over the Parsi community of Western India: with the Parsis of Bombay subject to the English law, and the Parsis of the provincial areas of the Presidency subject to the laws of usages and customs applicable to the Parsi community.

It was precisely such a scenario that the entreaties of Harry Borradaile to the Parsis in 1828, to devise a code of laws for the community, were designed to remedy. As Registrar of the Suddar Adawlut Court for Surat and Bombay, Borradaile set about to provide the Parsis with a set of questions on their laws and customs, as part of the Bombay government's reform of law in Western India. In his observations of the Parsis in 1825, clearly based on his partial contacts with them, Borradaile was of the opinion that the Parsis had no laws of their own, having lost them in their migration to India; and consequently Parsi custom differed "in few respects from that custom of the country founded on Hindu law."[8] In Borradaile's specific address to the Parsis three years later, his understanding of their situation had improved, as he was able to note the mixture of practices and customs the Parsis continued to adhere to based on their ancient books, and appeals to immemorial custom. However, the

---

[6] Report into the usages recognized as law by the Parsee Community of India . . . October 13, 1862, para. 2, in J.D. 1863 20/143:215-29.

[7] J. Duncan M. Derrett, "Justice, Equity and Good Conscience," in *Family Law in Asia and Africa*, no. 2, ed. J. N. D. Anderson (London, 1963), 114.

[8] From Borradaile's Report, vol. 1, p. 2, note, in Report into the usages recognized as law by the Parsee Community of India . . . October 13, 1862, para. 6, in J.D. 1863 20/143:215-29.

lack of a written record, Borradaile stressed, provided the potential for interminable disputes. It was the opinion of the government that the Parsis of Surat and Bombay should devise a code.[9]

It was not until 1836 that the Parsis of Bombay responded to Borradaile's request with a series of answers to his inquiries. Disagreements between the Parsis over such issues as: the division of intestate property, the rights of women to property, the rights of converts to inheritance, along with the lack of documentary evidence of usage and customary law, had prevented any agreement over the answers.[10] The exercise, however, did not prove futile as in attempting to answer the questions regarding their personal law, the Parsis had begun the process of re-examining their traditions and formulating answers that would one day provide the foundations for a code of laws. The event that occasioned a response provides insight into the dilemma facing the Parsis. In 1835, a Parsi taking advantage of the status of the Parsis under English law in Bombay claimed the right to be considered the sole heir to his intestate father's immovable estate under the English law of primogeniture." Unlike the Gheestas' inheritance case in 1811, where the Parsis were able to successfully appeal the application of the English law, the decision to apply the English law to the Parsis in the Presidency town since 1824, necessitated a direct appeal by the Parsis of Bombay to the Legislative Council of India.[12] The appeal by the Parsis resulted in Act IX of 1837, where in the instance of intestacy all immovable property was to "be taken to be and to have been of the nature of chattels real and not freehold."[13] In designating immovable property as in the nature of personal property, where an actual case of intestacy existed, property was made divisible through a scheme of partible inheritance based on the Eng-

---

[9] H. Borradaile, "Translation of a Goozerattee Letter ... to the Parsee Community of Surat and Bombay," January 1, 1828, in *Blue Pamphlets of 1843*, 30-1; Report into the usages recognized as law by the Parsee Community of India ... October 13, 1862, para. 6, in J.D. 1863 20/143:215-29.

[10] "Answers to a Series of Questions Put by H. Borradaile Esq. Relative to the Rights of Inheritance, no. 4, August 18, 1836, in *Blue Pamphlets of 1843*, 32-9.

[11] Report into the usages recognized as law by the Parsee Community of India ... October 13, 1862, para. 7, in J.D. 1863 20/143:215-29.

[12] "Humble Petition of the November 20, 1835, to the Hon. The Governor-General and Legislative Council of India," in *Blue Pamphlets of 1843*, 2-6.

[13] Ibid., 14-15: W. H. Macnaghten, Sec. to the Gov't of India, The Parsi Chattels and Real Act, No. IX of 1837, May 15, 1837.

lish Statute of Distribution. The Statute of Distribution provided to a third of property went to the widow and the remainder was divided equally among the children and their descendants.[14] In his draft proposal, His Lordship in Council acknowledged the property of the Parsis to have been inherited by them according to their national usages despite not being recognized in English law. He was of the opinion that to disturb that possession would be "one of those cases in which the strict enforcement of the Law would defeat the end for which Laws are made, would render property insecure, and would shake the confidence of the people in the Institutions under which they live."[15]

In securing for the Parsis of Bombay the legislative dispensation embodied in Act IX of 1837, the Indian Legislature had substituted one English legal custom for another. A partible system of distribution of an intestate's estate was permitted for the Parsis of Bombay over the English law of primogeniture. Act IX of 1837 subjected the Parsis of Bombay in all cases of intestacy to the English Statute of Distribution in addition to the application of English common law relating to husband and wife. The statute applied solely to the transmission of immovable property within the jurisdiction of the Supreme Courts; consequently creating a further distinction between the legal status of the Parsis of Bombay and of the Mofussil.[16] The actions of the Legislature had accommodated the concerns of the Parsis but only partially. It had provided a legal alternative to the strict application of primogeniture in favour of a system of distribution more in line with what the Parsis practised, yet left the Parsis subject to another set of social norms embodied in both English statue law and the common law. Whereas the Statue of Distribution provided for the rights of a widow, it rewarded a second wife over the Parsis' custom of recognizing the claims of the wife and children of a first marriage. The common law as regards husband and wife, similarly, did not recognize the right of a wife to any independent control during the life of the husband over any property, including that which came to her from her family, as was the custom of the

---

[14] P. L. Paruck, *The Indian Succession Act* (Bombay, 1953), 63.

[15] "Resolution of January 30, 1837," in *Blue Pamphlets of 1843*, 11.

[16] Report into the usages recognized as law by the Parsee Community of India. October 13, 1862, para. 8, in J.D. 1863 20/143:215-29.

Parsis. The diversity of application of substantive law to the Parsis continued until 1865. In 1868, Act IX of 1837 was repealed.

The actions of the Parsis in 1836 and 1837 were consonant with the pattern of petitioning government for redress they had practised since the eighteenth century. Yet, Act IX of 1837 clearly revealed to the Parsis the unsuitability of applying English law to their situation. In light of the unsuitability of the English law and their inability to agree over a standard law code, Parsis continued to put forward the reconstitution of the Punchayet as a remedy to the absence of a code of laws. Attempts in 1838 and 1841 were made to convince the government and the Indian Law Commission that the remedy implemented in the Act IX of 1837, remained unsuitable to the community. In 1841, there was a sense of urgency in their plea, as the signatories included an instance where Parsi children had been materially disadvantaged by the fact that their father had died intestate, and his estate passed to his second wife.[17]

Nothing was done in response to the Parsis' applications whether for a remedy to the application of English law or the reconstitution of the Punchayet. The Supreme Court of Bombay on behalf of the government expressed its objection to a new Punchayet, as its status in English law would be problematic: "If its authority were compulsory, questions might arise as to the legality and regularity of its proceedings before it; besides that, no longer depending for their force on general consent, its decisions would be much less likely, in the absence of any authentic standard of law, to give general satisfaction."[18] The Court had affirmed the legal custom that was evolving in India whereby, while instructed to be accommodating to the laws of the inhabitants, its authority was increasingly that of a court both temporal and spiritual.[19] As long as the Court held itself out as an alternative tribunal to the Punchayet, obliged to apply the English law in any dispute, the social control of the Punchayet to enforce the customs of the Parsis could not prevail over the Parsi community. The decision of the Court, furthermore, effectively confirmed the greatest misgiving of the Parsis, that in the absence of a code of laws their special relationship with the British authority would fail them.

---

[17] Petition to Rt. Hon. Lord Auckland, November 21, 1838, and Letter to Harry Borradaile Esq., March 5, 1841, in *Blue Pamphlets of 1843*, 22-8, 41-3.

[18] D. F. Karaka, *History of the Parsis*, 2 vols. (London, 1884), 1:239.

[19] Derrett, *Religion, Law and State*, 233-4.

The Parsis had had some reason to be encouraged in requesting a reconstitution of the Punchayet in framing their Petition to the Legislative Council in 1838, as in 1837 Chief Justice J. W. Awdry of the Supreme Court of Bombay had expressed his belief that a Punchayet should be invested with some definite authority in ecclesiastical and matrimonial questions. Awdry, however, did not intend the Punchayet to be a substitute for a code of laws, as had the Parsi leaders in framing their Petition, and Awdry amiably passed over the hope of resuscitating the Punchayet as regards to other powers. His insight would prove prescient thirty years later when the role of matrimonial courts for the Parsis was considered. The Chief Justice's response, however, does reveal the extent of the Parsis' attempts to deal with the question of their personal law. The Parsis had examined many issues relating to a code including controversial points such as: whether converts away from Zoroastrianism should forfeit the right to inherit, or whether a Parsi wife has the right to dispose of her property free from the consent of the husband. It remained for the Parsis to reach consensus on the aspects of a code:

> I will conclude, as I begun, by expressing my conviction that if the Parsees are really agreed on the proposed scheme of inheritance, the difficulty of framing a statue to that effect (though greater than would be anticipated by individuals unused to legislation) would be as little as can be expected in such cases, as the whole appears to be a very sensible and coherent system.[20]

The legal difficulties of the Parsis and the remedies that they pursued from 1836 to 1841 reveal the cultural conflict the minority experienced in its attempt to preserve its social identity. It is noteworthy that whereas British legal opinion continued to regard the Parsis as virtually devoid of anything deserving of the name of law,[21] the comments of the British officials to the petitions of the Parsis acknowledged that a culture of law existed among the Parsis. The cultural bias continued to regard the lack of codified law as a measure of the absence of any law. From Borradaile, to Justices Perry and Awdry of the Supreme Court of Bombay, the admission was that the Parsis did not lack altogether a custom of law as one intelligible to British justice in India. To present the issue in this way is to suggest that the

[20] Letter from Sir John Wither Awdry, Chief Justice, to Bomanjee Hormarjee, April 25, 1837, in *Blue Pamphlets of 1843*, 44-7.

[21] William Morley, *Administration of Justice in British India* (New Delhi, 1858), 326

difficulty for the Parsis in having their customs recognized under British justice represents in some measure the difficulties in accommodating British norms to India.

In 1856, the legal difficulties of the Parsis culminated with the judgement of the Judicial Committee of the Privy Council in the case of *Cursetjee* v. *Perozebai*, and reveal the contradictions of British jurisprudence in India. The details of the case were that Perozebai, 13, the daughter of Framji Cowasji Banaji, and Ardeseer Cursetjee, 15, married in 1830. From 1833 to 1836, the couple cohabitated together after which time the husband rejected the wife and remarried without benefit of divorce. In 1843, Perozebai instituted a suit against her husband in the Supreme Court of Bombay for the restitution of the conjugal bond and a nullification of the second marriage under the English Ecclesiastical Law. Contesting the jurisdiction of the Supreme Court to hear the case, the husband argued that as the Parsis could be construed as neither British subjects nor Christians, the Ecclesiastical Law and the jurisdiction of the Court could not apply. The counsel for the plaintiff countered that the law establishing the Court included Indians within its jurisdiction, and since the time of the Recorder's Court in Bombay ecclesiastical jurisdiction of the Church of England was extended to the inhabitants of Bombay.[22]

In 1843, Justice Perry of the Supreme Court of Bombay overruled the husband's protest against the Court's jurisdiction to hear the case. Perry recounted the history of the law courts in Bombay since the transfer of Bombay to the British in 1661, and upheld the jurisdiction of the Supreme Court to apply ecclesiastical law to all the inhabitants of Bombay. The decision affirmed the intention of British justice in India: "To afford to all who may be subject to the jurisdiction of the Court—a tribunal before which every difference, that could arise in civilized society, might be adjusted."[23] Perry had recited the history of the law courts in Bombay in part to establish the basis on which the judgement proceeded in the likely case of an appeal. An appeal to the Privy Council soon followed and a decision was rendered on July 17, 1856. The Privy Council exercised its prerogative to examine the details of the case and considered the implications of applying the Ecclesiastical Law. As the case involved a

[22] Erskine Perry, *Cases Illustrative of Oriental Life* (1853; reprint, New Delhi, 1988), 57-8.

[23] Ibid., 69.

request for the restitution of conjugal rights, Ecclesiastical Law would have to apply. The Privy Council, however, felt the wife's request for the re-establishment of conjugal relations with a husband who had re-married and was living in adultery to be unenforceable and, represented not the "administration of Ecclesiastical Law, but its violation."[24] The Ecclesiastical Law, the Privy Council held, was founded exclusively on the assumption that the litigants are Christian (and strictly Christians professing the doctrines of the Church of England). The Privy Council held open the hope that some remedy under civil law might be available to the wife, but sustained the protest of the husband and reversed the judgement of the Supreme Court.

The ruling of the Privy Council denying jurisdiction to a British court to decide a dispute between Parsis based on the Ecclesiastical Law, equally rendered any matrimonial remedy in a dispute between Parsis in English law uncertain.[25] To the distress over the issue of intestate inheritance and succession was added the dilemma of the lack of a matrimonial law. This decision had the potential to be particularly deleterious to the interests of the Parsis as the efforts made over the past half century to distinguish and protect the Parsi conjugal bond were now undermined. The Parsis noted the effect of the decision of the Privy Council:

> The temporal rights and incidents derived from marriage, nay, the very nature of the marriage contract itself, are left wholly unascertained; remarriages are without authority; the ties of family are relaxed; morality is infringed; successions are become uncertain; and the female sex amongst us is denied the certain protection and recognition which it enjoys amongst other communities.[26]

Between 1860 and 1861 alone, the incidence of bigamy among the Parsis of Bombay, at a minimum, totalled some twenty-six cases.[27]

---

[24] *Bombay Times*, August 28, 1856: "Ardeseer vs. Perozebaee, Judgement of the Judicial Committee of the Privy Council."

[25] Petition to the Legislative Council of India, from Managing Committee, Parsi Law Association, March 1, 1860, para. 10, in J.D. 1862 21/468:151-9; Report into the usages recognized as law by the Parsee Community of India ... October 13, 1862, para. 12, in J.D. 1863 20/143:215-29.

[26] Framjee Nasserwanjee, Chairman Managing Committee, Parsi Law Association, to Sir George R. Clerk, Gov. and Pres. in Council, March 9, 1861, para. 9, in J.D. 1862 21/468:429-59.

[27] Letter of Nowrozjee Furdoonjee to Kaikhusrow Hormusjee, Secretary to the Parsi Law Association, April 28, 1862, in J.D. 1863 20/143:325.

The *Rast Goftar* confirmed this fact, and noted the judgement of the Privy Council to have had "no mean influence on the social morality of the Parsees" in the years following the judgement.[28] The rise in the cases of bigamy threatened not only the importance of the marriage bond, but also the social identity of the Parsi community.

The decision of the Privy Council also exposed a contradiction in the consistency and rationalizations of British justice in India. In *Cursetjee* v. *Perozebai*, the Privy Council had deliberately declined to inquire into the nature of Parsi law, for the practical reason that "from the religion the Parsees profess it cannot be the remedy the Court Christian would afford."[29] Yet, in ruling the request of the Parsi wife as "utterly repugnant ... to the character, practice, and principles of the Ecclesiastical Law," the Privy Council had denied the Parsis the benefit of law relative to their social needs. The Privy Council had denied its right to interfere with matrimonial law as regarded Parsis while denying the Parsis the benefit of matrimonial law. In reversing the decision of the Supreme Court, the Privy Council effectively denied the Parsis the tribunal 'spiritual,' which the Supreme Court had held itself out to be, consequently contradicting the Supreme Court's justification in 1838 in refusing the restitution of the Punchayet. It was argued at the time that the Punchayet would find itself in opposition to the Supreme Court as a tribunal both temporal and spiritual.

The blemish the legal situation of the Parsis represented for British justice in India was periodically commented on, if at times grudgingly, by the British as the Parsis worked to devise a code. While squarely blaming the delay for a code on the Parsis, the *Bombay Times* acknowledged that it was English law that was violating "the immemorial usages of the people, and outraging those ideas of justice, which they have inherited from their fathers."[30] In 1861, the *Bombay Times* noted the contradiction in the English law as regarded the Parsis, when in an article charting the history of the Parsis' attempts to obtain a code, it commented that:

> By the highest legal authority, the Supreme Court is debarred from entertaining suits relating to marriage, divorce, and other kindred matters, arising in the Parsee community; the necessity of action there-

[28] *Rast Goftar*, October 2, 1864.

[29] *Bombay Times*, August 28, 1856.

[30] *Bombay Times*, January 7, 1859.

> fore is the more apparent on the part of Government to stay the current which at this moment is drifting Parsee society into anarchy.[31]

The vagaries of English law and the alien procedure of appealing to it, as well as the inability to satisfactorily agree over a code of Parsi laws explain both the residue of support for the Punchayet, and the lack of expeditious response to the government's call for a code by the Parsis.[32] For other Parsis, the Punchayet's reconstitution was altogether untenable. From 1835 to 1865, the changing social milieu contributed to the breakdown of the consensual cultural understanding that had been the basis of the Punchayet's success. The perception of the Punchayet's obsolescence and obstructionism to the cause of reform and progress was rife by mid-century:

> The present Parsee Punchayet has fallen so much into universal contempt, that the Parsees are no longer able to restrain their feelings. The farce of a Punchayet was allowed to continue as long as Sir Jamsetjee lived, but the growing independent spirit of the Parsees cannot now be checked and bridled with such restraints. The present weak state of the Punchayet, with its feeble powers of imparting justice, and a total want of energy on the part of its members, form a striking contrast to the Punchayet of bygone days, when justice was dispensed impartially, and everything was done in a business-like manner that afforded universal satisfaction.[33]

By mid-century, the picture of the Punchayet's decline stood as the story of its entire history. Despite contemporary misgivings about the Punchayet, both supporter and critic acknowledged the past effectiveness of the institution. Indeed, it was the memory of that effectiveness which turned supporter into ardent critic. The rise and fall of the Parsi Punchayet is representative of the unique social ideology that arose among the Parsis, and1 that had bound community to institution in the support of the Parsi identity for a time. The phenomenon that witnessed community and institution in mutual support of Parsi identity could only witness the rise of disaffection with the institutional method as it failed to safeguard identity. By mid-century, the efforts of the Parsi community had to turn to composing a code of laws in order to safeguard their social customs and norms in the new social and legal climate. If both code and tribunal are seen

---

[31] *Bombay Times*, May 12, 1861.

[32] Proceedings of the Legislative Council, March 31, 1860, in J.D. 1863 20/143:295.

[33] *Bombay Times*, August 23, 1859.

to be representative of the need to safeguard the Parsi identity, then the continued preoccupation with the idea of a Punchayet on the part of some Parsis is understandable. It is also consistent with the interpretation of the history of the Parsis as the continuous attempt by the Parsis of India to direct change in support of their identity.

In 1855, Parsi attempts began to resolve the legal status of the Parsis in Indian law. The creation of a Parsi law code marked the major feat of cooperation between Parsis in the nineteenth century. On August 1, 1855, Parsi leaders met under the authority of the Punchayet head Nowrojee Jamsetjee Wadia to make preparations for an Anjuman meeting. An Anjuman meeting was held on August 9, at Wadiaji fire-temple, and a subsequent meeting was planned.[34] On August 20, 1855, the Parsi Law Association was formed at a gathering of some 2,000 Parsis at Cowasjee Byramjee fire-temple. The initial fifty members that made up the Managing Committee were leaders of the community, including old Punchayet members such as Nowrojee Jamsetjee Wadia, Jamsetjee Jejeebhoy, Bomanjee Hormarjee Wadia, Cursetjee Jamsetjee Jejeebhoy, Sorabjee Jamsetjee Jejeebhoy (1825-82), Framjee Nasserwanjee Patel, Manakji Nasarvanji Petit, Kharshedji Nasarvanji Cama, Cowasjee Jehangir Readymoney, and Byramjee Jejeebhoy (1822-90). Reformers on the Managing Committee included Sorabjee Shapoorjee Bengallee, Nowrozjee Furdoonjee, Dosabhai Framji Karaka, and Ardesar Framji Moos. Nineteen Parsis from the educated class were included on the Managing Committee on the recommendation of Behramji Cursetji Gandhi, including Manockjee Cursetjee.[35] On September 4, 1855, at the first committee meeting of the Association, Nowrozjee Furdoonjee and Sorabjee Shapoorjee Bengallee were recognized as secretaries, and an additional seventy-five Parsis joined the Association. On September 19, 1855, a subcommittee of twenty was formed to prepare a draft code of laws with the aim of petitioning the Legislative Council of India for its enactment.[36]

The predominantly conservative composition of the Parsi Law Association reflected the limited nature of the task before the Parsis. Nowrozjee Furdoonjee explained the object of the meeting:

[34] *Parsee Prakash*, 2:678.

[35] Minutes of Proceedings of a Public Meeting of the Parsee Inhabitants of Bombay, August 20, 1855, in J.D. 1862 21/468:169-76.

[36] *Parsee Prakash*, 2:679n.

> But it is to be regretted that members of the Zoroastrian community, who live in this country under the British rule, are not in a position to enjoy, in the administration of justice, the same privileges with respect to their ancestral customs and usages [as those of the Hindus and Muslims]. The British authorities and the Courts of Justice have not hitherto recognized any of our laws. It is our bounden duty to endeavour to obviate the evils that, from time to time, arise from the want of such fixed laws, applicable to our people, as would be recognized and enforced by British authorities and Judges, and from the application of English Law in the adjudication of those cases in which Zoroastrians are concerned.[37]

The meeting of the Parsis primarily aimed to seek that relief from the application of English law as regards inheritance and succession which the Parsis of Bombay had longed for since 1837. At the same time, the unique nature of the task before the Parsis worked in favour of the modernization of Parsi tradition. The contemporary press followed the Parsis' attempts to secure a code of laws. The *Bombay Times* noted less the significance of the Parsis' aims than the precedent of the meeting.[38] *The Friend of India* went further and commended the Parsis for their initiative:

> But we have never had a Meeting like this. For the first time, a great body of Natives has met to remove a practical grievance by measures calculated to have a practical effect. The Parsees act under no European instigation, for no European has any personal interest in the question. They have benefited by no European guidance, for no European knew any thing of the matter in hand. They did their own work by themselves. They used their own language to express their own thoughts. They appointed a Committee entirely of their own race, and their speeches were, for the most part, the free expression of Parsee ideas. In short, they originated instead of merely imitating.[39]

If the opinions of the contemporary press reflected more the interest in the gathering of the Parsis than the proposals aimed at, the Draft Code of Laws settled and adopted by the Parsis on December 5, 1859, evinced many of the progressive changes the community had undergone in the course of the century. In particular, provisions provided for a partible system of intestate inheritance by the formula where a son received a share, a widow a half share and a daughter a

---

[37] Minutes of Proceedings of a Public Meeting . . . August 20, 1855, in J.D. 1862 21/468:171.

[38] Opinion of the Press, no date, in J.D. 1863 20/143: 431, Booklet No. 2.

[39] Ibid., 429.

quarter share. The right of a married woman to hold property during the life of her husband was also affirmed. Section XII, specifically provided that any property of whatever kind acquired by any woman whether married or single, who having attained the age of majority, set by the Parsis at twenty-one, shall be taken to be her sole and separate property, to be disposed of as if she were a *femme sole.*[40] On March 31, 1860, P. W. LeGeyt submitted the Draft Code accompanied by a Petition of the Parsi Law Association to the Legislative Council of India. At that time, a Select Committee consisting of Sir James Outram, Sir Bartle Frere, and Sir Charles Jackson was created to institute inquiries as to the need for special legislation.[41] On May 19, 1860, the Legislative Council further directed the Government of Bombay to distribute copies of the Petition at provincial centres in the Bombay Presidency and to invite the views and opinions of the entire Parsi community on the Draft Code. The inquiries were initially to be for a period of three months; however, due to representations from the Parsis of the Mofussil the Legislative Council extended the time for six months from September 1, I860.[42]

The Parsis of the Mofussil formed the chief opposition to the enactment of a code of laws. The demands of the rural society on the Mofussil Parsis, as well as their connection to traditional ways raised obstacles to provisions in the Draft Code. To some degree, it may be said that the Mofussil Parsis opposed the authority of the Bombay Parsis to speak on behalf of the Parsi community. Modee Rustomjee Khoorsedjee, the hereditary chief of the Surat Parsis, as the chief representative for the Mofussil Parsis, noted the objections of the Mofussil Parsis to the Bombay Parsis taking up the issue of a code of laws on behalf of the community. The Mofussil Parsis objected to what they considered the misrepresentation by the Bombay community that it had precedence over the other Parsi communities of the Presidency, from which the Parsis of Bombay had originally come. Moreover, the Mofussil Parsis regarded the code of laws proposed by the Parsi Law Association as principally aimed to suit the Bom-

---

[40] Draft Code, in J.D. 186221/468:160-9.

[41] Proceeding of the Legislative Council, March 31, 1860, in J.D. 1863 20/143: 497-500.

[42] Lord H. Ulick Browne, Under Sec. to the Gov't of India, to H. L. Anderson, Acting Chief Sec. to the Gov't of Bombay, May 19, 1860, in J.D. 1862 21/468:149; Letter of Modee Rustomjee Khoorshedjee and the Principal Members of the Parsee Community of Surat, to H. B. Lindsay, June 27, 1860, in J.D. 1862 21/468:187-9.

bay Parsis' fancy. A code that was inconsistent with the religion of the Parsis and contrary to their established usages and customs, to the point that Modee Khoorsedjee doubted that it met with the approval of "the whole of the Zoroastrians of Bombay."[43] The objections of the Mofussil Parsis indicated that there was disagreement over both the desirability of a uniform code of law on behalf of the entire Parsi community, as well as to the nature of Parsi law.

The Mofussil Parsis from the towns of Ahmedabad, Baroda, Poona, Sanjan, Thana and the other provincial centres of Parsi concentration all sent petitions and pamphlets containing their objections to the Draft Code, which they represented as parting from the injunctions of their religion and the usages and customs of their ancestors. The Mofussil Parsis' specific objections, however, were to those provisions of the Draft Code that altered the system of inheritance and succession as practised by them, and that disadvantaged them in their traditional way of life. Principally, the Mofussil Parsis as a whole objected to: the provisions that admitted the claims of widows and daughters to make a will and to inheritance; the right of married women to property; and the absence of provision for the recognition of adopting a son on behalf of the estate of a person who dies without a son, as was the custom in the Mofussil. The representatives of the town of Navsari noted that: "Those persons whose title to inheritance ought to have precedence are thrown to the background, and others occupy their place."[44] The objections of the Mofussil Parsis to the Draft Code highlighted both the change in the social outlook of the Parsi community of Bombay over the course of the century, as well as the extent to which the Mofussil Parsis had habituated to the conservative and traditional norms of the rural Gujarat setting.

The Parsi Law Association disputed the claims and objections of the Mofussil Parsis. The Bombay government submitted the documents containing the remarks and opinions of the Mofussil Parsis to the Managing Committee of the Parsi Law Association for its perusal and comment. Framjee Nasserwanjee Patel, the Chairman of

---

[43] Humble Petition of Modee Rustomjee Khoorshedjee and the Other Members of the Parsee Community of Surat, August 6, 1860, in J.D. 1862 21/468:231-41.

[44] Letters of Dastur Kaikobadjee Roostumjee, Dastur Cowasjee Nusserwanjee, Dessai Burjorjee Nowrozjee etc., and the whole Parsi Community of Nowsari, July 20, 1860, translation into English of October 29, 1860, in J.D. 1862 21/468:245-7; Petitions of the Parsis of the other Mofussil towns, in J.D. 1862 21468:279-378.

the Managing Committee, noted that the Mofussil Parsis were in error in presuming their legal predicament to be substantially different from that of the rest of the Parsi community to warrant an objection to the creation of a code of laws for the entire Parsi community. Framjee Nasserwanjee contended that despite the exemption of English law to them where usages and customs could be deduced (under the provisions of Regulation IV of 1827), the Mofussil Parsis were in fact subject to the same interpreters of that law as the Bombay Parsis. Framjee Nasserwanjee noted that the only choice practically applicable to the Mofussil Parsis in the present order of things was between the application of the customs of the Hindus on the one hand, and the English statutes and precedents on the other. Moreover, Framjee Nasserwanjee contended that the base of the Mofussil Parsis' objections lay in falsely presuming their usages and customs as based on the law of their Persian ancestors:

> The mistake of their authors lies in their assuming, without proof or argument, that the usages to which they wish to adhere in preference to the provisions now proposed for adoption, are the old usages of Persia.... The truth is that they are no such thing. They are Hindoo usages, adopted by the Parsees long after their landing in Guzerat.[45]

Framjee Nasserwanjee noted that the usages and customs the Mofussil Parsis adhered to and took to be consonant with the injunctions of religion, were in actuality the accommodations the rural Parsis had made long ago in Gujarat as means of safeguarding their material interests in the Indian rural setting. To illustrate his point, Framjee Nasserwanjee addressed the principal objection of the Mofussil Parsis to the inheritance of females. He noted that the ancestors of the Parsis of Gujarat had in fact innovated their usages as regards to inheritance, by adopting the pattern of inheritance in Hindu Gujarat aimed to safeguard property on behalf of males. The custom of debarring females from the inheritance of property, which the Mofussil Parsis took to be an ancient Persian usage, was more a Gujarati novelty. The Parsi Law Association contended that succession law among the ancient Persians never debarred females from inheritance, and that the Mofussil Parsis' ill-informed rationale could not be used as sufficient objection to a law code among the Parsis.

[45] Letter of Framjee Nasserwanjee, Chairman of the Managing Committee, Parsi Law Association, to Sir George R. Clerk, Gov. and Pres. in Council, Bombay, March 9, 1861, in J.D. 1862 21/468:429-59.

Framjee Nasserwanjee further noted that the opposition the Mofussil Parsis showed towards specific provisions in the Draft Code was neither consistently held among all the Mofussil Parsis nor justifiable under religious injunction. Framjee Nasserwanjee noted the very wide differences of opinion regarding the right of inheritance to the property left by a female dying intestate that prevailed among the Mofussil Parsis. To varying degrees, the various communities of the Mofussil had accorded to the daughters a right of inheritance to property left by married Parsi women, and often equal in extent to the share awarded to the sons. The only point on which the Mofussil Parsis were unanimous was concerning debarring females the right of inheritance to the property left by male Parsis dying intestate. This objection Framjee Nasserwanjee reiterated, however, had to do with the existing social and economic practices of the Mofussil Parsis and not religious injunctions found in any of the scriptures and texts of Zoroastrianism. None of the objections to specific provisions in the Draft Code put forward by the Mofussil Parsis, Framjee Nasserwanjee claimed, were sufficient to either justify the total exclusion of females from inheritance rights, nor sufficient to frustrate the creation of a Parsi law code. The remarks of Framjee Nasserwanjee evinced the progressive nature of the code of laws envisioned by the Parsi Law Association, and the great social change in the situation of the Bombay Parsis the code was meant to address.

The various opinions of the Parsis on the Draft Code moved the Select Committee appointed by the Legislative Council to recommend that the Government of Bombay appoint a commission to make a preliminary inquiry into the usages recognized as law by the Parsi community of India, and the necessity of special legislation in connection with them. Evidence was to be received from the Parsis, and a consultation of all the authorities, written or oral, to which reference has been or might be made, was to be undertaken.[46] A commission was appointed on December 26, 1861 headed by Justice Joseph Arnould, and comprising judges of the Supreme and Sudder Courts of the Presidency, and including representatives from the Bombay and Mofussil Parsi communities. The first public meeting of the Parsi Law Commission was held on February 15, 1862. The Parsi Law Association presented to the Commission the Draft of a

[46] Report of the Proceedings of the Legislative Council, August 10, 1861, in J.D. 1863 20/143:548-50.

'Supplemental Code of Betrothment, Marriage, and Divorce,' which the judgement of the Privy Council in the case of *Cursetjee* v. *Perozebai* of 1856 had made imperative during the Parsi Law Association's deliberations over the Draft Code of I860.[47]

The deliberations of the Commissicn from December 26, 1861, to the submission of its Report on the October 13, 1862, provided the Bombay Parsis the opportunity to systematically address both the objections of the Mofussil Parsis to the Draft and Supplemental Codes, and the necessity for the enactment of a code of laws uniformly applicable to the Parsis. The role of the Parsi reformers was perhaps pivotal to the conclusions of the Commission. Much of the evidence to support the draft proposals was gathered and presented by reformers such as Nowrozjee Furdoonjee and Sorabjee Shapoorjee Bengallee. As secretary to the Parsi Law Association, from its creation in August of 1855 until May of 1864, Nowrozjee Furdoonjee conducted his business on behalf of the Parsi Law Association without benefit of remuneration or honorarium.[48] Nowrozjee had articulated the need for a code of laws at the commencement of the Association, and worked to shape the code along a progressive course. Nowrozjee believed that where written evidence did not exclude the adoption of progressive rights, such as those for females to inherit, the code should favour a positive rule to be inclusive.[49] Nowrozjee Furdoonjee was effective in countering the objections of the Mofussil Parsis to provisions in the Draft Code as sufficient reason not to enact a code of laws on behalf of the Parsis. He characterized the objections of the Mofussil Parsis to the right of inheritance of females as unreasonable and "gross libels against the whole body of the female members of the Parsee Community." Nowrozjee detailed to the Law Commission instances that proved a lack of fixed rule and usage in the Mofussil concerning several of the provisions the Mofussil Parsis objected to in the Draft Code. Letters and references from Parsi communities outside Bombay in favour of the Draft Code were also presented as proof of the approval of the majority of the

[47] Address to the Parsee Law Commission and Draft Code of the Law of Betrothment, Marriage, and Divorce, February 15, 1862, in J.D. 1863 20/143:528-45

[48] *Rast Goftar*, December 7, 1862; Letter of Framjee Nasserwanjee to Rt. Hon. Sir Charles Wood, Secretary of State for India, London, May 31, 1864, in J.D. 1865 31/104:102-3.

[49] *Bombay Times*, May 13, 1861.

Parsi community of India of the enactment of a Code of Laws for the Parsis.[50] Nowrozjee Furdoonjee and other reformers, furthermore, brought about a change in the understanding of the effect of British policy on Indians. Nowrozjee provided the Law Commission with the necessary evidence of the unsuitability of the English law on the Parsis of Bombay, as well as the absence of a matrimonial law, which had led to the increased incidence of bigamy among the Parsis. The contributions of the reformers to the Commission provides credible example of the influence Indians benefiting from English education had on those whom they emulated.

The conclusions of the Parsi Law Commission reveal the extent to which the influence of the government and the Bombay Parsis ultimately shaped a code reflective of the contemporary requirements of the Parsis. The *Rast Goftar* eagerly anticipated the result of the Commission's inquiries and its favourable response to the demands of the Parsis.[51] The Parsi Law Commission had examined some ten major questions that sought to address the specific objections of the Mofussil Parsis to the Code of Laws, and the need for special legislation as regards to the enactment of the Code. A liberal rationalist interpretation was discernible in the opinions of the Commission, largely to the benefit of the Bombay Parsis. In particular, the Commission admitted the heritable right of females to the intestacy of a male Parsi, and accepted the amounts fixed in the Draft Code (½ of a share for the widow and ¼ of a share to each of the daughters). The right of adoption and inheritance was also recognized. The Bombay Parsis were held by the Commission to constitute the majority of the Parsi community by a ratio of four to one. It was the unanimous opinion of the Commission that the Parsi community of Bombay had established their claim for special legislation, and rejected the Mofussil Parsis' claim to be excluded from such legislation. A fixed code of positive regulations for the entire community was deemed in the interests of the Parsi community as a whole. The Mofussil Parsis, furthermore, were deemed not to have met the burden of having proved their objection to the Draft Code based either on religious scruple or apprehended inconvenience. Indeed, in agreeing with the substantial part of the Bombay Parsis' claims on behalf of the en-

[50] Letter of Nowrozjee Furdoonjee to the Parsee Law Commission and Petition of Calcutta Parsee Inhabitants to the Legislative Council of India, April 28, 1862, in J.D. 1863 20/143:314-31.

[51] *Rast Goftar*, December 7, 1862.

actment of a code of laws, the Commission commended the liberal values that imbued the Parsi law code.[52]

The Commission had also to address the need of a matrimonial code. The Supplemental Code submitted by the Parsis, with certain modifications, was accepted as the basis for the Parsi Marriage and Divorce Act, Act XV of 1865. The immediate requirement of a law providing the legislative security and finality to the settlement of matrimonial disputes favoured the emulation of a ready model. The Parsi marriage code was in large measure modelled on the English Statute Law encompassing the Matrimonial Causes Act of 1857, and with principles and provisions copied from the English Divorce Act of 1858. At the same time, Act XV of 1865 recognized certain usages and customs of the Parsis as law where the English law did not apply and was considered inappropriate to the Parsis, such as to the restitution of conjugal rights. A Parsi matrimonial law had to define what was believed to be the unique nature of the Parsi matrimonial union and, by extension, affected the definition of what it meant to be Parsi. A Parsi marriage, consequently, was defined to be a monogamous union between a Parsi husband and a Parsi wife. Furthermore, the validity and uniqueness of a Parsi marriage was based on: the recognition of thirty-three prohibitions of consanguinity and affinity; the solemnization of the marriage by the Parsi ceremony of Āshirvād, by at least one Parsi priest in the presence of a least two Parsi witnesses; and the parties to marriage being twenty-one, or having obtained the consent of the father or guardian for marriage prior to that age.[53] In the Draft Code of 1860, the term 'Parsi' or 'Parsis' was defined as a person or persons believing in and professing the religion of Zurthosht or Zoroaster, i.e., a Zoroastrian.[54] For all intents and purposes, among the Parsis, a Zoroastrian was taken to be a member of the Parsi community of India, i.e., an ethnic Parsi.

---

[52] Report into the usages recognized as law by the Parsee Community of India ... October 13, 1862, para. 22, in J.D. 1863 20/143:215-29; Abstract of the Proceedings of the Council of the Governor General of India, February 24, 1865, in S. S. Bengallee, *The Parsee Marriage and Divorce Act*, 1865 (Bombay, 1868), 218-27

[53] Address to the Parsi Law Commission and Draft Code of the Laws of Betrothment, Marriage, and Divorce, February 15, 1862, in J.D. 1863 20/143:528-45; Table of Relations put forward by Parsi Law Association, in J.D. 1865 31/104:185-6; Abstract of the Proceedings ... Governor General of India, January 20, 1865, in Bengallee, *Parsee Marriage and Divorce Act*, 199-214.

[54] Draft Code, para. 19, in J.D. 1862 21/468:160-9.

During the next half-century, the issues stemming from the legislative recognition of Parsi unions, as well as the issue of conversion, would force the debate over who was a Parsi, and the rights such a definition entailed.

The Parsi Marriage and Divorce Act reflected the progressive changes the Parsi community had undergone during the century. Bigamy was prohibited by penalty of the Indian Penal Code of 1860. The finality provided by legislation to an issue that had bedevilled the community since the time of the Punchayet was seen as preferable to the practice of adjudicating and sanctioning second marriages during the lifetime of a spouse by a tribunal. The prohibitions of consanguinity and affinity listed in the table of relations officially distinguished the nature of Parsi social relations from the other Indian communities, and along a recognizably Western basis. The Act further provided the terms for matrimonial relief, encompassing a declaration of nullity, dissolution of the marriage, divorce, judicial separation, and the restitution of conjugal rights. The Act, however, differentiated the grounds for divorce between husbands and wives. The differentiation in the rights of spouses encouraged reformist opinion to urge a revision of the provisions. In 1882, the Parsi journal the *Yajdan Parasat* noted the defects of the Parsi Marriage and Divorce Act and the embitterment of married life, which it believed such defects had caused in the past sixteen years. It also lamented the lack of interest for the removal of the defects among either the leadership of the Parsi community or the Parsi public.[55]

The acceptance of the substantial part of the Draft Code of 1860 and the Supplemental Draft Code of 1862 by the Parsi Law Commission recognized the leadership role of the Bombay Parsi community as regarded social change among the Parsis. The Government of Bombay also concurred with the findings of the Law Commission, and recommended that the law proposed on behalf of the Parsis have the character and sanction attached to an Act of the Indian Imperial Legislature. The government overrode the objections of the Mofussil Parsis, and expressed its belief that not only would the enactment of the proposals put forward by the Parsis of Bombay be in the overall interests of the Parsi community, but that the interests of government would also be well served. The expansion of the Bombay Parsi

[55] *Yajdan Parasat*, April 16, 1882, in *Reports on Native Newspapers*, J.D. 1882:10.

communiy beyond the Island of Bombay was believed beneficial to the State and could only be ensured if the family laws of the Bombay Parsis were safeguarded from being subject to a different and inferior law in the Mofussil.[56]

The opposition of the Mofussil Parsis to the Parsi law code had greatly affected the tone of the deliberations between the Parsis given the stakes, and evinced the ideological cleavage that continued to exist between reformers and traditionalists. The *Rast Goftar* blamed the waylaying of the code on the "absolute trash proceeding from an ignorant minority as the Mofussil Parsees who cling to the most antiquated absurdities, as if the progress of the world depended thereon."[57] The *Rast Goftar* took particular offence to the opposition to the right of female inheritance by the Mofussil Parsis, describing their claims as "the rankest absurdities," and "sentiments which are calculated to lower the entire Parsee community in the estimation of any civilized nation."[58] The opposition between the Bombay and Mofussil Parsis over the Draft Code, however, belied the process at work in support of Parsi identity. The creation of a Parsi code of laws was consonant with the historical process in support of identity the Parsis had followed. In 1865, the process witnessed as much the composition of a code of laws suited to the contemporary social requirements of the Parsis, as the record of their customs, ancient laws, and immemorial usages. The *Bombay Times* noted the unique nature of the Draft Code: "That while stamped by many peculiarities, and unfitted for a European type of civilization in some important particulars, it is a striking testimony, upon the whole, to the correct conceptions existing from olden time amongst this people, of the requirements of natural equity and justice."[59] The adoption of a uniform code of laws aimed to safeguard and strengthen Parsi identity consonant with similar attempts in the past.

The majority of the objections of the Mofussil Parsis were less objections of principle than of detail, as for example the necessity of a matrimonial law was acutely felt by all the Parsis. The Law Commission noted that in principle and substance the majority of the Mo-

---

56 Appendices to the Report of the Parsi Law Commission B and C, Minutes of Modee Rustomjee Khoorshedjee, in J.D. 1863 20/143:234-79; Resolution of the Honourable Board, October 20, 1863, in J.D. 1863 20/143:599-601.

57 *Rast Goftar*, June 28, 1863.

58 *Rast Goftar*, December 28, 1862, November 15, 1863.

59 *Bombay Times*, January 7, 1859.

fussil Parsis agreed with the vast majority of those in Bombay in desiring the Supplemental Code to become law.[60] The Parsis of the Mofussil, likewise, had completely agreed with the Bombay Parsis on the unsuitability of the English law to the requirements of the Parsi community. Their opposition to the Draft Code evaporated with the possibility that, in the absence of their adoption of a fixed code of laws, the English law might apply to them in certain circumstances. The latter point is significant as the *Bombay Times* was of the opinion that the Bombay Parsis would have to stand alone over the Draft Code, and get the law passed with exclusive reference to themselves, as to force the Mofussil Parsis to adopt the new code "would be to repeat the injustice it is intended to obviate."[61] The Bombay Parsis had accepted to maintain two different systems of substantive law between the Bombay and Mofussil communities if the objections of the Mofussil Parsis to the Draft Code could not be resolved. A Parsi code of law would apply only to the Bombay community.[62] The overwhelming preference of the Bombay Parsis and that believed to be the wisest course of legislation by the Commissioners, however, was for a code of laws uniformly applicable to all Parsis. The attempts by the Bombay Parsis to devise a code of laws aimed as much to socialize the Parsi community of India to a uniform, if progressive, code of laws aimed to safeguard Parsi identity, as to relieve the Parsis of the Bombay from the onerous application of the English law.[63] While the traditions of the Mofussil would be affected by a general Parsi code of laws, the original purpose behind the creation of the Parsi Law Association as well as the overall interests of Parsi identity would be served on behalf of both Parsi communities. Following the acceptance of the majority of the recommendations of the Law Commission by the Government of Bombay, the *Rast Goftar* predicted that despite their opposition, the Mofussil Parsis would benefit from the new code of laws.[64]

---

[60] Report into the usages recognized as law by the Parsee Community of India ... October 13, 1862, para. 19, in J.D. 1863 20/143:215-29.

[61] *Bombay Times*, January 7, 1859.

[62] Framjee Nasserwanjee to H. L. Anderson, Chief Sec. to Gov't of Bombay, June 27, 1860, in J.D. 1862 21/468:201-3; Framjee Nasserwanjee to Sir George R. Clerk, Gov. and Pres. in Council, Bombay, March 9, 1861, para. 38, in J.D. 1862 21/468:429-59.

[63] *Bombay Times*, January 10, 1859.

[64] *Rast Goftar*, November 1, 1863.

The Parsi Law Commission had accepted the majority of the provisions proposed by the Parsis for the enactment of a code by the Legislative Council. However, over two issues: the recognition of infant marriage, and the recognition of religious differences as grounds for voiding a marriage, the British members of the Parsi Law Commission differed with the Parsis. In their Supplement Draft Code on Marriage and Divorce, the Parsis appeared to sanction the practice of infant marriage and betrothals by including clauses providing for the duties and obligations arising from such a union, and the civil and criminal penalties for their violation. The British members of the Law Commission believed that neither Parsi scripture nor usage sanctioned such a practice, and further regarded it as injurious to the community. The British justices were buoyed in their decision by the support of Manockjee Cursetjee, the Anglophile reformer and member of the Parsi Law Association, opposing the practice of infant marriage and betrothal among the Parsis.[65]

The Parsis had also proposed that in the event of a difference of religious belief arising between parties before or after a Parsi marriage, grounds for declaring such a union void should be enacted. The British members also regarded this as a retrograde piece of legislation if proposed and, insightfully, believed such an enactment was unnecessary so long as the Parsis held strong views as regards interfaith unions. On October 20, 1863, the Government of Bombay in preparing its recommendations to the Legislative Council deferred final consideration of the two issues to the Government of India. The Government of Bombay remained conspicuously silent on the question of infant marriage making no recommendation for its prohibition in specific legislation. On the other question of religious differences as grounds for voiding a marriage, the Government of Bombay also made no provision for voiding a marriage entered into by two parties. The Government of Bombay, however, parted from the British members of the Law Commission over the more difficult question of a change of religious belief by husband or wife after marriage. The government concurred with the Parsis as to the desir-

[65] Report into the usages recognized as law by the Parsee Community of India ... October 13, 1862, para. 27, in J.D. 1863 20/143:215-29. On the details of Manockjee Cursetjee's comments, see Humble Memorial of the Managing Committee of the Parsee Law Commission, to His Excellency Rt. Hon. Sir John L. M. Lawrence, Viceroy and Governor General of India, January 21, 1865, in J.D. 1865 31/104: 14-46.

ability of voiding such a marriage at the insistence of either party, citing the need to be sensitive to Indians' religious beliefs.[66]

The Parsis urged the Legislative Council of India not to omit those sections and parts of sections of the Supplemental Draft Code, which referred to age limits or differences of religion between married persons.[67] Parsi opinion, however, remained divided over the provisions. The *Rast Goftar* concurred with the British members of the Law Commission in seeking to eradicate the "atrocious enormity" of infant marriage. However, the *Rast Goftar* agreed with the majority of the Parsi members of the Law Commission in objecting to making a Parsi marriage binding after the conversion of one of the parties to another faith.[68] The strength of the Parsi identity united reformers and traditionalists alike in opposing any attempt, however well intentioned, to redefine a Parsi marriage as other than between two Parsis. On passage of the Parsi Laws, the Legislative Council of India left legislation proscribing the practice of infant marriage silent, and the Parsi Marriage and Divorce Act of 1865 neither expressly condemned infant marriage nor recognized infancy as grounds for invalidity. No minimum age was provided for a valid marriage, though twenty-one was held as the age of consent and Parsi majority, and the consent of a father or guardian was requisite for a valid marriage between parties below that age. No reference to infant marriage appeared in the Act, with the exception of Section 37, which denied the enforcement of any matrimonial obligations if at the date of the suit the husband is not over sixteen or the wife not over fourteen. The Parsi Marriage and Divorce Act of 1865 also did not allow for voiding marriages, perhaps on the premise that the termination of an unwanted marriage should be left to other forms of relief, including the recourse to divorce.[69] The Act, however, perpetuated a belief in the validity of infant marriage.[70]

---

[66] Resolution of the Honourable Board, October 20, 1863, paras. 6 and 7, in J.D. 1863 20/143:599-601.

[67] Humble Memorial of the Managing Committee of the Parsee Law Association ... to His Excellency Rt. Hon. Sir John L. M. Lawrence, Viceroy and Governor-General of India, January 21, 1865, in J.D. 1865 31/104:14-46.

[68] *Rast Goftar*, November 8, 1863.

[69] See Abstract of the Proceedings ... Governor-General of India, December 23, 1864, January 20, 1865, in Bengallee, *Parsee Marriage and Divorce Act*, 227-34.

[70] A debate emerged as to the intentions of the framers and the consequences of their actions as regarded infant marriage. Pherozeshah Mehta contended that government had not rendered infant marriage legal by omitting any reference to it in the

The new Parsi law code finally settled the role of the Punchayet as an adjudicative tribunal. The Parsi Draft Code had called for a Punchayet of twelve to be elected every five years to grant divorce and adjudicate exceptional issues on behalf of the Parsi community of Bombay. The Parsi Law Commission accepted the idea subject to permitting appeals to the High Court.[71] The reformers opposed the reconstitution of the Punchayet. The Legislative Council proved instrumental in resolving the dispute by establishing special Parsi matrimonial courts. Matrimonial causes were to be adjudicated by Chief Matrimonial Courts composed of a High Court judge assisted by eleven Parsi delegates appointed by government on the nomination of the Justices of the Peace in Bombay, Calcutta, and Madras. District Matrimonial Courts were also to be established composed of a High Court judge and seven Parsi delegates.[72]

The new system, however, continued to provide opportunity for argument between the Parsis. By May 1865, Parsi delegates for the Matrimonial Courts were selected from the communities of the Presidency. The overwhelming majority of the delegates nominated

---

Parsi law code. See J. R. B. Jeejeebhoy, ed., *Some Unpublished Later Speeches and Writings of the Hon. Sir Pherozeshah Mehta* (Bombay, 1918), 3-4. Subsequent court rulings, however, favoured an interpretation of the validity of what was known as non-age (below the age of majority) Parsi marriage. The courts held the usage of the Parsis, as opposed to religious tenet, as accepting the validity of infant marriage. See *Peshotam v. Meherbai*, 1888, *Shirinbai v. Kharshedji*, 1898, in Framjee A. Rana, *Parsi Law: Embodying the Law of Marriage and Divorce and Inheritance and Succession Applicable to Parsis in British India* (Bombay, 1934), 22. In 1929, the Child Marriage Restraint Act became applicable to the Parsis. The Act prescribed fifteen years a minimum age for girls, and eighteen years for boys. Child marriage, however, continued to be neither void nor voidable, but once performed was treated as valid. The Parsi Marriage and Divorce Act of 1936 confirmed this. Further amendments to the Child Marriage Restraint Act raised the age limits yet again, without affecting the validity of child marriage. Finally, the Amendment of the Parsi Marriage and Divorce Act of 1988 set the completion of twenty-one years of age for males and eighteen years of age for females as requisite for the validity of a Parsi marriage. The Special Marriage Act of 1954, involving marriage between individuals of different faiths, does not recognize child marriage as valid, in the case of females below eighteen years of age and males below twenty-one years of age. On amendments to the Parsi Marriage and Divorce Act, see Mohammad Shabbir and S. C. Manchanda, *Parsi Law in India (As Amended by Act of 1988)* (Allahabad, 1991)

[71] Draft Code, in J.D. 1862 21/468:160-9; Report into the usages recognized as law by the Parsee Community of India ... October 13, 1862, para. 29, in J.D. 1863 20/143:215-29.

[72] A Bill to Define and Amend the Law relating to Marriage and Divorce among the Parsees, April 3, 1865, in J.D. 1865 31/104:76-92.

were traditionalists and leading members of the Parsi community.[73] The reformers objected to the hold of the *shetias* over the nomination to the Courts, and in particular the lack of a sufficient educational qualification. The merits of the new system were neither universally acknowledged nor apparent. The choice of candidates, who were usually elected in private chambers by a group of less than twenty influential individuals, gave the appearance of power among a privileged clique, and alienated progressive public opinion. Both Cursetjee Jamsetjee Jejeebhoy and his son the twenty-one-year-old Manockjee Cursetjee Jamsetjee (1851-98), the second and third Sir Jamsetjee Jejeebhoys respectively, and the nominal leaders of the Parsi community, were elected delegates.[74] The turnover of delegates due to various reasons, including old age, poor health and infirmity was also frequent. One priestly delegate by the name of Dastur Jamaspjee Minocherjee resigned citing both his inability to sit for long periods due to a disorder, and his inability to meet his priestly obligations due to having to serve as a delegate.[75]

The uniqueness of the Parsi Marriage and Divorce Act and the authority of the Parsi Matrimonial Court were confirmed in the case of *Ardeshir* v. *Avabai.* In 1869, Ardeshir Jehangir Framji obtained a decree from the Chief Parsi Matrimonial Court for the restitution of the conjugal bond with his wife Avabai. When the wife refused to return to the husband, in 1870 the Court sentenced her to a month's jail and Rs. 200 fine, enforceable under the Indian Civil Procedure Code. In 1871, the Court further held the limited punishment to have fulfilled the terms of the Parsi Marriage and Divorce Act. In 1872, the Supreme Court of Bombay upheld the ruling of the Parsi Matrimonial Court, and interpreted the progressive nature of the Parsi

[73] Names of Delegates, May 25, 1865, in J.D. 1865 31/104:112-17.

[74] Letter of Cursetjee Jamsetjee Jejeebhoy to J. Nugent, Under Secretary to Government, on election of Manockjee Cursetjee Jamsetjee, July 19, 1873, Letter to M.C.J. from Government, August 5, 1873, and acknowledgement of letter by M.C.J., August 7, 1873, in J.D. 1875 129/403:214-25; Letter of Cursetjee Jamsetjee Jejeebhoy to J. Nugent, acknowledging election of Hormusjee Nowrojee Laklatwalla to fill seat of late father, September 3, 1877, in J.D. 1877 90/827, no page.

[75] Letter of Dastoor Jamaspjee Minocherjee, July 16, 1874, in J.D. 1875 129/403:243. For various letters of appointment and resignation, see J.D. 1875 129/403:205-90. Debate continues on the elimination of this unique system, in favour of the uniformity of the personal law in the Indian Constitution, see Phiroze K. Irani, "The Personal Law of the Parsis of India," in *Family Law in Asia and Africa*, no. 6, ed. J. N. D. Anderson (London, 1968), 292.

Marriage and Divorce Act, as not intending to repeatedly punish a wife for refusing to live with a husband.[76]

It is significant that a Parsi law code emerged after mid-century, once the influence and the rationale of the new learning had been accepted. The task of safeguarding identity was also simplified by mid-century. The advancement of education among the Parsis and the new social outlook the reformers contributed to made a code relevant, while dispensing with the need to regulate, control, or compel the innumerable everyday points of caste, social custom and etiquette among the Parsis. The number of concerns relevant to safeguarding Parsi identity had been simplified and codified. The Parsis had defined those areas where in order to remain Parsis, particular laws would apply only to them. In so doing, they had also accepted and made easier their assimilation to the process of modernization in the wider span of their social activity.[77]

The remnant of infant marriage provided the conspicuous example of the limits of social reform among the Parsis in the late nineteenth century. The Parsis believed themselves to have socially progressed to the point where their situation compared to that of other communities was much advanced. In 1884, a Parsi named Ginwala disparaged the practice of infant marriage and adoptions, and enforced widowhood among Hindus, in a letter in the press.[78] Ginwala's letter incurred a judicious response from a Hindu reminding the Parsi of the magnitude of the task underway in India:

> How is it possible for one, who has so badly betrayed his ignorance of the society he is living in, to know the ins and outs of a society the de-

[76] See Rana, *Parsi Law*, 10, 89, 95-6.

[77] In those areas outside the Parsi Laws, a duality of legal standards continued to apply to the Parsis during British rule. This was confirmed by subsequent court rulings following the passage of the Parsi Laws. Except where special legislation affected the community, the English Common Law governed the Bombay Parsis. The Mofussil Parsis were still held subject to Regulation IV of 1827. The passage of the Parsi Laws had made possible the periodic updating and modernization of custom. In 1925, the Parsi Intestate Succession Act of 1865 was re-enacted as part of the Indian Succession Act, and amended in 1939. In 1925, a more equitable division of shares was devised, that, for example, improved the position of widows and daughters and added the parents of a Parsi male intestate as heirs. The formula under the revised Act was that a widow and son receive equal shares twice that of a daughter, and the father half that of a son, and the mother half that of a daughter. In 1991, a further revision provided for equal shares to women and men. See Paruck, *Indian Succession Act*, 66; Irani, "Personal Law of the Parsis," 296.

[78] *The Times of India*, August 30, 1884.

> fects of which he has very few chances of knowing? I admire the spirit in which the Parsees behave towards their fellow brethren the Hindus. Let them not be blind reformers. Let them know that a strong case needs no invectives. Does he think Government interference competent to effect any change in the customs of the Hindus? Does he expect outward force to improve at once the status of the Hindu society with all its traditional associations deeply rooted in the Aryan mind for centuries? If he thinks so, he is greatly mistaken. Outward force will only make the orthodox more obstinate and will only produce breaches, which it will be very difficult to heal.[79]

The Parsis were well advised to listen to the caveats of their fellow Indians on the consequences of rapid social advancement. The compilation of the Parsi Laws exemplified the compromises the community had made between tradition and modernity. With their economic, educational, and social progress underway, and identity among other communities better defined, the concerns of the Parsis increasingly turned to the sleeping question of their religious identity. Questions of conscience, sensibilities, belonging, as well as those of power, rights, obligations, and solidarity, came to preoccupy the community. A renewed religious debate commenced as to the nature of the community. It was only appropriate that from the high point of the achievement of the Parsi Laws in the nineteenth century, the Parsis faced the consequences stemming from the achievement in the twentieth century.

2. *Identity and the Law Courts: The Parsi Punchayet Case*

The enactment of the Parsi Laws of 1865 had raised a predicament as to the extent of the application of Parsi law. The Draft Code of 1860 had included a clause that sought to provide a definition of the term 'Parsi,' as applying to a person or persons believing in and professing the religion of Zoroaster.[80] This definition, however, did not provide that clarity necessary to determine the extent of its application to persons claiming to be Parsi not born in the community. This provision, moreover, was struck from the legislative enactment of the code of laws on the ground that as an imperfect definition its omission could do no harm. The failure of the Legislative Council of

---

[79] *The Times of India*, September 6, 1884.

[80] *Draft Code*, March 1, 1860, in J.D. 1862 21/468:160-9.

India to provide a legislative definition of Parsi provided uncertainty in assessing the rights and benefits of membership in the Parsi community, and a source of debate over the definition of who was a Parsi. The resolution of the question of identity was the subject of disputation in the courts. Once again, the debate over one's credentials as a Parsi came to involve the institution of the Punchayet in the Parsi Punchayet Case of 1906-08.

In 1906, a suit was filed in the High Court of Bombay against the trustees of the Parsi Punchayet of Bombay challenging the validity of their appointment and claim to managing the properties and funds of the Parsi community. The suit further claimed the right of all Zoroastrians to the use and benefit of those properties and funds. The suit was filed under Section 539 of the Civil Procedure Code with the consent of the Advocate General on November 15, 1906, but only began to be heard in March of 1908. The Parsi judge, Justice (later Sir) Dinshaw D. Davar (1856-1916) heard the case, and on his recommendation a second British judge, Justice Sir Frank Beaman, was added. The plaintiffs comprised Sir Dinshaw Petit, 2nd Bart., Sir Cowasjee Jehangir 1st Bart., Rustomjee Byramjee Jejeebhoy (1864-1922), Ratanji Jamsetji Tata (1871-1918), Bapuji Sorabji Patel (1861-1923), Ratanji Dadabhoy Tata (1856-1926), and Nanabhoy Nauroji Katrak, represented by counsel Basil Scot and George R. Lowndes, and instructed by Ardeshir Hormusji Dinshaw & Co. The defendants in the case included the five Punchayet trustees, Sir Jamsetjee Jejeebhoy, 4th Bart. (1852-1908), Hormusji Edaljee Albless, Jamsetjee Cursetjee Jamsetjee (1860-1916), Merwanji Mancherji Cama (1849-1935), and Bomanji Dinshaw Petit (1812-78), represented by counsel J. D. Inverarity, Sir Thomas Strangman, and Jamshedji Kanga.

The case was styled *Sir Dinshaw M. Petit* v. *Sir Jamsetji Jeejeebhoy*. However, from the start the inference was that the case involved a party not directly represented. The cause of the case was inferred to lay in the claim of a French lady, Suzanne Briere, converted to Zoroastrianism and subsequently married in 1903 to Ratanji Dadabhoy Tata, a plaintiff in the case. Having become a Parsi of the Zoroastrian religion, it was claimed, she and other legitimate converts were entitled to the use and benefit of all institutions and funds, including fire-temples and Towers of Silence, accorded to other Parsis. The claim of Mrs. Tata was not adjudicated in this case, but influenced the case and the arguments of counsel.[81] The two issues of the trustees' right to manage the properties and funds of the Parsi Punchayet, and the rights of Zoroastrians including converts to the benefit of those properties and funds were in fact separate if mutually relevant suits, which the court would feel compelled to address given the importance of the case to all parties.

The dispute in the High Court involved parties from the elite of Parsi society over issues that bore on the entire Parsi people. The plaintiffs' decision to test the validity of the trustees' position in court represented a challenge to the orthodox consensus over conversion and community membership among the Parsis. As the Parsis became inured to the pace of modernization, economically, socially, and intellectually, and as many of the social issues of the past century no longer held the attention of the community, the issue of religious identity in the midst of change came to bear more fundamentally on the community. By the latter part of the nineteenth century, the Parsi Punchayet had lost its legal authority to adjudicate issues on behalf of the Parsi community, and had been transformed into an institution of public charity and the overseer of the majority of the properties and funds of the Parsi community. The Punchayet, however, remained relevant in the discussion of Parsi identity and the rights that stemmed from it. In 1882, some eleven individuals from Mazagon in Bombay, born of Parsi fathers and non-Parsi mothers, petitioned the Parsi Punchayet to be recognized as Parsis. Nine of the eleven Mazagon converts had had their *Navjotes*, i.e., the religious confirmations, performed in June of 1882, with the financial support of some two hundred Parsis, leading reformers, and a prominent priest. The controversy in the Mazagon conversions came to centre on the religious procedure and rituals performed in the conversions, with objections raised by orthodox priests and Parsis. The Punchayet was content to let the priests debate and settle the issue.[82] The debate over religious ritual could not obscure the fundamental issue of identity, which the conversions had raised. For some Parsis, the denial to any individual born of a Parsi father of the benefit of the Zoroastrian religion was untenable. For other Parsis, the opposition to

---

[81] *The Parsi Punchayet Case: A Verbatim Report Reprinted from The Times of India* (Bombay, 1908), 29.

[82] Sapur F. Desai, *History of the Bombay Parsi Punchayet, 1860-1960* (Bombay, 1978), 13.

the admission of *juddīns* or non-Parsis to the community remained a social concern that went beyond an issue of ritual.

By the beginning of the twentieth century, a general debate over the admission of converts to the Parsi community had begun. In 1903, J. B. Petit and J. B. Wadia forwarded a requisition affixed with some 2,300 Parsi signatures to the trustees of the Parsi Punchayet, requesting a special committee to examine concerns relating to the admission of *juddīns*.[83] On August 2, 1903, an Anjuman of the Parsis met and appointed subcommittees to examine the issues relating to *juddīn* admissions. The subcommittees found there to be no bar to the admission of proselytes to Zoroastrianism, and that such admission was enjoined by the dictates of the religion. The Parsis, however, were divided as to the social advisability of permitting such conversions.[84] The Anjuman meeting of 1903 and its deliberations marked a significant point in the Parsis' efforts to deal with the issue of conversions. During the course of the meetings news of both the Tata marriage and *Navjote*, and the *Navjote* of a Rajput lady of fifty-eight, who was living with or had married a Parsi and desired to be recognized as Parsi, affected deliberations. The rapid pace of the celebrated cases of conversions, unsanctioned by the greater community, and performed by a high priest in the absence of consensus among the priests, concerned Parsis beyond the general question of the admission of converts.

In 1905, before the Parsi Punchayet Case was launched, the trustees of the Punchayet sought legal opinion over conversions and the admission of individuals to the Parsi community. The opinions of three lawyers were solicited concerning a lengthy list of queries. The lawyers were Basil Scot, Dinshaw Davar who would be judge in the Parsi Punchayet Case, and J. D. Inverarity who would be co-counsel for the defence in the same case. The opinions of the three lawyers in 1905 provided the first effort to find a definition of the term 'Parsi' since the passage of the Parsi Laws. In particular, the lawyers sought to address the rights of non-Parsis by birth, who converted to Zoroastrianism and had undergone the *Navjote* ceremony, to benefit of the properties and funds of the Parsi community. In counsel Scot's opinion, all non-Parsi converts were members of the Parsi community and entitled to the benefits of that membership. From an under-

[83] Ibid., 13: Requisition of July 13, 1903.

[84] Ibid., 14-5: Deliberations of March/April 1904.

standing of the Marriage and Divorce Act and the trust deeds of the Punchayet, it was Scot's understanding that the term Parsi meant a person professing the Parsi or Zoroastrian religion.[85] In counsel Davar's opinion, the term Parsi denoted a nationality or community and had no reference to religion. Davar defined a Parsi to be: an individual born of Parsis, a descendant of the band of Persians who left Persia due to religious persecution, or of an individual born of a Parsi father and non-Parsi mate who had undergone religious confirmation and was admitted by the community. In Davar's opinion, converts might claim to being Zoroastrian, but could not claim any rights as Parsis.[86] The contradictory opinions of Scot and Davar moved the trustees to solicit a third opinion from J. D. Inverarity. It was the opinion of counsel that Mrs. Tata, the Rajput lady, and other converts like them, were not Parsis and not members of the Parsi community, although they were converts to the Zoroastrian religion. He agreed as to the definition of Parsi offered by Davar in its limited ethnic sense; however, Inverarity expanded on the thought of Davar by reference to the case of a Parsi who converted away from Zoroastrianism. In such a case, Inverarity contended, a claim to being Parsi would be meaningless without an observance of the religious sense. While the convert would remain a Parsi in an ethnic sense, his being a Parsi would have little meaning or reference, as he would not be a functioning member of the community. Non-Parsi converts, according to Inverarity, were not entitled to the benefit of the trusts and funds as understood from the trust deeds applicable only to Parsis. To Davar's ethnic definition of birth from the male line, as a condition of being a member of the Parsi community, Inverarity had added the condition of having to follow the Zoroastrian religion.[87]

A clear divergence as to the nature of the Parsis of India was evident in the advice of the lawyers. For Scot, the synonymous nature of the religious and the ethnic identity of the Parsis was held to be similar to the compatibility of one's religious and national identity in the West, with a religious identity shared by individuals of various ethnic, cultural, and national identities. For Davar, the endogamous nature of Parsi society defined the community. His contention that a Parsi remained one despite a change in religion evinced his ethnic

[85] Ibid., 237: Appendix 'A' Opinions of Counsels Basil Scot, Dinshaw Davar and Inverarity.

[86] Ibid., 237, 242.

[87] Ibid., 238.

definition of identity. It was a definition Dhanjibhai Nauroji had adhered to even after his conversion to Christianity in 1839, when years later he claimed to have been born a Parsi, and remained one.[88] Counsel Inverarity's assessment of the Parsi community reflected his appreciation of the community-centred life of Indians. Inverarity acknowledged the ethnic sense of the term Parsi conveyed by Davar, yet reasoned that one's identity as a Parsi was dependent on one's religious affiliation as a Zoroastrian, without which the term Parsi lost its relevance. According to Inverarity, while a Zoroastrian need not be a Parsi, a Parsi could not but be a Zoroastrian.[89] In this sense, Inverarity's appreciation of what it meant to be a Parsi gave to the definition logic, which Davar's exclusively ethnic definition lacked. Inverarity's appraisal is also more true to the understanding of how the Parsis of India have historically defined themselves, as one who is not a Zoroastrian would not be acknowledged a Parsi.[90]

Notwithstanding the three lawyers' opinions, all the lawyers were agreed that as the definition of Parsi involved a matter of fact, no vote, edict, or action by the majority of the Parsi community intent not to accept converts could arbitrarily alter the rights of the minority seeking the benefits of community membership. Albeit, the Parsis were advised to state community opposition to conversions and the policy to deny converts to the Zoroastrian religion the benefits of the properties and trust funds of the community. While the resolution would have no legal effect and bind no court, it would establish a base of action in any future court challenge. At the same time, however, counsel Inverarity was of the opinion that resolutions of the community were unnecessary so long as, on a practical point, the original trust deeds that established the properties and funds of the community, intended only Parsis to benefit from the properties and funds.[91] The conclusions of the lawyers left any resolution of the issue of the rights that followed from identity to the law courts.

From the advice of counsel, it was clear that the claims of converts to the use and benefit of the properties and funds of the Parsi community of Bombay and India would largely depend on the construction given the definition of Parsi in the various trust deeds establishing them. It is an irony that while counsel held the definition

[88] Dhanjibhai Nauroji, *From Zoroaster to Christ* (London, 1909), 63.
[89] Desai, *History of the Bombay Parsi Punchayet*, 242.
[90] See Irani, "Personal Law of the Parsis," 274.
[91] Desai, *History of the Bombay Parsi Punchayet*, 247-50.

of Parsi to be a matter of fact, immutable by resolutions of the Parsis, the definition was left to a court of law to interpret. The Parsis, however, were determined to state their position on who was entitled to the rights associated with membership in the community. An Anjuman meeting of the community was called for April 16, 1905, at Albless Baug, in Bombay. In three resolutions, the Parsis ruled adversely on the admission of converts. In the first resolution, the Anjuman found the social consequences of admitting converts to be injurious to the Parsi Zoroastrian community. For the first time the term Parsi Zoroastrian community was used, signifying the ethnic and religious nature of the community. In the second resolution, the claims of non-Parsis to any of the facilities of the community were denied. The Anjuman further reiterated its opposition to the conversion of individuals by Parsi priests. The extreme displeasure at the conduct of the prodigal priests was made manifest by the Anjuman urging all Parsi authorities to ostracize and bar such priests from service to the community. The third resolution by the Anjuman, declared that the prior resolutions passed unanimously by the assembly equally applied to the children of Parsi fathers and alien women whether married or not, from the date of the Anjuman meeting.[92]

The resolutions of the Anjuman meeting of April 1905 reflected the attempt by many in the Parsi community to regain authority over the issue of conversion. By the unanimity of its voice, the Anjuman had overawed any lack of religious objection to conversion and proselytism, by holding the social consequences of conversion not to have been in the interests of the community. The Anjuman had demonstrated a passion and commitment to the safeguarding of the Parsi identity more reminiscent of the Anjuman meetings of the last century than the dawn of the twentieth century. Impressive for their clarity, consistency, and simplicity of presentation and application, the resolutions of the Parsis were intended for both internal and external notice. Confirming the identity of the Parsis of India as an endogamous community, the Anjuman had declared that the Parsis and their Irani kin were the only Zoroastrians entitled to participate in the life of the community through the benefit and use of its facilities. Moreover, in defining a Parsi as the product of two Parsi parents, the

---

[92] R. E. Enthoven, ed., *The Tribes and Castes of Bombay*, vol. 3 (Bombay, 1922), 195-6.

Anjuman had simplified the definition of the term and the debate around any definition, while imposing on Parsis both male and female the same moral and social responsibility of membership in the community. It reaffirmed a strict endogamy further distinguishing the Parsis from other Indian communities. In three resolutions, the Anjuman meeting of April 16, 1905 had made clear what it regarded as the *raison d'être* of the Parsis of India. The attempt to impose stricter conditions on the community corresponds to the tendency on the part of the Parsi orthodox in the twentieth century to reinterpret the customs and practices of the Parsis along a more conservative basis, and one more conservative than custom historically held to.

The clarity of vision of the Anjuman meeting of 1905 could not disguise the reactionary nature of the Parsis' pronouncements. The sanctions against priests who initiated non-Parsi converts belied the inability of the community to prevent conversions. Furthermore, not all the Parsis were in agreement with the resolutions or even with the procedures that led to them. The Anjuman meeting of 1905 ignored the extent of the pluralism of thought, including religious opinion, within the Parsi community by the twentieth century. Parsis who objected to community meetings being convened for such purposes opposed the calling of the Anjuman, and many prominent Parsis signed a petition to the trustees of the Parsi Punchayet to this effect.[93] The commentaries in the contemporary press reflected the split in the Parsi community. *The Times of India* noted the mass meeting of Parsis at Albless Baug and the "heart-bearing question of proselytism among the Parsees" that continued to exercise its hold over the community and disunite it.[94] The writer Rustom P. Karkaria (1869-1919) was a member of the committee assigned to investigate the advisability of admitting *juddīns* to the Parsi community in 1903. In a letter to *The Times of India*, Karkaria noted the unrepresentative nature of the Anjuman meeting, and how a distinguished segment of the community approved of admitting proselytes to the community:

> At such meetings everything except what falls in with the preconceived view is treated with scant consideration. A speaker must trim his sails to the prevailing breeze; otherwise he must be prepared to be hooted and hissed at, as in fact one speaker was hissed and hooted at last Sunday's meeting because, forgetting his audience, he uttered just

---

[93] *Parsee Prakash*, 4:14; The Rangoon Navjot Case of 1916, reprinted in *Journal of the Iranian Association* 9, no. 12 (April 1920-March 1921): 182.

[94] *The Times of India*, April 17, 1905.

> one short sentence which those assembled did not like. The dissidents had too much regard for their own dignity, as well as that of the community, to form part of such an assembly.[95]

Karkaria's remarks also drew letters and comments in support of the Anjuman's position. Some Parsis contested Karkaria's characterization of the meeting, while one Parsi chided the author for his "pro-conversion bias."[96] Other Parsis took a less sanguine view. A Nadirshaw H. E. Sukia opposed the notion that the religion of the Parsis sanctioned proselytism. While another Parsi believed the modern Parsi community had no practical necessity to admit proselytes.[97] An outside observer took a more noble view of the "solemn conclave" that had assembled to decide the fate of the Parsi community. Believing that the small and effete minority of the Parsis was destined to oblivion, the writer commended their intention to fade away remaining true to their beliefs in not admitting proselytes.[98] The debate over conversion that had arisen anew in the first decade of the twentieth century witnessed a polarization of sentiment and opinion within the Parsi community. The debate over admitting converts to the Parsi community now formed a permanent feature of the debate over religious identity. Traditionalist and orthodox Parsis opposed the admission of converts based on tradition and the social consequences to the community, and increasingly asserted their voice over the issue. For progressive Parsi opinion, the admission of converts had become the test for all the changes in religious outlook and understanding the Parsis underwent in the past half century.

Both the resolutions of the Anjuman meeting of 1905, and the opinions of counsel solicited prior to the meeting became subjects of contention in the Parsi Punchayet Case. It was in part the absence of a Punchayet legally and morally powerful enough to pronounce on Parsi identity and adjudicate claims to membership in the community that persuaded the Parsis to solicit legal opinion, and compelled the Anjuman of the Parsis to pass its orthodox resolutions. Soon after the Anjuman meeting, the plaintiffs in the Parsi Punchayet Case made request for inspection of the trust deeds from which the trustees of the Punchayet claimed their authority. The antagonistic tone of the

[95] *The Times of India*, April 21, 1905.

[96] *The Times of India*, April 25, 29, 1905.

[97] *The Times of India*, April 21, 1905.

[98] *The Times of India*, April 19, 1905.

correspondence reflected the importance of the issues at stake beyond an inspection of the trust deeds.[99]

In opening their court case, the plaintiffs repeated their claim to the defendants being invalid trustees who had deviated from the original intent and design of the trusts endowing the community with properties and trusts intended for all Zoroastrians. The plaintiffs characterized the trustees as a segment of the Punchayet who had arrogated to themselves the management of the properties and funds. They had filled vacancies on their own authority without accounting to the greater community whose representatives they were supposed to be, and had reserved the use and benefit of the properties and funds they managed for only a segment of the community, through a partisan and erroneous reading of the terms Parsi and Zoroastrian. Plaintiff counsel George R. Lowndes contended that a divergence had emerged between the trust deeds of 1851 and 1884, in which the properties and funds of the Punchayet were first comprehensively listed and from which the trustees claimed their authority, and the original construction of the bequests, which assumed the terms Parsi and Zoroastrian to be synonymous. From an examination of the history, documents, plaques and other evidence surrounding the original intent of the founders of the properties and trusts, it was contended that the properties and trusts of the community were originally intended for the benefit of an ethnically heterogeneous category of people. The plaintiffs limited the claim made by converts to the use of specific religious institutions of the Parsi community, essential to practising Zoroastrians. These included the Towers of Silence in Bombay, *sāgḍis* (shelters at the Towers), *nasā khānās* (mortuary houses), and one fire-temple, the Godavara agiary. The fund for consigning the dead to the Towers was also claimed by the plaintiffs as of benefit for all Zoroastrians. The plaintiffs asked the court to rule that the defendants were not validly appointed trustees, that the right to appoint trustees rested in the general body of Zoroastrians in Bombay, and that a scheme be framed for the appointment of trustees and for the proper administration of the properties and funds.[100]

The plaintiffs' case presented an essentially modernist understanding of the Parsis and their history. The Parsis were character-

---

[99] Letter of trustees to Messrs. Ardeshir Hormusji Dinshaw & Co., Trustees' Meeting of Laws Passed, No. 16, 26th April 1905 to 27th March 1906, 8-9, Parsi Punchayet of Bombay Records.

[100] *Parsi Punchayet Case: Verbatim Report*, 5-6, 10, 19, 37, 41, 53, 73.

ized as a heterogeneous community united principally by religion, and historically led by a democratic and representative internal government. The instigation of the suit by parties other than those individuals directly aggrieved, i.e., converts, also suggests the championing of a cause and an agenda as much as a demand for individual justice. Maintaining that the founders of the charities believed in the doctrine of proselytism as part of Zoroastrianism, the plaintiffs essentially opposed the notion of the Parsis as a caste. They believed that all Zoroastrians could claim to be Parsi.

Witness testimony supporting the claim that Zoroastrianism enjoined conversion formed a major part of the plaintiffs' case. Of the less than half dozen witnesses one convert, in particular, was produced in court to confirm the claim that Parsis converted full aliens to their religion. The plaintiffs claimed that a woman of twenty-five years named Soonabai was born a Hindu, converted at a young age to Zoroastrianism, and was living with her adopted father as a Parsi in Surat.[101] The example of Soonabai furthermore suggested that there was no distinction to be made as regards conversion by gender among the Parsis. The plaintiffs also produced religious and historical evidence as to customary conversion among the Parsis, before and after coming to India. They noted religious commandments attributable to Zarathustra urging proselytism, a *fatva* (injunction) from the Parsi/Iranian *Rivāyat* correspondence commending conversions of non-Zoroastrians, prayers of the Parsis that enjoined the conversion of the world to the Good Religion, as well as Parsi prayers celebrating the conversion of prominent Hindu pandits in the past. With such overwhelming evidence, counsel Lowndes felt that "it is almost impossible to conceive that it cannot be a part of the doctrine of the people to convert.... I say it is an essential part of their religion to convert."[102] The reformist/traditionalist confrontations of the past century debated in the press had found their way to the courtroom by the new century, such was the new urgency to address the question of identity in the midst of pluralism.

On presenting their case, counsel for the defendants Sir Thomas Strangman offered a vigorous defence of the trustees' position and actions, and challenged the claims upon which the plaintiffs brought the case to court. The defendants maintained their claim to being

[101] Ibid., 5-6.

[102] Ibid., 76.

valid trustees, and reiterated their legal and moral right to manage the properties and funds of the Punchayet. The defendants challenged the plaintiffs' version of the facts and maintained that they not only had always had the right to fill vacancies and reappoint trustees, but that this fact was known and accepted by the Parsis and those who bequeathed properties and funds to be managed by the Punchayet. Moreover, counsel Strangman contested the right of the plaintiffs to bring a case to court and seek a remedy for something that did not directly affect them. He held it was for the party who is directly affected, and in connection to whom the trusts were to be construed as regards the use of the religious institutions of the community, to bring the case to court. As all the litigants were Parsis, none of whose rights had been denied, people who were not parties to the suit were calling on the court inappropriately to entertain a suit. The two ladies on whose behalf the case was ostensibly initiated were not Parsis and could not argue about the trusts. Counsel maintained that the religious institutions and funds of the community were exclusively for benefit of Parsis, and were never contemplated for the use of all who called themselves Zoroastrian. Counsel for the defendants held that the Parsis used religious and ethnic terms freely and jointly in the past in reference only to the Parsi community. A person born outside the community but converted to Zoroastrianism was never within the contemplation of the founders of the charities. The bonds of religion and race united the Parsis, counsel Strangman contended, where Parsi denotes race and connotes religion. The defendants portrayed the merits of the suit as unfounded and yet involving a case of factional dispute within the Parsi community.[103]

It was left to the two justices to deliver a judgement whose impact would have consequences beyond the interests of the seven plaintiffs and five defendants. The court was wholly sensitive to this point. During the course of the trial, the court had intimated to the parties its willingness to offer a solution to the case, as it stood, without in any way prejudging the final result, should the suggestions of the court not be accepted by the parties. The court noted the effect of the course of the litigation on the Parsis:

> This course has given just offence and caused much indignation throughout the community whose social and private affairs have been drawn within the scope of the inquiry and we think that as it can be

[103] Ibid., 81-3, 103, 119, 123-4, 143, 155, 162, 173.

> stopped upon perfectly fair and satisfactory terms, it is in the interest of the parties and the public that it should be stopped as soon as possible.[104]

The court was prepared to reappoint the existing trustees while ordering a scheme for the filling of vacancies. It would also declare that Zoroastrianism permits conversion, while leaving to the Parsis the regulation of conversion by framing rules to safeguard against abuse. The court effectively left the definition of Parsi untouched.

In offering its compromise, it may be said that the court had recognized the unique circumstances it had been called on to adjudicate. As the old social mechanisms and community institutions that properly had settled questions of social, communal, and religious dispute had eroded away, the trend and recourse to turning to courts and the law to settle matters had begun. To some degree, the courts were ill-suited to their new task, while compelled to take it up. In offering its solution to expeditiously end the litigation, the court acknowledged the introduction into the case of matters well outside legal issues. The court had attempted to provide a compromise settlement along the lines of an old-line tribunal while mindful of the legalities at issue. The court's offer, however, was rejected and the case continued.

In delivering its final judgement, the court noted that the two questions of the valid appointment of the defendants, and the rights of converts to Zoroastrianism to the benefit of the properties and funds of the Parsi community to be separate suits. However, the great importance attached to the two issues warranted a decision by the court on both issues.[105] The justices presented two separate judgements. Justice Davar offered the legal judgement on behalf of the court on the first branch of the case, as to the status of the trustees, ruling that the trustees were invalidly appointed. On the second branch of the case, both justices were also in agreement, ruling against the interests of the plaintiffs. However, as this part of the judgement was in the form of *obiter dicta*, it was elaborated on by the justices separately, offering their individual perspectives on the issues. The judgements of the two jurists were not the first time a court had been called on to adjudicate the social and internal workings of the Parsis. However, the judgements in the Parsi Punchayet

[104] Ibid., 93.

[105] *Parsi Punchayet Case: In the High Court of Judicature at Bombay, Suit No. 689 of 1906: Judgment of the Hon'ble Mr. Justice Davar, Delivered Friday, 27th November 1908* (Bombay, 1908), 45 (hereafter cited as Davar).

Case would stand as the chief statement on the social and religious nature of the community in the modern history of the Parsis of India. The judgements came as close as a court had or would to giving a legal definition to the term Parsi, while providing the Parsi community with a point of reference around which to better debate and consider the future of the community.

Justice Davar delivered the more lengthy judgement addressing those points that concerned him predominantly. Addressing the primary branch of the case as to the validity of the trustees, and their ability to fill vacancies, Davar traced the history of the Parsi Punchayet, and examined the role and duties of the trustees. From the evidence, Davar was of the opinion that the history of the Parsi Punchayet of Bombay was one of a democratic institution, in which the principles of election and accountability were ingrained from its very origins. Davar held that the Punchayet trustees owed their existence to the Parsi community of Bombay, whose appointees they were.[106] In 1823, the informal position of trustee of the funds of the Punchayet was created, and four trustees controlled funds valued at Rs. 18,000. At the same time, although appointed trustees of the funds alone, the trustees also came into management of the immovable properties of the community. By 1851, the funds had grown to one and a half lakh or Rs. 1,50,000, and comprised fifteen funds. At that time, five Punchayet members executed a trust deed. From the examination of the trust deed of 1851 and other exhibits, it was apparent to Davar that the trustees had arrogated to themselves rights and duties unsanctioned by the community. They had no legal right to appoint trustees of property that belonged to the community, or to appoint their own successors. Davar held the right of the trustees to the management of the properties and funds both before and after 1851, to be dubious. From the examination of some twenty-six immovable properties held by the Punchayet, of which the most important was the Towers of Silence, Davar found that the defendants could claim no legal right or position as regarded all but two properties. This decision Davar reiterated was consistent as much with points of case law and those regarding charities as with an appraisal of the terms relating to the individual properties. Significantly, Davar found that as regarded their administration of the properties and funds, the trustees had acted soundly. Save for the second branch of

[106] Ibid., 9-10, 16.

the suit, which was deemed by far to be the more important of the questions before the court, Davar felt no case would have arisen. It was the decision of the court that the defendants were deemed not to have been validly appointed trustees, however, the court held that the existing trustees should be reappointed as a matter of both convenience and practical benefit to the community. A scheme for the appointment of new trustees was to be left to the Commissioner of Trusts, or a committee of the members of the Parsi community.[107]

The judgement of Justice Davar on the position of the trustees marked the culmination of commentary on the role of the Punchayet. To the commentaries by members of the Punchayet, contemporary Parsi observers, Parsi reformers, government officials, British jurists and legislators, was added the judgement of a modern law court presided over by a Parsi. The judgement of Justice Davar gave to the Punchayet a renewed relevance since the institution had lost the power and authority over the Parsis of India from the middle of the nineteenth century. As custodian of the majority of the religious institutions of the Parsi community, the Punchayet played a major role in determining their use, and, by implication, the practical definition of what it meant to be a Parsi in India. The judgement of Justice Davar no less demonstrated the ability of a court of law to shape historical understanding and perception through its own interpretation of the history of an institution.

Both Justices Davar and Beaman were well aware of the importance of the second issue to both the Parsi community as a whole, and the converts not directly represented in the case. Both men were intent on presenting unanimity on the major conclusions. The judgements of Justices Davar and Beaman provide parallel observations on the nature of the Parsis from Oriental and Occidental perspectives, each magnifying and simplifying different issues based on their cultural outlooks. Davar felt compelled to render detailed expositions on the customs and habits of the Parsis while often reducing other issues to minor points of debate within the Parsi community. Beaman, on the other hand, emphasized the general principles behind issues. Despite the importance of the case for all parties the opinions of the justices as to the rights of converts to the religious institutions of the Parsis stood less as legal judgements than as learned commentaries.

[107] Ibid., 21-4, 30-8, 43-4.

The differences in the justices' perceptions were initially apparent in their appreciation of the necessity to adjudicate the second branch of the case. The preliminary issue the justices had to deal with was the right of the plaintiffs to bring the suit, and the obligation of the court to hear the suit and if justified provide relief. Davar concurred with the defendants that the plaintiffs as Parsis, born of Parsis and raised in the religion of their forefathers, had no legal cause to maintain a suit where their rights were never denied, and no infringement either actual or threatened of their rights had occurred. Davar believed that the underlying reason why the plaintiffs had come to court had nothing to do with their own situation, but with the alleged grievances of the French and Rajput converts, neither of whom gave testimony in the case. The case was in Davar's opinion a strictly private suit for the parties caused injury to pursue. Consequently, Davar felt he could offer a judgement on the merits of the second branch of the case without prejudicing the cause of the plaintiffs, as any adverse ruling or error by the court would not apply to the converts, they not being parties to the case. The issues surrounding any future cause of action would also be clearer by his ruling.[108]

Beaman dissented from the opinion offered by Davar as to the rights of the plaintiffs to sue for legal relief. For Beaman, the suit did not concern solely the rights of any one convert, or an abstract right argued in the absence of the concerned parties, but centred on the profound religious question involved at the heart of the use of great public religious endowments. In Beaman's opinion, the plaintiffs had evinced sufficient cause under the provisions of Section 539 of the Civil Procedure Code to bring forward a suit. Beaman observed: "It is as certain as anything in human affairs can be, that no Convert yet to be made could have anything more to say to any Court on his own behalf than has bcen so ably said for the whole of his class ... at the instigation and expense of these Plaintiffs."[109] The plaintiffs as persons interested in a trust were agitating not on behalf of individuals but on behalf of a great principle of administration. On the preliminary issue, consequently, Beaman elevated the religious question of the place of converts in the Parsi community to a matter of fundamental rights. Beaman held that the sole issue of relevance in the

[108] Ibid., 48, 50, 52.

[109] *Parsi Punchayet Case: In the High Court of Judicature at Bombay, Suit No. 689 of 1906: Judgment of the Hon'ble Mr. Justice Beaman* (Bombay, 1908), 4 (hereafter cited as Beaman).

case was the intention and original design of the founders of the trusts as to who was entitled to the use of the religious institutions and endowments of the Parsi community. The religious, social, and cultural issues surrounding the case were relevant only to the extent that they provided an answer to this question.[110]

The judgement of Justice Davar reflected many of the rationales and justifications of traditional Parsi life and outlook. As a public official and particularly as a Parsi, Davar was sensitive to the concerns of the Parsis in the debate over conversion. Davar presented a didactic recitation of the customs of the Parsis and the factors that shaped their history. Davar ascribed particular importance to the usages and customs of the Parsis in determining the intent of the founders of the trusts. In his examination of the witness testimony of the plaintiffs' case, Davar dismissed all claims that the Parsis in the recent or distant past practised conversion. Davar described many of the alleged instances of conversion, as the convenient actions of unscrupulous Parsis who sought to introduce non-Parsi individuals into the community, in order to disguise relationships that are more clandestine. Such relationships included Parsi men taking mistresses and seeking to introduce the children from such liaisons into the community, despite the disapprobation of the community. In disbelieving the claims of witnesses as regarded customary conversions, Davar provided the rationale for disbelieving any claim of conversion, as the misunderstandings of deceived or gullible Parsis.[111]

The case of Soonabai was of particular concern to Davar as it was claimed that Soonabai was a full alien convert to Zoroastrianism. Raised as a Parsi from infancy by a Parsi man who had found her in a hospital, the twenty-five-year-old Soonabai gave evidence that she had been brought to Bombay prior to the trial to visit all the major fire-temples of the Parsis. The facts surrounding the life of the girl and her relationship with the adopted Parsi father struck Davar as highly inconsistent, and characteristic of those cases involving a suspicious relationship. Davar regarded the presentation of Soonabai by the plaintiffs with particular disdain, as both inappropriate legal behaviour by the plaintiffs and their counsel, and as vitiating their general contentions. Chiding the plaintiffs and their counsel, Davar re-

[110]Ibid., 8-10, 28, 41-2.

[111]Davar, 58.

flected on the feelings of the Parsis on the use of the religious institutions by non-Parsis:

> Each one of the Plaintiffs must have known perfectly well that such visit would be regarded by the great bulk of the Parsi community as a sacrilege, if she was an entire alien as they say. They must have known that such visits would wound the feelings of the major portion of the community. It would be idle to disguise the fact that this woman was made to go into the Fire Temples purely for the purpose of creating evidence in the case. It would be idle for the Plaintiffs to shirk their responsibility for the proceeding. They have lent their names to the case and they have entrusted the conduct of their case to responsible Solicitors, and their Counsel was deliberately instructed to examine the witness on these visits to the three most sacred Fire Temples in Bombay. I cannot sufficiently express my sense of disapprobation of tactics such as these.[112]

In directing his comments to the Parsi plaintiffs as much as to their counsel, Davar raised the internal debate over conversion among the Parsis in as high and open a forum conceivable.

It is not surprising therefore that Davar reserved his most vehement criticism for a Parsi priest from Surat who had testified on behalf of the plaintiffs, and sought to expose the indulgences of the Parsis as typifying their general behaviour. Sorabji Bomanji Punthaky had testified that it was common practice in the past and continued to prevail to a certain extent in the present among both lay and clerical Parsis, to rear children of non-Parsi mistresses as Parsis. Davar's contempt for the priest was undisguised, as he believed the priest had libelled the Parsis of Surat and his own class for the sake of pecuniary reward:

> If I have formed a low estimate of this man's morality and honesty, he himself is responsible for it.... That his own conscience in religious matters, when they touch his pocket, is as elastic as his sense of social morality is also clear from his own evidence.[113]

Davar's attack on the credibility of the priest reflected the importance attached to the priestly class in the conversion question. The lackadaisical manner in which Sorabji Punthaky had suggested he or any priest could convert a *juddīn* to Zoroastrianism jarred against the historical attempts of the Parsis to regulate the community in India. It was also testimony to the fact that social control found it difficult

[112] Ibid., 63.
[113] Ibid., 65.

to prevent a priest prepared to initiate an individual into the religion from doing so, particularly, unlike the example of Sorabji Punthaky, where the priest felt his actions to be sincere.

Davar also addressed the question of conversions in the distant past and the broader issue of Zoroastrianism and proselytism. As part of their evidence, the plaintiffs had noted three instances of celebrated conversions in the past. These included the conversion of three Hindu Pandits (wise men) whose names were recited in prayers of the Parsis, the conversion of the Mogul Emperor Akbar, and the more recent Mazagon conversions of 1882. All three instances, Davar held, could not be taken as instances of proof of full conversions. The most recent case of the Mazagon conversions was of children and adults by Parsi fathers, who had been religiously confirmed by a Parsi priest. Evidence for the conversion of the Hindu Pandits, cited in prayers of the Parsis, struck Davar as a case of 'ecumenical' custom to acknowledge the aid and contributions of non-Parsis in Parsi prayers. On the conversion of Akbar, the judge was at pains to take the case seriously beyond noting the famous occasion when the Parsi priest Dastur Meherji Rana of Navsari, had visited the Emperor to expound on the virtues of his religion, as had many learned religious figures from various communities.[114]

Davar's judgement was consistent in holding that no evidence existed to warrant any claim that in the history of the Parsis of India had the conversion of an individual born in another religion been known to the Zoroastrians of India. Far from it being customary to convert, the history of the Parsis did not admit of the attempt, encouragement, or permission of the conversion of *juddīns* to Zoroastrianism.[115] Davar's outlook on the nature of conversion in India distinguished the Oriental view of religious conversion and community from the Occidental outlook offered by the plaintiffs and their counsel, and reflected the social organization the Parsis had adopted ostensibly on arrival in India. In ruling that in the long history of the Parsis in India the cases of Mrs. Tata and the Rajput lady stood as the sole examples of full alien conversions, Davar conveyed the outlook among the communities in India, including the Parsis, to view individuals who were not born into the community as outside

[114]Ibid., 70-2.

[115]Ibid., 81.

the community. The testimonial evidence offered by the plaintiffs of individuals claiming to be converts did not reflect so much cases of formal conversion, as it did the nature of caste-centred community life in India to tolerate, overlook, or acquiesce to, in varying degrees, the presence of individuals from other communities without admitting them formally as members of the community.

Davar's commentary on conversion and the Parsis revealed the general perceptions and prejudices of the Parsis that had come to form a part of their culture in India. Davar reiterated that in the twelve centuries of the history of the Parsis in India, the Parsis had adapted to their social environment so much so that the religious tenet permitting conversion had come into complete disuse. Essentially, the Parsis had come to resemble a caste, in so far as they were an endogamous native community, ostensibly segregated in their social and religious interaction from the other Indian communities around them. Conversion in this milieu was meaningless as the barriers between Indian caste-based communities precluded the formal interfaith conversion of individuals. 'Conversion' occurred only with regard to expelling or readmitting an individual originally from the caste-community. Before 1903 when the case of Mrs. Tara arose, in Davar's opinion, the Parsis had given no thought to recognize the conversion of full aliens. The original construction of the properties and funds of the Parsis, consequently, would have had to exclude all those save Parsis from the use in the benefaction.[116]

Beaman also downplayed the importance of witness testimony as to present-day conversions among the Parsis as relevant to the greater issue of whether at some stage in their history the Parsis accepted conversion. Beaman, however, differed from Davar in his understanding of the implications of the evidence of customary conversion. Beaman held that the historical evidence cited strongly suggested that at some stage in the history of the Parsis in India the concept of conversion was accepted. The example of the Emperor Akbar, in particular, summarily dismissed by Davar, reflected for Beaman a widely spread popular sentiment among the Parsis of the past, and to some degree adhered to in the present, to credit the idea of explicating the virtues of the religion of the Parsis to outsiders. While in the early history of the Parsis in India there might have been a natural reticence or wariness on the part of the minority

[116]Ibid., 86.

community to openly proselytize, Beaman felt the Parsis would have welcomed the admission of influential and protective converts to the community. At a specific stage in their history in India, Beaman contended, the Parsis had come to place their community sentiments and identity above their religious sentiments, and abjured proselytism. Theoretically adhering to their ancient religion and avowing its principal tenets the Parsis, Beaman noted, had "undoubtedly become a caste, and a singularly powerful, influential, and, in every sense, superior caste; assimilated in every sense the caste idea, and made it the bulwark of their tribal or caste unity, so they were themselves hemmed in by it."[117]

For Beaman that stage appeared to have come about with the change in the Parsis' socio-political organization. The tribal or caste body politic of the Parsis, known as the Zoroastrian Anjuman, had naturally given birth to the Parsi Punchayet as a caste institution working the development of the caste sentiment. This process had in all likelihood taken place within the past 150 years, coinciding with the period in which the properties and funds were constructed. This suggested that the founders of the trusts could not have intended the religious institutions of the Parsis to be for the use of converts. Of the twenty-eight references and terms used to characterize the community, none employed the term Parsi. This suggested to Beaman, as it had to Davar, that the religious institutions and funds of the Indian Zoroastrians were reserved for those individuals who comprised the Anjuman of Parsis, under whose custodial control they belonged.[118] Justices Davar and Beaman's understanding of the evolution and nature of the Parsi community, particularly its social organization,was crucial to determining the original intention of the founders of the trusts of the Parsis. In actuality, the question of the original intentions of the founders of the trusts had become ancillary to the historical overview and interpretation of the two jurists.

The judgement of Justice Davar went far in defining who was a Parsi. Davar contended that the word Parsi had only a racial (i.e., ethnic) significance as distinct from the word Zoroastrian, which connotes a religious faith. Davar limited the definition of who was a Parsi to: the original descendants of the Persian emigrants, those born of Parsi parents who profess the Zoroastrian religion, the Iranis

---

[117]Beaman, 16-17, 25-31.

[118]Ibid., 29-35.

who settled in India either temporarily or permanently who profess the Zoroastrian religion, and the children of Parsi fathers by women from other communities who have been duly and properly admitted to the religion.[119] Since the enactment of the Parsi Laws of 1865, it was resolved that Parsi law applied in specific areas only to Parsis. The judgement of Justice Davar further clarified the definition of Parsi by resolving that not all Zoroastrians were Parsis. Since the case of Mrs. Tata, a distinction had arisen between the terms Parsi and Zoroastrian, so that for the purpose of definition Davar felt they could no longer be taken to mean the same thing, as they had prior to 1903 among the Parsis. By distinguishing the ethnic versus the religious roots of the Parsis, Davar had rejected the plaintiffs' claim that by being converted to Zoroastrianism Mrs. Tata, or any full convert, could be considered a Parsi or a member of the Parsi community.[120]

Yet, it should be noted that by defining the term Parsi on the basis of birth or ethnicity alone, the judgement of Justice Davar had left an ambiguity in the definition, and other issues open for debate. The

[119] Davar, 116-17.

[120] The definition of Parsi offered in the judgement of Justice Davar served as the basis of a definition of Parsi incorporated into the Parsi Marriage and Divorce Act of 1936, Section 2, Clause 7, where Parsi was defined as a Parsi Zoroastrian, (i.e., Indian Zoroastrian). The three categories of Zoroastrians, who were defined as Parsi, remained the guide and standard applied in law to the definition of Parsi by the Indian courts. Two subsequent court cases also clarified the status of Iranian Zoroastrians in Parsi law. In the case of *Yezdiar* v. *Yezdiar* of 1950, the High Court of Bombay refused to apply the standard established in the judgement of Justice Davar in the *Petit* case as regards the definition of Parsi, to Iranian Zoroastrian immigrants who were not permanently domiciled in India. On appeal, the Appeal Court avoided the question of domicile, and addressed the definition of Parsi. It limited the definition of Parsi to the descendants of the original Zoroastrian emigrants from Iran, and those Iranian Zoroastrians who were permanently domiciled in India as Indian citizens. In the case of *Jamshed Irani* v. *Banu Irani* of 1966, the decision in *Yezdiar* v. *Yezdiar* was ignored and declared bad law by the High Court of Bombay, specifically for the reason that the court had failed to take account of provisions in the Parsi Marriage and Divorce Act of 1936, Sections 4 and 52 (2), that provided for a change of domicile (among other things) to persons married under the Parsi Marriage and Divorce Act(s). The Court upheld the prescriptive standard as to the definition of the term Parsi in the judgement of Justice Davar, and included both the Zoroastrians of Iran and the Zoroastrians of India within the definition of Parsi applicable in law in India. To all intents and purposes, the decision(s) of the court(s) in 1950 not to regard Iranian Zoroastrians not permanently domiciled in India as Parsis in law was ignored by the Parsi community. The Parsis continued to regard Indian and Iranian Zoroastrians (when in India) as part of the Parsi community. See Irani, "Personal Law of the Parsis," 282; Shabbir and Manchanda, *Parsi Law in India*, 6-7.

reasoning of Davar implied that one could conceive of a Parsi professing a religion other than Zoroastrianism.[121] The Reverend Dhanjibhai Nauroji might be taken as an example. Yet, by the sensibilities of the Parsis of India, the example of a Parsi who was not a Zoroastrian might be said to have been inconceivable. The very overview of the history of the Parsis given by Davar logically implied that the incredibility of a Parsi not being a Zoroastrian would have been as far fetched in 1909 as in 1839. Where an individual such as Dhanjibhai Nauroji had consciously and deliberately renounced the religion of his birth, its tenets, dogma, and worldview, and had formally espoused Christianity by being baptized, it could be said that a conversion had taken place. By the customs of the East, and including among the Parsis, while born a Parsi, Dhanjibhai Nauroji in any meaningful sense had ceased to be Parsi. While Dhanjibhai might claim to be of Parsi background or to have been born a Parsi, to suggest that he was still a Parsi appears more a statement of sentiment than conviction, as his claim to being a Parsi would be meaningless without being a Zoroastrian. This was the point J. D. Inverarity made in 1905, in more accurately characterizing the Parsis as an ethnoreligious community.

The definition of Parsi offered by Davar had included the children born of Parsi fathers and non-Parsi women, who had been properly and duly admitted to the religion. This placed Davar's judgement in contradiction to the resolution of the Anjuman meeting of 1905, which acknowledged only children of Parsi parents as Parsis. Davar's interpretation, however, had not fundamentally differed from the traditional cultural framework of the Parsis. Davar had accepted the interpretation of the Parsis as a patriarchal community of the East, where family units and lineal descent is acknowledged as derived from the male. Davar understood that such children were Parsis as of birth, but did not enjoy the rights of the community until they were duly ritually confirmed, i.e., underwent the *Navjote*. The Parsis had passed resolutions periodically from 1818 to 1830, against the admission of children other than those of Parsi parents to the community. The community's actions reflected the disapproval of the introduction of children of Parsi fathers by non-Parsi women to the community without the formal consent of the community through the Punchayet, as much as it reflected the disapprobation of the

[121] Davar, 94.

community with the situation itself. It reflected the social and moral considerations, which for many Parsis impinged on the purely ethnic consideration, of acknowledging who was a Parsi and acceptance in the community. The same social, moral, and ethnic considerations, it should be noted, left open the question of accepting the children of Parsi mothers by non-Parsi men.

Davar acknowledged children born to Parsi fathers and non-Parsi mothers as Parsi, without sanctioning the practice. Davar's overview of the history of the Parsis, once again, logically implied that like the old Punchayet, Davar did not regard the situation as an invitation to intercommunity unions or adoptions, but as a practice of tolerance by the Parsis for a situation that should never have arisen and was regarded with disapprobation. The practice of 'acknowledging' the children born of Parsi fathers by non-Parsi women as Parsi, would be reinterpreted by the modern Parsis, so much so, that opinion would come to recognize as custom the 'rights' of Parsi men in such a situation. The judgement of Justice Davar aided in the clarification of identity among the Parsis. Significantly, his judgement came to stand as a support for traditional and orthodox Parsi values. Moreover, it came to be part of the historical aetiology of the Parsis' present customs, cited as validation for the nature and state of the contemporary community.

In their respective rulings, the two justices had come to similar findings from differing perspectives on the facts. In large part, they had not differed in their assessment of the course of the Parsis' cultural evolution. They had noted the assimilation of the Parsis to the cultural milieu and norms of the Indian setting as the defining characteristic of the community's history, so much so, that the observance of the tenets of an ancient religion were said to have been modified. Both came to support the notion of the Parsis having formed a group identity and, it may be said, nascent political philosophy of communal organization backed by a consensus on social norms and controls. Both justices equally appreciated the unique historical irony in the Parsis' ability to safeguard, strengthen, and distinguish their collective communal identity from the other Indian communities through the assimilation to the caste-based customs of India. However, whereas for Beaman history provided an explanation of the Parsis' situation, to Davar history provided as much a validation. It was here that the two justices parted company on the relevance of certain issues before the court. For Davar, the importance of custom, ritual, and the sensibilities of the Parsis were indicative of the very historical evolution the court had found itself addressing in taking up the issue of the validity of the trustees, and the use of the religious institutions by converts. For Beaman, the historical evidence was intended to determine a direct issue of right. He regarded collateral considerations by the Parsis of the consequences in admitting converts as expediency and sentiment, and of no concern to the court. Beaman expressed his lack of sympathy for what he regarded as the "most orthodox, the most bigoted champions of the Defendants' case," whose jealous bigotry, he felt, had instigated the case. The rationale of this party, Beaman found to be as inconsistent as it was foreign to him:

> The Defendants, expressing, as we now know the orthodox Parsi view, are prepared to overlook immorality, bastardy—anything but alienage. They are ready to admit any and every Irani Zoroastrian about whose antecedents they cannot possibly know anything. But they will not admit the purest most blameless foreigner, of whose character and conduct they may have the completest assurance.[122]

Beaman's commentary in this regard was significant as it was cited by reformist Parsis following the case as justification of their belief that the true religious question at the heart of the case had been frustrated by secondary questions of custom and legal procedure.

In concluding his judgement, Beaman remarked on the dichotomy of cultural perspectives that had animated the parties in the case:

> It is difficult for any Englishman—probably impossible for any English Churchman who has not been in years in close intimate contact with Orientals of all religions and castes—to put himself into the place of men situated as the Founders of these Trusts were situated.... No English Christian would think of regarding a place of worship desecrated, because a genuine believer happened to have come from a base trade; still less would he deny to such an one rites of Christian burial in a Christian cemetery. But in the Zoroastrian Community, the conditions are widely different. There, while the religion and its ritual purity are still the mainspring of the communal life, they are so intimately bound up with the exclusiveness and the purity of the tribe or caste, that they have become practically identical.[123]

The judgements of Justices Davar and Beaman as exposition of the law stood undisturbed for some forty years. In the absence of a clear

[122] Beaman, 30.
[123] Ibid., 40.

legislative definition, the judgements provided a working definition of identity among the Parsis, which had become the preoccupation of the law since the late nineteenth century. In offering their *obiter dicta* on the second branch of the case, the authors had intended to provide some legal clarity to the issues involved over identity and conversion. At the same time, however, the judgements left unresolved certain issues concerning conversion within the Parsi community that resulted in further legal confrontations, as in the Rangoon Navjote Case of 1914. More immediately, the judgements were the subject of commentary in the press by Parsis and others as to the nature of the contemporary Parsi community. The somewhat rival nature of the commentaries by the justices provided grounds for debate as they mirrored the reformist and orthodox cleavage within the Parsi community.

3. *Law and Ideology:* *The Debate Over Modernity and the Rangoon Navjote Case*

The judgements in the Parsi Punchayet Case came to have an impact on the modern Parsi community that went beyond an overview of the role of the Punchayet, or the issue of conversion. The early twentieth century witnessed the maturation of ideology among the Parsis since the process of educational reform had begun in the early nineteenth century. The judgements came at a time when Parsi intellectual opinion was taking account of the great changes the community had undergone in the previous century. The judgements intensified the debate over progress among the Parsis in which issues as varied as intermarriage, biology and race, education, religious dogma, and the differences between the East and the West were raised. Essentially this was a debate reflective of the concerns of the generation of Parsis that was heir to the debates and confrontations between the reformers and traditionalists of the previous century. At the same time, it exposed the universal tension surrounding change that affects all the generations of Parsis. The debate took account of the judgements in the Parsi Punchayet Case, while to a greater degree incorporating the judgements into a more contemporaneous discussion.

In June 1910, the barrister and future judge, Jehangir J. Vimadalal (1870-1931) urged the Parsis to remain faithful to their traditions, as exemplified by Zarathustra, against what Vimadalal characterized as the evils of Satan and the blackest aspects of Western civilization. Vimadalal's comments were reproduced in print and came soon after the Parsi Punchayet Case. While he did not raise the subject of the Tata conversion specifically, his comments had renewed the debate over conversion. Some Parsis criticized Vimadalal's invocation of the name and message of Zarathustra as inconsistent and hypocritical, in light of his and orthodox Parsis' opposition to accepting converts into the community:

> In the case of Mrs. Tata, Mr. Vimadalal quite forgot that what he now so strongly, so emphatically and so zealously speaks about Zoroaster and his self-sacrificing devotion for the propagation of his religion was thrown to the winds in the case of Mrs. R. D. Tata's admission to the fold of Zoroastrianism.[124]

For reformist Parsis, the refusal to admit *juddīns* or non-Parsis to the religion and community typified the Parsis' long-standing social elitism and resistance to social progress. Reformers regarded the refusal to accept *juddīns* into the community as, in Justice Beaman's words, "an opportunist gloss upon sound religious doctrine."[125] Increasingly, the judgement of Justice Davar came to be interpreted by reformers as the advantage of legalisms over true religion:

> So far as the Farmans [dictates] of Zoroaster as regards propagation of his religion are concerned, the religion has in the High Court suit triumphed in spite of all desperate attempts to the contrary. The success of the trustees lies in the fact of the interpretation and construction of legal documents under which they hold the properties and funds.[126]

To some degree, this appraisal obscured the point that the plaintiffs in the Parsi Punchayet Case had instigated the lawsuit on purely secular grounds. It, however, fostered the belief that the reformers were upholding the spiritual commandment of Zarathustra, the first reformer. It guided reformers in continuing the debate on the future of the Parsi community, and their opposition to the orthodox consensus, which the judgement of Justice Davar had contributed to.

The religious argument remained potent for the reformers in their opposition to the policy of the orthodox. By portraying the judgements in the Parsi Punchayet Case as based more on the cultural biases of conservative parties in the community than the tenets of the

---

[124] *Oriental Review*, June 22, 1910.
[125] Beaman, 24.
[126] *Oriental Review*, July 13, 1910.

religion, the reformers challenged the moral authority of the legal opinions. They also challenged the prevailing assumptions of society that conflicted with their assessment of ongoing social progress. The reformers linked the social evolution of the Parsis to the question of the community's religious outlook, including the resolution of contentious religious issues. They sought to turn the debate away from the cultural outlook implicit in the judgements in the Parsi Punchayet Case and towards an outlook relating to the social state of modern Parsis. Specifically, the reformers utilized the religious issue to counter the orthodox argument over the social consequences of permitting conversions. Whereas the orthodox identified safeguarding the religion with maintaining the race *(i.e.,* ethnicity), reformers identified the 'true' nature of Zoroastrianism as including proselytism and the continued social progress of the Parsis:

> It is no idle speculation to say that a race which has shown, and is showing, such remarkable enterprise, enlightenment and conspicuous abilities will always be found in the vanguard of civilization, and no reactionary forces will keep it back, though they may retard for a while its onward course. It is, therefore, doubtful whether it will quietly submit itself to be enclosed in a social and religious ring fence, albeit there is no lack of this tendency among the more orthodox members of the Community.[127]

Despite the setback the judgements in the Parsi Punchayet Case posed to reformist Parsis, their comments remained relevant to the question of Parsi identity. The renewed challenge of the reformers to orthodoxy established the lines along which debate over progress would proceed in future. It compelled the orthodox to take better account of the sentiments of all Parsis and the pressures of modernity on the community.

Much of the debate and literature of the early twentieth century among the Parsis composes a diverse if often acrimonious discussion on contemporary Western influences on the Parsi community. Contemporary Western ideas opened and shaped a dialogue on the future of the Parsi community. Most significantly, contemporary Western ideas were used by the Parsis to address issues of concern within the community. In the debate over modernity, which reached its height in the first decades of the twentieth century, both reformers and the orthodox took from Western thought arguments to support their

[127] *Oriental Review*, July 6, 1910.

basic interpretation of the nature of the modern Parsi community. Reformers believed their religious outlook to be particularly compatible with modern life.[128] The reformers continued to associate Zoroastrianism with a progressive outlook. By the twentieth century, a distinct reformist outlook on Zoroastrianism and Parsi life had emerged which accepted Western rationalist assumptions regarding religion and social life. A composite of Zoroastrian and rationalist religious concepts expressed itself in a reformist creed for Zoroastrians. The creed of the reformers accepted the fundamental articles of religious faith found in Zoroastrianism while redefining the religious life of the Parsis. Belief in the worship of Mazda, acceptance of Zarathustra as prophet, and an understanding of the ethical purpose of religious life formed the heart of the creed. At the same time, this creed was believed able to change and develop with the developing religious life of man, and the evolution of knowledge and social ideals. For the reformers, the uniqueness of Zoroastrianism lay in its inherent progressiveness and modernity as it had advanced from being a cult, dedicated to ritual and a crude material view of life, to a state where it was intrinsically intelligible to everyone.[129]

Religion, according to the reformers, was the proof of the evolution of humanity's knowledge and social ideals rather than its foundation. Consequently, where progressive understandings come to define a religion, redefinition of the articles of faith naturally occur. While initially a prophet or reformer was needed to guide humanity on its religious quest, the creed of the reformers held that the truths of Zoroastrianism were passed on to succeeding generations partly through authority, and largely through the liberty of thought. The authority and revelation of the prophet rested not on any authoritative communication of truth from God, but as the founder of a historical religion. By upholding the ethical, spiritual, evangelical, and prophetic message of Zarathustra above the ritualistic norms of priestly religion adhered to by the orthodox, the Parsi reformers of the twentieth century maintained the continuity of reformist religious belief since the middle of the nineteenth century. At the same time, they distinguished themselves from their predecessors in champion-

[128] *Oriental Review*, June 29, 1910.

[129] Reprint of a lecture delivered to the Rahnumai Sabha, November 1917, "The Creed of A Zoroastrian," *Journal of the Iranian Association* 7, no. 10 (January 1919): 343-51.

ing an outlook and an agenda against the orthodox religious consensus that had emerged since the Parsi Punchayet Case.

The creed of the reformers in redefining the nature of Parsi religious life had opened the way for further redefinitions and reinterpretations of religion and religious life. This itself made for a plurality of reformist thought. While some reformers upheld Zoroastrianism as the ideal expression of a living religion, others logically progressed to seeing Zoroastrianism as less a religion than a philosophy. Parsi religious scholarship reached its height in the early twentieth century with the works of M. N. Dhalla, who had studied Zoroastrianism under Professor A. V. Williams Jackson of Columbia University from 1905 to 1909. Maneckji Nusserwanji Dhalla (1875-1956) was probably the most influential Western-educated scholar of Zoroastrianism among the Parsis since K. R. Cama. Dhalla's masterly overview of the history and evolution of the religion acknowledges the debt to Western academic techniques and thought, while providing a progressive Parsi defence against the challenge of orthodoxy. *The History of Zoroastrianism* of 1938 was a revised and enlarged edition of Dhalla's first major work *Zoroastrian Theology* of 1914. Dhalla adheres to the concept that Zarathustra enunciated a new religion that encompasses an ethical monotheism. Dhalla placed Zarathustra's time and age at approximately 1000 B.C.E. Earlier scholarship placed Zarathustra in the fifth to sixth centuries B.C.E.[130]

The impact of Western religious and intellectual thought on Dhalla influenced him to broaden his perspective from that of other reformers and characterize and interpret many traditional Zoroastrian doctrinal beliefs in Christian, ecumenical, and moral rationalist terms. Dhalla's writings display a thoughtfulness and gentility in which scholarly research is coupled to liberal philosophical interpretation. Dhalla acknowledged how because of their demand for religious reform, the reformers had come to be termed Parsi Protestants charged by their detractors with thinking in terms of Christianity. The analogy between Parsi reformers and Protestants is appropriate given not only the reform and simplification of ritual the reformers demanded, but also the influence of predominantly Protestant scholars and Iranists on the reformers since the time of Haug. From his study of the history of the religion, however, Dhalla still maintained that the

[130]See M. N. Dhalla, *Zoroastrian Theology* (New York, 1914); idem, *History of Zoroastrianism* (1938; reprint, Bombay, 1963), xxxi.

reformers had remained true to their history and had looked to antiquity for models for their conduct and conclusions:

> Remember that the ancients had tackled the religious and ceremonial questions that arose in their own days according to light that had prevailed in the past. Those of that day had not done the thinking for all times to come, with injunctions to the future generations to act in strict accordance with them. They alone had not the monopoly to think, and had not given the final mandate to acquiesce in all that they had believed.[131]

Dhalla's writings reflect the growing tendency in reformist works by the twentieth century not just to present a favourable view of the religion to Westerners, as had the works of Parsis of the nineteenth century, but also to subscribe to the philosophical ideals of the West. Fundamentally religious in his outlook, Dhalla was initiated a priest, presiding as dastur in Karachi. At the same time, Dhalla defined humanity's goal as lying in finding a philosophy of life suited to its needs.[132] Dhalla's work marked a broadening of the reformist view of religion, which held the examination of other religions as bringing the Zoroastrian back to the uniqueness of his own. In contrast to other reformers, Dhalla was conservative in his religious outlook. For example, D. M. Madan upheld the virtues of independent analysis and philosophical inquiry over dogmatism and authority, noted the inadequacy of revelation, and portrayed Zoroastrianism as more rational philosophy than religion.[133] The plurality of thought within the reformist movement evinced the diversification of Parsi thought since the nineteenth century.

The creed of the reformers was implicit in the idea behind the Zoroastrian Conferences of 1910, 1911, 1912, and 1913, proposed by Dastur Dhalla following his return to India from America in 1909. Like K. R. Cama on his return to India in 1859, following his studies in Europe, Dhalla sought to apply the knowledge and techniques of Western scholarship to a reinvestigation of the beliefs of the Parsis. The idea behind the Zoroastrian Conference consisted in a review of the social and religious questions of modern Parsi life under the leadership and guidance of the reformers. Soliciting a gamut of opinions

---

[131] Dhalla, *History of Zoroastrianism*, 500-1.

[132] See M. N. Dhalla, *Our Perfecting World: Zarathustra's Way of Life* (Oxford, (1930)

[133] D. M. Madan, *Revelation Considered as a Source of Religious Knowledge With Special Reference to Zoroastrianism* (Bombay, 1909).

on issues ranging from restoring Zoroastrianism to its pristine simplicity, to schemes for the education of the priests, to projects to promote technical education, provide medical and charitable resources, and other social and educational causes, the first Conference in 1910 hoped to become a new congress for the Parsis. The Conference had adopted a policy to avoid controversial resolutions that would inflame sensibilities among the Parsis.[134] The *Jam-e-Jamshed* of August 28, 1909, initially welcomed the proposal for a conference, noting how "the suggestion of holding a conference is undoubtedly approvable."[135] However, the Conference's inevitable course to examine radical religious and social reform alienated orthodox opinion. The reform agenda included such contentious issues as the old reformist desire for a revision of the calendar, the question of replacing Parsi fire-temples with prayer halls, reform of religious ceremonies and offerings, and discussion of the *juddin* question. The Conferences also took place at a time of great social and religious agitation between reformers and orthodox in the community, particularly following the Parsi Punchayet Case. The Conferences incurred the displeasure of the traditionalists and orthodox who disrupted the Conferences from within and without, labelling them "pestilential organization[s], with the object of destroying all that is good and beautiful in the Zoroastrian religion."[136] The Conferences were attacked less for the actual opinions and agenda proposed than for the contemporary issues they became associated with. In 1911, Dhalla and Pestonji Ardeshir Wadia started the Iranian Association and in 1912, produced the *Journal of the Iranian Association*. The extent to which the confrontation of ideas defined the new reformist organization is evident in the three main aims of the Association: to maintain the purity of the Zoroastrian religion, to expose and counteract the teachings of the Theosophist and orthodox, and promote measures for the welfare of the Parsis.[137] The disruptions of the Conferences and the assaults by the orthodox in the conservative Parsi press had to some degree deflated the reformers' belief that they commanded the attention of the majority of Parsis. The opposition to the Zoroastrian Conferences confirmed that the orthodox challenge to the reformers remained potent in the twentieth century.

---

[134] *Journal of the Iranian Association* 4, no. 4 (July 1915): 138

[135] Ibid., 137.

[136] Ibid., 130.

[137] *Journal of the Iranian Association* l, no. 1 (April 1912).

The polemical debates of the early twentieth century reveal the extent to which Parsi intellectual and religious thought as a whole came to be influenced by modern and contemporary philosophies. While the interpretations of reformers and orthodox were a chasm apart, the pressure of modernity shaped the presuppositions of the two movements along similar lines. For orthodox Parsis, the judgement of Justice Davar had become a confirmation and validation of what they believed to be the nature of the Parsi community; in S. F. Desai's words "a *vade-mecum* of all orthodox Parsis."[138] Albeit, by 1910 the debate on the future of the Parsis had progressed beyond the historical and cultural analysis offered in the judgements. Both reformist and orthodox philosophies came to embrace more contemporaneous arguments, and utilize the current pseudo-scientific theories to understand and present a view of the Parsis. This was particularly noteworthy in the attempt to demonstrate the compatibility of orthodox thought with the new scientific knowledge.

J. J. Vimadalal put forward biological and racial arguments to justify his contention that conversions among the Parsis would necessitate intermarriages between Parsis and members of other communities, which would inevitably prove inimical to the well-being of the Parsi community:

> Now it is the opinion of biologists of eminence (Darwin, Spencer, Gustave Le Bon and others) that by intermarriage with people who have evolved along different lines and whose traits of character run therefore in different grooves (without regard to relative inferiority or superiority) there results a low type of progeny and the nation or community degenerates.[139]

Such comments incurred both ridicule and an educated response from Parsi and non-Parsi commentators. One critic noted his acquaintance with the works of Darwin, Huxley, Spencer, De Vries, Mendel, Weissmann, Fourens, Buffon, Lallemand, Maudsley, Haeckel, Eimer, Ward, Zehnder, Strahan, Lankester and Galton. From his knowledge of the works, he questioned Vimadalal's views on inter-ethnic unions, noting that he had "not, as yet, come across a statement in their works that goes to prove that only bad qualifies result in the offspring of crossing between two different races."[140] At times

[138] Desai, *History of the Bombay Parsi Punchayet*, 26.

[139] *Oriental Review*, June 29, 1910.

[140] *Oriental Review*, August 24, 1910.

the references by both reformers and orthodox to the panoply of works by contemporary Western writers, scientists, and sociologists (all too many to list here) turned the debate into a 'battle of theses'. The Parsis' familiarity with contemporary Western literature witnessed the aggravation of the ideological and rhetorical stalemate within the community.

The Parsis' utilization of Western ideas in support of their ideological outlooks went beyond the rationalization of the data and arguments by reformers and the orthodox to suit partisan needs, including in the conversion debate. Accusations of ignorance, inaccuracy, and bias and ill-conceived intentions as guiding the agenda of Parsis both reformers and orthodox were employed by the Parsis against one another. The interplay of Western and Parsi ideas in the twentieth century, however, was more complex. The Parsis both adopted and co-opted Western ideas in support and validation of existing ideological outlooks and agendas, while at the same time being shaped in their outlook by these ideas. For example, the biological and racial arguments were used by the orthodox to substantiate a cultural view long held by Parsis, while the extent to which the Parsis were increasingly preoccupied with the question of intermarriage and race evinces the impact of contemporary 'scientific' arguments on them. The articulation of what may be regarded as a Social Darwinist outlook by orthodox Parsis with reference to Western writers and sources, clearly represents the extent to which Parsi opinion followed Western thought, and at the same time represents the relevance of such arguments to the existing perceptions and circumstances of some Parsis.

J. J. Vimadalal's critique of the influence of the West on the spiritual life of the Parsis may also be said to have owed something to the general disillusionment with the idea of the West so prevalent in contemporary European thought. Refusing to have his mental vision blurred by the glamour of the West, as he phrased it, Vimadalal attacked predominantly what he saw as the moral failings of the West. He found corroboration for his outlook in the economic writings of Charles Booth and Robert Blatchford, and the philosophical commentaries of W. H. Hudson, W. J. Stead, and Edward Carpenter.[141] To a larger degree, Vimadalal's views represent a very conservative faith in traditional society felt by Parsis, including the same

[141] *Oriental Review*, July 13, 1910.

Parsis who welcomed and benefited from the material and social progress of the community as a whole. Vimadalal defended his position in stating:

> I never had at any time nor have I now the least intention of presenting the dark side of the picture only nor of ignoring the black side of Oriental Civilization. My protest was and is against those who advise our community to turn Western and up-to-date inside and outside and to let go all that is Eastern.... Let Parsi life be modelled on its own past and time-hallowed foundation, religious, moral and social and let us draw from the West such good points in Occidental Civilization as are capable of easy and natural assimilation with our own lines of growth. Let us do our best to clear our Community of all its evils and to warn it against thoughtlessly adopting a line of growth that would inevitably lead to the evils now experienced in the West.[142]

There is something essentially modernist in the lament for the passing of a world held dear. Such remarks convey the maturation and articulation of a body of Parsi orthodox thought in the twentieth century, and the consequences of defending the label. The debate in 1910 is different from the debates of the last century between the reformers and the orthodox in that the Parsis were no longer a community on the verge of change debating the transformation from traditional to modern society, but one inured to the process of change confronted with assessing the merits of the transformation.

Parsi orthodoxy in the early twentieth century evinced both its commitment to tradition, and its evolution in the debate over modernity. The strength of orthodoxy lay in its ability to tap the sentiment of contemporary traditionalist and conservative Parsi public opinion and represent it against the rival popularity of the reformers. Orthodoxy articulated the cultural threat an uncritical adoption of things Western posed to the Parsis, and the sense of alienation felt by traditionalist Parsis at the pace and consequence of change, particularly upon their right to dispose of their culture and customs. The strength and appeal of orthodoxy lay precisely in the championing of a cultural and religious identity intimately familiar to Parsis, and unadorned by intellectual artifices. Orthodoxy articulated the concept of 'Parseeism' (i.e., Zoroastrianism as practised by the Parsis) at a time when the new erudition among Parsis had come to deprecate such a colloquial term.

---

[142] *Oriental Review*, August 10, 1910.

> It is on a belief in these fundamental principles of our religion (upon which Zoroastrian morals are based), on a following of these Ethical precepts in life and on faith in the efficacy of the beautiful ritual that has fortunately been preserved to us still, that Parsee character has been moulded and formed through long ages and 'Parseeism' come to what it is—a force for good, capable of holding its own against heavy odds and withstanding many untoward circumstances. It was due to this 'Parseeism' that we gloried up to but a few years ago in having no beggar or public woman in the community, and we had amongst us that feeling of solidarity and union which tied together all the classes of the community in a noble bond of love, brotherliness, and unison.[143]

The impulse to stress the positive nature of traditional Parsi life had also welcomed Western religious scholarship. While on one level, orthodoxy conveyed the Parsis' basic feelings regarding their tradition and identity, in order to meet the challenge of modernity to tradition Parsi orthodox thought came to adopt more and more the assumptions in religious debate associated with modern Western religious traditions in confrontation with secularism. Chief among the assumptions was the compulsion to substantiate the basis of religious belief. Zoroastrianism as a world religion with ancient precepts and value system was represented as compatible with modern life.[144]

It was equally characteristic of Parsi orthodox thought in the twentieth century to adopt and rely on foreign concepts unfamiliar to traditional Parsi belief in defence of faith. This in part involved an attack on the assumptions of reformist belief that went beyond producing rationalist counterarguments, and to the espousal of pseudo-scientific, antirationalist, and sensationalist philosophies. A strong anti-intellectualism and even contempt for scholarship is often present in orthodox works. This tendency distinguishes the evolution of a segment of Parsi orthodox thought in the twentieth century from that of the nineteenth century, as well as from moderate Parsi conservative opinion of the twentieth century. Whereas nineteenth century Parsi orthodox thinking shared a suspicion for academic learning

---

143 *Oriental Review*, September 7, 1910. 'Parsiism' refers to the religion of the Parsis, synonymous with Zoroastrianism. With the new scholarship into Zoroastrianism, particularly by the reformers, Parsiism may be said to have taken on a pejorative meaning. Whereas Zoroastrianism properly referred to the religion of the Parsis, Parsiism was associated with the mixture of religious and social practices the Parsis had adopted over the centuries in India. Davar, 94, had noted how the concept of a 'Parsi religion' was meaningless.

144 J. C. Coyajee, *The Future of Zoroastrianism* (Bombay, no date), 21.

that attacked tradition, twentieth century orthodox remarks reflect a cynicism with 'objective' knowledge in general:

> It is high time that Parsees should be made clearly to understand the nature of the claims of 'experts' of various sorts, so as to get rid of a kind of thraldom to so-called expertism. I repeat, and I will take every opportunity of repeating, that the mere understanding of the languages of our scriptures is by itself no qualification at all for the exposition of religion. It often times is the reverse.[145]

Orthodox opinion had come to redefine the new learning much more broadly than academic scholarship alone, and came to adopt rival philosophies to that of the reformers in support of tradition.

It is a measure of the influence of modernity on Parsi thought that among both reformers and orthodox, religious belief had become a matter of intellectual debate where arguments were marshalled in support of the credibility of one's belief and faith. The reliance on Theosophy by the Parsi orthodox for a defence of age-old traditional Parsi religious practices, further reflects the change Parsi ideological thought was undergoing in the twentieth century in the debate over modernity. Antirationalist critiques were often coupled to the fascination with Theosophical ideas in the reactionary confrontation between Parsi orthodoxy and reformism. In the Western Theosophists' criticisms of contemporary European Orientalist scholarship and the reform movement within Zoroastrianism, Parsi orthodoxy had found an ally that offered both what appeared as a critical counterargument to Western scholarship, and a spiritualist approach to learning. H. P. Blavatsky noted how the European Orientalists had only touched the "sediments of genuine Zoroastrianism," and that the key to the true understanding of Zoroastrianism lay with those who were willing to join the very, very few true Occultists.[146] Theosophy's claim to be able to tap extrasensory and supersensible knowledge and reality found particular appeal among those Parsis who believed themselves intuitively connected to their religion by virtue of their devotional practice. The Parsi orthodox contention that academic scholarship was an impediment to genuine religious experience can better be appreciated in light of the belief in the efficacy of more metaphysical forms of knowledge:

---

[145] *Oriental Review*, August 17, 1910.

[146] H. P. Blavatsky, "Zoroaster in 'History' and Zarathustra in the Secret Records," in *H. P. Blavatsky: Collected Writings, 1881-82* (Wheaton, Ill., 1968), 455-6.

> Students of Western Science should never forget that its investigations are confined to what can be observed by our limited senses aided by such instruments as have been brought to their aid, and it is only of very recent years that the phenomena of hypnotism, telepathy, spiritualism and the rest are bringing the borderland of the invisible worlds within the purview of its investigations, and that therefore it would be nothing but presumption on its part to venture to pronounce any opinion on these deep subjects which are quite outside its sphere.[147]

Parsi orthodoxy's stance on conversion further demonstrates the Theosophical impact on Parsi beliefs by the twentieth century. Parsi Theosophists maintained that those who did not have a proper appreciation for 'the spirit of Zoroastrianism,' in fact misunderstood the enjoinment to proselytize in Zoroastrianism. The Parsi Theosophists held out spiritual experience, knowledge and realization as counterbalance to the expertise of the modern Iranist scholars. Proselytism as properly understood by the Parsi Theosophists meant preaching the doctrine of morality to the world, though not incorporating the people to whom the moral doctrine is preached into the Zoroastrian fold.[148] By turning the debate over conversion into a debate about the spiritual powers of the debaters, the Parsi Theosophists evinced more conviction than rationalist argument. They had elevated traditional belief, knowledge, and practice to a higher plain, in an attempt to resist the encroachment of modernity on traditional faith. This antirationalist viewpoint, however, earned the Parsi orthodox and Theosophists the strong invective of their critics:

> Do you expect entire ignoramuses to come and teach us religious truths? If Avestan students are not fully capable, it is one thing. But if, as the fact is, Theosophists know still less or not at all, how are they better fitted to enlighten the community? It is nothing else but silly to put forward a claim of this character in favour of the Theosophists as such.[149]

By 1907, a unique Parsi version of Theosophy emerged known as *Ilm-i-Khshnoom* or the Science of Satisfaction. Behramshah Shroff of Surat started *Khshnoomism* after returning from a visit to Iran, and claiming to have been befriended by a secret, Utopian Zoroastrian sect that had preserved ancient Zoroastrian knowledge and wis-

---

[147] *Oriental Review*, September 7, 1910.

[148] The Rangoon Navjot Case, reprinted in *Journal of the Iranian Association* 9, no.12 (April 1920-March 1921): 99-100.

[149] *Oriental Review*, August 3, 1910.

dom.[150] Shroffs works in Gujarati gained him a following among the orthodox, though it never openly characterized itself as a separate sect among the Parsis. *Khshnoomism* reflected the Parsi fascination for Zoroastrian folklore and mysticism combined with traditional Theosophical ideas. It represents a movement in opposition to Western values as can be found in the history of Parsi thought.[151]

The fascination on the part of Parsi orthodoxy for Theosophy further distinguished orthodox thought from traditional Parsi opinion, and towards beliefs that are more ultra-orthodox. By the twentieth century, Parsi Theosophy came to incorporate a variety of influences in its belief system. Such influences included the belief in mysticism, reincarnation, and the transmigration of souls, vegetarianism, and many forms of abstinence. The espousal of Theosophy by Parsis has been interpreted as both a religious challenge to traditional Parsiism for the allegiance of Parsis dissatisfied with the spiritual answers of traditional belief, and as a potentially divisive force from a movement outside the community.[152] While the former assessment is based on the appraisal of the growing popularity of Theosophy and sees its emergence as a distinct religious tendency or movement within Parsi belief, the latter presupposes the intrinsic antagonism of Theosophy to indigenous Parsi beliefs. Both assessments however reflect the broadening of Parsi religious outlook. The plurality of ideological and religious outlook that emerged in the Parsi community by the twentieth century may perhaps be said to have rendered Theosophy less a religious challenge and rival to traditional Parsiism, than the progression of Parsi religious thought in alternative directions.[153]

---

[150] See N. F. Mama, *A Mazdayaznan Mystic: Life Sketch of the Late Behramshah Navroji Shroff the Twentieth Century Exponent of Zarthoshti Elm-e-Khshnoom* (Bombay, 1944). A Khshnoomist reaction to Parsi reformism is offered in a review of Dhalla's Zoroastrian Theology, see P. S. Masani, *Zoroastrianism: Ancient and Modern* (Bombay, 1917).

[151] In the history of the Parsis there is no movement as distinct and articulated as the Arya Samaj, in reaction to Christianity and modernism. See J. N. Farquhar, *Modern Religious Movements in India* (London, 1929), 29-45, 101-29.

[152] Eckehard Kulke, *The Parsees in India* (Munich, 1974), 99; John R. Hinnells, "Social Change and Religious Transformation Among Bombay Parsis in the Early Twentieth Century," in *Traditions in Contact and Change*, eds. P. Slater and D. Webe (Winnipeg, 1983), 118.

[153] On Parsis and Theosophy, see N. F. Bilimoria, ed., *Zoroastrianism in the Light of Theosophy* (Bombay, 1898); J. B. Sanjana, *Parsis and Theosophy* (Bombay, 1954).

The adoption of Theosophy by some Parsis reflects the dichotomy already noted in the Parsis utilizing contemporary ideas in support of their beliefs, while influenced in their beliefs by the ideas and movements. Supernatural and magical claims and justifications for the belief in Parsi devotional practices have always formed an intrinsic part of Parsi and Zoroastrian tradition. To the extent that the Parsi Theosophists defended such practices as the use of rituals, efficacy of Avestan in prayer, and the practice of purity laws, it reflected the fidelity to that tradition. On the other hand, to the extent that Parsi orthodoxy had come to espouse Theosophical foundations as the basis for Parsi religious devotion, it had come to distance itself from traditional belief. Theosophy reconfirmed orthodoxy's basic faith in Parsi religious outlook and practices, while providing new rationales and justifications for them. Theosophy's appeal among Parsis rested on the unabashed confidence in and innovative reinterpretations of traditional religious beliefs. Theosophy confirmed for some Parsis that their beliefs were both meaningful and relevant in the modern world. The adherence to Theosophical ideas among some Parsis, in fact, reflected the emergence of an ultra-orthodox viewpoint or faction among Parsis, which shared with orthodoxy the belief in tradition, yet in adopting contemporary rationales and philosophies parted from conventional Zoroastrianism. As in the case of the reformers, ultra-orthodox thought had reinterpreted traditional Parsi beliefs while remaining part of the Parsi tradition. As in the case of the reformers, ultra-orthodoxy's creative innovations of Parsi religious thought earned them the criticism of their opponents.[154]

The evolution of Parsi thought in the twentieth century reflected that ideological debate had become a permanent feature within the Parsi community and tradition. The intensity of the debate between the social and religious viewpoints of the reformers and orthodox demonstrated the desire by both sides to shape Parsi opinion towards a uniform social and religious outlook. However, the philosophies of reform and orthodoxy had come to form distinct movements that were expanding further and further to the peripheries of the religious ideological spectrum. Significantly, despite the emergence of Parsi religious pluralism, Parsi religious practices remained unchanged, and divisions had not formed to segregate Parsis in their religious observances and worship.

[154] *Oriental Review*, August 3, 31, 1910, September 7, 1910.

The Rangoon Navjote Case

The perceptions of the Parsis as to their religious, social, and cultural evolution were very much relevant in the case of the Rangoon Navjote controversy, and its investigation will provide a conclusion to the analysis of Parsi thought in the first half of the twentieth century. On the surface, the Rangoon Navjote Case of 1915-18 was the antithesis of the Parsi Punchayet Case. However, the issues conerning conversion and identity were the natural corollary to the 1906-08 case. Whereas the Parsi Punchayet Case ostensibly involved a court challenge on behalf of converts claiming admission to the Parsi fold and its religious institutions, the Rangoon case involved a court challenge by Parsis seeking to exclude and restrain an initiate from the use of a fire-temple. In 1915, a fifteen-year-old girl named Bella on entering the Rangoon fire-temple for the first time since her *Navjote*, found herself and her adopted father the defendants in a court case contesting her right to the premises of the fire-temple. The suit was filed on March 31, 1915, in the court of Lower Burma by four plaintiffs including Merwanji Cowasji, the brother of the second defendant, seeking to exclude Bella from entering the fire-temple, and prevent the second defendant who was a trustee of the Rangoon fire-temple from assisting her to do so. It was claimed by the plaintiffs to the suit that the defendant Bella was not validly converted or initiated into the Zoroastrian religion, and could not be, and that her presence in the fire-temple had both wounded the religious feelings of the Parsis, and had resulted in a desecration of the sacred temple.

Bella was the child of a Parsi widow who had died when Bella was three months old and a Goanese Christian father named Jones who died prior to Bella's birth. Sapurji Cowasji adopted Bella following her parents' death. When Bella was fourteen, arrangement was sought to initiate her a Zoroastrian by having her *Navjote* performed. The head priest at Rangoon refused to conduct the ceremony given Bella's background, and given the sentiments of the Parsi community towards such a *Navjote*. Dastur Kaikobad of Poona subsequently performed the *Navjote*. While the case involved the Rangoon Parsis it affected all Parsis, and the Bombay Parsis played a major role in it. The case once again refocused the ideological and philosophical outlooks of reformers and orthodox on the question of conversion and identity, with each side presenting the rationale and evolution of thought since the judgements in the Parsi Punchayet Case. The orthodox Parsis sought to present the consensus of opinion they believed had emerged on the issue of conversion since 1908, and sought to both challenge Bella's status as a Parsi, and obtain a legal declaration excluding Bella from the use of the temple. For the reformers, the case presented the opportunity to challenge all the presuppositions of traditional belief that had formed around the Punchayet Case judgements, and challenge the very basis on which the Parsis of India continued to claim an understanding of their history, culture, and religion.

The Bombay Parsis had taken an interest in the events in Rangoon shortly prior to Bella's *Navjote*. News had reached the Bombay community of the *Navjote* to be performed of a girl believed to be twelve years of age and whose father, and possibly mother, were not Zoroastrians. The orthodox Parsis of Rangoon were noted to be indignant at the course of events but without remedy. The Parsi community of Bombay was urged to publicize the case and express its displeasure over the *Navjote*, and use its influence on the Parsi priest who intended to perform the ceremony.[155] The Rangoon Anjuman of Parsis along with Dastur Kaikobad of Poona were notified by the Secretary of the Parsi Punchayet of Bombay of the feelings of the Bombay community on the issue of *juddīn* conversions and the decision of the High Court of Bombay in 1908.[156] The Parsi Punchayet of Bombay believed the decision of the High Court of Bombay in 1908, which declared the properties and funds of the Bombay Parsi community for the benefit only of Parsis, to be applicable not only to the Parsi community of Bombay but to the entire Parsi community of India (including Burma). The Parsi Punchayet of Bombay was instrumental in influencing the Rangoon Anjuman to debar Bella from the Rangoon fire-temple and restrict her father from aiding her entry.[157] A requisition was also signed by a number of Parsis against Dastur Kaikobad in April 1914, encouraged it appears by the trustees of the Punchayet and supported by the conservative Parsi press.[158]

---

155 Letter of G. K. Nariman to J. J. Modi, Secretary Parsi Punchayet of Bombay, March 6, 1914, Trustees' Meeting Book, 7th June 1912 to 16th October 1914, 496, Parsi Punchayet of Bombay Records.

156 Ibid., 497-8: Letter of J. J. Modi to G. K. Nariman, and letter to Dastur Kaikobad c/o Nariman, no date.

157 Ibid., 509-10: J. J. Modi to Merwanjee Cowasjee, Rangoon, April 2, 1914.

158 Ibid., 535-9: Letters of Punchayet to Dastur Kaikobad, May 1, 1914.

Dastur Kaikobad, for his part, noted his sadness that the elders of the community were against the *Navjote*, but that he had conducted it in good faith. He agreed, however, to cause no further discomfort to the community by performing similar *Navjote* ceremonies.[159]

The actions of the Bombay community and its leadership were all a matter of scrutiny for the defence in the Rangoon Navjote Case. The defence challenged the assumptions on which the Parsis had come to define their identity, portraying the assumptions as less the result of the historical and cultural evolution of the community than based on popular opinion, notions, and contemporary sensibilities. The judgement of Justice Davar in 1908 also came under scrutiny with the defence seeking to destroy the foundations for the judgement, and the moral authority that surrounded it. Whereas the Parsi Punchayet Case involved an overview of the history and evolution of the Parsis' traditional concept of identity, the Rangoon Navjote Case focused on the Parsis' accommodations and adaptations as regards identity. The defence in the Rangoon Navjote Case challenged the credentials, knowledge, and understanding of Parsi custom of the plaintiffs' witnesses, examined the historical evidence for the Parsis' beliefs, noted the inconsistencies of custom, and raised questions that suggested that the evolution of custom and identity among the Parsis was an ongoing process.

The defence challenged the basis on which the Parsis maintained their definition of Parsi and its application in its examination and cross-examination of many prominent orthodox witnesses. Each witness repeated the definition of a Parsi as applicable to those individuals born of two Parsi parents, those descended from the original Persian immigrants to India, and noted the custom of accepting the duly initiated children of Parsi fathers and non-Parsi mothers. Their definition clearly did not include the children of Parsi women by non-Parsi fathers. The defence sought to establish that what was taken to be Parsi custom and the definition of who was a Parsi, was in fact variable, characterizing it as a definition based on hearsay.[160] The defence further suggested that as regards the situation of the children of Parsi women and non-Parsi fathers, no specific resolution, judgement, or argument existed in the history of the Parsis to

---

[159] Ibid., 540: Letter of Dastur Kaikobad to trustees, May 6, 1914.

[160] The Rangoon Navjot Case of 1916, reprinted in *Journal of the Iranian Association* 8, no. 12 (April 1919-March 1920): 4, 14.

specifically deny this class of children a place in the community. The defence noted that neither in the Anjuman resolutions of 1905 nor in the judgement of Justice Davar had a special class of people that included the children of Parsi women by non-Parsi fathers been listed as outside the community. The only references to Parsi women who married outside the community were by implication.[161]

It was only since the passing down of the judgement of Justice Davar, the defence contended, that the Parsis had come to form their understanding or 'constitution' on the definition of a Parsi, and specifically accepting children of Parsi men and non-Parsi women in the community, while denying the children of Parsi women and non-Parsi men. The defence represented the judgement of Justice Davar as the validation for orthodox sensibilities, a catch-all tool to answer the opposition of those who did not accept the definition, and a "bludgeon ... in the shape of the High Court decision."[162] The defence strategy sought to tie the issue of Parsi identity to the contemporary ideological battle within the Parsi community. A vociferous and bias segment of the Parsis had been able to determine membership in the community, and convince a court presided over by an orthodox Parsi of their claim. The defence inferred that the admission of converts to the Parsi community was part of an ongoing debate over the question of identity and rights among the Parsis. The defence claimed that a sizeable opposition among the Parsis existed to the orthodox policy on membership in the community, and that the court was inappropriately being called on to debar an individual initiated a Zoroastrian and equally accepted by a segment of the Parsi community.[163]

The defence in the Rangoon Navjote Case also examined the historical evidence to substantiate its claim that the Parsis had misinterpreted the religion, and the customs of the past as regards conversion. The defence examined both the history and customs of the ancient Iranians, and the traditions of the Parsis since arriving in India. From an examination of the religious and historical documents, the defence sought to convey that aside from the Punchayet Case judgements, the Parsis could rely on no historical fact for their policy, and that they had deviated from the custom of their ancient Iranian ancestors to intermarry and proselytize. The Parsis' objections to con-

[161] Ibid., 45.

[162] Ibid., 42.

[163] The Rangoon Navjot Case of 1916, reprinted in *Journal of the Iranian Association* 9, no. 12 (April 1920-March 1921): 99-102, 122, 158, 164, 182, 217.

version, and in particular their opposition to intermarriage, the defence claimed, were based on a false premise that historically such things never happened. The defence also cited many 'exceptions' the Parsis of the past had made in admitting converts to the community, as proof of the inconsistency of application of the definition of Parsi.[164]

Significantly, the defence's presentation of the historical evidence largely ignored the representation of the Parsis as a caste opposed to conversion, including the findings of Justices Davar and Beaman. The historical outlook presented by the defence appealed to those Parsis who had never regarded the historical analysis offered in the Punchayet Case judgements as either historically accurate or offering an actual historical analysis. What the defence regarded as exceptions and inconsistencies in the Parsis' approach to membership in the community, the judgements of Justices Davar and Beaman had both recognized as the evolution of the Parsis' social norms in India. Those social norms the justices held had a direct bearing on the construction of the trust deeds applicable to the use of the properties and funds of the Parsi community of Bombay and by extension India, including in Burma. The Parsis' efforts to define identity and the nature of the community, particularly in juxtaposition to the other communities around them, had historically entailed making accommodations, which as a result of the flexibility of their application were characterized by the defence in the Navjote Case as inconsistencies, or at worst, the deliberate biases of partisan interests in the community.

The chief accommodation the Parsis had made, as noted by High Court of Bombay in 1908, was accepting children born of Parsi fathers and non-Parsi mothers in the community. In the Rangoon Navjote Case, the rights and position of children born of Parsi mothers and non-Parsi fathers was the underlying theme. The opposition to Bella's entry into the fire-temple in Rangoon had focused attention on the difference in treatment between Parsi males and females in the community. The level of debate over the situation of half-caste children in the community was measure of the contemporary reappraisals of their history and customs the Parsis were now engaged in. Among progressive Parsis, the invidious practice of accepting the

---

[164] *Journal of the Iranian Association* 9, no. 12:86, 89, 150-2, 217-20

children born of Parsi fathers and non-Parsi mothers as part of the community while excluding children born of Parsi mothers and non-Parsi fathers symbolized a regressive view of community life which was incompatible with their outlook on Parsi social progress. Among orthodox Parsis, the inclusion of children born of Parsi fathers and non-Parsi mothers in the Parsi community had come to be accepted as a legitimate practice, at least in legal theory. They had come to accept the three-fold definition of Parsi contained in the judgement of Justice Davar, while reinterpreting the historical framework of that definition. Davar had acknowledged as Parsi the children of Parsi men by non-Parsi women who were duly confirmed into the religion, while conveying that the Parsis of the past had regarded such a situation with disapprobation and one that should never have arisen. Given this evolution of outlook, it is but a little jump in logic to presume that new generations of Parsi men could regard as a 'right' marrying women from outside the community and having their children recognized as Parsis with full rights in the community. In light of such case, it is equally little wonder Parsi women would seek to make a similar claim on the community.

The defence sought to illustrate the inconsistency of accepting a one-sided practice to Parsi men only, while offering its own historical interpretation of custom. The defence argument in the Rangoon Navjote Case was one of the first to challenge the basis for the dissimilar treatment of Parsi men and women over the issue of marriage, children, and community acceptance. Arguments since then have increasingly stressed modern-day concepts of equality and the equality of treatment as regards the acceptance of children of Parsi women who have married non-Parsis in the community. The defence had gone well beyond a claim for Bella to use the fire-temple of Rangoon. The Rangoon Navjote Case had offered the defence the opportunity to challenge the perceptions and presuppositions of modern Parsis as to identity. The defence had provided a reassessment of the history of the Parsis' cultural and social evolution. The defence exposition may well be seen as a counter opinion to the judgements in the Punchayet Case. The judgement in the Rangoon Navjote Case reflected the extent to which the defence had succeeded in conveying its perception of events.

Mr. Justice C. Young offered the preliminary judgement in the Rangoon Navjote Case.[165] The case for the Burma court revolved chiefly around whether Bella was a Zoroastrian and whether her religious confirmation was valid. The court felt it did not have to consider the status of Bella as a Parsi, as if it was shown that Zoroastrianism permitted conversion, it was immaterial to a declaration of Bella's rights. The Rangoon court consequently refrained from any discussion of caste or the history of the properties and trusts of the Parsis. In reducing the issues to an examination of the religious question alone, the Burma court had little difficulty in citing the very judgements in the Parsi Punchayet Case in favour of regarding Zoroastrianism as a proselytizing religion. The court subsequently ruled that Bella had in fact been properly confirmed into the Zoroastrian religion, and that the plaintiffs could not legitimately sustain any claim to a 'moral' trespass by Bella into the temple.

Having to some degree negated the social and cultural considerations attached to identity and the use of religious institutions, the court came to accept the reformist outlook concerning religious life and identity, and confirmed the greatest misgivings of the orthodox. Applying an equal standard to males and females, the court ruled that as Bella was virtually raised a Parsi she was only technically a convert: "Really she was as much a Zoroastrian as if she had been the actual instead of being only the adopted child of Mr. S. Cowasji."[166] Furthermore, as a priest had been satisfied to the defendant's religious conviction, the question of the propriety of the *Navjote* was accepted. The Rangoon decision confirmed the fact that in the absence of community sanction, or notwithstanding community sanction, the right and ability to initiate an individual into the faith rested with individual Parsi priests.

The evolution of philosophical and ideological outlooks coupled to social and cultural changes, had permitted a plurality of opinion and argument to emerge among the Parsis that came to influence the resolution of disputes by the community in a non-communal forum. The arguments that underlay the judgement in the Rangoon Case, as much as based on law, were influenced by the debate over identity within the Parsi community, which the law naturally took into ac-

---

[165] Judgement in the Rangoon Navjot Case, April 23, 1918, reprinted in *Journal of the Iranian Association* 8, no. 9 (December 1918):302-25.

[166] Ibid., 316.

count in the arguments of the parties. While citing parts of the Parsi Punchayet Case in support of its judgement, the latter had effectively challenged the cultural outlook of the Parsis offered in the Punchayet Case judgements. Even Justice Beaman while desirous to adjudicate only on an issue of right had been compelled to note the significance of the historical and cultural evolution of the Parsis in ruling against the plaintiffs in that case. If the preliminary judgement in the Rangoon Navjote Case reflected an appreciation of the historical and cultural evolution of the Parsis of India, it was certainly the appreciation of a much more recent evolution. In separating the religious issue from the social and cultural question, the Rangoon decision acknowledged the legitimacy of the debate and dispute over Parsi identity of the Parsi reformers. Where the defence in the Rangoon Navjote Case had determinedly assailed the consistency of the Parsis' customs, the doubt was raised sufficient to open the question of adjudicating on custom and history, as a court would any point in law. When historical questions become the discussion of 'non-historical' disciplines too often the standards of the discipline, including the legal profession, take precedence in the analysis.

The case underwent two appeals. The Chief Court of Burma permitted the plaintiffs to enlarge their cause of action and contend that the presence of Bella within the temple precincts to be a violation of the temple trust, and their sensibilities as Parsi beneficiaries of the trust. The Court, consequently, examined the question of who are entitled to the benefits of the fire-temple trust. The Court construed the effect of the documents to impose a trust for the benefit of persons professing the Zoroastrian religion and no others. The Court held the trust to be reserved for a religion and not a race, and agreed with the judgement of Justice Young that Bella could be and was converted or initiated into the Zoroastrian religion. The Chief Court, consequently, dismissed the case of the plaintiffs.

The case was eventually appealed to the Judicial Committee of the Privy Council, and decided by Justices Lord Phillimore, Lord Blanesburgh, and Sir John Edge, on October 22, 1925.[167] Lord Phillimore offered judgement on behalf of the court and ruled that the

[167] Judgement in *Saklat and Others* v. *Bella, in The Times Law Reports*, vol. 42: *1925-1926*, ed. J. Ferguson Walker (London, 1926), 25-9.

trusts of the Parsi fire-temple of Rangoon were to be construed as being confined to persons who are not only of the Zoroastrian religion but also racial Parsis. In their examination of the temple trust documents, as well as the judgements of the Parsi Punchayet Case, their lordships held the double qualification of an individual being a racial Parsi professing the Zoroastrian faith as essential to an appreciation of for whom the temple use was primarily intended.

The judgement of the Judicial Committee of the Privy Council confirmed the view of the Parsi community and its evolution offered by the defendants in the Parsi Punchayet Case. It upheld the threefold definition and prescriptive standard of who is a Parsi elaborated by Justice Davar. Their lordships finding as regards the trust documents, however, did not conclude their commentary and judgement on the qualifications and beneficiaries to the religious institutions of the Parsis. Their lordships held Bella not entitled, as of right, to the use of the temple, and may therefore be excluded or extruded from the temple by the trustees as a trespasser. Nothing, however, compelled and bound the temple authorities to do so, in their lordships' judgement. Indeed, their lordships elaborated the standard applicable where a charity or trust renders some convenience or service of such a nature that it will not hurt the lawful recipients if others share in the service of the trust with them. Examples and illustrations of this form of 'public accommodation' were drawn by their lordships from the history of British institutions, including libraries, gardens, and universities. Consequently, their lordships felt the plaintiffs had failed in the greater part of their suit, and they did not warrant either a declaration against Bella's use of the temple, or a claim of compensation for damage as a result of the trespass from the court.

The judgement of the Judicial Committee of the Privy Council had to some degree thrown back the issue of conversion and community acceptance to the Parsis. While it recognized the claims of tradition regarding the use of the religious institutions of the Parsis of India, it upheld the standard that by extension, if progressively applied, left to Parsi Anjumans and temple authorities the choice not to object to the presence of Zoroastrians not regarded as Parsis within the temple precincts. The Rangoon Navjote Case had once again raised the question of the identity of the Parsis and their perceptions of that identity. In his judgement, Justice Young touched on a sentiment that has continued to resonate in the Parsi community, giving palpable weight to the debate over identity and the Parsis' treatment of one another. Justice Young in referring to the eighteen-year-old girl noted: “All that the defendant asks is permission to pray in the temple of her faith.”

Summary

The process of defining identity through the law had come full circle by the second decade of the twentieth century. What had begun in the middle of the nineteenth century as the attempt to give the Parsis the security of law as regards their customs through legislation in a code, ended with challenges to the meaning of being Parsi in the law courts. With the composition of the Parsi Laws of 1865, it was established that Parsi law applied only to Parsis. The Parsis were able to secure the core issues surrounding their identity while accommodating social change to the many other aspects of identity. The Parsis gained a legislative and constitutional definition of marriage, and were the first Indian community to legally recognize property rights for women. At the same time, the question of the Parsis' religious identity gained renewed focus. The religious issue was no longer a matter of communal debate regarding observances, regulating minor issues, and forming consensus, but now involved issues of heated adversarial confrontation and polemical argument, including in the law courts. Initially, the law courts felt constrained to adjudicate on the issue of religious identity. This was clear in the comments of Justices Davar and Beaman in the early part of the Parsi Punchayet Case when their preference had clearly been to reach a compromise settlement, in as much as a court could, being both sensitive to the needs of the community and the requirements of law. With the erosion of the existing Parsi institutions of social authority and social control, the courts were called on to settle matters not predominantly the preserve of the law and the courts. The social tensions within the Parsi community, which included the growing ideological and philosophical cleavage, made the recourse to the courts and the law to settle religious issues the alternative and the preference of modern Parsis. Couched in trust deeds and restraining orders, the legal suits of the Parsis could not disguise the debate between reformers and orthodox in the new arena, with each side presenting the standard arguments that distinguished their contemporary and modernist presuppositions on the subject of religion and identity.

The law courts provided limited answers to the issues of the Parsis. In the Parsi Punchayet Case, the judgements of Justices Davar and Beaman provided traditionalist and orthodox Parsis with the authority and social sanction for their beliefs, as well as a legal convention on the issue of the Parsi identity. A working and prescriptive definition of Parsi was established, as well clarifying that not all Zoroastrians are Parsis. In the preliminary and secondary judgements of the Rangoon Navjote Case, progressive and reformist Parsis also found some comfort, as the internal debate over Parsi identity remained litigable. If, however, the courts had provided certain answers for partisan interests they cannot be said to have provided any resolution to the debate over identity within the greater Parsi community. The same pressures and forces that made for the Parsi Punchayet and Rangoon Navjote Cases could not but continue the debate over identity within the community. It can well be argued that even in the two court cases, the issues raised were neither novel nor unadjudged previously, but had simply been raised in a new forum. In this respect, yet another aspect of the Parsis' habituation to modernity lies in their short memories and unwillingness to remember their history. The inability of the law courts to provide a solution to the debates of the Parsis, moreover, did not lie in any lack of legal authority, but in its lack of moral relevance. The judgements of the justices in the two cases clearly indicate the capacity of the law and the courts to provide judgements over an issue of rights, while providing no resolution to internal community debates. By the early twentieth century, the Parsis' internal disagreements moved them to seek answers from the law for a resolution of their identity only to have the issue thrust back at them. By that time, it should have become abundantly clear that the resolution of the issues of concern to the Parsis would have to come from the Parsis.

CHAPTER SIX

IDENTITY AND POLITICAL NATIONALISM

By the nineteenth century, the Parsis had proved to be the beneficiaries of colonial rule par excellence. Their economic, political, and social state had been radically transformed under British rule. The early Parsi leaders, the *shetias*, had cooperated and welcomed ties to the British resulting in them being recognized as the leaders of the Parsi community. They had first hand experience of the opportunities available under British rule and their political philosophy, if it may be so described, held to the sufficient exercise of British power in India in benefit of Indians. It was from the ranks of the Parsis that the most loyal of colonial subjects emerged and, equally, it was from their ranks that emerged individuals who would shape and lay the foundations for the self-government of India.

The political maturation of Indians was the natural outgrowth of the social and educational changes taking place under British colonialism, and to which Parsis and Indians had contributed. The Parsis had taken part in politics on the municipal and provincial levels, and an articulated Parsi opinion had emerged within the vernacular and English-medium press on political issues. The early Indian nationalists among the Parsis such as Dadabhai Naoroji, Pherozeshah Mehta and Dinsha Wacha were the quintessential examples of the benefits the next generation of Indians had put English education to. Their outlooks, identities, and material advancement had been shaped by their educational background and opportunities. At mid-century, they adhered to the corporatist reformist vision of social reform within caste communities in benefit of social advancement of Indians in general. And by the latter nineteenth century, Naoroji, Mehta, Wacha and the other educated reformers while loyal to British rule sought a greater independent role for Indians in public affairs, and often in competition with the British. Ultimately, the early leaders of the nationalist movement came to see the progress of Indians to lie in the gradual evolution of India towards self-government. They would be the architects of Indian nationalism guiding it along a moderate course and giving it its calling as a movement dedicated to the interests of all Indians.

The rise of Parsis within the Indian nationalist movement, however, while seemingly consonant with the intellectual maturation and politicization of educated Indians throughout the nineteenth century, posed a dilemma for the Parsis and their sense of identity. The public lives of Dadabhai Naoroji and the other Parsis within the Indian nationalist movement offer a picture of the process of change within Parsi society and the reassessment of identity among Parsis. For the first time issues ostensibly not solely of concern to the Parsis would come to impact on the Parsis' sense of identity. The careers of the nationalists exemplify the transition some Parsis made to a sense of greater identity, as much as they do the difficulties with that transformation.

1. *Dadabhai Naoroji*

Of the many Parsis who would rise to prominence in the nineteenth century, Dadabhai Naoroji holds pre-eminent place. In his introduction to the volume of correspondence between Dadabhai Naoroji and Dinsha Edulji Wacha, R. P. Patwardhan hazards the opinion that of all the great Parsis of the past century, Dadabhai Naoroji was "the brightest and best."[1] Dadabhai achieved renown unparalleled among the Parsis since the first Jamsetjee Jejeebhoy. In large measure, this was a result of Dadabhai Naoroji taking part in public life beyond the confines and concerns of the Parsi community, as well as beyond the parameters of Bombay. As the first Indian subject to run for Parliament, lose, again run and succeed in becoming a Member of Parliament at Westminster, Dadabhai Naoroji achieved a celebrity and influence on behalf of all Indians. The acclaim of his long public life earned him the accolade of the Grand Old Man of India. Yet, while he was the leading representative of India for a time, and is of the first generation of nationalist politicians, Dadabhai Naoroji's association with the name of other leading Parsis of the century attests to the ties of community and identity that continued to define his public and private world. Dadabhai Naoroji along with individuals like Pherozeshah M. Mehta and D. E. Wacha represent the culmination

---

[1] R. P. Patwardan, ed., *Dadabhai Naoroji Correspondence*, vol. 2, part 1 (Bombay, 1977), xiii.

of the efforts undertaken through the nineteenth century by the Parsis to transform their social state, resulting in the rise of public figures comfortable on a community, regional, national, and international level.

Dadabhai Naoroji, consequently, was as much the product of the Parsis' social change as he was its advocate and champion. Born on September 4, 1825, in Bombay, Dadabhai was from a family of priestly background and modest means by the name of Dordi, originally from the region near Navsari. An only child who lost his father at the age of four, Dadabhai was raised by his mother who was a major influence on him, and who saw fit to educate Dadabhai for a secular career. Dadabhai attended the government-run Native Education Society School begun in 1825, which offered a free education to Indian youths. Dadabhai's most famous and still best biographer, R. P. Masani, notes that the experience of the NES School instilled in Dadabhai an ardent appreciation for the benefits to be derived from access to free education.[2] The career of Dadabhai Naoroji is testimony to the task Indians put English education to. Dadabhai's first job following graduation was as Head Native Assistant Master at the Elphinstone College. This was soon followed by his elevation to Professor of Mathematics and Natural Philosophy at age twenty-seven. Dadabhai's academic appointment had owed something to his having to forgo the opportunity to travel to Britain to study as a barrister, offered to him by Sir Erskine Perry in 1845. Due to the recent row over the Parsi boys' conversion case, the Parsi leadership was not agreeable to join in the offer. The appellation of 'Dadabhai Professor' was one that delighted Dadabhai throughout his life, and certainly gave meaning to his didactic efforts on behalf of educating Indians and the British on various subjects.[3]

Dadabhai Naoroji took part and was in some way associated with every social concern and reformist endeavour in Bombay in the early to mid-nineteenth century. Dadabhai's participation within the reform groups and societies at mid-century was the natural outgrowth of a life influenced by education. The apprenticeship for his political career lay in the social politics of the Parsis of Bombay. Dadabhai was a member and/or leader within the Native Literary Society, Students' Literary and Scientific Society, the Dnyan Prasarak Society,

[2] R. P. Masani, *Dadabhai Naoroji* (Delhi, 1960), 5-9.

[3] *Parsee Prakash*, 1:503; Masani, *Dadabhai Naoroji*, 10-13.

the Rahnumai Mazdayasnan Society, the Parsi Law Association, and the Bombay Association. In 1851, Dadabhai started the *Rast Goftar* newspaper as the first reformist newspaper, which sought to move Parsi-run journalism away from purely community concerns. While the newspaper was started in reaction to the *shetias'* ineffectual leadership during the Parsi/Muslim riots of 1851, Dadabhai maintained respect for the great traditionalist leaders of the community like Jamsetjee Jejeebhoy and Framji Cowasji Banaji.[4] Dadabhai's open-mindedness to the *shetias* reflected his desire to be inclusive of all elements in the cause of reform.

The *shetias'* financial support of socially reformist causes and projects was essential particularly in the early years when most endeavours were all close-run things. The network of interests and support developed between generations of Parsis was one Dadabhai was familiar with and came to rely on after he left for Britain. The name of Cama was often associated with the support, both moral and financial, of reformist causes. It was at the behest of the Camas that Dadabhai Naoroji accompanied Kharshedji and his brother Mancherji to Britain in 1855. The Camas established the first successful Indian mercantile business house dealing in a variety of goods in London and Liverpool, which for three years Dadabhai ran in partnership with them. While unsure of his abilities as a businessman, Dadabhai accepted the offer as a means to further the contacts between Indians and Britons. Dadabhai's journey to Britain beginning in 1855 began a twenty-five year relationship with that country, during which he ventured back and forth several times. In 1858, Dadabhai severed his business ties to the Camas, and began his own firm under the name of Dadabhai Naoroji & Co., which operated until 1881.[5] His career choice signified the route some Indians followed, including among the educated intelligentsia, to achieve financial independence. During the time his firm was in operation, Dadabhai made many contacts that served to expand his knowledge of the economic ties between India and Britain.

A major aspect of Dadabhai's role in Britain was to aid the passage of other Indians to Britain who would be able to compete and take part in business, educational, and other professional opportuni-

---

[4] K. N. Banaji, *Memoirs of the Late Framji Cowasji Banaji* (Bombay, 1892), 101; C. M. C., *The Framjee Cowasjee Institute: Its Origin, Its Work and Its Future* (Bombay, 1917), 9.

[5] Masani, *Dadabhai Naoroji*, 26-30.

ties. The first Parsi to come to England is recorded to be Nowroji Manockji in 1724. The son of the Parsi trader Rustam Manock of Surat, Nowroji had come to England to settle the uneasy business affairs of his family with the East India Company. Not until the nineteenth century did other Parsis venture to Britain, when in 1840 Ardeseer Cursetjee Wadia arrived by permission of the Government of Bombay and guest of the East India Company. A member of the Wadia shipbuilding family, Ardaseer came to Britain to enhance his engineering expertise. His visit was followed by that of his cousins, Jehangir Nowroji and Hirjibhoy Meherwanji in 1841, for similar educational reasons. The travel of the Wadias to Britain was still somewhat an exceptional undertaking among Parsis and Indians, and their recollections provide unique account of their experiences.[6] By the middle of the 1850s, Parsis and other Indians began to come to Britain on a steady basis. In large part this was for educational purposes, both formal and informal, to study medicine, law, and industry; and for business reasons and private excursions. A steady stream of Parsi and Indian arrivals to Britain made the potentiality for a solid network of contacts and interests that would expand into both formal and informal business, social, and political ties.

Dadabhai Naoroji became a magnet for Indians seeking to come to Britain. Requests were made to Dadabhai directly or indirectly to aid in the passage, settlement, and introductions of Indians. Many requests were of course from Parsis and Dadabhai, no doubt in the generous spirit of the pupil-master, was never remiss to return to others the goodwill and support he had benefited from. Requests came in from many diverse quarters as well as from Dadabhai's friends and reformist colleagues. Sorabjee Shapoorjee Bengallee wrote to him on many occasions urging him to accommodate individuals. Bengallee noted the interest Dadabhai had shown in the advancement of young men over a span of a decade, and requested from him assistance for young Indians seeking entrance to the Indian Civil Service, studying for the Bar, entering a profession, and seeking to take the examination for the Indian Medical Service.[7] The

[6] R. A. Wadia, *Scions of Lowjee Wadia* (Bombay, 1964); A. C. Wadia, *Diary of an Overland Journey from Bombay to England* (London, 1840); J. N. and H. M. Wadia, *Journal of a Residence of Two Years and a Half in Great Britain* (London 1841).

[7] S. S. Bengallee to Dadabhai Naoroji (hereafter cited as D.N.), in Dadabhai Naoroji Papers, 2B89(1) 22.5.1888, 2B89(2) 6.3.1889, 2B89(4) 13.5.1891, 2B89(5)

backgrounds of the many Parsis requesting Dadabhai's assistance attest to his practice to accommodate a pool of talent and goals. Individuals such as Phirozesha Kersaspji Dadachanji, whom Bengallee described as "a deserving young man of our community" from a family of modest means, and a Jehangir R. Vakharid, both sought entrance into the Indian Civil Service.[8] Other Parsis coming to Britain included Jamsetjee Cursetjee Jamsetjee, the youngest son of the second Jamsetjee Jejeebhoy, and Banaji Sorabji Wadia, a member of the Wadia shipbuilding family.[9] On an even more personal note, Bengallee requested the services of Dadabhai to accommodate Furdoonjee Nowrozjee Furdoonjee, the adopted son and grandnephew of their friend Nowrozjee Furdoonjee, who had not particularly excelled at his education in Bombay and now sought a chance in Britain.[10] Dadabhai also aided young women such as a Miss Dhanjibaiji Banaji, a promising art student who had won prizes, held exhibitions of her work, and was the daughter of Merwanji Furdoonji Banaji. In addition to aiding a Banaji, Dadabhai and Bengallee would have felt gratified in their lives' efforts to aid an educated and talented woman, as Bengallee noted that D.N. had "many young male students from India introduced to you, but none drawing and painting, specially a lady of the arts."[11]

Assistance to Indians was a pattern Dadabhai followed all his life whether in Britain or in India. This was the case whether the individual requesting aid was hard up as in the case of Mr. Abessiain, who wrote to Dadabhai for financial assistance to come to Britain, as he was unemployed and unable to pay his passage; or whether he was the son of a Maharaja, who was advised by his great father to in all things take Dadabhai's advice.[12] One individual Dadabhai assisted in Britain was a little known Gujarati who came to study law in 1888, by the name of Mohandas K. Gandhi. The demands on Dadabhai's assistance increased with his years in Britain, and corresponded to the rise of Dadabhai's public profile. The measure of support Indians

---

4.3.1892, microfilms, University of Toronto, Robarts Library (hereafter cited as Naoroji Papers).

[8] Naoroji Papers, 2B89(6) 25.3.1892, 2B89(9) 20.2.1893.

[9] Naoroji Papers, 2B89 23.4.1885, 2B89(8) 15.6.1892.

[10] Naoroji Papers, 2B89(3) 15.4.1890.

[11] Naoroji Papers, 2B89(7) 3.5.1892.

[12] C. Abessiain to D.N., Naoroji Papers, 1A3 11.1895; S. K. Acharaya to D.N., Naoroji Papers, 1AS(1) 28.6.1906, 1A5(2) 19.7.1906.

could expect in Britain was to an extent dependent on the successful ability of Dadabhai to popularize the concerns of Indians whether in Britain or India. The rise of Dadabhai's public image served the dual goal of creating a more welcoming atmosphere in Britain for Indians, and providing the basis for the reform of issues important to Indians in Britain, India, and the Empire. His liberal education served Dadabhai particularly well in presenting facts and cogent arguments to a Victorian audience struck by the sincerity of tone and the novelty of example represented by a product of their British Indian Empire. Dadabhai was connected with many public bodies and scholarly societies in Britain, including the Liverpool Literary and Philosophical Society, the Philomatic Society, the Council of the Liverpool Athenaeum, the Cotton Supply Association of Manchester, the Royal Institution of London, the Royal Asiatic Society of Great Britain and Ireland, the Ethnological and Anthropological Societies, the Society of Arts, and the National Indian Association. These institutions provided the forum in which to combat the notions and opinions of the day concerning India, and were reminiscent of the Bombay societies Dadabhai had taken part in his early academic years.

A subject Dadabhai was particularly enthusiastic to place before the British was the civilization and religion of the Parsis. This was done in part to present a better understanding of the Parsis to a wider audience, which incidentally also included other Indians, while putting forward the cultural case for all Indians. In 1861, before the Liverpool Philomatic Society, Dadabhai read papers on the 'Manners and Customs of the Parsees' and the 'Parsee Religion'. The works were in large part reformist tracts in the spirit of other Parsi writings desirous to present a favourable portrayal of the Parsis' social progress. Unlike other Parsi reformist writers such as Dosabhai Framji Karaka and Manockjee Cursetjee, however, who tended to distinguish the social and educational progress of the Parsis from that of other Indians, Dadabhai defended the moral and social progress of all Indians.

In 1866, Dadabhai read a paper before the Ethnological Society of London entitled 'The European and Asiatic Races,' in which he endeavoured to address what amounted to aspersions on Indians by the President of the Society, John Crawfurd. In his article, Dadabhai brought to bear a vast knowledge of subjects and researches from the histories of cultures and civilizations, to the commentaries of learned scholars, to a review of parliamentary reports. Addressing the accusation that Indians were morally unequal to Europeans and unfit for education, Dadabhai questioned the basis of Crawfurd's argument. It was an error of British perception and of cultural perspectives in general, Dadabhai argued, that assumed Indians were incapable of progress based on the limited evidence offered by the initial British attempts at education in India. To underscore the fragility of cultural conclusions, Dadabhai noted the example of a Parsi resident in Britain for eight years who was so thoroughly disillusioned by his experiences that he believed "scoundrelism" of every kind to be rife in English daily life.[13]

To foster understanding between cultures on December 1, 1866, Dadabhai along with W. C. Bonnerjee set up the East India Association as a forum to discuss subjects relative to Britons and Indians. The Association had its counterparts in India as the Bombay, Calcutta, and Madras Branches begun in 1869. The E.I.A. marked the coming to influence of the middle class and educated segment of Indian leaders on a national and international level.[14] The E.I.A. was the successor to the London Indian Society begun in 1865. The Society had limited its official membership to Indians. The E.I.A., however, brought together a wider audience of supporters and an all-India focus to issues.[15] The experiences of the Parsi reformers had demonstrated that viable support for reformist causes often necessitated the participation of more traditionalist elements in the process of organization. Dadabhai sought to be inclusive of a spectrum of opinion in the E.I.A., as he believed that inclusiveness served to promote the general interests of all Indians, while ultimately political leadership remained under the control of the educated interests. Consequently, Dadabhai was able to draw into political organization Parsis, educated Indians, the British, as well as Indian princes and potentates.[16] The E.I.A., in particular, associated itself with British Liberal opinion capable of eliciting the attention of British politicians such as Henry Fawcett and David and William Wedderburn. Mid-Victorian Liberalism was the natural ally to Dadabhai's politics as he shared with the movement the commitment to reform, removal of

---

[13] Dadabhai Naoroji, "The European and Asiatic Races," *in Essays, Speeches, Addresses, and Writings, of the Hon'ble Dadabhai Naoroji*, ed. C. L. Parekh (Bombay, 1887), 1-25.

[14] *Journal of the East India Association* l, no. 1 (1867): 38.

[15] W. Hamilton Burn, Sec. of E.I.A., to D.N., Naoroji Papers, 8E2 5.2.1886.

[16] G. A. Natesan and Co., ed., *Famous Parsis* (Madras, 1930), 110.

disadvantages on social non-conformists, and a rational optimism and belief in progress. The Liberal philosophy also appealed to the spirit of cooperation that Dadabhai believed India's tie to Britain ultimately rested on: as he held an implicit faith in the fair-mindedness and sense of justice of the British.[17] The E.I.A. existed till 1907, by which time Dadabhai had honed the skills of conciliating a variety of interests within an organization.

The success Dadabhai achieved in publicizing Indian topics, issues, and concerns before the British public is evident in the enormous public interest he generated. British fascination with the Parsis was particularly evident. British interest in the Parsis was occasionally evident in biographical accounts and sketches of prominent and interesting Parsis in the public prints.[18] Dadabhai in Britain, however, transformed a passing curiosity as regards the Parsis into an ardent interest. Interest in the religion of the Parsis attracted many solicitations from individuals fascinated by the motivations that drove Dadabhai. Commending Dadabhai on a lecture he delivered on the Parsis and their religion, C. A. Baultes from Clerkenwell acknowledged the mutuality of experiences between Christians and Parsis: "Perhaps you are not aware that there has been in England the same kind of reform and investigation of Christianity with just the same result as you described concerning the Parsee religion."[19]

Wonderment at the "unique position of the Parsi nation in India" compelled a missionary on his way to India to request further information from Dadabhai.[20] He was joined by many others for more information on the Parsis from Dadabhai, including from Indians.[21] Other interested parties were struck by the coup Dadabhai had achieved in publicizing his interests, and sought to add to the renown by requesting interviews with Dadabhai for the purposes of writing

[17] *Journal of the East India Association* 3, no. 3 (1869).

[18] *The Parsee Prakash* lists accounts of many Parsis in the British prints during the nineteenth century. For a list of the accounts in the British papers, see John R. Hinnells, *Zoroastrians in Britain: The Ratanbai Katrak Lectures, University of Oxford, 1985* (Oxford, 1996), 103-4. See also Manockjee Cursetjee, *A Few Out of the Many Letters and Extracts of Letters, Addressed to Manockjee Cursetjee Esq., and to Others Regarding Him; Also Selections from the Newspapers of the Day* (Bombay, 1849).

[19] C. A. Baultes to D.N., Naoroji Papers, 2B37 Oct. 1888.

[20] Edwin Greaves to D.N., Naoroji Papers, 10G103 5.1.1893.

[21] Herbert Baynes to D.N., Naoroji Papers, 2B67 30.1.1890; Aziz Ahmed to D.N., Naoroji Papers, 1A91(5) 18.2.1890, 1A91(37) 22.3.1897; Romesh Dutt to D.N., Naoroji Papers, 8D161(17) 17.6.1901.

biographical sketches in local newspapers.[22] Another writer requested of Dadabhai the details necessary to construct an account of the life of Indians in Britain so that he could in a small way, "arouse a sense of justice and energy in the minds of some of my countrymen towards India."[23]

In addition to the novelty surrounding the subject, the information on the Parsis placed the nature of Dadabhai's activism in context. In his correspondence with Dadabhai, Aziz Ahmed, a Muslim convert to Christianity, commented on the importance and significance of Dadabhai's background and writings to the latter's electoral prospects. Dadabhai's works, Ahmed noted, would reveal to the British who Dadabhai is, what he is, what he wanted, and in the case of Dadabhai's religion, what his principles were. Aziz Ahmed believed Dadabhai's identification as a Parsi would also aid his quest for a parliamentary seat in Britain, as the Parsis were popularly believed to have a good reputation, and as a minority were "practically neutral" or considered "an impartial community . . . less formidable to timid Britons and to Anglo-Indians than a Bengalee, a Hindu, or a Mussalman." Offering up his own cultural 'expertise,' Aziz Ahmed suggested to Dadabhai that he seek a safe seat in Scotland where the quality of the population would serve him better than among an unthinking Irish constituency in London. To maximize his impact on the British, Ahmed urged Dadabhai to make his speeches interesting, that is he elaborated, "within the easy comprehension" of his audience.[24] Dadabhai's electoral prospects ultimately depended upon a variety of factors in addition to publicity, most importantly, his political contacts and supports. At the same time, the cultural affinity and ease between Dadabhai and the British, which the comments of Aziz Ahmed touched on, account for the relative success Dadabhai and other Parsis enjoyed above other Indians in British politics. The example and composure of Dadabhai in Britain, his accounts of the Parsis and the culture of India had served to animate interest in Dadabhai's audience, and enlist it in the concerns of Indians.

Dadabhai's presence in Britain was of considerable consequence to the establishment of the Parsi community in Britain. Dadabhai

---

[22] L. B. Baker to D.N., Naoroji Papers, 2B47 29.9.1886; Robert Dell to D.N., Naoroji Papers, 8D75(2) 12.12.1888.

[23] J. T. Anderson to D.N., Naoroji Papers, 1A48(1) 6.7.1900.

[24] Aziz Ahmed to D.N., Naoroji Papers, 1A91(15) 7.10.1891.

was the first Parsi to make Britain the centre of his public activity, and demonstrated to Parsis their ability to have an influence on matters of concern to them beyond the parameters of Bombay. The arrival of prominent Parsis to Britain such as Dadabhai, Nowrozjee Furdoonjee, and the Camas highlighted the need to make Britain a centre of organization for Parsis. In 1861, the Religious Funds of Zoroastrians of Europe or London Zoroastrian Association was established. Mancherji Hormusji Cama had originated the Association through his own efforts, as Dadabhai reminded other Parsis who credited him with its creation.[25] Under the direction of M. H. Cama, Nowrozjee Furdoonjee, and Dadabhai, the Association looked to the religious and social welfare of the Zoroastrians of Britain and Europe. The Association devised a working constitution with M. H. Cama as the first chairman and established six funds. The funds provided for burials, material assistance to Zoroastrians, purchasing educational material on Zoroastrianism, assisting Zoroastrian scholars, the establishment of a meeting and prayer centre, and other miscellaneous expenditures. By 1889, a General Fund was created by subscription for the benefit of Zoroastrians in Europe.[26]

The Association's major accomplishment was securing an *aramgah* or burial site for Parsis in London in 1863, in connection with Brookwood Cemetery. Dadabhai was chairman of the Association from 1864 until 1908, after which time M. M. Bhownaggree came to influence the Association and transform it into a social body. With the establishment of a quasi-religious and social forum, the Zoroastrians of Britain had to deal with the level of contact between the community and non-Zoroastrians. In 1892, the decision was taken to permit non-Zoroastrians access to the chapel in the Parsi burial ground at the time of a funeral. Parsis had previously to deal with the issue of death and funerals while resident outside India, and accommodations had been made wherever Parsis settled.[27] On January 30, 1915, Dastur Dhalla performed the first *Navjote* in Britain, at the Caxton Hall, London, of a Parsi girl, Goolcheher R. R. Desai.[28] The nascent Zoroastrian community in Britain was the first significant

---

25 D. R. Colah to D.N., Naoroji Papers, 6C212 12.7.1889.

26 Meetings of Charitable Fund of the Zoroastrians of Europe, Naoroji Papers, C212(l) 6.11.1889.

27 On the Association and other Parsi based organizations in Britain, see Hinnells, *Zoroastrians in Britain*, 108-9.

28 H. D. Darukhanawala, *Parsi Lustre on Indian Soil* (Bombay, 1939), 392.

Zoroastrian community to deal with the active and greater association of Zoroastrians with non-Zoroastrians outside the East. The issues of identity, religion and society in the new settings would now come to be debated among Zoroastrians in all the centres of Zoroastrian concentration that were to follow in the twentieth century.

The number of Parsis in Britain encouraged the organization of various associations, and the assistance of Dadabhai and other Parsis was of considerable influence in extending the capacities of Parsis to function outside India. In 1896, it is reported that fifty-three Parsis out of 326 Indians visited Britain.[29] Law and medical students in particular made the major cities of Britain including London, Oxford, Cambridge, Edinburgh, and Aberdeen centres of Parsi activity. Other Parsis came to Liverpool and Manchester to learn and conduct the commercial trade, and all the newcomers looked to Dadabhai, the Camas, and other prominent Parsis who had made the successful transition from India to the West for guidance and coordination of the interests of the Parsis. The moral and material supports of community were transferred from the confines of India to the fledgling community in Britain. In 1863, Cowasjee Jehangir Readymoney set up a prize fund valued at Rs. 5,000 to assist Parsis studying law in Britain. In the same year, Rustomjee Jamsetjee Jejeebhoy (1824-72) established a scholarship valued at Rs. 1,50,000 for Indians studying law in Britain.[30] The Edinburgh Parsi Union was started to assist the accommodation, education, and morale of Parsi Medical Students in the Scottish capital, and communicated to Dadabhai its desire to coordinate its efforts with the London based Zoroastrian Fund.[31] A contribution from the Parsi businessman, millowner, and philanthropist Sir Shapurji Bharucha aided the efforts of the Edinburgh Parsi Union by the establishment of a fund and a property.[32] The house functioned as a hostel, but was sold by 1947. The combined efforts of Parsis in Britain and India also made possible the purchase of a permanent property for the London Zoroastrian Association. The Asso-

---

[29] Delphine Menant, *The Parsis*, vol. 3, trans. Anthony D. Mango (Bombay, 1996), 173.

[30] Parses Prakash, 2:64, 81; Jal H. Wadia, *Sir Jamsetjee Jejeebhoy Parsee Benevolent Institution Centenary Volume* (Bombay, 1949), 157.

[31] Rustom H. Appoo, President Edinburgh Parsi Union, to D.N., Naoroji Papers, 8E17 no date.

[32] H. M. Dadachanjee, *Life Sketch of Sir Shapoorjee Bharucha* (in Gujarati) (Bombay, 1928).

ciation did not have a permanent headquarters, and from its beginnings held annual meetings predominantly at the offices of Messrs. Cama Moolla and Co. During the 1920s, a site in South Kensington and alternately a building in Kensington were purchased that served as a hostel and social and religious centre, and was the headquarters for the Zoroastrian community of Britain. In 1969, a new property was purchased at Compayne Gardens, in large measure to accommodate the growth of the Zoroastrian community.[33]

The organization of Parsis in Britain aimed to transcend differences in political affiliation and ideology, and utilize Parsi efforts on behalf of issues of importance to Zoroastrians in Britain and abroad. The Conservative Muncherjee M. Bhownaggree worked with Dadabhai on issues of concern to Parsis, despite their clear political differences. The ability to cooperate over issues and projects was evident in the efforts of the Persian Zoroastrian Amelioration Society. The Amelioration Society and Fund had begun in Bombay in 1855, to work for the redress of the treatment and conditions of the Zoroastrians of Iran. Reformist and traditionalist Parsis had united to start the Society, which from 1857 to 1882 sent deputations to the Shah in Persia and Britain. In 1873 and 1882 Dadabhai, Nowrozjee Furdoonjee and other Parsis travelled to Britain for audiences with the visiting Shah and, on the latter occasion, secured the elimination of a long-standing religious tax on the Iranian Zoroastrians. The efforts of the Amelioration Society illustrates the ability of the Parsis to utilize the social changes they had undergone through the century, unite as a community and influence events in their interest. The Parsis in Britain, at the turn of the century, continued in the spirit of community interest and cooperation begun at mid-century in Bombay, while their political and ideological allegiances came to diverge. Bhownaggree and Dadabhai as members of the Zoroastrian Fund maintained contacts and in 1902, Bhownaggree communicated to Dadabhai the arrangements made for the reception of the Shah of Persia in London.[34] Both worked to continue to ameliorate the conditions of the Zoroastrians of Iran into the twentieth century.

The involvement of Dadabhai Naoroji in the growth of the Parsi community in Britain was one aspect of the overall objective of as-

---

[33] Naoroji Papers, C212(9) 11.10.1894; Hinnells, *Zoroastrians in Britain*, 123-5.

[34] Bhownaggree to D.N., Naoroji Papers, 3B130(14) 14.7.1900; Bhownaggree to D.N., Naoroji Papers, 3B130(19) 20.8.1902.

sisting Indians in Britain. Indeed, efforts on behalf of the Parsis were a deliberate expression on Dadabhai's part of the unity of Indian aims in Britain. The disabilities placed on Indians who desired to join the Indian Civil Service jarred with the fundamental tenets Dadabhai understood to underlie Britain's role in India. In 1855, a new system of recruitment by open competition was adopted for the I.C.S., replacing in part a system of patronage nominations. The system, however, required Indians to pass entrance examinations in Britain, imposing on Indian applicants the burdens of travel and time not visited on British candidates. For much of his public life Dadabhai endeavoured to create a coalition of support and influence public policy towards raising the age limit on the competition for the examinations for Indians to permit them sufficient opportunity to prepare, and to have simultaneous exams in India and Britain.[35] One of Dadabhai's first actions on arriving in Britain was to seek the readmission of the Parsi R. H. Wadia (1837-71) to the examination for the I.C.S in 1859. Wadia was the first Indian candidate for the I.C.S. examination since the new rules, and had been denied admission due to an unannounced reduction in the age limit from twenty-three to twenty-two, and subsequently to nineteen. Dadabhai protested to the Secretary of State for India the invidious nature of the regulations for the I.C.S., and with Sir Erskine Perry's help was able to gain the support of John Bright and his friends in the matter. In 1859, Dadabhai's agitation over the age limit issue was enough to gain Lord Stanley's assurance that no further changes to the Civil Service rules would be made without prior publicity being given.[36] Wadia was ultimately unsuccessful in his attempts to take the I.C.S examination, and after some years died prematurely at age thirty-four.[37] It was not until 1876 that the first Parsi, C. R. Wadia (1855-1941), passed the Civil Service examinations, at the age of eighteen.[38] In 1893, Dadabhai and his Liberal supporters were able to secure a majority in Parliament in favour of simultaneous exams. The resolution was ultimately defeated by a hostile British officialdom, however, the

---

[35] Dadabhai Naoroji, "Admission of Educated Natives into the Indian Civil Service," Essay before E.I.A., April 17, 1867, and Memorandum to Sir Northcote of May 2, 1868, in Parekh, *Essays. Speeches, Addresses, and Writings*, 75-96, 490-500.

[36] Masani, *Dadabhai Naoroji*, 31-2.

[37] *Parsee Prakash*, 2:362 (obituary).

[38] Ibid., 496.

passage of the initial resolution marked a major achievement of the efforts of Dadabhai and his supporters, and provided the impetus for rallying renewed support to the cause of Indian issues in Britain and India.[39]

Indian opinion had followed Dadabhai's efforts on behalf of the issue of simultaneous exams in Britain. The issue of simultaneous exams directly affected only a very privileged minority of Indian society, yet the nationalists had managed to make it the major feat of nationalist organization in Britain and India. As a member of the Indian National Congress, Dadabhai had made the holding of simultaneous exams in Britain and India the major goal of Indian nationalists and their supporters. At the Inaugural Congress in Bombay in 1885, Dadabhai referred to the issue as the question of questions for educated Indians, and upon which all other political reforms depended.[40] In July 1889, the British Committee of the Indian National Congress was formed. It was open to all those interested in the cause of Indian reform, and maintained the interests of the Indian National Congress in Britain up until 1920.[41] Dadabhai maintained contact with all the major nationalist leaders in India such as Surendranath Banerjea, Subramaniam Iyer, and G. K. Gokhale, the great Indian leader from Maharashtra, and closely followed the political agitation in India over the issue of simultaneous examinations and other issues.[42] These men continued to shape the nationalist movement along a moderate course in benefit of greater political, administrative, and social reforms for Indians. The issue of simultaneous exams evinced how very far Dadabhai and educated Indian opinion had come from community and local based politics.

Parsi opinion also supported the breakdown of barriers to qualified Indians competing for the I.C.S. The major Parsi-run newspapers *Rast Goftar*, *Bombay Samachar*, and the *Jam-e-Jamshed* supported the equal treatment of Indians with Europeans, and advocated a rise in the age limit for Indian candidates to the I.C.S. The *Jam-e-Jamshed* urged all the political associations in India to keep agitating on behalf of reform of the age question as an expression of the edu-

---

[39] Munni Rawal, *Dadabhai Naoroji: A Prophet of Indian Nationalism (1855-1900)* (New Delhi, 1989), 45; *The Times of London*, June 3, 1893.

[40] Rawal, *Dadabhai Naoroji*, 25.

[41] Ibid., 30-1; Eckehard Kulke, *The Parsees in India* (Munich, 1974), 223-4.

[42] G. K. Gokhale to D.N., Naoroji Papers, 10G64 9.11:1894; Gokhale to D.N., Naoroji Papers, 10G64(3) 25.2.1897.

cational maturity of Indians. The *Jam-e-Jamshed*, however, parted from liberal Indian opinion in believing twenty-one years to be a sufficient threshold for qualification, and it opposed the concept of simultaneous exams as a disability for Indians seeking to compete alongside and gain the confidence of Europeans.[43] The qualified support of the *Jam-e-Jamshed* on the I.C.S. question highlighted the resistance Dadabhai had begun to face from conservative Parsis over liberal political reforms. Other conservatives reacted against any reform of imperial institutions. For example, the Parsi N. S. Ginwalla wrote against the Congress' approach to simultaneous exams and the Indian Civil Service, as against the interests of the Empire. He advocated a two-tier civil service in which entry was completely based on merit, yet segregated for Indians in their own separate and independent branch. Lower grade appointments were to be reserved for Indians subordinate to the main service to which no Indian could compete to enter. Reminiscent of the opinions held by British officials on the capabilities of Indians, Ginwalla believed his system to be in the best interests of the peace, well-being, and administration of India:

> Not that I doubt for one moment the qualification by ability, education and integrity of the Natives to hold and discharge to the entire satisfaction of their rulers the duties of these high offices of State, but I fear that the Native of this country seldom possesses the self reliance, firmness of character, and tact so necessary in cases of emergency.[44]

Ginwalla's opposition to Dadabhai was not personal, as he conveyed his admiration for Dadabhai and his belief that Dadabhai was a proud representative of India in Britain.[45] Ginwalla, albeit, represented a clear example, particularly as would be found among Parsis, of the opposition that existed to the Indian nationalists' attempts to in any way upset the status quo between Britain and India.

From the mid-1860s, Dadabhai had also begun to give lectures and write on economic subjects. Dadabhai Naoroji's writings in critique of the moral and economic relationship between Britain and India form the keynote of Indian economic nationalism. Significantly, the progress of Dadabhai's economic outlook followed his own progression from Parsi businessman to nationalist leader. Dada-

---

[43] See *The Voice of India*, May 15 and July 15, 31, 1884, 305, 409, 429-30, 459.

[44] Nusserwanjee S. Ginwalla, "The Indian Civil Service," Naoroji Papers, 10G52 1.12.1884.

[45] Ginwalla to D.N., Naoroji Papers, 10G52(2) 18.12.1893.

bhai had followed the course of many a Parsi to economic independence, including among the educated, by going into business or the financial world. S. S. Bengallee initially began his career as a bank employee, and D. E. Wacha was active in accounting and the banking world.[46] R. P. Patwardhan notes that before 1855 economic issues had not attracted Dadabhai's attention.[47] Indeed, it was following his partnership in business with the Camas and the establishment of his own company in 1859 that Dadabhai began to appreciate the economic situation of India. The strength of the ties forged among Indians in business with one another profoundly affected Dadabhai's appreciation of the potentialities of Indian economic independence.

In one form or another, throughout his life Dadabhai maintained some business link to his Parsi and Indian associates. The strength of the ties crossed political allegiances, and was evident whether in the face of financial fortune or failure. When Dadabhai lost three lakhs (Rs. 3,00,000) and his firm collapsed, it is reported that his Indian creditors sympathized with him to the extent that they promptly released him from the debt and engaged him in the liquidation, while others obliged him with fresh loans.[48] By the new century, Dadabhai joined in business with G. K. Gokhale to produce a new typewriter from a patent of S. A. Bhise, and to be backed by money from J. N. Tata, the Parsi businessman and pioneer of Indian industry. Dadabhai had supported the scheme from conception investing some £2,600 over eight years, and his friends sought to refund his investment and provide him a share of the future proceeds of four per cent from Bhise and three per cent from Tata, once profits were realized.[49] From the mid-1860s, the influence of British thinkers increasingly affected Dadabhai. It was soon after the establishment of the East India Association in December 1866 that Dadabhai met John Dickinson, Evans Bell, and John Bright, and that economics became an all-absorbing preoccupation for him. The three men had written on the moral and economic ties between India and Britain, and Bell had encouraged Dadabhai to raise "an articulate public opinion in our

---

[46] N. S. Bengallee, *The Life of Sorabjee Shapoorjee Bengallee* (Bombay, no date), 11-13; Natesan, *Famous Parsis*, 82, 292; D. E. Wacha, *Shells from the Sands of Bombay* (Bombay, 1920), 671.

[47] Patwardhan, *Dadabhai Naoroji Correspondence*, vol. 2, part 1, xxi.

[48] See Parekh, *Essays, Speeches, Addresses, and Writings*, 4.

[49] S. A. Bhise to D.N., Naoroji Papers, 3B126 (12) 22.10.1901, 2B136(63) 29.1.1910; G. K. Gokhale to J. N. Tata, Naoroji Papers, 10G64(21) 12.5.1909.

Eastern Empire," on the impact of British political and economic administration on Indians.[50] Both Dadabhai's business experiences and the writings of British social and economic theoreticians combined in the formulation of a potent indictment of the political economy of empire in India.

Dadabhai's economic writings constitute the first major reassessment of the moral and economic relationship between Britain and India since the beginnings of the colonial economy. By the late nineteenth century, Indian nationalists believed the amelioration of the moral condition of India to be increasingly tied to meeting the economic aspirations of India under imperialism. Beginning with papers entitled 'England's Duties to India,' 'The Wants and Means of India,' and 'The Commerce of India,' delivered before the E.I.A. in 1867, 1870, and 1871 respectively, Dadabhai presented the major theme of his economic writings: the economic and moral consequences of the drain of wealth from India to Britain.[51] Dadabhai acknowledged the mutuality of dependence of the two countries, and the benefits and obligations imposed on India by the relationship. At the same time, he reiterated that the evils of a "material and moral drain," could only be alleviated by even-handed economic dealings on the part of the British in India, befitting the trust they held in India.[52] Dadabhai's impact on public policy was evident when in 1871 he appeared before the Fawcett Committee on East India Finance, where he contended that almost a quarter of India's national capital was lost each year to Britain.[53] He also detailed for the first time to an astonished public opinion the average income in India to be Rs. 20 p.a.[54] Dadabhai's economic argument had the greatest impact with his essay on 'The Poverty of India' of 1876, read before the Bombay Branch of the E.I.A., and his *Poverty and Un-British Rule in India* of 1902, in which he detailed the full economic and moral drain British imperialism was having on India. By the turn of the century, Dadabhai believed the imperial system to have a detrimental influence on the progress of India. It was in contact with Parsis that he candidly articulated his view that India was a nation being bled, and had been reduced to a nation of drawers of water and

---

[50] Evans Bell to D.N., Naoroji Papers, 2B81(1) 23.1.1869, 2B81(2) 8.2.1869.

[51] See Parekh, *Essays, Speeches, Addresses, and Writings*, 26-50.

[52] Ibid., 123.

[53] Ibid., 175-6.

[54] Natesan, *Famous Parsis*, 113-14.

hewers of wood. Dadabhai believed Indians lacked neither enterprise nor industry in comparison to other peoples, save that India was not a self-governing nation in command of its resources, and was under the rule of a foreign people.[55] The subject of the condition of India overwhelmingly preoccupied his public and parliamentary speeches. His economic works were the subject of much notice and publicity and requests for publication; and gained Indian questions an audience around the world.[56]

It was with Dadabhai's runs for Parliament that he and his cause achieved an abiding public profile. Dadabhai's first attempt at a seat in Parliament was in 1886 shortly after gaining the Liberal nomination for the London riding of Holborn, in December 1885. Dadabhai had established himself as the chief spokesman for Indian political interests, and it was for that cause that he attempted to enter Parliament. In his first address to the voters of Holborn, Dadabhai professed his support for and faith in the ties between Britain and India, while asking of them the opportunity to serve his Indian countrymen in Parliament.[57] Dadabhai was defeated in his first quest for a seat, however, he had shown the strength of his political ties in obtaining the nomination for the riding, the ability to organize and prepare in what was a very short period following his return to Britain, and the decision to make Parliament the centre of his political efforts. In seeking and obtaining the nomination for his second attempt at Parliament in the riding of Central Finsbury in 1892, Dadabhai called on the political ties he had made while in British political circles. He gained the support of the National Liberal Club, which represented the Central Association, National Federation, and Radical Union, and which urgently pressed the Associations "to give their invaluable assistance to the candidature of Mr. Dadabhai Naoroji."[58] Despite a difficult nomination in which his ballot victory was disputed, he gained the nomination and went on to win the seat. Dadabhai retained the seat until the general election of 1895, at which time he and the Liberals were defeated. In 1906, Dadabhai again attempted to re-enter Parliament but was unsuccessful.

---

[55] Dadabhai Naoroji to J. N. Tata, December 9, 1891, London, in miscellaneous letters, University of Bombay Library.

[56] A. J. Comridge and Co. to D.N., Naoroji Papers, 1A1 23.6.1898; Oscar Eisengarten to D.N., Naoroji Papers, 8E30 29.11.1891.

[57] See Parekh, *Essays, Speeches, Addresses, and Writings*, 302-10.

[58] Memorial of National Liberal Club, Naoroji Papers, 6C86(1) no date.

Dadabhai Naoroji's candidacy for Parliament highlighted the question of 'race' and prejudice in politics. In a celebrated incident in 1888, the Conservative Prime Minister Lord Salisbury accounted for his party's victory in 1886 by questioning the ability of a British constituency such as Holborn to elect a 'black man'. Lord Salisbury's remarks exposed the undercurrent of racial intolerance against Indians, and squarely brought to attention the issue of Dadabhai's identity. The remarks also starkly demonstrated the racial prejudice that could confront Parsis outside India, and perturb the illusion that the Parsis were immune to prejudice because of their affinity to the British. The remarks in reference to Dadabhai were the most overt expression of the bigotry faced by those still regarded as 'natives' or black men by the British. The issue of Dadabhai's identity as a Parsi, moreover, was raised to question whether he could represent Indians generally. In drawing attention to his Parsi background, the more conservative political interests clearly sought to deprive Dadabhai of the authority and legitimacy in representing all Indians. The Anglo-Indian press was particularly critical of Dadabhai and the nationalist movement. The press' perpetual opposition to the grievances and concerns of Indians with British administration in India earned from Dinsha Wacha the reproof of being rabid and foaming at the mouth.[59] Wacha singled out *The Times of India*, which he described to Dadabhai as "malignant in spirit" and motivated with a "view to belittle you in the eyes of your own countrymen."[60] *The Times of India* had been cool to Dadabhai's initial foray into British politics, and regarded his stand in what was an Irish constituency like Holborn with as much enthusiasm.[61]

The remarks surrounding Dadabhai's identity gave to Dadabhai's candidacy in 1892 a renewed publicity, and helped to unite support behind it. Dadabhai's Parsi identity had not been an obstacle to his position in the Indian nationalist movement, and he enjoyed widespread support from his fellow Indians in his bids for Parliament. The *Hindu Patriot* declared that there existed no one better qualified to represent India than Dadabhai.[62] In the latter half of the nineteenth

---

[59] Patwardhan, *Dadabhai Naoroji Correspondence*, vol. 2, part 2, September 27, 1895, 459.

[60] Ibid., September 17, 1904, 871.

[61] *The Times of India*, July 5, 1888.

[62] *Hindu Patriot*, January 31, 1889, in *Report on Native Papers*, 1889, no. 5, 5, Department of Archives, Government of Maharashtra, Bombay.

century, communal and religious identifications among nationalists had not assumed the potency or relevance they would in the twentieth century. The tendency in the early Congress movement was to stress the national identity of Indians while conscious of the divergent groups that made up the movement. Where disputes arose, they were usually attributable more to conflicts of personality and strategy than to one's ethnic, religious, or regional background. Parsi public opinion, on the other hand, which was usually dispassionate over nationalist politics, gave a vigorous defence of Dadabhai's character and worthy qualities as a candidate. Indeed, it was the Parsi press that attached significance to Dadabhai's background as a Parsi. The *Bombay Samachar* noted the displeasure of the Parsis at the remarks of Salisbury, and the *Jam-e-Jamshed* noted the need to give Indians a larger share in the public service of the Empire.[63] In the wake of the remarks of Lord Salisbury, the *Rast Goftar* remarked on Dadabhai's unmistakable identity as a Parsi, given his qualities of culture, simplicity, honour, and energy.[64]

The level of support Dadabhai enjoyed among the British could also be gauged following Salisbury's remarks. In an attempt to diffuse the race issue, the Liberals stressed Dadabhai's character as a "genuine Englishman."[65] In fact many Britons, for whom Dadabhai had gained a certain affinity, had poorly received Salisbury's remark. The Edinburgh Labour Association offered Dadabhai a ready platform from which to reply to Salisbury and bring the grievances of Indians before a Scottish audience. Even in the midst of the controversy over Dadabhai's role in politics, the Association appraised a connection with Dadabhai to be worthwhile.[66] Other influential figures also lent their support. Lord Ripon, who had an especial following and affection among Indians, and Parsis in particular, came out in support of Dadabhai. The Irishman H. H. Champion, who was of aid to Dadabhai in building a coalition of support from behind the scenes, regaled in the benefit Salisbury's intemperate remark would reap.[67] Captain F. T. Penton, the Conservative candidate, also challenged Dadabhai's victory in Central Finsbury, in a petition for

[63] *Bombay Samachar*, March 2, 1889, Jam-e-Jamshed, March 2, 1889, ibid., no. 9, 7.

[64] *Rast Goftar*, October 5, 1888.

[65] Kulke, *The Parsees in India*, 221.

[66] Henry C. Noble, Sec. E.L.A., to D.N., Naoroji Papers, 8E16 15.12.1888.

[67] H. H. Champion to D.N., Naoroji Papers, 6C99(6) 15.4.1889.

recount. Dadabhai succeeded in the recount, and earned additional support from those who believed the action to have been "most un-English."[68] The backlash to Lord Salisbury's comment and Penton's sorry defeat, were the most conspicuous expressions of the well-spring of support Dadabhai had been able to tap since his involvement in public activity. It had galvanized most Indian opinion to Dadabhai, and emphasized to the British the invidious situation that existed for Indians.

Victory for Dadabhai in Central Finsbury brought him the authority and vindication he had sought in pressing the cause of India. A constituency had accepted a 'black man,' while cognizant of his broader representative goal, and now gravitated to him to address and support their concerns. The question of Dadabhai's ability to represent anyone other than those of his background appeared to have been settled, as he was accepted as "a Parsi by birth, an Englishman by habit and association."[69] Even the difficulty with Dadabhai's surname was rendered less formidable in pronunciation to the British when after his victory in 1892, he was referred to as Dadabhai "Narrow Majority."[70] Dadabhai and the Liberals had won the general election over the issue of the Irish Question, yet it may be added that given Dadabhai's pledge to be the representative of India in Parliament and stand as a Liberal, various constituencies and interests had actually warmed to his candidacy and his support for what could be regarded as other deserving interests. Champion had expressed as much to Dadabhai in surmising the extent of support to be expected.[71] Whereas Dadabhai had solicited support for his causes, now causes vied for his attention. Requests for assistance, speeches, and donations to various causes often associated with the Liberals poured in from women's missions and interests, labour and trades societies, temperance societies, heath care sponsors, and even the Asylum for Idiots, in whose services on behalf of the handicapped Dadabhai had shown interest.[72]

Dadabhai's election also appeared to rejuvenate the hopes of Indians in British values. In his maiden speech in the House of Com-

[68] N. D. Albless to D.N., Naoroji Papers, 1A31 14.12.1892.

[69] *Indian Spectator* in *The Times of India*, October 13, 1892.

[70] V. S. Srinivasa Sastri, *Life and Times of Sir Pherozeshah Mehta* (Madras, 1945). 21; Kulke, *The Parsees in India*, 221.

[71] H. H. Champion to D.N., Naoroji Papers, 6C99 21.6.1886.

[72] Naoroji Papers, 1A6, 1A23, 1A34, 1A37, 1A37(6), 1A38(1), 1A78(2).

mons on August 9, 1892, Dadabhai summed up the mood of Indians in noting the "everlasting gratitude of the millions of India" for the voters of Central Finsbury, and the renewed tie that had been forged between Britain and India.[73] Congratulations deluged Dadabhai from India and Britain. A typical letter from an Indian supporter in Bengal read: "Congratulate you most heartily on your success.... Trusting you will spare no pains to render your own native country the services for which she looks to you as one of her worthiest sons."[74] The extent of Dadabhai's new duties and obligations was implicit, and signified the role Dadabhai had made for himself as a figure not confined to championing any one interest or community, but bringing together many constituencies. Dadabhai represented the early generation of nationalist Indians who favoured India's connection with Britain, albeit, on a more equitable plain; and his inclusive vision of politics would continue to be shared decades after communal and sectarian interests would take the stage.

2. *The Parsis and Nationalist Politics—The Contributions of Pherozeshah Mehta and D. E. Wacha*

The Parsis had followed Dadabhai's career and shared in the rejoicing over his election to Parliament. They had taken part along with the inhabitants of Bombay in the first public address to Dadabhai in 1869 on his initial return to India. On December 16, 1893, Sir Dinshaw Petit and Pherozeshah Mehta arranged a public meeting in honour of Dadabhai's election victory.[75] The Parsi community and press generally supported Dadabhai's efforts on behalf of the rights of Indians to equal treatment in Indian administration. However, the participation of Dadabhai and other Parsis in nationalist politics witnessed the growing divergence of Parsi opinion over political allegiances. In his political philosophy, Dadabhai had sought to exemplify the compatibility of his Parsi and Indian identities. As the President of the Indian National Congress in 1893, Dadabhai had stated his first allegiance to be to India as an Indian, as he believed

[73] Cited in Natesan, *Famous Parsis*, 119-20. See also Memorial of People of Chikmagalur to Electors of Central Finsbury, Naoroji Papers, 6C132 25.7.1892.

[74] B. K. Chatterjee to D.N., Naoroji Papers, 6C121 16.1.1893.

[75] J. R. B. Jeejeebhoy, ed., *Some Unpublished and Later Speeches and Writings of the Hon. Sir Pherozeshah Mehta* (Bombay, 1918), 68.

India was the first allegiance of all the members of Indian communities.[76] His philosophy was shared by the other two great Parsi figures of the nationalist movement, Pherozeshah M. Mehta and D. E. Wacha. All three believed the interests of the Parsis lay in identifying with the greater Indian identity, and by the same token having Indian nationalism identify with the concerns of all Indians. It is an interesting point that the experiences of Naoroji, Mehta, and Wacha, as Parsis in mid-century Bombay, had shaped their appreciation for their greater Indian identity, and influenced them to shape the Indian nationalist movement towards a non-communal character.

The Parsis had undergone the process of educational, social, and religious reform alongside yet separate from the other Indian communities. As advocates of what is referred to as a secular nationalism in the Indian nationalist movement, Naoroji, Mehta, and Wacha believed in the parallel process of social reform within communities, and broad cooperation over issues of national character and interest by all Indians. The appeal to secular nationalism, where the gradual demand for political power from the British became the chief goal, served the interests of the educated elite who composed the leadership of the Indian nationalist movement, and remained the philosophy employed to unite Indians behind the movement. Secular nationalism had as its goal the uniting of Indians behind the goal of greater political expression and power, while making that goal the expression of identity. Differences of ethnicity, religion, and region were accepted as part of the nationalist movement, while downplayed in the interests of unity. It was a philosophy and policy that the Parsi leaders strove to foster within the movement, along with other Indian leaders of similar backgrounds and experiences, distinguishing them as the 'moderates' within the movement.

Other nationalist leaders like B. G. Tilak and, more particularly, M. K. Gandhi would modulate the theme of nationalism by an appeal to religion, tradition, and cultural identity, in the interests of democratizing the process. In the case of Gandhi, who was also a moderate, the love of religion and the pride in cultural identity was the appeal made on behalf of uniting all Indian communities in the appreciation of their Indian identity, and each community's contributions to that identity. For Gandhi, religion was not an expression of political

---

[76] G. A. Natesan and Co., ed., *Congress Presidential Addresses: From the Foundation to the Silver Jubilee, First Series, 1885-1910* (Madras, 1935), 161.

identity, as it was for Tilak, who more and more identified being a Hindu with one's identity as an Indian. For Gandhi, however, the expression of one's religious identity, whatever that might be, posed no bar to one's political identity as an Indian. For Gandhi, political identity as an Indian reposed in accepting the multiplicity of identities within India. To some degree, Gandhi's philosophy was an ingenious play on the pronouncements of the secular nationalists. Indeed, Gandhi professed his political consciousness was inspired by Dadabhai, and that he had learned his first practical lesson in *ahimsa* (non-violence) from the example of Mehta.[77] Whereas a Parsi like Mehta could claim his background to be no bar to leadership of the movement, so Gandhi claimed the expression of a religious affiliation to equally pose no bar to one's nationalist commitment.

It was in the first period of nationalist organization from 1885 to 1915, that the Parsis' influence on Indian nationalist politics was most conspicuous, and aimed to accommodate the aspirations of a minority community like the Parsis to the nationalist movement. Pherozeshah Merwanjee Mehta was the leading Parsi in nationalist politics in India. He was educated at Elphinstone College, was the first Parsi barrister at the Bar in England, and among his many accomplishments was President of the Bombay Municipal Corporation in 1884, 1885, 1905 and 1911, a member of the Bombay Legislative Council in 1886 and the Imperial Legislative Council from 1894 to 1895, an officer of the University of Bombay Senate, and was knighted in 1904. While Dadabhai was chiefly concerned with representing Indian opinion in Britain, Mehta strove to shape nationalist policy in India. As a member of the Indian Nationalist Congress from its inception in 1885, and as its president in 1890, Mehta sought to make the I.N.C. the moderate and legitimate voice of Indian political opinion. He defended the nationalist cause from both antinationalists who challenged the Congress' claim to be the legitimate representative of Indians, and from radical Congress members who believed in violent agitation as a political tool. Mehta devised and delivered the nationalists' best retort in response to the antinationalists who held the size of the movement to be a disqualification to its ability to represent Indians. Mehta noted that the "microscopic minority" of the I.N.C. was better qualified to guide their fellow

[77] See the Incident at Rajkot, in M. K. Gandhi, *An Autobiography or The Story of My Experiments with Truth* (Ahmedabad, 1927), Ch. 4.

Indians than the "still more microscopic minority" of English district officers and officials whose understanding of things Indian, including the language, "seldom rise above the knowledge of English possessed, for instance, by French waiters at Paris Hotels which proudly blazon forth the legend: *Ici on parle Anglais.*"[78] Mehta gave the nationalist movement an ideological relevance and a sense of pride in its unique *raison d'être*, as he described it to be a movement dedicated to putting forward rights and interests which are national in character, and which concern all the 'nationalities' or inhabitants of the Indian peninsula.[79] Of haughty demeanour and quick wit, Mehta was equally exacting in his criticism of the more radical Congress members, whom he believed through their tactics diminished the legitimacy of the movement in the eyes of the movement's critics and potential supporters.[80] The differences in tactics came to a head in the years 1906-07, when at the Twenty-second Congress a tumult occurred. The intercession of the Grand Old Man averted a schism in the movement's ranks, providing the movement with the necessary facade of unity.[81] After 1908, Mehta's influence in the Congress declined, though by that time the Congress had been steered towards the moderate course Mehta had always envisioned.[82]

D. E. Wacha shared Mehta's goal to guide the Congress movement along a moderate path. Dinsha Edulji Wacha had attended Elphinstone College but left before graduation to help his father's business. He began work in the Bank of Bombay, and proceeded to join Bombay's first accountancy firm as an assistant. He was a managing agent with Morarji Goculdas and Sholapur Mills & Co., and a lifelong member of the Bombay Mill Owners' Association. He was President of the Bombay Municipal Corporation in 1901, and a member of the Bombay Legislative Council in 1915 and the Imperial Legislative Council in 1916. He was knighted in 1917. Wacha's expertise lay in financial matters which he wrote frequently on in monographs and various publications, including the *Indian Spectator*

---

[78] Pherozeshah Mehta, "Sixth Congress-Calcutta-1890-Presidential Address," in Natesan, *Congress Presidential Addresses*, 62.

[79] Ibid., 63.

[80] Homi Mody, *Sir Pherozeshah Mehta: A Political Biography* (1921; reprint London, 1963), 249-51; John R. McLane, *Indian Nationalism and the Early Congress* (Princeton, 1977), 168; Srinivasa Sastri, *Life and Times of Sir Pherozeshah Mehta*, 94-109.

[81] Davendra Prasad Ghose to D.N., Naoroji Papers, 10G38 20.9.1906.

[82] McLane, *Indian Nationalism*, 367-9.

which he helped his friend Behramji M. Malabari keep going.[83] His knowledge of financial matters was of benefit to the nationalist movement in scrutinizing Britain's management of Indian finances, and in providing Congress with a conservative base of support from the Indian financial community. Wacha was witness and participant to the creation of many political associations in Bombay, and believed Congress to provide the best forum in which to bring together Indian opinion.[84] He shared with Mehta the fear and distrust of both the conservative Anglo-Indian establishment, and the radicals in Congress like Tilak, whom he called a "hot fire-brand" and the head of a "rabid following," who through personal motives would damage the base of support the movement had built up.[85]

Both Mehta and Wacha sought to include the Parsis in the base of support for nationalism. Mehta was most pronounced in his support for the nationalist cause to the Parsis, seeking to convey to them what he believed to be the compatibility of their community identity as Parsis and their national identity as Indians. His Presidential Address to the Sixth Congress of 1890, in Calcutta, is often cited as the premier expression of the creed of nationalism. Mehta sought to confront the issues of his leadership, minorities in the nationalist movement, and the support for nationalism among minorities:

> In speaking of myself as a native of this country, I am not unaware, that incredible, as it may seem, Parsis have been both called and invited to call themselves, foreigners.... To my mind, a Parsi is a better and truer Parsi, as a Mahomedan or a Hindu, is a better and truer Mahomedan or Hindu, the more he is attached to the land which gave him his birth, the more he is bound in brotherly relations and affections to all the children of the soil, the more he recognizes the fraternity of all the native communities of the country, and the immutable bond which binds them together in the pursuit of common gains and objects under a common Government.... The birthright, therefore, Gentlemen, which the Parsis thus possess of so indefeasible and glorious a character, they have refused and will always refuse to sell for any mess of pottage, however fragrant and tempting.[86]

Mehta's remarks on his leadership role in the Congress, and his reminder to the Parsis of their place in the nationalist movement were

---

83 Wacha, *Shells*, 671; Natesan, *Famous Parsis*, 422.

84 Patwardhan, *Dadabhai Naoroji Correspondence*, vol. 2, part 1, January 6, 1893, 316.

85 Ibid., vol. 2, part 2, November 15, 1895, 462.

86 Natesan, *Congress Presidential Addresses*, 59-60.

meant to reassure all those who believed the inhabitants of India could work on behalf of national interests in one movement. Mehta's views equally affirmed the mutuality of interests and compatibility between Hindus and Muslims, whom he believed had historically lived together in peace in India.[87] Furthermore, Mehta believed in equality of treatment for all the subjects of the Empire, including Indians in South Africa.[88] In this regard, he was one of the first to validate the idea of an Indian national movement welded together by a common alliance of nationality.

Mehta and the other leaders' appeals to national identification, however, did not find an immediate audience among the majority of Parsis. Parsi public opinion could not agree on the consequences allegiance to the nationalist movement would have on the Parsis' identity and interests. Moreover, Parsi public opinion did not share in the growing sense of distance and alienation it believed nationalist politics to be fomenting between Indians and the British. The Parsis continued to regard the relationship between the community and the British as beneficial to its interests, and with a sense of gratitude and sympathy. This sense of sympathy had been strong throughout the century as Parsi and British values coalesced in many areas, notably on education and social mores. With the assumption of direct rule of India by the British government from 1858, and its personification in the figure of Queen-Empress, Parsi public opinion had come to politically identify with British rule.

The loyalty to Queen-Empress and the Royal Family particularly symbolized the personal identification the Parsis had made to the political tie with Britain. Both Framji Cowasji Banaji and Jamsetjee Jejeebhoy had sent gifts to Victoria as token of the close ties between the Parsis and the British.[89] Jamsetjee Jejeebhoy had acknowledged with "deep gratitude ... the gracious goodness of Her Majesty the Queen," for the bestowal of his knighthood, and its significance for all Indians in 1842.[90] The third Sir Jamsetjee Jejeebhoy led the Bombay contingent as representative of the Parsis and greater Indian

[87] Ibid., 63.

[88] Mody, *Sir Pherozeshah Mehta*, 2, 3, 6; Natesan, *Famous Parsis*, 391-2; Jeejeebhoy, *Some Unpublished and Later Speeches and Writings of the Hon. Sir Pherozeshah Mehta*, 96, 212.

[89] D. F. Karaka, *History of the Parsis*, 2 vols. (London,1884), 2:117-18; J.J. MSS, 354.

[90] J.J. to J. Rivett-Carnac, April 18, 1842, J.J. MSS, 369:116-18.

community of Bombay at the Imperial Assemblage in December 1877, held in Delhi to mark the recognition of Victoria as Empress of India.[91] The Parsis had remained steadfast in their loyalty to the British and the Crown during the Mutiny of 1857, and gave public thanks for the end of the Mutiny.[92] Various endowments and patriotic funds had been raised by Parsis on behalf of British soldiers who had defended the Crown in conflicts, including the war with Russia at mid-century.[93] Forty-six Parsis are listed as having died in the name of the Crown in the Great War of 1914-18.[94] Many Parsis were passionate and romantic royalists. The connection with royalty symbolized as much a sense of stability, continuity, and cultural relevance for the Parsis as for any of the Empire's subjects. D. F. Karaka noted "the Parsis take as much interest in the royal family of England, and have as much love for them, as their ancestors had for their ancient [Persian] kings." So much so that the Parsis offered prayers for the ailing Prince of Wales during his periodic illnesses. It is not unusual therefore that it was a Parsi, K. N. Kabraji, who translated God Save the Queen into Gujarati, as 'Raksh Dev Rani'.[95] In 1911, the Parsis had prepared a commemorative casket detailed with a coronation scene of an ancient Persian king, for the royal durbar of George V and Queen Mary. And the Parsi community offered prayers and congratulations on the coronation of the last King-Emperor and Imperial Majesties of India in 1937.[96] A Parsi reminded the Indian nationalists of the Parsis' attachment to monarchy, including among reformers, that political nationalism threatened to upset.[97] In the twentieth century, a diversity of political opinion took shape among the Parsis. However, the lack of mass participation in the nationalist movement among the Parsis before Independence lies in their ambivalence towards nationalism's motives, and their interests in the movement.[98]

---

[91] Bernard S. Cohn, "Representing Authority in Victorian India," in *The Invention of Tradition*, eds. Eric Hobsbawm and Terence Ranger (Cambridge, 1983), 195.

[92] *Bombay Times*, July 22, 1857.

[93] G.D. 1855 579/59:21-41; G.D. 1856 90/562:11-17; Karaka, *History of the Parsis*, 2:273-82.

[94] Sohrab K. H. Katrak, *Who Are the Parsees*? (Karachi, 1965), 294-5.

[95] Karaka, *History of the Parsis*, 2:283-91.

[96] *Parsee Prakash*, 5: 59-60; ibid., 7: 365.

[97] N. S. Ginwalla, "An Appeal to My Countrymen for Our Beloved Queen," Naoroji Papers, 10G52(1) 24.4.1885.

[98] The career of Madame Bhikaji R. K. Cama (1861-1936) is example of a Parsi who was a passionate advocate of Independence operating outside traditional polit-

The Parsis in the nationalist movement shared the regard for the British tie. The reformist Parsis of the Bombay Association had been some of the first inhabitants of Bombay to affirm their loyalty and appreciation to the Crown following the Royal Proclamation of 1858, which declared the British government's intention to follow a liberal policy in India." In 1884, Pherozeshah Mehta started the Ripon Club, named in honour of the liberal-minded Marquis of Ripon, Viceroy of India, 1880-84. The Club was a venue for the discussion of opinion among Parsis of diverse political backgrounds and philosophies, and its creation was an expression of the political Anglophilism of the Parsis.[100] The Parsis in the nationalist movement, at the same time, sought progressive political reform that was inclusive of Indians in Indian affairs. The Congress Parsis shared the goals and methods of an evolving national movement towards political self-rule or *swaraj*, first advocated by Dadabhai in 1906.

The opposition to Naoroji, Mehta, and Wacha came from those who clearly believed there to be no interest in the Parsis' flirtation with nationalist politics. The opposition, moreover, transcended the traditional/conservative resistance within the Parsi community to social reform as even liberal and reformist Parsis opposed nationalist political organization. The *Rast Goftar*, under its publisher K. N. Kabraji from 1858 to 1902, opposed the Parsis' participation in the Congress movement.[101] Kabraji who shared Dadabhai's idea of social reform within the Parsi community parted terms with Dadabhai over his belief that the latter had forsaken the commitment to social re-

---

ical forums. From a well-to-do background, Cama sympathized with radical nationalist elements. She is remembered for unfurling the Indian tricolour (future national flag) at the International Socialist Conference in Stuttgart in 1,907. See B. R. Chowdhury, *Madame Cama: A Short Life-Sketch* (Delhi, 1977). The career of Shapurji D. Saklatvala (1874-1936) provides example of a Parsi on the Left of the political spectrum. Saklatvala was a critic of British rule, though, less concerned with political nationalism in India than with the international workers' struggle. Saklatvala was the third Parsi elected to Parliament'at Westminster as a member of the National Labour Party for the constituency of North Battersea in 1922, and represented the Communist Party of Great Britain in the same constituency from 1924 to 1929. See P. Saha, *Shapurji Saklatvala: A Short Biography* (Delhi, 1970); M. Squires, *Saklatvala: A Political Biography* (London, 1990).

[99] Address from the Bombay Association to the H.M the Queen, December 16, 1858, in G.D. 1859 1/80:403-4; Address from the Inhabitants of Bombay to H.M the Queen, January 10, 1859 G.D. 1859 1/80:431-2.

[100] See *Ripon Club, Golden Jubilee 1884-1934* (Bombay, 1934).

[101] *Rast Goftar*, November 18, 1888.

form in favour of a movement that would divert the energies of the Parsis, and undermine the strength of identity the efforts at social reform had endeavoured to produce.[102] The non-Congress Parsis' arguments consisted in portraying the Parsis as different from other Indians, and as virtual foreigners sojourning in India, as more loyal to British rule, and dubious as to the viability of the nationalist movement.[103] To some degree the arguments against the Parsis' participation in the nationalist cause resembled the arguments put forward by the Muslims, in the early pre-Independence decades, as to the fear of the loss of identity and influence in a movement where they were a minority.[104] This line of argument re-enforced by the strong social and cultural identification with the British augured for the Parsis to remain at best neutral between political interests.[105]

The Parsis' reaction to political nationalism grew more critical and in opposition as the principles and methods of Indian nationalism developed and intensified. Political allegiances among the Parsis became polarized between the Congress Parsis and their supporters on the one side, and both liberal and conservative Parsis led by the Parsi elites on the other. In particular, the non-Congress Parsi leadership opposed both the principle of manhood suffrage and the politics of agitation that the Congress Parsis came to support. The opposition to the democratic principle largely lay in the Parsis' fear of losing influence and being inundated by the power of majorities. The non-Congress Parsis opposed the Congress Parsis' advocacy of *swaraj* from the early years of the new century, as totally against their interests. The Parsis' concern over politics in India intensified with the mobilization and agitation of the masses begun in the 1920s, particularly under Gandhi. The Parsis admired Gandhi's principles and actions on behalf of the downtrodden and the citizens of the Empire, particularly his efforts on behalf of Indians in South Africa, but opposed his ideas and course for political nationalism in India believing them to be misguided. Parsis opposed the non-cooperation movement led by Gandhi from 1920 to 1921 that sought to boycott Indians' participation in public institutions, as militating against the Parsis' interests established over years, as well as disloyal to the

[102] *Rast Goftar*, January 4, 1891.
[103] *Rast Goftar*, May 12, 1889.
[104] *Rast Goftar*, June 2, 1889.
[105] *Rast Goftar*, January 31, 1897.

government and disrespectful of the law.[106] The *Jam-e-Jamshed* criticized Gandhi's methods as both ill-conceived and naive: "We have great respect for Mr. Gandhi's abilities, but it must be borne in mind that in any movement the followers are always more enthusiastic and less wise than their chief and that they bring trouble upon themselves and the country by their excess of enthusiasm."[107] The Parsis would grow more alienated from Gandhi and the Congress as political agitation took what they believed a predictable course:

> The Parsi Community was greatly perturbed owing to numerous assaults having been made on Parsi ladies and gentlemen. We are grieved to see that a certain section of the turbulent element in Bombay has not respected the principle of 'non-violence' and has indulged in wrong and despicable acts.... [The Parsi Community] expresses the hope that the bitter experiences gained in Bombay will induce Mr. Gandhi to give up his intention of commencing civil disobedience....[108]

Gandhi, for his part, praised the Parsis for their accomplishments as a community, while he sought to appeal to their Indianness as a people, often addressing them as his fellow countrymen, whose right and responsibility was to India as much as that of any other Indian community.[109] While in South Africa, Gandhi's principle patron, friend, and fellow jailmate had been the Parsi philanthropist Rustomjee J. Ghorkhodu (1864-1924). 'Parsi Rustomjee,' as Ghorkhodu was popularly known, and the Parsis' support for Gandhi in South Africa had been conspicuous for a small community.[110] Gandhi noted the self-sacrifice and bravery of the Parsis of South Africa, as exhibiting the prestige of all Indians.[111] Whereas Gandhi sought to democratize the Indian national movement among the masses, the Parsis represented to Gandhi and the other nationalists a community that was also very typical of the moderate Indians who had to be

---

[106] J. R. B. Jeejeebhoy, *Non-Cooperation, Its Pros and Cons* (Bombay, 1921); idem, *Bribery and Corruption in Bombay* (Bombay, 1952), 293, 306.

[107] *Jam-e-Jamshed*, September 28, 1920, in *Report on Native Papers*, 1920, no. 40, 417.

[108] *Bombay Samachar*, November 18, 1921, ibid., no. 47, 1346-7.

[109] "Speech at the Opening of Lokamanya National School," Anklesvar 10.11.1920, in *The Collected Works of Mahatma Gandhi*, vol. 18, July-November 1920 (Ahmedabad, 1966), 419-20.

[110] *Indian Opinion*, 19.2.1910, ibid., vol. 10, November 1909-March 1911, 158-9; Darukhanawala, *Parsi Lustre*, 145.

[111] *Indian Opinion*, 20.2.1909, in *Collected Works of Mahatma Gandhi*, vol. 9, September 1908-November 1909, 193-4. See also Gandhi, *An Autobiography*, vol. 2, 157-66.

brought into the nationalist movement for its success. The Parsis' caution, compactness, and solidarity as a community, and their insistence on abundant proof of the stability and morality of any movement before committing to it, appealed to Gandhi. Gandhi urged the Parsis to join the movement and guide it along a thoughtful course, as non-cooperators anxiously awaited the Parsis' lead.[112]

Gandhi's appeals to the Parsis acknowledged the Parsis' relevance to the debate over nationalism in India, and the press confirmed this fact:

> Mr. Gandhi, in our view, is rightly anxious to enlist Parsi sympathy in favour of his propaganda. The patriotism of the Parsis is, from the nature of causes, temperate and rational. It would be easy to rouse a body of Hindus or of Muhammadans against the foreign rulers, by a mere appeal to history irrespective of moral and practical considerations. Not so the Parsis. If the Parsis then are induced to join any political movement it must gain moral support by that fact. They cannot easily be influenced by racial and historical hatred against the British irrespective of the merits of the actual situation.... Mr. Gandhi is on firmer ground when he appeals to the Parsis to help him in combating social evils.[113]

At the same time, the incompatibility of Gandhi's aims and the general interests of the Parsis were also apparent. The support among Parsis of such policies and goals as rapid industrialization and capital accumulation, as well as their hostility to prohibition, divided Gandhi and the Parsis.[114] Above all, the Parsis opposed the fundamental premise of Gandhi's movement, to remove the British from India: "You intend getting rid of the British Government by means of non-cooperation. We Parsis, along with other Indians, are of the opinion that we cannot do without the British for some years to come."[115]

---

[112] "To the Parsees," from *Young India*, 23.3.1921, in *Collected Works of Mahatma Gandhi*, vol. 19, 1920-1, 469-71.

[113] *Praja Mitra and Parsi*, April 11, 1921, in *Report on Native Papers*, 1921, no. 16, 434.

[114] The participation of the Parsis in the liquor trade made them opponents of Gandhi's temperance movement and other prohibitions on the alcohol trade. See *Jam-e-Jamshed*, April 2, 1921, ibid., No. 14, 386. See Press Communique issued by the Punchayet in the matter of Prohibition introduced by the Congress-led government in 1939, in Sapur F. Desai, *The History of the Bombay Parsi Punchayet, 1860-1960* (Bombay, 1977), 311-12; *Parsee Prakash*, 7: 494-502.

[115] *Jam-e-Jamshed*, April 2, 1921, in *Report on Native Papers*, 1921, no. 14, 386.

As discussion began on India's constitutional evolution, the Parsis reacted slowly to change, in part, dependent and confident in the British government's ability to safeguard and represent their interests. The Parsi community showed some interest in the idea of 'separate representation' or franchise under separate electorate, in the new councils proposed for Indians under both the reforms of Morley-Minto of 1909 and Montagu-Chelmsford of 1919, but nothing came of their representations. The initial ambivalence with which the Parsis regarded constitutional change, including the idea for special separate electoral representation of Indian minority communities, soon gave way to reaction to the tremendous changes progressing around them, and an attempt to safeguard loss of their influence. Throughout the 1930s and 1940s, the non-Congress Parsis sought to represent themselves at the various conferences in Britain and India discussing constitutional change for India; however, their presence and contribution were marginal in the prevailing political circumstances. The political developments in India of the twentieth century had witnessed the drift of the Parsis towards communal-interest politics and exposed their precarious situation. The infinitesimally small size of the Parsi community rendered its claims for special representation problematic, particularly given the opposition to such a proposal on the part of the Congress Parsis. The advent of Independence witnessed the Parsis reconcile themselves to the new political reality, while maintaining a sense of nostalgia for the *ancien regime*. On August 14, 1947, the Parsis of Bombay held an Independence celebration, and the Parsi Punchayet on behalf of the Parsis of India sent congratulations to both Prime Minister Nehru and the Governor-General of Pakistan M. A. Jinnah. With Independence, Parsis came to share and support the idea of Indian nationalist identity, and emerged as enthusiastic supporters of Indian patriotism. They came to see their inevitable interests to lie in the progress of India.[116]

The ambivalence of the general body of Parsis towards Indian nationalism witnessed the divergence between Parsi and Indian public opinion over the overall progress of India for the first time in the history of the modern Parsi community. Whereas the Parsis had been at the vanguard of public opinion on social progress throughout the

[116] On the constitutional and political developments relative to the Parsis, see Kulke, Parsees in India, 190-216; Desai, *History of the Bombay Parsi Punchayet*, 121-8.

nineteenth century, by the last decade of the century their political stance appeared increasingly anachronistic. The newspaper *Kannada Suvarte* noted the "incorrect notions of loyalty and nationality," that it believed sustained the Parsis' opposition to Indian nationalism. The Parsis could claim to be neither different from other Indians nor unconcerned with the progress of politics. The *Bombay Samachar*, likewise, noted the Parsis' fears to be groundless and based on imaginary suppositions. The Phoenix astutely commented that the paucity of Parsis joining the Congress would rather damage the interests of the Parsis than hurt the cause of nationalism. And the *Gujarati* was bemused at "professedly the most forward race in modern India" ignoring its self-interest.[117]

The Parsis in the nationalist movement joined with Indian opinion in seeking to both alleviate and discount the Parsis' political concerns. Both Mehta and Wacha sought to convey the self-interest of the Parsis in identifying with the nationalist movement. In 1889, Mehta noted that it was the very situation of the Parsis as a minority, which compelled them to join the nationalist movement:

> To ask the Parsees to isolate themselves and their interests from those of the other natives of his country is to preach something not only equally selfish, but a great deal more short-sighted and unwise. In our case, it would be almost a suicidal policy.... Isolated as Parsees, pure and simple, holding ourselves aloof from the other natives of the country without common interests, common sympathies, and common cooperation, we might still remain an interesting community, but of no account whatsoever in the great march of events moulding the lofty destinies of this magnificent land.[118]

The inability to break the Parsis' ambivalence to nationalism was reflected in the nationalist Parsis' growing antagonism towards the community. The Parsis in the nationalist movement were particularly disdainful of the conservative Parsi press. The focus on political nationalism by the Parsi press reflected the maturation of the journalistic profession during the course of the century. At the same time, the Parsi press diverged over the level of Parsi commitment to the political process. Wacha noted the Parsi papers' lack of fidelity to the na-

[117] *Kannade Survate*, May 17, 1889, in *Report on Native Papers*, 1889, no. 21, 6-7; *Bombay Samachar*, May 24, 1889, ibid., no. 21, 6; *Phoenix*, May 29, 1889, ibid., no. 23, 9; *Gujarati*, July 7, 1889, ibid., no. 28, 7.

[118] Natesan, *Famous Parsis*, 332.

tionalist cause.[119] The opposition by the *Rast Goftar* had focused attention on its publisher and editor. Wacha described Kabraji as "writing a quantity of nonsense," while engaged in a "mischievous campaign."[120] Wacha particularly reviled what he regarded as the inconsistency and turncoat nature of the *Rast Goftar's* editorial opinion in not supporting a progressive cause like the nationalist movement.[121] The nationalist Parsis also singled out the conservative *Jam-e-Jamshed.* The influence of the paper was particularly annoying to the nationalist Parsi leaders as it had a considerable audience among Parsis. Writing to Dadabhai, Wacha described the *Jam-e-Jamshed* as "the most vicious and mischievous paper now going."[122] Wacha accused the paper of undermining not only the support for the nationalist cause, but the progress of the Parsis:

> If any community tries to bring about bad feeling it is the shallow class of the Parsis under the guidance of the superficial *Jame.* I hate the paper and its gimcrack politics.... And as the Parsi community has abandoned thinking for itself I find that in political matters it is not only growing imbecile but positively reactionary which can never bode any good.[123]

The reactions of Mehta and Wacha towards the Parsis' resistance to nationalism to some degree reflected their own ambivalent position within the Parsi community, and the incongruity of the task they had undertaken. Mehta and Wacha sought to reconcile a recalcitrant Parsi opinion to Indian nationalism amidst their own distancing from community-interest politics. The difficulties experienced by Mehta and Wacha with the Parsis reflected the fact that the nationalists had never sought to be the representatives of the Parsis and their interests within the nationalist movement. Pherozeshah Mehta's own reputation among the orthodox segment of the Parsi community did not commend him as the voice of authority. As Sir Homi Mody suggests the resentment reigned among Mehta's detractors that he was "studiously indifferent to the interests of his co-religionists, and that he

---

[119] Patwardhan, *Dadabhai Naoroji Correspondence,* vol. 2, part 1, May 7, 1904, 862.

[120] Ibid., vol. 2, part 1, May 28, 1889, 163; ibid., vol. 2, part 2, September 17, 1904, 871.

[121] Ibid., vol. 2, part 1, June 4, 1889, 165, August 2, 1892, 294.

[122] Ibid., vol. 2, part 2, December 3, 1904, 880.

[123] Ibid., vol. 2, part 2, September 24, 1904, 873-4.

had given to the country what was meant for his community."[124] The insularity and parochialism of the most orthodox Parsis had always regarded the cosmopolitanism of Parsis with disdain. Both the first Sir Jamsetjee Jejeebhoy and J. N. Tata were at some point in their lives criticized for the catholic nature of their charities.[125] The indictment against Mehta by orthodox Parsis overlooked a record of activity in the community and an abiding concern for the interests of the Parsis, yet aptly illustrated the dilemma new political allegiances raised for the Parsis in the nationalist movement.

Mehta, characteristically, was not averse to confront the opinions of his critics publicly. In 1912, Mehta addressed the accusation levelled against him by the orthodox that he was more an Indian than a Parsi, and was not an orthodox Parsi. Incredulous at the charge, Mehta chided those who called themselves orthodox for their dilettante concern for everything except what should have genuinely occupied them. He held the true aim of orthodoxy was to look to things directly of concern to the Parsis while allowing for the full expression of a plurality of opinion to all Parsis. The situation of the Parsis in India, Mehta held, had permitted them to appreciate what were the real needs of the community, while conscious of their obligations to the general social environment. Using the example of the charitable nature of the Parsis, Mehta alluded to the spirit that should guide the Parsis in all their dealings:

> I can never bring myself to agree with those who think that charity should begin at home and be confined to home. I would say that charity should begin at home and end abroad. By all means let the Parsis provide for all that is necessary for their community but after supplying the needs of their own co-religionists, let them look beyond their own narrow sphere.[126]

The reactions to Mehta on the part of Parsis are reminiscent of those prevalent within any group whether religious, ethnic, racial, linguistic, or nationalist in identification, towards the growth of a plurality of interest among its members. What is interesting to note is the extent to which the political debate among the Parsis was both an extension of the general debate over identity, and an illustration of how comprehensive the debate had become.

---

[124] Mody, *Sir Pherozeshah Mehta*, 344-5.

[125] See Jeejeebhoy, *Some Unpublished and Later Speeches and Writings of the Hon Sir Pherozeshah Mehta*, 315.

[126] Ibid., 313-16.

The arguments of the Parsi leaders, therefore, at times only served to remind a large segment of Parsi opinion as to the lack of relevance of joining a movement that broke from their traditional allegiances.[127] The nationalist Parsis' inability to influence majority Parsi opinion would widen the political divide between Parsis, and perhaps accounts for the inability of a Parsi to gain a solid political constituency in the community in the early years of nationalist politics. Parsi political opinion had diverged sufficiently to witness the candidacy and election of a second Parsi to the British House of Commons in 1895, on a Conservative ticket. Muncherjee M. Bhownaggree represented the constituency of Bethnal Green, and in 1897 was the fifth Parsi to be knighted. His victory reflected a strategy to dissociate himself from the Indian nationalist movement while sufficiently confident of a Conservative base of support in India. Bhownaggree was on cordial personal terms with Dadabhai, and offered his congratulations on Dadabhai's election in 1892 as a triumph for Indians, which transcended mere political or party terms.[128] Bhownaggree shared the concern for the treatment of colonial subjects in the Empire, and worked for the interests of Parsis in Britain as a member of the Zoroastrian Fund.[129] Bhownaggree was involved in, the famous case of the Parsi George Edalji, who was sentenced to seven years imprisonment in 1903, for the alleged maiming of a pony and other animal mutilations in Great Wyrley. The attention of Bhownaggree and many others led to Edalji's release in October 1906, and moved the author Sir Arthur Conan Doyle to investigate the case and attempt to clear Edalji's name.[130] Bhownaggree, however, was the antithesis to Dadabhai on the issue of India and political reform. Bhownaggree supported Conservative British imperial policy, and opposed the Congress movement.[131] He earned the derision of progressive Indian opinion for his stance, gaining the reputa-

---

[127] *Rast Goftar*, November 21, 1889.

[128] Bhownaggree to D.N., Naoroji Papers, 3B130(5) 7.12.1900; See Speech of Bhownaggree as chairman at a dinner in celebration of Dadabhai's election, Naoroji Papers, 3B130(30) no date.

[129] Bhownaggree to D.N., Naoroji Papers, 3B130(20) 8.4.1903; 3B130(21) 7.5.1903.

[130] Bhownaggree to D.N., Naoroji Papers, 3B130(23) 12.11.1903. See also Daniel Stashower, *Teller of Tales: The Life of Arthur Conan Doyle* (New York, 1999), 254-60.

[131] Patwardhan, *Dadabhai Naoroji Correspondence*, vol. 2, part 1, May 20, 1893, 346; ibid., vol. 2, part 2, June 28, 1895, 444.

tion of being in league with the "pensioned politicians who rule India from Westminster,"[132] or more disparagingly Mr. M. M. "Bow the Knee and Agree."[133] His claim to be the representative of 'Conservative India' was discounted by nationalist opinion no sooner than he was elected.[134] Yet, despite the opposition to Bhownaggree, he represented a significant segment of opinion in India, which opposed involvement in the Congress movement and desired the maintenance of the political status quo.[135]

The support the nationalist Parsis could expect from the Parsi community consequently was small. In 1890, Wacha wrote optimistically that, "the Congress has made many new friends and I am certain that there has been a strong revolution in the attitude of the Parsis."[136] The actual number of Parsi delegates to the Congresses, however, remained small even for a small community. The number of Parsi delegates to the four Congresses held in Bombay from 1885 to 1915, where it would be expected the Parsis would be at the height of their attendance, included: 8 Parsis out of 72 delegates in 1885; 44 Parsis out of 1,889 delegates in 1889; 70 Parsis out of 1,010 delegates in 1904; and 96 Parsis out of 1,259 delegates in 1915.[137] The attendance numbers of Indians to the early Congresses in general were a source of concern to the nationalists.[138] Wacha nevertheless conceded that waverers had reduced the number of Parsis prepared to join and attend Congress meetings.[139] The delegate lists of Parsis attending Congresses are not a clear indication of the depth of support for nationalism among the Parsis. Albeit, the Parsis' active commitment to nationalist politics was not comparable, for example, to their commitment to municipal politics in Bombay City from the

---

[132] Ibid., vol. 2, part 1, August 12, 1892, 294.

[133] Kulke, *The Parsees in India*, 227.

[134] Patwardhan, *Dadabhai Naoroji Correspondence*, vol. 2, part 2, December 20,1895,469.

[135] Ibid., vol. 2, part 1, May 10, 1889, 158, November 15, 1889, 198-9.

[136] Ibid., vol. 2, part 1, January 3, 1890, 204.

[137] A. Moin and Shaheda Zaidi, *The Encyclopaedia of the Indian National Congress, Volume 1, 1885-1890: The Founding Fathers* (New Delhi, 1976), 324; *Volume 4, 1901-1905: On the Road to Self-Government* (New Delhi, 1978), 641-6; *Volume 6, 1911-1915: In Search of a Creed* (New Delhi, 1979), 717-32; B. B. Majumdar, *Indian Political Associations and Reform of Legislature, 1818-1917* (Calcutta, 1965), 203.

[138] McLane, *Indian Nationalism*, 91-2, 118-19.

[139] Patwardhan, *Dadabhai Naoroji Correspondence*, vol. 2, part 1, January 3, 1890, 204.

mid-to-late nineteenth century, where they formed a sizeable proportion of the electoral role relative to their numbers.[140]

The ambivalence towards the nationalist cause among Parsis also affected the material support the Parsi leaders could hope to see from the community. The conservative Parsi establishment of Bombay shared the ambivalence of the general community. Wacha and Mehta clearly believed the support of someone like J. N. Tata, who was the new generation of rising entrepreneurial stars among the Parsis, was the key to bringing in other financial patrons.[141] While the business community did not forsake its options where political interests were concerned, the active support for nationalist politics remained tepid. J. N. Tata contributed sizeably to Dadabhai's elections in Britain, and was in contact with Mehta.[142] Tata's active support for the Congress movement, however, was not forthcoming. Wacha attributed this to Mr. Tata being "carried away by the stream of popular idols," i.e., by the prevailing sentiment among the majority of Parsis against the nationalist cause.[143] Gandhi worried that Tata and the Parsis might become oblivious to the wants and aspirations of the multitude of their countrymen, as the "Rockefeller spirit" seemed to be overtaking the great House of the Tatas.[144] It was left to Tata's sons to support the Congress.[145] Ratanji J. Tata gave Rs. 50,000 in support to the Indian freedom fight in South Africa between 1909 and 1912. Gandhi hailed the donation, in large measure, for the implication it carried in laying the entire Parsi community under obligation.[146]

J. N. Tata sought to contribute to the welfare of Indians in the more usual way of the Parsi philanthropist. He supported the education of Indians for the Civil Service to a sum of five lakhs. In addition, he would endow a polytechnic research university to the sum of thirty lakhs.[147] Tata's economic vision and support for the Indian do-

---

[140] See J. C. Masselos, *Towards Nationalism* (Bombay, 1974); Christine Dobbin, *Urban Leadership in Western India* (Oxford, 1972).

[141] Patwardhan, *Dadabhai Naoroji Correspondence*, vol. 2, part 1, November 1, 1889, 196.

[142] Ibid., vol. 2, part 2, July 5, 1895, 446.

[143] Ibid., vol. 2, part 1, November 15, 1889, 200.

[144] *Collected Works of Mahatma Gandhi*, vol. 19, 1920-21, 469-71.

[145] Patwardhan, *Dadabhai Naoroji Correspondence*, vol. 2, part 2, September 24,1904, 873.

[146] *Indian Opinion*, 11.12.1909, in *Collected Works of Mahatma Gandhi*, vol. 10, November 1909-March 1911, 98-9; ibid: *Indian Opinion*, 19.2.1910, 158-9.

[147] Patwardhan, *Dadabhai Naoroji Correspondence*, vol. 2, part 2, June 1, 1896, 491; Natesan, *Famous Parsis*, 268-9.

mestic economy shared with political nationalism the idea of self-sufficiency and autonomy. The Tata firms profited from the movement for Indian self-sufficiency initiated by Gandhi known as *swadeshi.* Tata mills in Bombay were renamed under the *swadeshi* banner in recognition of the movement. The difficulties in encouraging prominent Parsi supporters to the nationalist cause, however, was one of the reasons the Parsi nationalists increasingly turned away from concentrating on Parsi support in the nationalist cause.

The political divisions between Parsis had its effect on the nationalist Parsis' appreciation of their role within the Parsi community. The commitment to Indian nationalism evinced their drift away from the majority sentiment among the Parsis. Wacha at times despaired over the Parsis' disinterest in nationalist politics, and was candid about the divisions in the Parsi community. He wrote to Dadabhai:

> *If any community* is deceived it is the rising generation of PARSIS. Don't be surprised at it. The Parsi is going down the incline fast enough. There will be no hope for him a few years hence. *It has lost its thinking faculty....* The silly and mischievous cry still goes forth that the Parsis should not dabble in politics. They must cast their lot with the Anglo-Indian or hold themselves aloof from the Hindus.... I had a talk with half a dozen such in the Ripon Club the other day. They are typical of the less educated and ignorant class in the community. Of course, when I really explained the matter and put things in their right attitude they were quite convinced. But this shows which way the Parsi wind blows.[148]

Wacha had to admit that the size of the opposition to the movement was from "not an inconsiderable class of Parsis."[149] His hope lay in the gradual but perceptible progress of nationalist aims among Indians and Parsis.

Summary

The lives and public careers of Dadabhai Naoroji and the other nationalist Parsi leaders offer a picture of the changing nature of identity, and the changes in the Parsi community into the twentieth century. While their educational elevation distinguished them from pre-

---

[148] Patwardhan, *Dadabhai Naoroji Correspondence*, vol. 2, part 2, September 17, 1904, 871.

[149] Ibid., vol. 2, part 1, May 10, 1889, 158.

vious generations of Parsis, in large measure, the early Parsis in the nationalist movement shared with previous generations the understanding that the Parsis had to direct social change to their benefit. They appreciated that the Parsis had to be actively involved in shaping those factors that bore directly on the welfare of the community and Parsi identity. And like previous generations, they exploited the opportunities available in their time. In this sense, they appreciated the history of the Parsis in India as much as they contributed to it.

It is an axiom of the historiography of modern India that the rise of the Indian nationalist movement owed to the very conditions created by British colonial rule. In particular, the advancement of English education and the coalescence of British and Indian values from the nineteenth century had predisposed a new class of Indians to be loyal in its allegiance yet desirous of the rights and opportunities presented by Western culture and colonial rule. The shape and character that nationalism first assumed in India equally owed to the characters and backgrounds of individual nationalist leaders. The ability of the Parsis to foresee change and adapt to it in part accounts for the rise of Parsis within the nationalist movement, and their reassessment of the interests of the Parsis within a changing India. The Parsis' political identity had come to diversify by the latter nineteenth century. Dadabhai Naoroji's faith in the value of British rule was as constant as the first generation of Parsis to interact with the British, the *shetias*. However, whereas the *shetias* were essentially apolitical in character, Dadabhai and his nationalist partners Pherozeshah Mehta and Dinsha Wacha sought a role in actively guiding British rule towards a better understanding of Indians and the their needs, and eventually sought political responsibility from British rule.

The public career of Dadabhai and his nationalist contemporaries also marked the natural progression of Parsis away from purely Parsi concerns, and to the Parsis' involvement in the last major sphere of activity: party politics. To some degree, the participation of all the Parsis in party politics in Britain and India reflected a commitment to the very basic Zoroastrian values of justice and active participation in the affairs of the world for its betterment. Nevertheless, the example of Parsis in nationalist politics implied that few things could be termed purely Parsi concerns. This often created difficulty for the nationalist leaders within the Parsi community. Dadabhai Naoroji, Pherozeshah Mehta, and Dinsha Wacha sought to place their nationalist credentials above their ethnic and religious identity as Parsis, though never renouncing the latter. All three men were the clear products of their Parsi background, and came to nationalist politics with a record of involvement in the Parsi community. At the same time, none of the nationalist leaders claimed or could have claimed the Parsis as a solid constituency. Their involvement in nationalist politics was problematic for a large segment of Parsi opinion, which still clung solely to the expression of their community identity. Early in his public life in 1877, Pherozeshah Mehta realized as much as the Parsis debated recognizing a nominal leader of the community:

> If the Parsees can manage to merge in the general mass of the Queen's Indian subjects, then there is no such necessity. But whatever may be the future destiny of the Parsees, such a thing is not possible in the present. On the contrary, Parsees, as at present constituted, are distinguished as inferior only to the Jews in the tenacity with which they cling to an exclusive nationality.[150]

While the nationalist Parsi leaders sought to involve the Parsis in the nationalist movement, and to some degree shape the movement in a moderate course favourable to the involvement of a community like the Parsis, they had not sought to simply be the representatives of the Parsis, or accommodate their concerns in the movement. For Naoroji, Mehta, and Wacha whose activities as Parsis in cosmopolitan Bombay had conditioned them to appreciate the expansion of the interests of the Parsis beyond the Parsi community, this would have been anathema. Naoroji, Mehta, and Wacha sought to represent Indian nationalist aspirations while sensitive to the community ethos that had contributed to shaping their political backgrounds. To some degree, Naoroji, Mehta, and Wacha presaged the great nationalist leaders to come to prominence such as Gandhi and Jawaharlal Nehru, who were also well-educated, professionally trained, continental, and coming from a strong sense of community, while continually and tenuously in search of the perfect constituency. The Parsi nationalist leaders had taken the lead in arguing the value of broadening the Parsis' sense of identity, while themselves unbound by the limitations of any one identity.

---

[150] C. Y. Chintamani, ed., *Speeches and Writings of the Honourable Sir Pherozeshah M. Mehta, K.C.I.E.* (Allahabad, 1905), 128.

EPILOGUE

IDENTITY AND THE PRESENT-DAY PARSIS

In his novel *Such a Long Journey*, Rohinton Mistry's protagonist Gustad Noble laments the passing of traditions in modern life. Putting aside his ballpoint pen in favour of his fountain pen, Gustad muses:

> No one wrote with them anymore, not even in schools. But at one time that was how children made the transition from pencil to ink. That was the bloody problem with modern education. In the name of progress they discarded seemingly unimportant things, without knowing that what they were chucking out the window of modernity was tradition. And if tradition was lost, then the loss of respect for those who respected and loved tradition always followed.[1]

By the twenty-first century, the Parsis continue to debate the balance of tradition and change and Parsi identity. The processes that have historically shaped the Parsis identity continue to shape the modern community. The Parsis' responses to the plurality of thought over social and religious issues continues to be shaped by the process of assimilation and adaptation to their environment; and, increasingly, in the case of overseas Parsi communities, to their new environment. At the same time, Parsi attitudes to identity in the twenty-first century vary widely. Progressive Parsi attitudes towards identity reflect the prevailing attitudes in society, including modern Indian society, over issues of individual rights and equality. Traditionalist Parsi attitudes, equally, have been affected by the phenomenon of the rise of conservatism worldwide in recent decades. The recourse to independence of action on the part of parties dissatisfied with the continuing discussion has also increased. Parsi priests, particularly orthodox priests, have taken a greater role in seeking to have their opinions heard as a means of providing some resolution to interminable debates over the admission of converts to the community. At the same time, Parsis in India who have married outside the commu-

[1] Rohinton Mistry, *Such a Long Journey* (Toronto, 1991), paperback edition, 80-1.

nity but who continue to regard themselves as active members of the community, principally Parsi women, have increasingly banded together and have sought to gain recognition of their and their families' place in the community. Meanwhile, Parsi communities outside India in Europe and North America, in particular, have begun to re-examine and reshape Parsi traditions.

The issues surrounding the Parsi identity and conversion have in large measure been driven by famous controversial cases among the Parsis. The issue of conversion did not end with the case of Bella. As late as 1942, Dastur Framroze Bode and other Parsi priests performed the *Navjote* ceremony of seventy-seven children in Bansda in India. Like the Mazagon *Navjotes* in 1882, the children were believed to have Parsi fathers. However, the public reaction was such that it appeared to upset even the tacit understanding that had emerged regarding the admission of children by Parsi fathers to the community since the Parsi Punchayet Case. Dastur Bode and his priestly colleagues were censured by the Anjumans of various Parsi communities in India, the society of Parsi priests known as the Athornan Mandal, and the Navsari Bhagarsath Anjuman.[2] It appears that while the Parsis had become inured to the pluralism of thought within the community, actual cases of 'conversion' continued to upset the conservative status quo in the community.[3]

In 1990, the most serious community dispute, perhaps since the Parsi Punchayet Case, began when a Parsi woman by the name of Roxan Darshan Shah, 25, was killed in an automobile accident on the Bombay/Poona road, and her remains were refused consignment to the Towers of Silence in Bombay. The Parsi Punchayet authorities, who have authority over the *dakhma* in Bombay, had refused to consign Roxan's body to the *dakhma*, on notification by the *dakhma* authorities that Roxan Shah was married to a Jain and, consequently, was believed to have renounced Zoroastrianism. The facts of the case were that Roxan Nadir had married Darshan Shah under the provisions of the Special Marriages Act of 1954, which recognizes marriage between individuals of different religions. The couple had

[2] *Parsee Prakash*, 8:38.

[3] The debate over conversion and the acceptance of non-Parsis into the community is ongoing. See H. K. Mirza, *Conversion Caucus* (Bombay, 1971); K. Antia, *The Argument for Acceptance* (Bombay, 1985); H. K. Mirza, K. M. Jamaspasa and F. M. Kotwal, *Conversion: A Myth Exploded* (Bombay, 1985); idem, *Antia's 'Acceptance': A Zoroastrian 'Ahrmogih'* (Bombay, 1985).

undergone a "symbolic ceremony," according to Roxan's father Dr. Adi Nadir, consisting of Hindu marriage observances.[4]

The refusal of the Punchayet authorities to consign Roxan's body to the doongerwadi (Parsi-Gujarati for Tower of Silence) led to a heated controversy within the Parsi community over the treatment of Roxan and her family, the subject of intermarriage and the rights of Parsis, specifically women, who marry outside the community. Dr. Firoze M. Kotwal, Dastur at H. B. Wadia fire-temple, Bombay, offered his opinion and that on the part of the orthodox Parsi priesthood, noting that both the tradition and religious custom of the Parsis regarded a woman who had married outside the Parsi community as having embraced her husband's religion. Dastur Kotwal noted both the right of the community and its priesthood to pass laws for the preservation of its identity and customs, and stated his belief that modern legislation, such as the Special Marriages Act, or the judgements of law courts could not affect the religious laws of the Zoroastrians.[5] Dastur Kotwal's comments reflected the historical and traditional understanding that had prevailed within the Parsi community over the issue of conversion and religious innovation for much of its history to the present. The liberal press, however, roundly criticized his comments. The editor of the *Bombay Samachar*, Jehan Daruwala, in particular, attacked both Dastur Kotwal and his opinions, referring to him as obscurantist and fanatical in his approach to religion.[6]

The issues in the dispute, of course, were not new. The decision to refuse a body into the *dakhma* by the *dakhma* and Punchayet authorities had occurred in the past. One of the 'accommodations' the Parsis of the past had made, and which the defence in the Rangoon Navjote Case assailed, was to place the bodies of individuals of doubtful Parsi background in the *chotra* or alternate place of con-

---

[4] The dispute was covered in both the Parsi and general Indian press for over a year. For an introduction to the dispute, see Arnavaz S. Mama, "An Injustice at Doongerwadi," *Parsiana*, August 1990; idem, "The Controversy Continues," and "The Orthodox Response," *Parsiana*, October 1990; Island, August 1991. The Parsi-Gujarati weekly *Jam-e-Jamshed* and the Anglo-Gujarati newspaper *Bombay Samachar* ran many articles and letters starting from August 1990.

[5] See *Parsiana*, September 1990.

[6] See *The Case of Roxan Darshan Shah: Articles and Letters Reprinted in the Bombay Samachar: Parsi Tari Arsi* (Bombay, 1990), 13-14.

signment to the *dakhma* proper.[7] In 1918, the body of Soonabai Edulji R. Mehta, who had married a Dr. Underwood under the Indian Christian Marriage Act, was denied consignment to the *dakhma* and was placed in the *chotra.* Up to the middle of the twentieth century, the opinion of legal counsel was solicited by the Parsi Punchayet on the rights of Parsis marrying outside the community under the provisions of various Marriage Acts of Parliament. The legal opinions all denied or placed conditions on the rights of Parsis marrying outside the community.[8] Many of the arguments and responses by the Parsis, whether based on religious, historical, or contemporary progressive ideas put forward during the Roxan episode and after, were reminiscent of those put forward by traditionalists and reformers many times in the past. In the atmosphere of the late twentieth century, however, the dispute was both unique and significant. The extent to which progressive Parsi opinion had come to reflect the changes in modern life, the shock over the Roxan episode was clear. Indeed, the belief on the part of the editor of the *Samachar* that "no sensible Parsi subscribes to such anachronistic, anti-religious and idiotic ideas,"[9] as those expressed by Dastur Kotwal and the orthodox, reflected the extent to which 'reformism' had given way to a general progressive attitude among many Parsis in the late twentieth century.

The dispute was also significant given the repetition of the issues surrounding the Parsi identity and community membership. On the one hand, the debate reflected that the Parsis held their religious identity as important as at any time in the past. On the other hand, the Parsis remained deadlocked over actual changes to the social and religious practices of the community. The Parsis were no longer a community discussing and debating their identity in the midst of adapting to and directing social change in their favour. By the twenty-first century, the Parsis are in the midst of a decline, both relative and absolute, in comparison to their social environment, economically, educationally, and demographically. The need to confront and resolve issues relative to their identity that include the issues of intermarriages and the acceptance of converts to the community continue to weigh heavily on the small community. The Roxan

---

[7] See *Journal of the Iranian Association* 9, no. 12 (April 1920-March 1921): 88-9, 106-9, 184-8.

[8] See Appendices J, K, Kl, in Sapur F. Desai, *The History of the Bombay Parsi Punchayet* (Bombay, 1977), 294-303

[9] *The Case of Roxan Darshan Shah*, 13-14.

case once again led to the soliciting of legal opinions, pronouncements by the priesthood, and resolutions by the Punchayet. The Parsi Punchayet of Bombay remained the focus of attention for the community. More than a century after the Punchayet had lost its legal authority to adjudicate disputes among the Parsis, to some degree, it remained significant in the discussion of the Parsi identity. The Punchayet was finally compelled by the public scrutiny and mood to seek some compromise to the situation. On April 9, 1991, the Parsi Punchayet took the decision to permit Parsi women married to non-Parsis the right to be consigned to one of the Towers of Silence "specifically earmarked for the purpose."[10] The use of the *dakhma* was conditional on the family of the deceased having to submit an affidavit that confirmed that the deceased had continued to follow the Zoroastrian religion until her death. This decision, however, placated neither liberal nor orthodox sentiments. The orthodox condemned the resolution, while the liberals viewed the resolution of the Punchayet as discriminatory against Parsi women who had married outside the community while requiring no such undertaking from Parsi men in similar situations. The majority of Parsi opinion, which loathed the spectacle of Parsis publicly attacking one another, was relieved at the attempt to dissipate the dispute. The decision was too late to benefit the family of Roxan Shah, whose remains were interred in a Parsi cemetery in Mahableshwar. The episode, however, illustrated all too well the paradox involved in attempting to address an issue that would not go away, and the clear difficulties involved in reopening the issue of identity.

Since the Roxan case the recourse to independence of action on the part of liberals and conservatives over issues relative to the Parsi identity is the striking feature of the changes occurring in the community. In large part, as a reaction to steady progressive attitudes in Parsi and Indian society, a new conservatism has emerged among some Parsis. A stronger conservative defence of traditional Parsi religious practices and values has emerged, which often appears in the press and in print. Letters and articles in both the Gujarati and English language Parsi press appear in support of orthodoxy and range from passionate polemics against the reformers, to thoughtful arguments on the history and future of Parsi identity.[11] On other occa-

---

10 Statement of B.P.P. in *Parsiana*, March 1991.

11 Articles in support of orthodoxy regularly appear in the Parsi press. See Adi

sions, some Parsis have come to openly oppose practices they regard as innovations or against the traditions of the community. Priests supported by trustees of Zoroastrian Anjumans have refused the children of mixed marriages entrance into fire-temples.[12]

Following the Roxan controversy, Parsis who have married outside the community in India have banded together to form the association of intermarried Parsis and their supporters. During the Roxan episode, thirty-two Parsi women and their supporters signed a petition to the Parsi Punchayet of Bombay seeking the reassurance that upon their deaths they could be consigned to the *dakhma*.[13] The intention of Parsis who have married non-Parsis to remain part of the community and keep their concerns before the Parsis reflects the persistent tension over identity. For many, the old concept of the Parsis as a 'caste' community has no meaning whatsoever, as caste has come to be viewed pejoratively by modern Parsis and other Indians. Among progressives, the tendency has also been to seek legal relief and legislative clarification to issues surrounding the Parsi identity. This approach while clarifying the individual rights of Parsis marrying non-Parsis provides no relief to the general debate over community membership and interfaith marriages. The Special Marriages Act of 1954, in particular, has often been cited by progressives as recognizing the right of Parsis to marry non-Parsis while remaining active members of the Parsi community. The Special Marriages Act applies to marriages between persons of different as well as the same religion, and provides for the registration of marriages celebrated and solemnized under different religions. A Parsi marriage, can also be registered under the Special Marriage Act and be regarded as a marriage under the Act, and be terminated under its provisions. While the Special Marriage Act recognizes the validity of interfaith marriages as a general law, it does not supersede the Parsi Act of 1865 and the revisions of 1936 and 1988, in the recognition of what constitutes a Parsi marriage.[14] The Special Marriages Act,

---

F. Doctor, "The State of Zoroastrian Orthodoxy," *Parsiana*, August 1988. The orthodox viewpoint also appeared in the new publication *Deen Parast*, N. H. Dadrawala, General Editor. See Jal N. Birdy, "The Parsi Identity," *Deen Parast*, September 1991.

[12] *Parsiana*, August 1992, notes the refusal of Zoroastrian Anjumans in India to admit children born of Parsi mothers and non-Parsi fathers entrance to the fire-temples of the Parsis.

[13] *Parsiana*, October 1990, February 1991.

[14] Phiroze K. Irani, "The Personal Law of the Parsis of India," in *Family Law in*

consequently, has no bearing on the Parsi community's traditional practices as regards the recognition and acceptance of interfaith marriages and membership in the community.

Public controversy arose among the Parsis following the death of J. R. D. Tata. On November 29, 1993, Jehangir Ratanji Dadabhoy Tata, the pioneer of twentieth century Indian industry, founder of Tata Air Services in 1932 (the airline that eventually became Air India), and the head of India's Tata business and industrial conglomerate, died in Geneva. J. R. D. Tata was heir to the Tata textile and commercial enterprise started by Jamsetjee Nusserwanjee Tata in the nineteenth century, and the son of Ratanji Dadabhoy and Suzanne (Briere) Tata, the French lady whose *Navjote* in 1903 was the spark to the Parsi Punchayet Case. Born in 1904 in Paris, 'JRD' as he was popularly referred to, or 'Jeh' to his associates, had become an Indian citizen, and as one of India's leading businessmen and philanthropists was the first Zoroastrian to be awarded India's highest civilian honour, the Bharat Ratna, in 1992. Upon his death accolades from around the world poured forth for the man *The Daily Telegraph* hailed as the "Henry Ford of India."[15] In honour of JRD, the Government of Maharashtra proclaimed a three-day state mourning period, and announced plans to establish awards in the memory of Tata. Upon JRD's death, however, another public controversy arose among the Parsis over the performance of the *Uthamnā* ceremony in memory of the departed. JRD was interred in Pere Lachaise, in Paris; however, twelve Parsi priests, performed an *Uthamnā* ceremony in his memory on December 1, 1993, in Bombay. When two prominent Parsi priests, Dastur Dr. Firoze Kotwal and Ervad Dr. Peshotan Peer publicly objected to the *Uthamnā* ceremony being performed on behalf of JRD, whom they did not regard as Parsi or, at best, regarded as a half-caste Parsi, the community was once again under scrutiny over its beliefs and practices.

The comments by the priests reflected their belief that the priesthood is the ultimate arbiter of faith and identity among the Parsis, particularly in the face of progressive challenges to the revision of tradition, and the perceived ineffectual leadership of the Punchayet in safeguarding the Parsi identity. The tendency to apply a strict endogamy to the definition of who is a Parsi, by defining a Parsi to be

---

Asia and Africa, no. 6, ed. J. N. D. Anderson (London, 1968), 294.

[15] *The Daily Telegraph*, November 30, 1993.

the product of two Parsi parents, to oppose interfaith marriages, and to show no regard for the celebrity or credentials of those who act contrary to the customs of the Parsis, also reflects a stronger response among Parsis in recent years. Letters in support and against the opinions of the priests reflected the division in the Parsi community. On the whole, however, it may be said that many Parsis were dismayed and embarrassed over the episode, particularly as it had begun when the priests' comments were carried in the general Indian press. The heated nature of such disputes is increasingly moving a segment within the community not to want to broach such contentious subjects altogether. One letter in the Parsi press noted the spectacle the Parsis were offering up India:

> JRD symbolized the best among human beings and we are fortunate that he belonged to our community. Instead of recognizing this and honouring this great man, we are making a controversy! The whole nation is saluting him; in Bombay there are posters saying 'JRD—the Jewel of India,' and in our community we are squabbling over whether we should pray for his departed soul![16]

The question of community membership and conversion forms a paradox at the heart of the issue of identity and the modern Parsi community. The accommodation to social change conforms to the process of adaptability the Parsis have historically adhered to in India and that has sustained a sense of identity; yet, the accommodation to social change at times seemingly contradicts the very efforts of past generations of Parsis to preserve a unique sense of identity.

The independent actions of the Zoroastrian communities outside India will perhaps have the greatest influence on Parsi tradition in the years to come. Parsi migration outside India had followed along Parsi trade and commercial routes. The earliest Parsi settlements outside India were along the South China coast at Canton and Shanghai beginning from the first half of the nineteenth century, and Hong Kong after mid-century. From the 1830s and 1840s, settlements had expanded to countries and territories around the Indian Ocean basin, such as Sind, the southern Arabian coast, East and South Africa, as well to Britain. It is largely from the 1960s and 1970s that the major waves of emigration of Parsis from India and Africa began to areas of settlement in Europe, North America, and Australia. From 1979,

[16] On the comments of Dastur Kotwal and Ervad Peer, see Arnavaz S. Mama, "JRD: The last rites and wrongs," *Parsiana*, January 1994. See letter of Anu Aga, and other letters in Parsiana, February-March 1994.

these new world communities were augmented by the migration of Zoroastrians from Iran. As these communities have grown they have seen fit to shape the evolution of Parsi tradition. The Zoroastrian communities in Britain and North America formed general associations and organizations to meet the requirements of the their local Zoroastrian populations, and formed larger organizations to communicate and coordinate discussion among Zoroastrians worldwide. The Zoroastrian Trust Funds of Europe (ZTFE) was formed in 1861, to meet the modest needs of British Zoroastrians, and the Federation of Zoroastrian Associations of North America (FEZANA) was formed in 1987, as an umbrella organization of the associations in North America.[17] In 1980, the London-based World Zoroastrian Organization (WZO) was formed with the aim to protect the interests of Parsi Zoroastrians worldwide. It is in local Zoroastrian associations and organizations that change to tradition is also occurring. The Parsis of the diaspora outside India have come to celebrate their identity as Parsis and their membership in a historically accomplished community. At the same time, some Zoroastrian Associations have acknowledged the need to better accommodate themselves to their social environments. Local Parsi communities in major cities have successfully accommodated many of their basic social and religious requirements in the new settings, such as the establishment of community centres that contain a prayer room in the absence of a fully consecrated temple, and the consecration of *aramgahs* or burial and scattering grounds in cemeteries for Zoroastrians. In 1863, the British Zoroastrian community obtained burial rights for Zoroastrians in Brookwood Cemetery. In 1989, the Toronto Zoroastrian community consecrated burial and scattering grounds in Glen Oaks Memorial Gardens.

Many associations also prefer to acknowledge themselves by the religious identification of Zoroastrian, so as to be more inclusive of the Zoroastrians of Iranian background, for whom the designation of Parsi is not relevant. At the same time, the stress upon religious identification among diaspora communities aims to downplay issues and tensions relative to Parsi communal concerns. The participation

[17] The first North American Zoroastrian Conference was held in Toronto, Canada, in 1975, with successive conferences following approximately every two to three years. FEZANA was also started at the Sixth North American Congress in Toronto, in April 1988. *See Parsiana*, July 1988.

of Iranian Zoroastrians within the associations and organizations founded and predominantly run by Parsis, consequently, adds a further cultural perspective. Attempts are made to respect differences while fostering integration. Many Zoroastrian organizations provide for organizational literature in both English and Farsi, and provide facilities for each culture's particular social functions. At times, however, the clash of cultures between Iranians and South Asian Zoroastrians has led to separate groups being formed. This is especially the case in cities such as New York and Los Angeles where the large numbers of Iranians permits of viable separate associations. Differences of religion also exist, as Iranian Zoroastrians are less ritually orientated and less amenable to recognize the authority of the Parsi priesthood.

As regards intermarriage and conversion, Zoroastrian associations outside India welcome non-Zoroastrian spouses at social gatherings and certain religious observances.[18] Individual Parsi priests bless civil marriages between Parsis and non-Parsis of both genders, and perform the *Navjotes* of children of mixed marriages, whether the father or mother is Parsi. The advocates of *Navjotes* for children of mixed marriages either regard such children as Parsi by right entitled to initiation, or make a more academic distinction noting such children to be Zoroastrian (as Zoroastrianism permits conversions) if not ethnically Parsi. None of these marriages, however, can be considered Parsi marriages by Parsi custom or law, and the situation of 'half-Parsi' children religiously confirmed as Zoroastrians also remains problematic as regards the use of religious facilities in India. Generally, the Zoroastrian communities outside India have adopted no general role or principle to guide the issues of intermarriage and the initiation of children. In April 1993, the World Zoroastrian Organization approved resolutions to amend its constitution to open its membership to the non-Zoroastrian spouses of Zoroastrians and their children. The changes to the membership clause of the WZO was noted to have been passed by an overwhelming majority of the members, however, the decision attracted criticism from Parsis in

[18] In 1986, ill will arose among the British Zoroastrian community when the ZTFE (U.K.) passed a resolution requesting non-Zoroastrian spouses to refrain from attending the *Muktad* ceremonies, in August, in memory of the departed, at Zoroastrian House. Those excluded, however, conducted their own *Fravardigan Jashan* or remembrance ceremony at Brookwood Cemetery. See *Parsiana*, January 1988.

India and the British Zoroastrians of the Zoroastrian Trust Funds of Europe, under whose direction the WZO was originally started. The ZTFE noted the unnecessary controversy the decision of the WZO would create within the world Zoroastrian community, and the contradiction implicit in permitting non-Zoroastrian as members and potentially leaders of a Zoroastrian organization.[19]

The conversion of individuals of other faiths to Zoroastrianism has also been a subject among the diaspora Zoroastrian communities. On March 5, 1983, the Parsi priest Noshir Hormuzdiar and an associate, at the Zoroastrian Darbe Mehr in New York City, performed the conversion of a 'full alien' by the name of Joseph Peterson. In spite of the opposition from Parsis inside and outside India, the priests were convinced of Peterson's sincerity to embrace Zoroastrianism, and saw no religious bar to the conversion.[20] On September 24, 1994, Neville Wadia (1911-96) had his *Navjote* performed over objections in the Parsi community. Wadia was the son of Sir Ness Wadia (1873-1952), the heir to a textile empire and philanthropist, and a Christian mother. Wadia had been baptized and raised as an Anglican, and had also married outside the Parsi community, to the daughter of M. A. Jinnah. The case of Neville Wadia represented an individual born of Parsi background raised in another religion seeking 'readmission' to the Parsi community. Five Parsi priests confirmed Wadia's suitability for readmission to the Parsi community, however, orthodox Parsis objected to what they regarded as the admission of a convert. Both Neville Wadia and his father's claims to being Parsi were disputed, as both were baptized Christians. The opposition to Wadia reflected the Parsis' fundamentalist sense of strict endogamy, as barring even the readmission of a convert born of a Parsi father to the community.[21] While not a cause célēbre on the level of the Roxan case, the case of Neville Wadia was significant as it represented a potential trend whereby individuals who had some claim or tie to being of Parsi background, sought to 'return' to the

---

[19] *Parsiana*, June 1993.

[20] *Parsiana*, March, April, May, August 1983. *Parsiana*, December 1988, published a letter from William H. Brawner, who claimed to be living as a Zarathustrian for the past seven years, and detailed his reasons for eventually seeking full conversion to Zoroastrianism

[21] Wadia noted his own reasons for his desire to return to the Parsi fold. See *Parsiana*, October 1994. See also *The Sunday Afternoon Despatch* and *Courier*, December 11, 1994; *Deen Parast*, November-December 1994.

Parsi fold, at any time in their lives. It also reflected that any hope of reaching a consensus on conversion among the Parsis in future must involve all elements within the community, including the priesthood. In 1990, the 'Zarathustrian Assembly' in California had declared its goal to convert 20,000 individuals of all races to Zoroastrianism within ten years. While the question of conversion among the Parsis has largely centred on intermarriages and the religious confirmations of half-Parsi children, the conversion of new Zoroastrians (what may in a purist sense be regarded as a true conversion) presents an important issue of principle in present-day Zoroastrianism. The sincere desire on the part of such potential converts confronts Zoroastrians and the Parsi community with as potent a need to revisit the issue of conversion in contemporary times as in 1903.[22]

Zoroastrian communities outside India have also felt the need to re-examine the relevance of Parsi traditions and practices both in the new settings and as a whole. Both their discussions and actions have tremendous consequences for the Parsi community as a whole. Religious practices in the diaspora communities have also undergone subtle changes, as centres have adopted more congregational practices and colloquial methods, such as English in reciting prayers. Some diaspora communities have also attempted to take the lead in unifying Parsi tradition such as, for example, in advocating adoption of the Fasli calendar, which is more in line with the Gregorian and Iranian calendars.[23] Diaspora communities in large cities such as London, Toronto, Vancouver, and Houston have also attempted to stem the loss of religious education and promote a sense of religious and community identity among the young by conducting religious

[22] *Parsiana*, June 1991. On perspectives and change among contemporary Zoroastrians, see H. B. M. Homji, *O Whither Parsis? Placate and Perish or Reform and Flourish* (Karachi, 1978); Rashna Writer, *Contemporary Zoroastrians: An Unstructured Nation* (Lanham, Maryland, 1994); Homi B. Dhalla, "Contra Conversion: The Case of the Zoroastrians of India," in *Religious Conversions: Contemporary Practices and Controversies*, eds. Christopher Lamb and M. D. Bryant (New York, 1999), 115-35; John R. Hinnells, "The Zoroastrian Diaspora in Britain, Canada, and the United States," in *The South Asian Diaspora in Britain, Canada, and the United States*, eds. H. Coward, J. R. Hinnells, and R. B. Williams (Albany, 2000), 35-54.

[23] In 1929, the Parsis of India rejected adopting the Fasli or seasonal calendar that began the New Year on March 21, in line with the custom of the Iranian community. Those Parsis or Faslis who adopted the Iranian calendar built their own fire-temples in Bombay in the first half of the twentieth century. See Desai, *History of the Bombay Parsi Punchayet*, 91-5.

and cultural classes for children. Religious education among diaspora Parsis, however, is not comprehensive and is meant to supplement a general state-run education. The classes are conducted periodically, usually once a month on a weekend and on a voluntary basis by adults; and are not in separate religious schools given the size of Zoroastrian populations and, unlike many immigrant and ethnic communities, the general disinclination on the part of Parsis to segregate themselves from the greater population.

The novelty of such innovations in the Zoroastrian communities outside India largely corresponds to the desire to be more accommodating, inclusive, and relevant in contemporary life on the part of Zoroastrians. However, as the centre of authority between the Indian and overseas communities changes, amidst the demographic decline of the Parsis in India and the rise of wealthy and prominent overseas communities, pressure will either mount on the Indian community to adopt some form of modus vivendi on issues such as intermarriage and membership in the Parsi community, or the Indian and overseas communities will substantially diverge in their customs and ways, ultimately, to fragment the unity of Parsi tradition. This would be an extraordinary occurrence in the evolution of the Parsi community as a whole. For all the 'layers' the Parsis have added to their identity as a community, and the changes that have been accommodated, the Parsis have maintained one Parsi tradition. While the Parsi community throughout its history in India avoided splintering into subcommunities, the divergence of ways between the Indian and more progressive overseas community may well, ultimately, see the fragmentation of the Parsi community along divergent courses and traditions. While the different communities will maintain contact with one another, and specifically with the community in India, their membership and evolution will clearly take different paths.

In recent years, the re-establishment of ties with individuals and communities that acknowledge themselves as Zoroastrian in the former Soviet Central Republics has also added a novel element to the discussion of identity among Parsis and world Zoroastrians. Interest in the legacy of Zoroastrianism has been renewed by archeological discoveries of ancient fire-temples in Southern Russia, Azerbaijan, and Uzbekistan, as well as the tales and experiences of Zoroastrians in the Republics of Armenia, Azerbaijan, and Tajikistan, and renewed speculation and discussion as to the ties to Zoroastrianism of the Kurdish peoples.[24] The ties between many of the Central Asian communities and Zoroastrianism must be regarded as nominal at best in certain circumstances, particularly as regards the Kurds whose culture is diverse and complex. The presence of purportedly thousands and tens of thousands of 'new-found' Zoroastrians from Central Asia presents the Parsi and world Zoroastrian communities with the sense of both wonderment and dread at the prospects for learning more about Zoroastrianism and potentially accommodating new cultures within the world Zoroastrian community. Despite the logistical difficulties of contact, the world Zoroastrian communities have taken notice of the new communities. The disparities between the world Zoroastrian communities and the Central Asian communities are as great as that between the Parsis and the Iranians of the nineteenth century, and has spurred attempts to alleviate the conditions of the Central Asian Zoroastrians. The contemporary plight of the Kurds has struck the international community, and, in particular, the world Zoroastrian communities, not least of all given the Kurds' (nominal) Zoroastrian ties, and has resulted in the creation of aid projects.[25] Organizations have also been formed to encourage contacts between the Central Asian and Bombay communities. Discussions have revealed the legacy of ancient communities that endured Islamic incursions, Soviet domination, and economic hardship, and that managed to maintain aspects of Persianized Zoroastrian culture and language, while in search of the sense and source of their Zoroastrian religious roots.[26] These communities provide unique contrast to the Parsis who in large measure assimilated to the culture of India, while maintaining their ancient religious observance.

The historical processes that have shaped the Parsi community of India continue to offer the opportunities and risks associated with accommodating identity to social change. The mechanisms and strategies the Parsis have relied on to preserve a sense of identity, and that witnessed the rise of a wealthy, influential, and accomplished community during the course of the nineteenth century, must

---

[24] See *Parsiana*, April 1988, March 1992. For a history of Zoroastrianism in Central Asia, see James R. Russell, *Zoroastrianism in Armenia* (Cambridge, Mass., 1987).

[25] On the plight of the Kurds and the Parsis, see *Parsiana*, September 1991.

[26] The Tajik-Indo Zoroastrian International Development Friendship and Cultural Association (TIZIDFCA) held a conference in Bombay in 1992. See *Parsiana*, May 1992.

now be reassessed in terms of contemporary pressures. The Parsis' progress has been tempered in post-Independence India. Parsi enterprise no longer commands predominance in any single industry. Historically, Parsi dominance in business was of a transitional nature. Parsis pioneered and dominated specific fields and industries for a time, while often vacating them as greater competition arose and diversifying into other fields. Parsi dominance and expertise in the shipbuilding industry, described as perhaps India's first proto-industry, had ended by the first decade of the twentieth century with not a single Parsi firm recorded in the field.[27] The many Parsi small-scale enterprises that once defined the character of Bombay have also largely disappeared. The rise of large-scale industrial and commercial enterprises, such as those of the Tata and Godrej conglomerates, now defines the Parsi perception of success in contemporary India. At the same time, the influence of old families such as the Jejeebhoys, Petits, and Readymoneys, has passed from the scene.

Parsi charity to Parsi and non-Parsi objects continues to be a hallmark of Parsi identity in Bombay and India. The Parsi Punchayet remains the central organization involved in Parsi charity in Bombay, among a wide network of support. Parsi charity to the centres of Zoroastrian migration has also aided the growth of these new communities, including in co-financing temple and community projects in various locales. In Bombay, close to a thousand Parsi charities have been listed in the Directory of Public Trusts under the Public Trusts Act since 1950. At the same time, the level of Parsi dependency on charity continues to grow, and cautionary tales and criticism continue to be heard regarding its liberal availability, its misuse, and enervation of Parsi initiative. In 1935, in the first major attempt to assess the coordination of Parsi charity, it was estimated that close to 14 per cent of the Bombay Parsi population of some 57,765 individuals was dependent on Parsi charity of some form. While this figure represented Parsis taking advantage of charity for various reasons, it also highlighted the actual cases of want in the Bombay Parsi community.[28] The need to better coordinate and administer the panoply of Parsi charities in Bombay and India, and meet the requirements of a largely aging population and a community under eco-

[27] See Census of India 1911, in *Parsee Prakash*, 5:24.

[28] See Jal F. Bulsara, *Parsi Charity Relief and Communal Amelioration* (Bombay, 1935), 330ff.

nomic competition from other communities remains the primary goal of the present-day Parsis.[29]

The Parsis continue to make education an important tool in their social progress as a community. In 1931, the Census of India noted a 79.1 per cent literacy rate among Parsis, with 84.5 per cent of Parsi men and 73.4 per cent of Parsi women listed as literate. This was the highest standard of literacy, both in vernacular and in English languages, recorded among Indian communities. The Parsi community was further stated to have the only satisfactory level of female literacy among Indian communities.[30] In the Census of India of 1961, the literacy rate of Parsi men and women was 89.89 per cent and 90.45 per cent respectively.[31] At the same time, Parsi youth today are faced with stiff competition from other communities in placement at educational institutions and in the job market. Both emigration and migrant work outside India are the preference of growing numbers of Parsis. Achievement among the Parsis, albeit, remains a marker of identity. Parsi contributions to independent India are noteworthy. The most prominent examples of Parsis who have achieved a national renown include Homi J. Bhabha (1909-66), the pioneer of India's nuclear program; Sam H. F. J. Manekshaw (1912-), India's first field marshal; and Feroze Gandhi (1912-60), the parliamentarian, husband of Indira Gandhi and father of Sanjay and Rajiv. Parsi achievement in the past decades also has extended outside India, as Parsis have excelled in various fields of endeavour.[32] The recitation of Parsi accomplishments and unparalleled feats, consequently, remains a feature of Parsi identity. Both the community in India and the overseas communities regularly acknowledge and publicize Parsi feats of excellence and accomplishment.

Demographically, the Parsis have long been seen as a stagnant group. From 1951 to 1961, while the population of India exploded, the Parsi population declined by 10 per cent. The Census of India of

[29] On the functions and organization of Parsi charity in the twentieth century, see R. K. Sidwa, *Scheme to Remove Poverty and Unemployment from the Parsee Community* (Bombay, no date); P. A. Wadia, *Ere the Shadow Thickens* (Bombay, 1949); Sapur F. Desai, *A Changing Social Structure* (Bombay, 1945); idem, *A Community at the Crossroads* (Bombay, 1948); idem, *The Parsi Punchayet and Its Workings* (Bombay, 1963); idem, *History of the Bombay Parsi Punchayet*, Chs. 16-20.

[30] See Census of India 1931, in *Parsee Prakash*, 7:30ff.

[31] See *Census of India 1961, X: Maharashtra*, 13.

[32] See Piloo Nanavutty, *The Parsis* (New Delhi, 1977).

1951 recorded 111,791 Parsis, while in the Census of India of 1961 that number was reduced to 100,687. By 1981, the population of Parsis in India was 71,630. This is in part due to migrations of Parsis out of India, and largely due to a low birth rate and a high mortality rate among an aging population. Present-day marriage patterns, furthermore, particularly among urban Parsis, contribute to low birth rates. Late marriage, and hypergamy or a sense of discernment in partners, particularly among females, reflects the Parsi habituation to modern social patterns.[33]

Notwithstanding the many challenges that confront them, the sense of community and religious devotion remains strong among the present-day Parsis. For all the difficulties the preservation of a sense of identity has entailed, the Parsis perseverance remains. The fact that the community has survived with a sense of pride and hope reflects their historical triumph. Symbolic of that triumph, at the dawn of a new millennium, on December 21, 1999, the Parsis of Bombay re-enacted an 'ancient' rite reminiscent of the actions of their first ancestors in India. An early morning, pre-dawn, stately procession of priests and Parsis from across Bombay and India, resembling of an imperial Achaemenian assemblage replete with swords, maces, lances and shields, transported a sacred fire, through the streets of Bombay for 'enthronement' in a new fire-temple at Godrej Baug. The 'enthronement' at night was enacted in accordance with Parsi religious ritual and theory to ensure that the holy flames were not exposed to any other source of light. The streets of Bombay along the route were cleaned and covered with copious amounts of sand, as to signify the untrodden and undisturbed path taken by the fire. The new fire-temple was built through the donation of the Parsi philanthropist Shapoorji Fakirji Jokhi of Hong Kong, at a cost of some seventy-five lakh rupees. The intricacies and difficulties in consecrating a new holy fire in modern times had delayed the installation until a consecrated fire could be located and acquired.

The one hundred and thirty-year-old fire first consecrated in the small village of Tavri, had resided at the Sir Jamsetjee Jejeebhoy Agiary in Navsari since 1964. A convoy of cars, trucks and buses accompanied the fire from Navsari to Bombay, in a two-stage jour-

---

[33] On population and social statistics of Parsis of India, see *Census of India 1961*; Eckehard Kulke, *The Parsees in India* (Munich, 1974), 35; Malini Karkal, *Survey of Parsi Population of Greater Bombay, 1982* (Bombay, 1984), 67-85; K. Gould, "An Aging, Dwindling Community," *Parsiana*, March 1987.

ney over two nights. The installation of the sacred fire in a new temple marked the first such occasion in over a quarter century.

On the *Jamshedi Navroz* celebration of the Parsis on March 21, 1913, the British reporter for *The Times of India* mused on the greatness and strengths of the Parsis of India. Noting the many accomplishments in various fields of endeavour associated with their name, the reporter speculated that the Parsis' success lay in the virtue of their blood and exclusive ancestry, not altogether dissimilar to virtues enjoyed by the British. Whatever the actual reasons, the reporter concluded by adding that: "There are in the present-day as good men and women amongst your community as there were in earlier days; and there is no reason to doubt that there will be as good in the days to be."[34] For all the apparent controversy and discussion in the present-day Parsi community over aspects of identity, the Parsis have at heart maintained their faith in the conclusions of the British reporter. The fervour of discussion and debate within the present-day Parsi community, and among its supporters in other communities, shows that it refuses to see itself as a dying community. History reflects that while the unforeseen course of events ultimately determines the destiny of peoples and nations, it has always remained within the Parsis' ability, when they are so united, to reshape their circumstances and influence events to their benefit.

[34] *The Times of India*, March 21, 1913.

GLOSSARY

In regards to the general orthography used in the text, the orthography is that used in modern English. Thus, the modern spelling would be: Parsi, Punchayet, suffix -ji, etc. The preference for the short /a/ (e.g. Panchayet) and the letters /ee/ and /oo/, in place of the vowels /i/ and /u/ respectively, is the older and somewhat outdated version reminiscent of the genius of English orthography of the nineteenth century. Quotations and sources that employ the older orthography are maintained in the original. The phonetic nature of Parsi names lends to numerable ways for their spelling, including among contemporaries. Parsi proper names have not been standardized, and names are rendered in the original form used by contemporary Parsis. Non-English words that appear in the text and in the glossary are rendered in the form used more commonly among Parsis. Diacritical marks over vowels are employed to assist in the pronunciation of less commonly used non-English words. Iran is used rather than Persia, to describe the ancestral land of the Zoroastrians. Persia better describes a province of the greater Iranian Plateau that gave its name to a larger political entity. Abbreviations: Ar. Arabic, Av. Avestan, In. Indian, N.P. New Persian, O.P. Old Persian, Phl. Pahlavi, P.Gj. Parsi-Gujarati, V. Vedic.

āfargāniun	(P.Gj.): a covered urn or censer upon which fire is kindled.
agiari/agiary	(P.Gj): fire-temple.
Ahura Mazdā	(Av.): 'Wise Lord'; name of God for Zoroastrians.
ahura	(Av.): 'lord' or heavenly being; equivalent of (V) asura.
anjuman	(N.P.): assembly; term used by Parsis in India.
aramgah	(N.P): 'place of rest'; a Zoroastrian burial or scattering ground.
Āshirvād	(In.): 'benediction' or 'blessing'; Parsi marriage ceremony.
Ashōdād	(P.Gj.): 'what is given to the righteous'; payment to priests in money or kind for sacerdotal services rendered.
Ātash Ādarān	(N.P.): sacred fire of second grade; also name of fire-temple.
Ātash Bahrām	(N.P): 'Fire of Victory'; sacred fire of highest grade; also name of cathedral fire-temple.
Ātash Dādgāh	(N.P.): fire of household or minor fire-temple.
Ātash Niyāyesh	(N.P.): ceremony of prayer to fire,
āthornan	(P-Gj.): Parsi priesthood; (O.P.) āthravan.
Avestā	composite book of holy texts of the Zoroastrians; and Zend or commentaries on Avestā.
bāj/vāj	(N.P.): various prayers recited by Parsis and priests daily, on special occasions and ceremonies, or before engaging in certain activities; also utterance in suppressed tone.
Barashnom	(Phi. and N.P.): Zoroastrian ceremony of abultion and purification.
behdin	(N.P.): '(of the) Good Religion'; a Zoroastrian, commonly a term for lay person; derivative of din-i behi or the Religion of Goodness
Būi/Būy	(N.P): fire-oblation ceremony performed by Parsi priest five times a day; 'feeding the fire' according to its grades, with san-

dalwood, frankincense, and aromatic materials; derived from esm-o-buy or 'fuel and smell'; (Av) baodha or 'odour' or 'smell'.

chotra — (P.Gj.): place for consignment of Parsi dead comprising a plinth and a pit; alternative to dakhma in past, in times of emergency or cases where individuals' Parsi background is doubtful.

bundobast — (P.Gj.): regulation enacted by Parsi Punchayet.

daēva — (Av): demon; (O.P.) daiva; equivalent to Latin deus for heavenly one.

dakhma — (P.Gj.) variant of (Av) daxma, (N.P) daxme for Tower of Silence or place where Parsi dead are consigned for exposure.

Dakhmenashini — (P.Gj.) variant of (N.P) daxme-neshīnī; funerary rites that include method of exposure of dead in Tower of Silence.

Dar-e-Meher — (N.P.): 'Gate of Mithra'; (Phl.) Dar-i Mihr; inner sanctum of fire-temple.

dashtānestān — (Phl.): place of isolation for menstruating women.

dastūr — (N.P.): highest rank of Zoroastrian priest; can perform all ritual ceremonies; (Phl.) dastwar.

doongerwadi — (P.Gj.): Tower of Silence precinct,

gāh — (Phl.): period of the day; five gāhs of day, beginning of each is observed with prayers by Parsis; specific prayer for each gāh.

gahambār — (P.Gj.) variant of (N.P.) gahanbār or six seasonal festivals of obligation celebrated for five days each among the Parsis.

Gāthās — (Av.): hymns or songs of Zarathustra; oldest part of religious literature and liturgy of Zoroastrianism.

gōmēz — (Phl.): unconsecrated bull's urine used in rituals and ceremonies; (Av.) gaomaēza.

hērbad/ērbad — (P.Gj.) variant of (Phl.) hērbed; Zoroastrian priest of minor order.

Jādi Rana — Hindu rajah of Qisseh-i Sanjan.

jaziya/jizya — (N.P.): head tax on non-Muslims in Muslim controlled area,

juddīn — (N.P.): a non-Zoroastrian; also darvand.

khāndhiās — (P.Gj.): pall-bearers who carry corpse on a iron bier after death to mortuary place; from khānd or shoulders, describing how corpse is borne; hold (Phl.) paiwand or cloth between each other to symbolize contact and united task performed.

khrafstras — (Phl. and N.P.): 'noxious' creatures; the killing of such creatures observed as part of Zoroastrian purity laws.

kustī — (N.P): thread cord worn tied around waist by religiously confirmed Zoroastrian; composed of seventy-two woven threads.

Martab — (N.P): second degree of Parsi priesthood, and ceremony associated with it; initiated priest may perform all Zoroastrian priestly rituals, including in inner sanctum of fire-temple.

Mazdāyasnān — (N.P): worshipper of Ahura Mazdā; i.e., a Zoroastrian.

mōbad — (P.Gj.) variant of (Phl.) mōbed; Zoroastrian priest qualified to perform all ceremonies.

Muktād — (P.Gj.) variant of Zoroastrian religious period of (N.P) Fravardigān, in memory of the departed, observed in last five days of the Zoroastrian calendar year.

nasāsālār(s) — (Phl. and N.P.): corpse-bearer responsible for collecting corpse at death, and after funeral exposing corpse in Tower of Silence; also services and maintains the Tower; also a crier for Punchayet; derivative of nasā for carrion or dead matter, and sālār for master.

Nāvar/Nābar — (N.P): initiation ceremony of Parsi priest; first degree of priesthood; known among Iranians as Nozud.

Navjéte — (P.Gj.): 'new birth'; ceremony of initiation and confirmation into Zoroastrianism; performed for youths from seven to fourteen years of age.

nīrang — (N.P.): consecrated bull's urine used in certain religious and ceremonial rites.

Nīrangdīn — (P.Gj.): ceremony to consecrate bull's urine.

padān — (P.Gj.) variant of (Av.) paitidāna; piece of white cloth of cotton worn by priest as form of mouth-veil when praying before fire and sacred objects so as not to defile object(s) with breath.

Pādyāb — (Phi. and N.P.): ritual ablution originally with unconsecrated bull's urine before performance of prayers and rites.

panthak — (P.Gj.): ecclesiastical district and jurisdiction of Parsi priest; hence panthaky for title of priest; derivative of (In) panth.

Qisseh-i Sanjan — (N.P.): 'Story of Sanjan'; narrative of Parsis' departure from Iran and landing and settlement in India.

Rīman — (P.Gj.) variant of (Phl.) rēman or 'polluted'; Parsi ceremony of ritual ablution against carrion.

Rivāyat — (Ar. and N.P.): 'epistle'; correspondence between Parsis and Zoroastrian priests of Iran from the fifteenth to the eighteenth centuries.

Sedra-pushun — Dari or Irani dialect form for 'putting on the sacred shirt'; religious confirmation ceremony of a Zoroastrian, known among Parsis as Navjote.

shetia — (In): merchant-prince, man of influence and standing in Bombay society; derivative of Gujarati and Marathi appellation of 'sett' or 'shet,' to denote gentleman; may be transliterated in alternate ways, sethia is more usual form used by Parsis.

sudra/sedra — (N.P. and P.Gj.): white cotton undershirt worn by religiously confirmed Zoroastrian around which kustī is tied.

Tānā/Thānā — (P.Gj.): Parsi ceremony to lay and consecrate foundation for dakhma; from tana or very fine thread used to mark the circumference of dakhma and its sections.

Tower of Silence — English term for dakhma; attributable to Robert Zavier Murphy, the oriental translator for the Government of Bombay; tower describes circular structure, and silence as attribute of dead.

Uthamnā — (P.Gj.): ceremony of prayer and remembrance performed by priest on third day following death of a Parsi.

varasyo — (P.Gj.): white bull whose urine and tail hair (vara) are used in Parsi purification and religious rites.

yasna — (Av.): sacrificial ritual; prayers and liturgy of Zoroastrians; (V) yajña.

Zarathustra — (Av.): prophet of Parsis; also Zardost, Zarthost.

Zarthosti — (P.Gj.): followers of Zarathustra; i.e., a Zoroastrian/Parsi.

BIBLIOGRAPHY

PRIMARY SOURCES

A. MANUSCRIPT SOURCES

Department of Archives, Government of Maharashtra, Bombay;

General Department:	1832 15/260	1853 42/665.
	1833 13/284	1855 579/59.
	1848 63/209	1856 90/562.
	1853 15/264	1859 1/80.
Judicial Department:	1843 81/935	186531/104.
	1852 25	1866 15.
	1862 21/468	1874110/291.
	1863 20/143	1875 129/403.
	1864 18	1877 90/827.

University of Bombay Library, Bombay;

Jamsetjee Jejeebhoy Manuscripts, Volumes 349, 354, 357, 359, 369, 375.

Miscellaneous Letters.

University of Toronto, Robarts Library, Toronto;

Dadabhai Naoroji Papers, microfilm, reels 1-12, section number A(l)-G 116(1145).

B. PRINTED SOURCES

(i) Newspapers and Journals

Bombay Gazette
Bombay Samachar
Bombay Times
Calcutta Review
The Daily Telegraph
Been Parast
East and West
The Bulletin of the World Zoroastrian Organization
The Indian Antiquary
Island
Jam-e-Jamshed
Journal of the East Asia Association
Journal of Iranian Association
Journal of the Royal Asiatic Society of Great Britain and Ireland

Oriental Christian Spectator
Oriental Review
Parsiana
Rast Goftar
The Sunday Afternoon Despatch and Courier
The Times Law Reports
The Times of India
The Times of London
The Voice of India

(ii) Official Publications

Census of India 1961, 1981. Government of India.
The Gazetteer of Bombay City and Island. Vol. 1. Bombay, 1909.
Gazetteer of the Bombay Presidency. Vol. 9, part 2. Bombay, 1899.
Report of the Board of Education, Bombay, 1847-48. Bombay, 1850.
Report of the Board of Education, Bombay, 1850-51. Bombay, 1852.
Report on Native Papers, 1889; 1920; 1921.
Report on Native Newspapers, 1882. In Judicial Department, Department of Archives, Government of Maharashtra, Bombay.
United Kingdom *Hansard's Parliamentary Debates*, 3rd series, vol. 187(1867).

(iii) Non-Official Records

Parsi Punchayet Daftar—All Parsi Zarthosti Anjuman Meeting Minutes No. 1, 1859-1916. Parsi Punchayet of Bombay.
Trustees' Meeting of Laws Passed, no. 16, 26th April to 27th March 1906, Parsi Punchayet of Bombay.
Trustees' Meeting Book, 7th June, 1912 to 16th October, 1914. Parsi Punchayet of Bombay.

(iv) Non-Official Publications

First Report of the Bombay Native School and School Society, Bombay. Bombay, 1825.
Fourth Report of the Proceedings of the Bombay Native Education Society, 1827. Bombay, 1828.
Proceedings of the Students' Literary and Scientific Society for the year(s): *1853*. Bombay, 1853; *1854-55 and 1855-56*. Bombay, 1856; *1856-57 and 1858-59*. Bombay, 1860.
Sixth Report of the Bombay Native Education Society, 1830. Bombay, 1831.
Twelfth Report of the Proceedings of the United Institution of the Elphinstone College, and the School of the Native Education Society, 1839. Bombay, 1840.
Annual Report of the Elphinstone Institution, 1852. Bombay, 1853.

(v) Other Contemporary Published Sources

Banaji, K. N. *Memoirs of the Late Framji Cowasji Banaji*. Bombay, 1892.
Bengallee, S. S. *The Parsee Marriage and Divorce Act, 1865*. Bombay, 1868.
A Brief Account of the Framjee Cowasjee Testimonial and the Principal Correspondence Relating to the Framjee Cowasjee Institute. Bombay, 1871.
Cama, K. R. *A Discourse on Mithraic Worship and Rites and Mysteries Connected With It, Delivered at the Freemasons' Jamshedi Naoroz Festival, Scottish Masonic Hall*. Bombay, 1876.

Chintamani, C. Y., ed. *Speeches and Writings of the Honourable Sir Pherozeshah M. Mehta, K.C.I.E.* Allahabad, 1905.

Correspondence, Deed, Bye-laws etc., Relating to 'Sir Jamsetjee Jejeebhoy Parsi Benevolent Institution,' Established in Bombay, 1849. Bombay, 1849.

Cursetjee, Manockjee. *A Few Out of Many Letters and Extracts of Letters, Addressed to Manockee Cursetjee Esq., and to Others Regarding Him; Also Selections from the Newspapers of the Day.* Bombay, 1849.

——. *On the Admission of Natives to Offices of Trust and Emolument Hitherto Exclusively Held by Europeans.* Bombay, 1850.

——. *On the Admission or Otherwise of the Natives Into Literary Institutions.* Bombay, 1850.

——. *The Parsee Panchayet, Its Rise, Its Fall and the Causes that Led to the Same: Being A Series of Letters in the Bombay Times of 1844-45, Under the Signature of Q in the Corner, Published at the Request of Some Gentlemen of the Parsee Community and With the Permission of the Author.* Bombay, 1860.

——. *Few Passing Ideas for the Benefit of India and Indians.* London, 1862.

Falkland, The Viscountess. *Chow-Chow.* Vol. 1. London, 1857.

Forbes, James. *Oriental Memoirs, A Narrative of Seventeen Years Residence in India.* Vol. 1. London, 1834.

Forrest, George W., ed. *Selections from the Letter Despatches and Other State Papers Preserved in the Bombay Secretariat.* Vol. 1. Bombay, 1887.

Gidumal, Dayaram. *The Life and Life-Work of B. M. Malabari.* Bombay, 1888.

Graham, Maria. *Journal of A Residence in India.* Edinburgh, 1813.

Greenfield, M. Rose. *Education versus Evangelization.* Amritsar, 1888.

Grose, John H. *A Voyage to the East Indies.* Vol. 1. London, 1766.

Hamilton, Walter. *East-India Gazetteer.* Vol. 1. London, 1828.

Jeejeebhoy, J. R. B., ed. *Some Unpublished Speeches and Writings of the Hon. Sir Pherozeshah Mehta.* Bombay, 1918.

Jehanghier, J. Cowasjee. *Life of Sir Cowasjee Jehanghier Readymoney.* London, 1890.

Karaka, D. F. *The British Raj, Contrasted With Its Successor.* London, 1858.

——. *The Parsees: Their Manners, Customs, and Religion* (under the name of Dosabhoy Framjee). London, 1858.

——. *History of the Parsis.* 2 vols. London, 1884.

Malabari, B. M. *The Indian Problem.* Bombay, 1864.

——. *An Appeal to the Daughters of India.* London, 1890.

——. *The Indian Eye on English Life: Or Rambles of a Pilgrim Reformer.* Bombay, 1895.

The Missionary Controversy: Discussion, Evidence and Report 1890. London, 1890.

Morley, William. *Administration of Justice in British India.* New Delhi, 1858.

Naoroji, Dadabhai. *The Manners and Customs of the Parsees: Paper Read Before the Liverpool Philomatic Society.* London, 1862.

Nauroji, Dhanjibhai. *From Zoroaster to Christ: An Autobiographical Sketch of the Rev. Dhanjibhai Nauroji the First Modern Convert to Christianity From the Zoroastrian Religion.* Edinburgh, 1909.

Nazir, C. S. *The First Parsee Baronet.* Bombay, 1866.

Obituary Notices of the Late Cursetjee Manackjee, Esq., As they Appeared in All the Native and English Newspapers of Bombay. Bombay, no date.

Ouseley, William. *Travels in the East More Particularly Persia.* London, 1813.

Parekh, C. L., ed. *Essays, Speeches, Addresses, & Writings, of the Hon'ble Dadabhai Naoroji.* Bombay, 1887.

Parsi Punchayet Case: A Verbatim Report Reprinted from The Times of India. Bombay, 1908.

Parsi Punchayet Case: In the High Court of Judicature at Bombay, Suit No. 689 of 1906: Judgment of the Hon 'ble Mr. Justice Davar, and Judgment of the Hon'ble Mr. Justice Beaman, Delivered 27th November, 1908. Bombay, 1908.

Patell, B. B. *The Parsee Patells of Bombay: Their Services to the British Government.* Bombay, 1876.

——. *Parsee Prakash: Being A Record of Important Events in the Growth of the Parsee Community in Western India, Chronologically Arranged.* Vols. 1 and 2. Bombay, 1888; Vols. 3-8, compiled by R. B. Paymaster (in Gujarati). Bombay 1913–43.

Perry, Erskine. *Cases Illustrative of Oriental Life: Decided at H.M. Court at Bombay, The Application of English Law to India.* 1853. Reprint, New Delhi 1988.

Ramsay, Williamson. *Memorandum on the Life and Public Charities of Jamsetjee Jejeebhoy.* London, 1855.

Seervai, K. N. and B. B. Patell. "Gujarat Parsis from Their Earliest Settlement to the Present Time (A.D. 1898)." In *Gazetteer of the Bombay Presidency.* Vol. 9, Part 2, edited by J. M. Campbell, 183-254. Bombay, 1899.

Tennant, William. *Indian Recreations: Consisting Chiefly of Strictures on the Domestic and Rural Economy of the Mahomedans and Hindoos.* London, 1804.

Wacha, D. E. *A Financial Chapter in the History of Bombay City.* Bombay, 1910.

——. *Premchund Roychund: His Early Life and Career.* Bombay, 1913.

——. *The Life and Work of J. N. Tata.* Madras, 1915.

——. *Shells from the Sands of Bombay: Being My Recollections and Reminiscences, 1860-75.* Bombay, 1920.

Wadia, A. C. *Diary of an Overland Journey from Bombay to England.* London, 1840.

Wadia, J. N. and H. M. *Journal of a Residence of Two Years and a Half in Great Britain.* London, 1841.

Warden, Francis. *Report on the Landed Tenures of Bombay.* Bombay, 1814.

Wilson, John. *A Lecture on the Vendidad Sade of the Parsis Delivered at Bombay On the 19th and 26th June, 1833.* Bombay, 1833.

——. *The Doctrine of Jehovah.* Edinburgh, 1847-

Yule, Henry, ed. "Miscellaneous Papers." In *The Diary of W. Hedges.* Vol. 2, no. 75. London, 1888.

OTHER WORKS

Ahmad, Imtiaz, ed. *Caste and Social Stratification Among the Muslims.* Delhi, 1973.

Altekar, A. S. "The Extent of the Sassanian Political Domination in India." In *M. P. Kharegat Memorial Volume.* Vol. 1, 215-25. Bombay, 1953.

Amighi, J. K. *The Zoroastrians of Iran: Conversion, Assimilation, or Persistence.* New York, 1990.

Antia, K. *The Argument for Acceptance.* Bombay, 1985.

Bagchi, Amiya Kumar. "European and Indian Entrepreneurs in India, 1900-30." In *Elites in South Asia,* edited by E. Leach and J. N. Mukherjee, 223-56. Cambridge, 1970.

Ballhatchet, Kenneth. *Social Policy and Social Change in Western India, 1817-1830.* Oxford, 1957.

Barnouw, Erik and S. Krishnaswamy. *Indian Film.* Oxford, 1980.

Bathena, B. N. *Kisseh-i-Sanjan: A Palpable Falsehood.* Benares, 1944.

Bausani, Alessandro. The *Persians: From the Earliest Days to the Twentieth Century.* 1961. Translated from the Italian by J. B. Donne. London, 1971.

Bengallee, N. S. *The Life of Sorabjee Shapoorjee Bengallee, C.I.E.* (in Gujarati). Bombay, no date.

Benjamin, S. *The Bene-Israels of the Bombay Presidency.* Bombay, 1873.

Bhandarkar, D. R. "Parasikas." In *M P. Kharegat Memorial Volume.* Vol. 1, 196-8. Bombay, 1953.

Bickerman, E. "The Zoroastrian Calendar." *Archiv Oriental* 35 (1967): 197-209.

Bilimoria, F. N., ed. *Zoroastrianism in the Light of Theosophy.* Bombay, 1898.

Bohman-Behram, B. K. "The Parsis and Other Communities in India." In *The Sugar in the Milk,* edited by Nancy and Ram Singh, 52-67. Bombay, 1977.

Boyce, Mary. "On the Sacred Fires of the Zoroastrians." *Bulletin of the School of Oriental and African Studies* 31, no. 1 (1968): 52-68.

——. "The Pious Foundations of the Zoroastrians." *Bulletin of the School of Oriental and African Studies* 31, no. 2 (1968): 270-89.

——. "Maneckji Limji Hataria in Iran." In *K. R. Cama Oriental Institute Golden Jubilee Volume,* 19-31. Bombay, 1969.

——. "On the Calendar of Zoroastrian Feasts." *Bulletin of the School of Oriental and African Studies* 23 (1970): 513-39.

——. "On the Zoroastrian Temple Cult of Fire." *Journal of the American Oriental Society* 95 (1975): 454-65.

——. "The Continuity of the Zoroastrian Quest." In *Man's Religious Quest,* edited by W. Foy, 603-19. London, 1978.

——. *Zoroastrians: Their Religious Beliefs and Practices.* London, 1979.

——. *History of Zoroastrianism.* 3 vols. Leiden, 1975, 1982, 1991.

——. *Textual Sources for the Study of Zoroastrianism.* Manchester, 1984.

——. *Zoroastrianism: Its Antiquity and Constant Vigour.* Costa Mesa, 1992.

——. "Corpse, Disposal of, in Zoroastrianism." *Encyclopedia Iranica* 6 (1993): 279-86.

Buillet, Richard W. *Conversion to Islam in the Medieval Period: An Essay in Quantitative History.* Cambridge, Mass., 1979.

Bulsara, Jal F. *Parsi Charity Relief and Communal Amelioration.* Bombay, 1953.

Cannon, Garland. *Oriental Jones: A Biography of Sir William Jones (1746-1794).* Delhi, 1964.

——. "The Reconstruction of the European Image of the Orient: A Bicentenary Reappraisal of Sir William Jones As Poet and Translator." In *Comparative Criticism,* edited by E. S. Shaffer, 167-88. Cambridge, 1986.

Carson, Penelope. "Missionaries, Bureaucrats and People of India, 1793-1833." In *Orientalism, Evangelicalism and the Military Cantonment in Early Nineteenth Century India: A Historiographical Overview,* edited by Nancy G. Cassels, 125-55. Lewiston, 1991.

Carter, Mary. "The Parsis in Bombay." *The Empire Review* 53 (1931): 129-31.

The Case of Roxan Darshan Shah: Articles and Letters Reprinted in the Bombay Samachar, Parsi Tari, Arsi. Bombay, 1990.

Cereti, Carlo G. *An 18th Century Account of Parsi History: The Qesse-ye Zartoštiān.* Naples, 1991.

——. "The Qesse-ye Zartoštiān-e Hendustān and the Qesse-ye Sanjān: Notes on Parsi History." In *Proceedings of the Second European Conference of Iranian Studies,* 141-52. Rome, 1995.

Chaudhuri, K. N. *Trade and Civilization in the Indian Ocean: An Economic History of the Rise of Islam to 1750.* Cambridge, 1975.

Choksey, R. D. *Mountstuart Elphinstone the Indian Years, 1796-1827.* Bombay, 1971.

Choksy, Jamsheed K. "Zoroastrians in Muslim Iran: Selected Problems of Coexistence and Interaction During the Early Medieval Period." *Iranian Studies* 20 (1): 17-30.

——. *Purity and Pollution in Zoroastrianism: Triumph Over Evil.* Austin, 1989.

——. *Conflict and Cooperation: Zoroastrian Subalterns and Muslim Elites in Medieval Iranian Society.* New York, 1997.

Choudhury, M. L. R. *The Din-i-Ilahi, or the Religion ofAkbar.* Calcutta, 1952.

Chowdhury, B. R. *Madame Cama: A Short Life-Sketch.* Delhi, 1977.

C. M. C. *The Framjee Cowasjee Institute: Its Origin, Its Work and Its Future.* Bombay, 1917.

Cohn, Bernard S. "Representing Authority in Victorian India." In *The Invention of Tradition,* edited by Eric Hobsbawm and Terence Ranger, 165-209. Cambridge, 1983.

Commissariat, M. S. *A History of Gujarat.* Bombay, 1938.

——. "The First Parsi in England (1724-25): Nowroji Rustom Manek of Surat and His Relations With the East India Company." In *M. P. Kharegat Memorial Volume.* Vol. 1, 221-57. Bombay, 1953.

Coorlawalla, D. N. "The Last Kabisah." In *Dastur Hoshang Memorial Volume,* 143-60. Bombay, 1918.

Coyajee, J. C. *The Future of Zoroastrianism.* Bombay, no date.

Da Cunha, J. G. *The Origin of Bombay.* Bombay, 1900.

Da Orta, Garcia. *Colloquies on the Simples and Drugs of Indians.* Translated from the Portuguese by Sir Clements Markam. London, 1913.

Dadachanjee, H. M. *Life Sketch of Sir Shapoorjee Bharucha* (in Gujarati). Bombay, 1928.

Dandamaev, M. A. and V. G. Lukonin. *The Culture and Social Institutions of Ancient Iran.* Translated from the Russian by P. Kohl and D. J. Dadson. Cambridge, 1989.

Daniel, Norman. *Islam and the West: The Making of an Image.* Edinburgh, 1960.

Darukhanawala, H. D. *Parsi Lustre on Indian Soil.* Bombay, 1939.

——. *Parsis and Sport.* Bombay, 1935.

Das, Satyajit, ed. *Selections From the Indian Journals.* Calcutta, 1963.

Das Gupta, Ashin. "The Merchants of Surat, c. 1700-50." In *Elites in South Asia,* edited by. E. Leach and J. N. Mukherjee, 201-22. Cambridge, 1970.

——. *Indian Merchants and the Decline of Surat,* 1700-1750. Wiesbaden, 1979.

Davar, Sohrab P. *The History of the Parsi Punchayet of Bombay,* Bombay, 1949.

David, M. D. *History of Bombay, 1661-1708.* Bombay, 1973.

——. *John Wilson and His Institution.* Bombay, 1975.

——. "History of the Church in India." In *Asia and Christianity,* edited by M. D. David, 162-73. Bombay, 1985.

——. "The British Colonialism in South Asia and Christianity." In *Western Colonialism in Asia and Christianity,* edited by M. D. David, 83-91. Bombay, 1988.

De Jong, Albert. *Traditions of the Magi: Zoroastrianism in Greek and Latin Literature.* Leiden, 1997.

——. "Purification *in absentia*: On the Development of Zoroastrian Ritual Practice." *In Transformations of the Inner Self in Ancient Religion,* edited by Jan Assmann and Guy G. Stroumsa, 301-29. Leiden, 1999.

Derrett, J. Duncan M. "Justice, Equity and Good Conscience." In *Family Law in Asia and Africa,* no. 2, edited by J. N. D. Anderson, 114-53. London, 1963.

——. *Religion, Law and State in India.* London, 1968.

——. *History of Indian Law.* Leiden, 1973.

Desai, Ashok V. "The Origins of Parsi Enterprise." *The Indian Economic and Social History Review* 5 (1968): 307-17.

Desai, Sapur F. *A Changing Social Structure*. Bombay, 1945.

——. *A Community at the Crossroad*. Bombay, 1948.

——. *The Parsi Punchayet and Its Working*. Bombay, 1963.

——. *Statistics of World Zoroastrians with Special Reference to Indian Zoroastrians*. Bombay, 1964.

——. *History of the Bombay Parsi Punchayet, 1860-1960*. Bombay, 1977.

Dhabhar, B. N. *Saddar Nasr and Saddar Bundehesh*. Bombay, 1909.

——. *The Persian Rivayats of Hormazyar Framarz and Others*. Bombay, 1932.

Dhalla, Homi B. "Contra Conversion: The Case of the Zoroastrians of India." In *Religious Conversions: Contemporary Practices and Controversies*, edited by Christopher Lamb and M. D. Bryant, 115-35. New York, 1999.

Dhalla, M. N. *Zoroastrian Theology: From the Earliest Times to the Present Day*. New York, 1914.

——. *Our Perfecting World: Zarathustra's Way of Life*. Oxford, 1930.

——. *History of Zoroastrianism*. 1938. Reprint, Bombay, 1963.

Dirks, Nicholas B. "Introduction," In *Colonialism and Culture*, edited by N. B. Dirks, 1-25. Ann Arbor, 1992.

Divekar, V. D. "Western India." In *The Cambridge Economic History of India*. Vol. 2, c. *1700-1970*, 332-51. Cambridge, 1983.

Dobbin, Christine. "Competing Elites in Bombay City Politics in the Mid-Nineteenth Century (1852-1883)." In *Elites in South Asia*, edited by E. Leach and S. N. Mukherjee, 79-94. Cambridge, 1970.

——. "The Parsi Punchayet in Bombay City in the Nineteenth Century." *Modern Asian Studies* 4, no. 2 (April, 1970): 149-64.

——. *Urban Leadership in Western India*. Oxford, 1972.

Douglas, James. *Bombay and Western India*. Vol. 1. Delhi, 1893.

Duchesne-Guillemin, Jacques. *The Hymns of Zaruthustra*. London, 1952.

——. *The Western Response to Zoroaster*. Oxford, 1958.

——. *Religion of Ancient Iran*. Translated from the French by K. M. JamaspAsa. Bombay, 1973.

——. *The New Encyclopaedia Britannica*, 15th ed., s.v. "Zoroastrianism and Parsiism."

Embree, Ainslie T. *Imagining India: Essays on Indian History*. Oxford, 1989.

Eduljee, H. E. *Kisseh-i-Sanjan*. Bombay, 1991.

Enthoven, R. E., ed. *The Tribes and Castes of Bombay*. Vol. 3. Delhi, 1922.

Farquhar, J. N. *Modern Religious Movements in India*. London, 1929.

Fawcett, Charles. *The First Century of British Justice in India*. Oxford, 1934.

——. *The English Factories in India*. Vol. 1. Oxford, 1936.

Firby, N. K. *European Travellers and Their Perceptions of Zoroastrians in the 17th and 18th Centuries*. Berlin, 1988.

Fisch, Jorg. *Cheap Lives and Dear Limbs: The British Transformation of the Bengal Criminal Law, 1769-1817*. Wiesbaden, 1983.

Forrester, Duncan B. *Caste and Christianity: Attitudes and Policies on Caste of Anglo-Saxon Protestant Missions in India*. London, 1980.

Furher, Holden. *Bombay Presidency in the Mid-18th Century*. London, 1965.

Gajendragadkar, S. N. *Parsi-Gujarati: A Descriptive Analysis*. Bombay, 1974.

Gandhi, M. K. *An Autobiography or The Story of My Experiments With Truth*. Ahmedabad, 1927.

——. *The Collected Works of Mahatma Gandhi*. Ahmedabad, 1966.

Gershevitch, Ilya. "Zoroaster's Own Contribution." *Journal of Near Eastern Studies* 223 (1964): 12-38.

——. "Approaches to Zoroaster's Gathas." *Iran* 33 (1995): 1-29.

Giara, Marzban J. *Global Directory of Zoroastrian Fire Temples.* Bombay, 1998.

Gignoux, Philippe. "Dietary Laws in Pre-Islamic and Post-Sasanian Iran: A Comparative Survey." *Jerusalem Studies in Arabic and Islam* 17 (1994): 16-42.

Gnoli, Gherardo. *Zoroaster's Time and Homeland: A Study on the Origins of Mazdeism and Related Problems.* Naples, 1980.

——. *The Idea of Iran: An Essay on its Origin.* Rome, 1989.

Greenberg, Michael. *British Trade and the Opening of China, 1800-42.* Cambridge, 1951.

Greenway, P. and D. St. Vincent. *Iran.* Lonely Planet Series. May 1998.

Guha, A. "Parsi Seths as Entrepreneurs, 1750-1850." *Economic and Political Weekly* 5, no. 35 (1969): 107-15.

——. "The Comprador Role of Parsi Seths, 1750-1850." *Economic and Political Weekly* 5, no. 48 (November, 1970): 1933-8.

H. P. Blavatsky: *Collected Writings 1881-82.* Vol. 3. Wheaton, Illinois, 1968.

Hamilton, Alexander. *A New Account of the East Indies*, London, 1930.

Hao, Yen-p'ing. *The Commercial Revolution in Nineteenth Century China: The Rise of Sino-Western Mercantile Capitalism.* Berkeley, 1986.

Haug, Martin. *Essays on the Sacred Language, Writings and Religion of the Parsis.* London, 1884.

Heesterman, J. C. *The Broken World of Sacrifice: An Essay in Ancient Indian Ritual.* Chicago, 1993.

Heismath, C. *Indian Nationalism and Hindu Social Reform.* Princeton, 1964.

Hinnells, John R. "Zoroastrian Influence on the Judaeo-Christian Tradition." *Journal of the K. R. Cama Oriental Institute* 45 (1976): 1-23.

——. "The Parsis and the British." *Journal of the K. R. Cama Oriental Institute* 46 (1978).

——. "The Parsis: A Bibliographical Survey." *Journal of Mithraic Studies* 3 (1980): 100-49.

——. "Social Change and Religious Transformations Among Bombay Parsis in the Early Twentieth Century." In *Traditions in Contact and Change*, edited by P. Slater and D. Wiebe, 105-25. Winnipeg, 1983.

——. "The Flowering of Zoroastrian Benevolence." In *Papers in Honour of Professor Mary Boyce, Hommages et Opera Minora.* Vol. 10, 261-326. Leiden, 1985.

——. "South Asian Diaspora Communities and Their Religion: A Comparative Study of Parsi Experiences." *South Asia Research* 14, no. 1 (Spring 1994): 62-104.

——. *Zoroastrians in Britain: The Ratanbai Katrak Lectures, University of Oxford, 1985.* Oxford, 1996.

—— "The Zoroastrian Diaspora in Britain, Canada, and the United States." In *The South Asian Religious Diaspora in Britain, Canada, and the United States*, edited by H. Coward, J. R. Hinnells, and R. B. Williams, 35-54. Albany, 2000.

Hodivala, S. H. *Studies in Parsi History.* Bombay, 1920.

Hodivala, S. K. "The 16 Sanskrit Shlokas." In *Dastur Hoshang Memorial Volume*, 70-97. Bombay, 1918.

——. *Parsis in Ancient India.* Bombay, 1920.

Homji, H. B. M. *O Whither Parsis? Placate and Perish or Reform and Flourish.* Karachi, 1978.

Humbach, Helmut. *The Heritage of Zarathustra: A New Translation of the Gāthās.* Heidelberg, 1994.
Hutton, J. H. *Caste In India: Its Nature, Function and Origins.* New York, 1963.
Ignatieff, Michael. *The Needs of Strangers: An Essay on Privacy, Solidarity, and the Politics of Being Human.* London, 1984.
Inden, Ronald. "Orientalist Constructions of India." *Modern Asian Studies* 20, no. 3 (1986): 401-46.
Ingham, Kenneth. *Reformers in India, 1793-1833: An Account of the Work of the Christian Missionaries on Behalf of Social Reform.* Cambridge, 1967.
Inostransev, K. "The Emigration of the Parsis to India and the Musalman World in the Midst of the VIIIth Century." Translated from the Russian by L. Bogdanov. *Journal of the K. R. Cama Oriental Institute* 1 (1922), 33-70.
Irani, Phiroze K, "The Personal Law of the Parsis of India." *In Family Law in Asia and Africa*, no. 6, edited by J. N. D. Anderson, 273-300. London, 1968.
Isenberg, Shirley Berry. *India's Bene Israel: A Comprehensive Inquiry and Sourcebook.* Bombay, 1988.
Jackson, A. V. W. *Zoroaster: The Prophet of Ancient Iran.* New York, 1899.
——. *Zoroastrian Studies.* New York, 1928.
Jeejeebhoy, J. R. B. *Non-Cooperation, Its Pros and Cons.* Bombay, 1921.
——. "A Survey of Bombay Journalism." In *Jam-e-Jamshed Centenary Memorial Volume*, 272-86. Bombay, 1932.
——. *Bribery and Corruption in Bombay.* Bombay, 1952.
——. "Communal Discipline Among the Parsees in Olden Times." In *M. P. Kharegat Memorial Volume.* Vol. 1, 295-323. Bombay, 1953.
Jessawalla, Dosabai Cowasjee. *The Story of My Life.* Bombay, 1911.
Jhabvala, C. H. *Cowasjee Dinshaw Adenvala C.I.E.* Bombay, 1920.
Jones, Kenneth. *The New Cambridge History of India: Socio-Religious Reform Movements in British India.* Cambridge, 1989.
Joshi, A. N. *The Life and Times of Sir Hormusjee C. Dinshaw.* Bombay, 1939.
Kanga, K. E., trans. *Extracts From the Narrative of Mons. Anquetil Du Perron's Travels in India.* Bombay, 1876.
Karkal, Malini. *Survey of the Parsi Population of Greater Bombay.* Bombay, 1984.
Karkaria, R. P. "Article II—The Oldest Paper in India: The Bombay Samachar." *Calcutta Review* 106 (1898): 218-36.
——. "Article III—The Revival of the Native Press in Western India: The Rast Goftar." *Calcutta Review* 107 (1898): 226-41.
Katrak, Sohrab K. H. *Who Are the Parsees?* Karachi, 1965.
Kennedy, Robert E. "The Protestant Work Ethic and the Parsis." *American Journal of Sociology* 68 (1962-63): 11-20.
Kopf, David. *British Orientalism and the Bengal Renaissance: The Dynamics of Indian Modernization, 1773-1835.* Los Angeles, 1969.
Kotwal, Firoze M. "The Authenticity of the Parsi Priestly Tradition." *Journal of the K. R. Cama Oriental Institute* 45 (1979): 24-33.
Kotwal, F. M. and J. Boyd. *A Guide to the Zoroastrian Religion.* Harvard, 1982.
Kreyenbroek, Philip G. "The Zoroastrian Priesthood After the Fall of the Sasanian Empire." In *Transition Periods in Iranian History: Actes du Symposium de Fribourg-en-Brisgau, 22-24 Mai 1985*, 151-66. Paris, 1987.
——. "On the Concept of Spiritual Authority in Zoroastrianism." *Jerusalem Studies in Arabic and Islam* 17(1994): 1-15.
Kulke, Eckehard. *The Parsees in India: A Minority as Agents of Social Change.* Munich, 1974.

Lockwood, Stephen C. *Augustine Heard and Company, 1858-1862.* Cambridge, Mass., 1971.

Luhrmann, T. M. *The Good Parsi: The Fate of a Colonial Elite in Postcolonial Society.* Cambridge, Mass., 1996.

McCully, B. T. *English Education and the Origins of Indian Nationalism.* New York, 1940.

Mackichan, D. *The Missionary Ideal in the Scottish Churches.* London, 1927.

McLane, John R. *Indian Nationalism and the Early Congress.* Princeton, 1977.

Madan, D. M. *Revelation Considered as a Source of Religious Knowledge With Special Reference to Zoroastrianism.* Bombay, 1909.

Madgaokar, G. N. *Mumbaiche Varnan* (in Marathi). Bombay, 1863.

Majumdar, B. B. *Indian Political Associations and Reform of Legislature, 1818-1917.* Calcutta, 1965.

Malabari, Phiroze M. B. *Bombay in the Making.* London, 1910.

Mama, N. F. *A Mazdayaznan Mystic, Life Sketch of the Late Behramshah Novroji Shroff, the 20th Century Exponent of Zarthoshti Elm-e-Khshnoom.* Bombay, 1944.

Managan, J. A. *The Games Ethic and Imperialism: Aspects of the Diffusion of an Ideal.* New York, 1986.

Manickam, Sundararaj. *Studies in Missionary History: Reflections on a Culture/Contact.* Madras, 1988.

Marshall, P. J. "The Moral Swing to the East: British Humanitarianism, India and the West Indies." *In The East India Company 1784-1834,* edited by C. H. Philips, 69-93. Oxford, 1961.

——. *The British Discovery of Hinduism in the Eighteenth Century.* Cambridge, 1970.

——. *The Great Map of Mankind: British Perspectives of the World in the Age of Enlightenment.* London, 1982.

Marzban, Jehangir B. *Jam-e-Jamshed Centenary Memorial Volume.* Bombay, 1932.

Masani, P. S. *Zoroastrianism Ancient and Modern: Comprising a Review of Dr. Dhalla's Book of Zoroastrian Theology.* Bombay, 1917.

Masani, R. P. *Dadabhai Naoroji.* Delhi, 1960.

——. *N. M. Wadia and His Foundation.* Bombay, 1961.

Masselos, J. C. *Towards Nationalism.* Bombay, 1974.

——. Changing Definitions of Bombay: City State to Capital City." In *Ports and Their Hinterlands in India (1700-1950),* edited by Indu Banga, 273-316. Bombay, 1992.

Mehta, S. D. *The Cotton Mills of India, 1854 to 1954.* Bombay, 1954.

Menant, Delphine. *The Parsis.* Vol. 3. Translated from the French by Anthony D. Mango. Bombay, 1996.

Mirza, H. K. *Conversion Caucus.* Bombay, 1971.

Mirza, H. K., K. M. Jamaspasa and F. M. Kotwal. *Conversion: A Myth Exploded* Bombay, 1985.

——. *Antia's 'Acceptance': A Zoroastrian 'Ahrmogih'.* Bombay, 1985.

Mistry, Rohinton. *Such a Long Journey.* Toronto, 1991.

Mitchell, J. M. *In Western India.* Edinburgh, 1899.

Modi, J. J. "The Parsis at the Court of Akbar and Dastur Meherji Rana." In *Contributions on Akbar and the Parsees,* edited by B. P. Ambashthya, 1-177. Delhi, 1976. Originally published in *J.B.B.R.A.S.* 21, no. 57 (1903): 69-245.

——. *A Few Events in the Early History of the Parsees and Their Dates.* Bombay, 1905.

——. *A Glimpse Into the Work of the Bombay Branch Royal Asiatic Society, During the Last 100 Years, from a Parsee Point of View*. Bombay, 1905.
——. *Anquetil du Perron and Dastur Darab*. Bombay, 1916.
——. *The Religious Ceremonies and Customs of the Parsees*. Bombay, 1922.
——. *A Glimpse Into the History and Work of the Zarthoshti Din-ni Khol-Karnari Mandli*. Bombay, 1922.
——. "A Note on the Parsee Massacre at Variav." *Journal of the K. R. Cama Institute* 2 (1923).
——. "Rustom Manock and the Persian Quisseh: A Study." In *Asiatic Papers*. Vol. 4, 101-320. Bombay, 1929.
——. "Darab Hormazdyar's Rivayat: A Few Notes in the Study of an Early Part of its Contents." *Journal of the K. R. Cama Oriental Institute* 22 (1932): 109-238.
——. "Qisseh-i Zarthustian-i Hendustan." *Journal of the K. R. Cama Oriental Institute* 17 (1930): 1-63; 19 (1931): 45-57; 20 (1933): 1-147.
Mody, Homi. *Sir Pherozeshah Mehta: A Political Biography*. 1921. Reprint, London, 1963.
Mody, Jehangir R. P. *Jamsetjee Jejeebhoy the First Indian Knight and Baronet*. Bombay, 1959.
Monserrate, Father Anthony. *The Commentary of Father Monserrate S.J. On His Journey to the Court of Akbar*. Translated from the Portuguese by J. S. Hoyland. London, 1922.
Morgan, David. *Medieval Persia, 1040-1797*. New York, 1988.
Morris, Morris D. "The Growth of Large-Scale Industry to 1947." In *The Cambridge Economic History of India*. Vol. 2, c. *1700-1970*, edited by Dharma Kumar, 552-676. Cambridge, 1983.
Moulton, J. H. *The Treasure of the Magi*. London, 1917.
Mulla, D. F. *Jurisdiction of Courts in Matters Relating to the Rights and Powers of Castes*. Bombay, 1901.
Murzban, M. M. *The Parsis: Being An Enlarged and Copiously Annotated, Up to Date English Edition of Mile. Delphine Menant's Les Parsis*. 2 vols. 1917. Reprint, Bombay, 1994.
Naik, J. P. and Syed Nurullah. *A Student's History of Education in India*. Bombay, 1962.
Nariman, G. K. "Was it Religious Persecution Which Compelled the Parsis to Migrate from Persia to India?" *Islamic Culture* 7. Hyderabad, 1933.
Natesan, G. A., and Co., ed. *Speeches and Writings of Sir Dinshaw Edulji Wacha*. Madras, 1920.
——. *Famous Parsis: Biographical & Critical Sketches*. Madras, 1930.
——. *Congress Presidential Addresses: From the Foundation to the Silver Jubilee, First Series, 1885-1910*. Madras, 1935.
Neusner, Jacob. *Judaism and Zoroastrianism at the Dusk of Late Antiquity: How Two Ancient Faiths Wrote Down Their Great Traditions*. Atlanta, 1993.
The New Encyclopaedia Britannica, 15th ed., s.v. "Middle Eastern Religion."
Nightingale, Pamela. *Trade and Empire in Western India, 1794-1806*. Cambridge, 1970.
O'Hanlon, Rosalind. "Cultures of rule, communities of resistance: gender, discourse and tradition in recent South Asian historiographies." In *Identity, Consciousness and the Past*, edited by H. L. Seneviratne, 94-114. Adelaide, 1988.
——. and D. Washbrook. "After Orientalism: Culture, Criticism and Politics in the

Third World." *Comparative Studies of Society and History* 34, no. 1 (1992): 141-67.

Palsetia, Jesse S. "The Development of the Parsi Community of Ontario." *Polypbony: The Bulletin of the Multicultural History Society of Ontario, South Asians in Ontario* 12 (1991): 125-9.

——. "Mad Dogs and Parsis: The Bombay Dog Riots of 1832." *Journal of the Royal Asiatic Society*, series 3, Vol. 11, part 1 (2001), pp. 13-30.

Pandey, B. N. *The Introduction of English Law into India.* London, 1967.

Paruck, P. L. *The Indian Succession Act.* Bombay, 1953.

Parulekar, R. V. *Survey of Indigenous Education in the Province of Bombay, 1820-1830.* Bombay, 1951.

Patel, B. B. "A Brief Outline of Some Controversial Questions that Led to the Advancement of the Study of Religious Literature Among the Parsis." In *K. R. Cama Oriental Institute Memorial Volume*, 170-82. Bombay, 1900.

Patel, J. M. F. *Stray Thoughts on Indian Cricket.* Bombay, 1905.

Patel, M. K. *History of Parsee Cricket.* Bombay, 1892.

Patwardhan, R. P., ed. *Dadabhai Naoroji Correspondence.* Vol. 2, parts 1 and 2. Bombay, 1977.

Paymaster, R. B. *The Early History of the Parsees in India.* Bombay, 1954.

Philips, C. H., ed. *Historians of India, Pakistan and Ceylon.* London, 1961.

Piacentini, V. Fiorani. *L'Emporio ed il Regno de Hormuz.* Milano, 1975.

Pissurlencar, P. S. S. *Portuguese Records on Rustom Manock.* Translated from the Portuguese by S. B. D'Silva. Bombay. 1936.

Prakash, Gyan. "Writing Post-Orientalist Histories of the Third World: Indian Historiography Is Good to Think." In *Colonialism and Culture*, edited by N. B. Dirks, 353-88. Ann Arbor, 1992.

Rana, Framjee A. *Parsi Law: Embodying the Law of Marriage and Divorce and Inheritance and Succession Applicable to Parsis in British India.* Bombay, 1934.

Rangoonwalla, Firoze. *Seventy-five Years of Indian Cinema.* New Delhi, 1975.

Rankin, George Claus. *Background to Indian Law.* Cambridge, 1946.

Rawal, Munni. *Dadabhai Naoroji: A Prophet of Indian Nationalism (1855-1900).* New Delhi, 1989.

Raychaudhuri, Tapan. "The Eighteenth Century Background." In *The Cambridge Economic History of India.* Vol. 2, c. *1700-1970*, edited by Dharma Kumar, 3-35. Cambridge, 1983.

Ripon Club, Golden Jubilee 1884-1934. Bombay, 1934.

Roland, Joan G. *Jews in British India: Identity in a Colonial Era.* Hanover, N.H., 1989.

Rudolph, L. I. and S. H. *The Modernity of Tradition: Political Development in India.* Chicago, 1967.

Russell, James R. *Zoroastrianism in Armenia.* Cambridge, Mass., 1987.

Rutnagar, S. M. *Bombay Industries: The Cotton Mills.* Bombay, 1927.

Saha, P. *Shapurji Saklatvala: A Short Biography.* Delhi, 1970.

Sanial, S. C. "History of the Press in India, X. Bombay—IV." *Calcutta Review* (1910): 264-94.

Sanjana, J. B. *Parsis and Theosophy.* Bombay, 1954.

Sankhdher, B. M. *Press, Politics, and Public Opinion in India: Dynamics of Modernization and Social Transformation.* New Delhi, 1984.

Sarkar, U. C. *Epochs in Hindu Legal History.* Hoshiarpur, 1958.

Schmidt, Hans-Peter. "The Sixteen Sanskrit Sanjan Slokas of Ākā Adhyāru." *Bulletin of the Deccan College Research Institute* 21 (1960-61): 157-96.

Schwartz, Martin. "The Religion of Achamenian Iran." In *The Cambridge History of Iran*. Vol. 2, edited by Ilya Gershevitch, 664-97. Cambridge, 1985.

Sen, Sunil Kumar. *The House of Tata, 1839-1939*. Calcutta, 1975.

Seth, Jalbhoy A. *Genealogy and Brief Account of the Seth Family* (in Gujarati). Bombay, 1900.

Shabbir, M. and S. C. Manchanda. *Parsi Law in India (As Amended by Act of 1988)*. Allahabad, 1991.

Shaked, Shaul. *Dualism in Transformation: Varieties of Religion in Sasanian Iran*. London, 1994.

A Short History of the 'Empress Mills,' Nagpur, Started Work 1st January 1877, Golden Jubilee Volume. Bombay, 1927.

Siddiqi, Asiya. "The Business World of Jamsetjee Jejeebhoy." *The Indian Economic and Social History Review* 19, nos. 3 & 4 (1982): 301-24.

Sidhwa, R. K. *Scheme to Remove Poverty and Unemployment from the Parsi Community*. Bombay, 1955.

Singer, Milton, ed. *When A Great Tradition Modernizes: An Anthropological Approach to Indian Civilization*. New York, 1972.

Singh, Dilbagh and B. Rajshirke. "The Merchants of Surat: Trade, Trade Practices and Institutions in the Late Eighteenth Century." In *Ports and Their Hinterlands in India (1700-1950)*, edited by Indu Banga, 181-98. Bombay, 1992.

Slapak, Oprah, ed. *The Jews of India: A Story of Three Communities*. Jerusalem, 1995.

Smith, George. *The Life of John Wilson, D.D.F.R.S.* London, 1879.

Spear, Percival. *The Nabobs*. Oxford, 1972.

Squires, M. *Saklatwala: A Political Biography*. London, 1990.

Srinivasa Sastri, V. S. *Life and Times of Sir Pherozeshah Mehta*. Madras, 1945.

Stashower, Daniel. *Teller of Tales: The Life of Arthur Conan Doyle*. New York, 1999.

Stokes, Eric. *The English Utilitarians and India*. Oxford, 1959.

Stoler, Ann Laura. "Rethinking Colonial Categories: European Communities and the Boundaries of Rule." In *Colonialism and Culture*, edited by N. B. Dirks, 319-52. Ann Arbor, 1992.

Strizower, S. "Jews as an Indian Caste." *Jewish Journal of Sociology* 1 (1959): 43-57.

——. *The Children of Israel: The Bene Israel of Bombay*. Oxford, 1971.

Sullivan, R. J. F. *One Hundred Years of Bombay, 1836-1936*. Bombay, 1937.

Thapar, Romila. *A History of India*. New York, 1966.

Tikekar, Aroon. *The Cloister's Pale: A Biography of the University of Bombay*. Bombay, 1957.

Tirmidhi, B. M. "Zoroastrians and Their Fire Temples in Iran and Adjoining Countries from the 9th to the 14th Centuries as Gleaned from the Arabic Geographical Works." *Islamic Culture* 24, no. 4 (1950): 271-84.

University of Bombay (1857-1957) Centenary Souvenir. Bombay, 1957.

Vaid, K. N. *The Overseas Indian Community in Hong Kong*. Hong Kong, 1972.

Vitalone, Mario. *The Persian Revayat 'Ithother': Zoroastrian Rituals in the Eighteenth Century*. Naples, 1996.

Wadia, D. F. *History of Lodge Rising Star of Western India No. 42 S.C.* Bombay, 1912.

Wadia, Jal H. *Sir Jamsetjee Jejeebhoy Parsee Benevolent Institution: Centenary Volume*. Bombay, 1949.

Wadia, P. A. *Parsi Ere the Shadows Thicken*. Bombay, 1949.

Wadia, R. A. *A Forgotten Friend of India: Charles Forbes 1st Bart*. Baroda, 1946.

——. *The Bombay Dockyard and the Wadia Master Builders.* Bombay, 1955.

——. *Scions of Lowjee Wadia.* Bombay, 1964.

Wagle, N. K. "Government, the Jāti, and the Individual: Rights, Discipline and Control in The Pune Kotwal Paper 1766-94." *Contributions to Indian Sociology*, 34 (2000) pp. 321-60.

Waley, Arthur. "Anquetil-Duperron and Sir William Jones." *History Today* (January 1952): 23-33.

White, David. "Parsis in the Commercial World of Western India, 1700-1750." *The Indian Economic and Social History Review* 24, no. 2 (1987), 183-203.

——. "From Crisis to Philanthropy: The Dynamics of Eighteenth Century Parsi Philanthropy." *Modern Asian Studies* 25, 2 (1991): 303-20.

Wink, Andre. *Al-Hind: The Making of the Indo-Islamic World.* Oxford, 1990.

Wright, Arnold. *Annesley of Surat and His Times.* London, 1918.

Writer, Rashna. *Contemporary Zoroastrians: An Unstructured Nation.* Lanham, Maryland, 1994.

Yarshater, Ehsan, ed. *The Cambridge History of Iran: The Seleucid, Parthian, and Sasanian Periods* 3 (2). Cambridge, 1983.

Zaehner, Robert C. *The Dawn and Twilight of.Zoroastrianism.* London, 1961.

Zaidi, Shaheda and A. Moin. *The Encyclopaedia of the Indian National Congress, Volume 1, 1885-1890, The Founding Fathers.* New Delhi, 1976; *Volume 4, 1901-1905, On Road to Self-Government.* New Delhi, 1978; *Volume 6, 1911-*1915, *In Search of A Creed.* New Delhi, 1979.

Zaveri, Rasik, ed. *Bombay Samachar: One Hundred and Fifty Years, 1822-1972* (in Gujarati). Bombay, 1972.

INDEX

1. Fire-temple precinct of Iranshah in Udwada, Gujarat.

2. Parsi *dakhma* in background in Nargol, Gujarat.

3. *Tānā* ceremony to lay foundation for new *dakhma*, in Calcutta, December 25, 1910.

4. First *Navjote* performed in Britain, at Caxton Hall, January 30, 1915, of Parsi girl Goolcheher R. R. Desai, by Dastur M. N. Dhalla.

5. Parsi procession for 'enthronement' of sacred fire in new fire-temple at Godrej Baug, December 21, 1999.

6. *Navjote* ceremony of Parsi boy in Bombay in January 2000.

7. Parsis offer prayers at the Bhikha Behram Parsi well in Bombay to mark 275 years in March 2000.

8. Parsi and Hindu cotton traders in Bombay in the nineteenth century.

9. Parsi children in the middle of nineteenth century.

10. Two Parsi youths.

11. Parsi youth initiated as *Nāvar*.

12. Parsi husband and wife in late nineteenth century.

13. Parsi lady in sari in early twentieth century.

14. Students at Parsi Ladies' School in early twentieth century.

15. Parsi children with musical instuments in early twentieth century.

16. Rustam Manock of Surat (*c.* 1635–1719).

17. Sir Jamsetjee Jejeebhoy, 1st Baronet (1783–1859).

18. Jamsetjee Nusserwanjee Tata (1839–1904).

19. Sir Dinshaw Manakji Petit, 1st Baronet (1823–1901).

20. Framjee Nasserwanjee Patel (1804–1892).

21. Nowrozjee Furdoonjee (1817–1885).

22. Manockjee Cursetjee Shroff (1808–1887).

23. Pirozebai Shapurjee Dhunjeebhoy (1834–1906).

24. Dadabhai Naoroji (1825–1917), the first Indian Member of Parliament, at Westminster.

25. Sir Pherozeshah M. Mehta (1845–1915).

26. Sir Dinsha E. Wachta (1844–1936).